THE IDEA OF FREEDOM

BOOKS BY ISAIAH BERLIN

Karl Marx
The Age of Enlightenment
Four Essays on Liberty
Vico and Herder

—

SELECTED WRITINGS
Edited by Henry Hardy

Russian Thinkers
Concepts and Categories:
Philosophical Essays
Against the Current:
Essays in the History of Ideas
Personal Impressions
forthcoming

THE IDEA OF FREEDOM

Essays in Honour of Isaiah Berlin

Edited by Alan Ryan

Oxford New York Toronto Melbourne
OXFORD UNIVERSITY PRESS
1979

Oxford University Press, Walton Street, Oxford OX2 6DP
OXFORD LONDON GLASGOW
NEW YORK TORONTO MELBOURNE WELLINGTON
KUALA LUMPUR SINGAPORE JAKARTA HONG KONG TOKYO
DELHI BOMBAY CALCUTTA MADRAS KARACHI
NAIROBI DAR ES SALAAM CAPE TOWN

British Library Cataloguing in Publication Data
The idea of freedom.
1. Liberty – Addresses, essays, lectures
I. Ryan, Alan II. Berlin, *Sir Isaiah*
123 JC585 74-40534

ISBN 0-19-215859-7

Printed in Great Britain by
Billing & Sons Limited,
Guildford, London and Worcester

Contents

Introduction 1
Alan Ryan

Capitalism, Freedom and the Proletariat 9
G. A. Cohen

Freedom as an Aesthetic Idea 27
Patrick Gardiner

Freud and Freedom 41
On a Fox in Hedgehog's Clothing
Peter Gay

Freedom and Explanation 61
or Seeing Double
Stuart Hampshire

Between Utility and Rights 77
H. L. A. Hart

Politicians and the Freedom to Choose 99
The Case of July 1914
James Joll

Heroes of their Time? 115
Form and Idea in Büchner's *Danton's Death* and Lermontov's *Hero of our Time*
Robin Milner-Gulland

Persian Empire and Greek Freedom 139
Arnaldo Momigliano

Two Liberal Traditions 153
Larry Siedentop

What's Wrong with Negative Liberty 175
Charles Taylor

'Venise et, par occasion, de la liberté' 195
Franco Venturi

Oughts and Cans 211
Morton White

Conflicts of Values 221
Bernard Williams

Rousseau's Perfectibilian Libertarianism 233
Robert Wokler

John Stuart Mill and Isaiah Berlin 253
The Ends of Life and the Preliminaries of Morality
Richard Wollheim

A Bibliography of Isaiah Berlin 271
Henry Hardy

Notes on contributors 289

Index 291
Patricia Utechin

ALAN RYAN

Introduction

I

Convention dictates that the introduction to a collection of essays such as this should be devoted to a description and assessment of the achievements of the person whose work is being celebrated. Cowardice – as well as a more avowable sense of what is practicable – prompts me otherwise. I say cowardice, because the standards which Isaiah Berlin himself has set for anyone who undertakes such an enterprise are dauntingly high. His ability to catch the allegiances and the emotional tone of the authors he has written about, as well as his ability to meet the commentator's first duty to the subtleties of their thought, has always meant that their personalities and ideas alike have remained intact and alive. But these are abilities easier to admire than to describe, and easier to describe than to acquire; on this occasion at least, reticence seems a sincerer form of flattery than imperfect imitation.

Even the boldest commentator might hesitate, however. For Isaiah Berlin's contribution to our intellectual lives has been notable for its great richness, variety and colour; indeed, to talk of it as simply a contribution to our intellectual lives is already to describe it in too pallid a fashion and to seem ungrateful for the sheer pleasure that his work has given. Part of his achievement has been the way in which he has firmly ignored the frigidly pious notion that intellectual respectability means a dry detachment from the world; his essays on men and ideas have always engaged the heart as well as the head. To try to write about the dry bones of his views on this or that subject without capturing the spirit which has breathed life into them would be a folly and an injustice.

The scope of Isaiah Berlin's work has been wide; he has gone his way without very much regard to conventional academic boundaries. To talk illuminatingly about his work, therefore, would be the task for a book, not an essay. One would have to begin with his work in philosophy, where to take one instance only he was influential in undermining logical positivism's standing as a philosophical orthodoxy by showing how the phenomenalist's old difficulties in accounting for the existence of the material world were unresolved in their modern form too. One would equally have to set about explaining why his work in the history of ideas matters so much – why, for example, it is such an achievement to have rescued Vico from the obscurity into which he had fallen, at least for almost all English readers. For this is not just a matter of bringing Vico back to life as a figure who was both a stranger to us and yet concerned with issues in historical and cultural studies which are still unresolved; it is also part of Berlin's running argument with the advocates of 'scientific history', with those who think that the goal of historical studies is to produce something akin to a natural science of history.

The same need to show the unity of his work as an intellectual historian and as a philosopher arises with his studies of Russian thinkers such as Belinsky, Herzen or Tolstoy. And this would be a complicated task, since part of the moral of such essays as 'A Remarkable Decade' lies in their reminder of the differences between Russian and Western ways of feeling and thinking, while part lies in their bringing home to us the aspiration to a unity of thought and emotion which was common to numerous Romantics, East and West. To make proper sense of the resonances of these studies would also be a sociological enterprise of some awkwardness; it is a cliché that in the 1950s Berlin's readers would have looked for the contrast between the aspirations of Herzen, say, and the achievements of Lenin and Stalin, but at the end of the 1960s, when a large part of the Western world was experiencing a rebellion of the young against almost anything and everything that could be attributed to 'the system', Berlin's essays on the youthful Russian intelligentsia of a hundred and twenty years earlier were as fresh as ever. And I have always thought, without being able to explain the fact, that English moral philosophy and political theory were invigorated by these essays in intellectual history, and stimulated to thought about moral and political pluralism, in a way that they would not have been by direct argument alone. It is as if examples of uninhibited grappling with the pressures of a desire for intellectual order and unity on the one side and perception of the chaos of the world on the other were what was needed to underpin Berlin's more obviously 'philosophical' essays such as 'Two Concepts of Liberty' or 'Does Political Theory Still Exist?'

To get anywhere with this would already be a considerable task. But it would scarcely be more than a foundation for much more besides. To be sure, Berlin's studies of Moses Hess, Chaim Weizmann and Lewis Namier are distinguished studies of very remarkable men. But they are also studies in the strange phenomenon of Jewishness – 'strange', that is to say, in the sense that a running theme of the essay on Moses Hess is just the way in which Hess's Jewishness defied the rationalist analysis to which he supposed it must yield. The whole subject of national identity and national character, not simply in its modern Zionist shape, is, of course, another permanent concern of Berlin's work, and one which reflects his willingness to cross the conventional academic boundaries. Anyone who is sympathetic to the doctrine – which Berlin calls 'expressivism' and claims as one of Herder's main insights – that cultures express their 'spirit' or 'character' in all their activities, is sure to want to account for what it is that the literature, the philosophy, the art and the music of an epoch and a society unite to express. To mention one last implication of this, any comprehensive account of Berlin's work would have to include his concern with music, and this not merely in the *Who's Who* sense of observing that he has for many years been a director of the Royal Opera House, but in the sense of showing how an interest in the philosophy of history and the philosophy of nationalism illuminates the work of that passionate nationalist Verdi. It is, however, a pretty stiff requirement that we should do as much justice to *Don Carlos* as to *Karl Marx*.

II

The demands which daunt the commentator are a little daunting even to an editor. To try to cover all of Isaiah Berlin's interests in one volume would have resulted in something which I imagine would have been unique among Festschriften – a volume physically too large and too heavy for its contributors to offer to its subject. More manageably, we have set ourselves the task of offering Isaiah Berlin some thoughts on issues raised by his *Four Essays on Liberty*.[1]

Although I have declined to meet the obligation to summarise Isaiah Berlin's achievements in a few terse paragraphs, I have no doubt that the widespread association of his name with these four essays is a proper recognition of a central theme in his work. Of course, as a glance at the contents of this volume suggests, 'freedom' is hardly the name of a single entity, even if there is no other single word which better captures what we want to talk about in different contexts. Often what Berlin has been concerned to argue *for* in the particular case emerges most clearly by contrast with what he is concerned to argue against. So, for example, arguments against scien-

[1] (London, 1969). This work is referred to subsequently in footnotes throughout this book as *F.E.L.*

tific history, and particularly against deterministic theories of history which claim that the historical process is governed by laws which dictate what must inevitably take place, bear on two sorts of freedom rather than one. The historian's concern with freedom is partly a concern with the sheer indeterminacy of the process of history, with an open-endedness on the part of human history which contrasts with the closed and repetitive character of mechanical, deterministic systems, so that unless men are forced into some single and uniform course of behaviour, there will be no single, predictable pattern to be discerned. In other words, freedom in the sense of non-interference yields indeterminacy in history. But the historian's concern with freedom is also a concern for the moral dimension in the writing of history in contrast with the merely technical questions which we would raise about machines. Success and failure alone matter about the workings of a piece of machinery. As 'Historical Inevitability' argues, if the future were closed in the way inevitabilist accounts of history suppose it to be, and if human behaviour was merely the behaviour of complex machines, then it is hard to see what room there could be for writing history as we now do, lavishing praise and blame on historical actors on other than merely technical grounds. There could, however, be quite different combinations of beliefs about indeterminacy in history and about the applicability of moral and quasi-moral judgements to human behaviour. One might hold that individual behaviour was merely mechanically caused but with some randomness in the way the various causes operated, and so believe both in the openness of the future in the sense of its unpredictability, so long as men were not forced into uniformity, and in the eliminability of moral terms in the description and explanation of individuals' behaviour. The variety of contrasts at issue, therefore, makes it impossible to do without some general label, while making it worth while to say something about what that label adheres to in particular cases. *Four Essays on Liberty* is certainly a book of essays on liberty, but there is no single thing that 'liberty' refers to.

If there is a thread on which we might hang the issues with which *Four Essays*, and, therefore, this volume, are concerned, it is to be found in the connection between choice, diversity and happiness (as distinct from contentment). That is, the burden of 'Two Concepts of Liberty' is that the importance of negative liberty – the preservation of an area within which an individual may do as he chooses without interference – lies in large part in the fact that goals conflict, not merely in the sense that one man's aims interfere with another's in such a way as to require policing to prevent them coming to blows, but in the sense that there is no one true answer to the question of what the right goals are for a given individual. Positive liberty – the freedom which consists in our behaviour being under the control of our 'true' or 'real' or 'higher' selves – presupposes that there is some uniquely correct answer to the question 'What should I do?' or to the same question in different guise, 'What sort of creature am I?' The simplest characterisation of positive libertarian doctrines is that they identify freedom with control; it is the source of the control over our actions with which positive libertarians are concerned, whether they identify freedom with a Stoic mastery of our everyday desires, or with obedience to Rousseau's General Will, or with submitting ourselves to Historical Necessity. The conviction that there is *no* resolution of the conflict that honest, decent, undeluded men and women incessantly discover between one good thing and another must mean that extreme versions of positive libertarianism are misguided. Of course, even the most enthusiastic defender of the claims of the empirical and everyday self against the demands of the supposed 'higher' or 'real' self will admit that some element of rational self-mastery is needed before anyone can be free; the person whose reactions are random, or whose impulses sweep him away regardless, can hardly be said to act freely. The defender of negative liberty does not have to deny that some self-control is required of a free agent; what he has to resist is the temptation to press the search for what controls the self to the lengths of discovering another and better self to do the controlling.

If the denial of the claims of positive liberty is in large part dependent on a pluralistic theory of the ends of life, then all monistic theories of morality will come to look deeply unattractive. Any simple utilitarian theory of morality, for instance, will have at least two characteristics which will seem at least odd, and probably dangerous. In the first place, the denial of a genuine plurality of moral demands means that what we normally think of as the pull of conflicting requirements has to be reconstructed as simply a problem about calculating what is for the best. The man who feels remorse at betraying a secret, even when he has decided that his duty *is* to betray it, would on the utilitarian view be irrational to feel any such thing. If he had reached the right answer, he should have no room for guilt. On Berlin's account of the moral life, it is the sense of remorse which accurately reflects the genuineness of moral conflict, not the utilitarian attempt to do away with it. Secondly, a blindness to the genuineness of the good that is sacrificed in a particular case is part and parcel of a tendency to underestimate the reality of sacrifice in general. Because the simpler forms of utilitarianism suggest that a policy is to be justified in terms of the quantity of pleasure achieved without paying any attention to who experiences that pleasure, it permits any amount of sacrifice of the present for the sake of a sufficient quantity of pleasure hereafter. On Berlin's view, it is only in very simple cases that any such calculations make sense; all too often there is no way in which what is lost and what is gained can be measured, and all we know is that when people are conscripted to be sacrificed, it is they who make the sacrifices and it is not they who gain from them.

Any account of the importance of pluralism makes two sorts of assumptions, even if they are not always very near the centre of the argument. The first set of assumptions are psychological, the second sociological. They are needed in order to provide a background which explains why people both need freedom and find it hard to bear, why their lives suggest both that there must be some right answer to their questions about what to do and that there cannot be any such thing; and they provide a background which goes some way towards explaining what sorts of society will tolerate and even enjoy diversity. It is very much the psychology and the sociology of the modern world that Berlin describes – not so much in *Four Essays on Liberty*, perhaps, as in his essays on Machiavelli and Montesquieu, but at any rate glancingly in almost everything he has written. What Karl Popper has characterised as the closed society is, on Berlin's view too, the sort of society which reflects and sustains the belief that each person has some niche waiting for him; primitive societies and closed selves sustain each other. By contrast the characteristic tension of the Western world is the tension between the hope that scientific (rather than religious) revelation will show that we have that niche waiting for us after all, and the hope that we can live without any such assurance, and, indeed, that we shall come to find happiness in abandoning the search for mere contentment.

III

The essays that follow take up these themes in a variety of ways; some of them are fairly directly critical of one or another claim advanced in *Four Essays on Liberty*. Richard Wollheim, for example, accepts Berlin's account of Mill's concern with diversity and freedom, but denies that Mill's pursuit of that concern amounted to the abandoning of utilitarianism; rather, it required a considerable sophistication of utilitarianism. Morton White takes up Berlin's claim that there is a conceptual inconsistency involved in any attempt to square our ordinary notion of moral responsibility with a belief in determinism, and doubts whether the plain man or the logician would really concur in this. Charles Taylor suggests that there is more to be said against negative liberty than Berlin has yet allowed, while G. A. Cohen argues that a class may lack freedom in ways which are hard to characterise in the terms offered by 'Two Concepts of Liberty'. James Joll agrees with Berlin that in so far as there is anything inevitable in history it is not because there are large-scale historical laws determining what happens; but he shows that the room for manoeuvre enjoyed by politicians may sometimes be so restricted that what they do is to all intents what they have to do. And Bernard Williams takes up Berlin's insistence on the inevitability of conflicts of values in order to argue that the different ways in which governments and individuals are obliged to resolve conflicts poses institutional problems of a kind which those who accept Berlin's views have not yet considered with the seriousness they deserve.

Others of these essays reflect on issues which *Four Essays on Liberty* provokes, albeit less directly. Stuart Hampshire provides further reasons for supposing, as Isaiah Berlin does, that the point of studying history is not to provide or test causal explanations of the kind we find in the natural sciences – though, as he says, his reasons are not ones he supposes that Isaiah Berlin has himself relied on. H. L. A. Hart takes up two conflicts that Berlin has often discussed, the conflict between utility and natural rights, and the conflict between liberty and equality, and suggests that the recent enthusiasm for rights, whether to liberty or equality, has produced at least as much confusion as it has cleared up.

Arnaldo Momigliano discusses the difficulties the Athenian commentators experienced in their efforts to explain to themselves just what it was that distinguished the social and political arrangements of imperial Persia from those of republican Athens, while Franco Venturi discusses the eighteenth century's doubts about the nature of that other great source of sociological reflection on political and social liberty, the Venetian Republic. A notable contributor to those reflections was Rousseau, who here appears in Robert Wokler's essay in his character of the philosophical anthropologist who saw beneath the diversity and chaos of the desires of civilised man a basically simple creature, whose gifts of free will and educability had turned out to be a curse to him. Larry Siedentop, however, praises those French social theorists who turned away from Rousseau's concern with human nature towards a more piecemeal political sociology, and who in the process created a foundation for political liberalism – as an intellectually serious doctrine – that the English contemporaries of de Tocqueville, Mill in particular, could only obtain at second hand. Peter Gay takes up the theme of the tension between an aspiration to capture the full complexity of human motivation, and the natural scientist's aspiration to explain that complexity with the bare minimum of causal apparatus, in perhaps its most interesting example in the past century – the case of Freud. Robin Milner-Gulland returns to some of the literary sources on which Isaiah Berlin has drawn so effectively; he discusses some of the connections between the formal organisation of two strikingly innovatory works – Büchner's *Danton's Death* and Lermontov's *Hero of our Time* – and what they have to tell us about character and its expression in word and action. And Patrick Gardiner sets out from what one might call a characteristic antipathy of *Four Essays on Liberty*, namely Berlin's dislike of Kant's identification of freedom with doing one's duty; he does so in the company of Schiller, and suggests that there is a good deal to be got from Schiller's emphasis on the possibilities of an aesthetically satisfying harmony of mind and heart as opposed to the Kantian emphasis on the dictatorship of the rational will.

After evading some of the duties which convention imposes upon editors, I am more than happy to fulfil a final duty. I ought to thank the authors of the essays that follow for their quite remarkable promptness and self-discipline; I have also enjoyed, and learned a good deal from what they wrote, and I am very grateful to them. All the credit that does not belong to them belongs to Henry Hardy of the Oxford University Press.

G. A. COHEN

Capitalism, Freedom and the Proletariat

In capitalist societies everyone owns something, if only his own labour power, and each is free to sell what he owns, and to buy whatever the sale of what he owns enables him to buy. Many claims made on capitalism's behalf are questionable, but here is a freedom which it certainly provides.

It is easy to show that under capitalism everyone has some of this freedom, especially if being free to sell something is compatible with not being free not to sell it, two conditions whose consistency I would defend. Australians are free to vote, even though they are not free not to vote, since voting is mandatory in Australia. One could say that Australians are forced to vote, but that proves that they are free to vote, as follows: one cannot be forced to do what one cannot do, and one cannot do what one is not free to do. Hence one is free to do what one is forced to do. Resistance to this odd-sounding but demonstrable conclusion comes from failure to distinguish the idea of being free to do something from other ideas, such as the idea of doing something freely.

Look at it this way: before you are forced to do A, you are, except in unusual cases, free to do A and free not to do A. The force removes the second freedom, not the first. It puts no obstacle in the path of your doing A, so you are still free to. Note, too, that you could frustrate someone who sought to force you to do A by making yourself not free to do it.

I labour this truth – that one is free to do what one is forced to do – because it, and failure to perceive it, help to explain the character and persistence of a certain ideological disagreement. Marxists say that working-class people are forced to sell their labour power, a thesis we shall look at later. Bourgeois thinkers celebrate the freedom of contract manifest not only in the capitalist's purchase of labour power but in the worker's sale of it. If Marxists are right, working-class people are importantly unfree: they are not free not to sell their labour power. But it remains true that (unlike chattel slaves) they are free to sell their labour power. The unfreedom asserted by Marxists is compatible with the freedom asserted by bourgeois thinkers. Indeed: if the Marxists are right, the bourgeois thinkers are right, unless they also think, as characteristically they do, that the truth they emphasise refutes the Marxist claim.

Freedom to buy and sell is one freedom, of which in capitalism there is a great deal. It belongs to capitalism's essential nature. But many think that capitalism is, quite as essentially, a more comprehensively free society. Very many people, including philosophers, who are known to speak carefully, use the phrase 'free society' as an alternative name for societies which are capitalist.[1] And the doctrine which recommends pure capitalism is widely called 'libertarianism', not, as might be more apt, 'libertarianism with respect to buying and selling'.

It is not only the libertarians themselves who think that is the right name for their party. Many who do not share their aims concede the name to them: they agree that unmodified capitalism is comprehensively a realm of freedom. This applies to *some* of those who in North America are called 'liberals'.

These liberals assert, plausibly, that liberty[2] is a good thing, but that it is not the only good thing. So far, libertarians will agree. But liberals also believe that libertarians wrongly sacrifice other good things in too total defence of the one good of liberty. They agree with libertarians that pure capitalism is liberty pure and simple, or anyway *economic*[3] liberty pure and simple, but they think the various good things lost when liberty pure and simple is the rule justify restraints on liberty. The capitalism they want is modified by welfare legislation and State intervention in the market. They advocate, they say, not unrestrained liberty, but liberty restrained by the demands of social and economic security. They do not question the libertarian's description of capitalism as the (economically) free society. But they believe that economic freedom may rightly and reasonably be abridged. They believe in a compromise between liberty and other values.

I shall argue that libertarians, and liberals of the kind described, misuse the concept of liberty. This is not a comment on the attractiveness of the institutions they severally favour, but on the rhetoric they use to describe them. They see the freedom which is

[1] See, e.g., Jan Narveson, 'A Puzzle About Economic Justice in Rawls' Theory', *Social Theory and Practice* 4 (1976), p. 3; James Rachels, 'What People Deserve', in C. J. Arthur and W. Shaw (eds), *Justice and Economic Distribution* (Englewood Cliffs, 1978), p. 151.

[2] I shall be using 'liberty' and 'freedom' more or less interchangeably.

[3] See pp. 13–14 below on what might be meant by *economic* liberty.

intrinsic to capitalism, but they do not notice the unfreedom which necessarily accompanies it.

To expose this failure of perception, I shall criticise some paragraphs from a recent piece by the philosopher Jan Narveson, a representative liberal in the present sense. Early in the piece Narveson characterises liberty as 'doing what we wish without the interference of others'.[4] This is not intended as a strict definition, so we need not complain about its roughness.[5] We can certainly accept this much: when a man cannot do what he wishes, because others will interfere, he is unfree.

Having characterised liberty, Narveson proceeds to maintain that those who question the identity between a free market and a society of economic liberty abuse language. Only by illicitly misdefining the term 'liberty' can they avoid the truth that capitalism maximises economic freedom:

> . . . some will doubtless insist that free enterprise does not constitute economic liberty and is, indeed, not even compatible with it. Thus they will claim that a system in which economic roles are centrally and coercively allocated[6] is actually in the interests of liberty . . . this is a thesis which could hardly be made out without redefining the term 'liberty' . . .

According to Narveson, those who favour 'the public welfare or the general good' should say so. They should not pretend that what they are advocating is freedom. They should stop locating values different from liberty (e.g. equality or happiness) in the constitution of liberty itself.[7]

I shall show that Narveson, and liberals like him, mishandle the term 'liberty', in much the same way to which he objects here. Narveson allows something different from what 'liberty' denotes, namely private property, to govern his use of that term. He is able to imagine that a market economy is *ipso facto* a free society, or, more modestly, a domain of economic liberty, because he is the victim of an unreflective association of ideas. The ideas in confused association are those of freedom and private property.

Let us suppose that I wish to take Mr Morgan's yacht, and go for a spin. If I try to, then it is probable that its owner, aided by law-

[4] op. cit. (note 1 above), p. 3.

[5] For good criticism of that kind of definition, see Isaiah Berlin, *F.E.L.*, pp. xxxviiiff., 139–40.

[6] This is not, of course, the most favourable way of describing what opponents of free enterprise recommend.

[7] Narveson, op. cit. (note 1 above), p. 6.

enforcing others, will stop me. I cannot do this thing that I wish to do, because others will interfere. But liberty, Narveson reasonably said, is 'doing what we wish without the interference of others'. It follows that I lack a liberty here.

Patently, the point is generalisable. Private property always limits liberty, as in the Morgan example. But free enterprise economies rest upon private property: you can sell and buy only what you respectively own and come to own. It follows that such economies pervasively restrict liberty. They are complex structures of freedom and unfreedom. The sentence 'free enterprise constitutes economic liberty' is demonstrably false.

This demonstration comes so quickly on Narveson's definition of liberty that we must pause to consider whether we have not misunderstood it. Perhaps it is elliptically expressed. Perhaps what is intended by 'doing what we wish without the interference of others' is 'doing what we wish without the *unjustified* interference of others'.[8] Call this the *moralised* definition.

Suppose now that, as many would assert, Morgan and others may justifiably prevent me using his yacht, since he is its legitimate owner. If that is so, then, on the new definition of liberty, their interference does not prejudice my liberty.

The moralised definition, combined with a moral endorsement of private property, yields the result that private property does not restrict liberty. Note that the moralised definition does not by itself deliver this conclusion. For if it is not morally right that Morgan have private property in the yacht, then his interference with me might be unjustified. The marriage of liberty and private property requires not only a moralised definition of liberty but also a moral endorsement of private property.

And now Narveson is in a dilemma. If we take his definition of liberty literally, as we first did, then it is easy to deny that free enterprise constitutes economic liberty. Free enterprise might still be best for economic liberty, but there is too much unfreedom built into the foundation of free enterprise, private property, for any simple identification of the two to be credible. If, on the other hand, we moralise the definition of liberty, as some do, then the charge that critics of capitalism misassimilate alien values to that of liberty rebounds on the prosecution. For the second definition harmonises

[8] Philosophy's most considerable libertarian is committed to some such characterisation of liberty, since for him a person's freedom is not compromised by restrictions on his choices which do not come from the unjustified behaviour of others. See Robert Nozick, *Anarchy, State and Utopia* (New York, 1974), p. 262.

free enterprise and economic liberty only under a certain evaluation of private property.

Recall that the liberal, unlike the libertarian, does not say that he supports a policy of economic liberty pure and simple. He says he thinks it right to restrict liberty in the interest of social and economic security. But if he stays with the morally neutral definition, he cannot call the policy he wishes to modify one of pure economic liberty. And if he passes over to the moralised definition, he cannot say that taxation for social services and State direction of the market interfere with liberty, since they are, *ex hypothesi*, given the policy he favours, justified. Neither definition entitles him to describe his political recommendations as fruit of a compromise between liberty and other values, not, at any rate, without far more argument than is standardly supplied.[9]

Much familiar liberal rhetoric is strictly incoherent, using 'liberty' in a morally neutral way in respect of taxation, and in a morally fraught way in respect of Morgan's yacht. Libertarians, like Nozick, can consistently use a moralised definition, because they think the public interventions liberals allow are justified. But liberals, thinking them justified, must vacillate between competing identifications of freedom.

Now I hope it will be agreed that the moralised definition is incorrect: even justified interferences reduce freedom.[10] We may therefore conclude that private property restricts liberty. So, of course, does

[9] Isaiah Berlin once praised Roosevelt's New Deal as 'the most constructive compromise between individual liberty and economic security which our own time has witnessed' (in an essay of 1949: see *F.E.L.*, p. 31), and the idea that the New Deal reduced the first of these values for the sake of the second is not uncommon in liberal circles. I contend that no coherent concept of individual liberty justifies these descriptions. When a man's economic security is enhanced, there typically are, *as a result*, fewer 'obstacles to possible choices and activities' for him (ibid., p. xxxix), and he therefore typically enjoys more individual liberty. Perhaps the individual liberty of already economically secure people was reduced by the New Deal, but how do liberals know, what talk of 'compromise' between liberty and competing values implies, that individual liberty as such (not just that of members of certain classes) was reduced? I do not think the quoted characterisation of the New Deal is compatible with Isaiah Berlin's later acknowledgement (see ibid., p. xlvi) that 'the case for social legislation or planning, for the welfare state and socialism' can be based on consideration of liberty.

My criticism of Isaiah Berlin respects his distinction between liberty and the conditions for it (ibid., p. liii), of which economic security is one. I do not say that economic security *is* liberty, but that typically, and certainly in the context of Berlin's comment, it causes liberty to increase, just as equality in education (also not a form of liberty) does, to take Berlin's own example (ibid., p. liv).

[10] For defence of this rather obvious claim, see my 'Robert Nozick and Wilt Chamberlain', in Arthur and Shaw, op. cit. (note 1 above), p. 259.

communal property. All property rules do. Which set is best for liberty is a difficult question, briefly addressed below. From liberal discourse the answer would appear easy, but liberal discourse is conceptually untenable.

I now need to consider a possible liberal response to what has been argued. It might be granted that if I cannot use Morgan's yacht, then this restricts my liberty, but not, it could be said, my *economic* liberty. If the connection between capitalism and liberty has been overstated, the possibility that capitalism is *economic* liberty still requires consideration.

The resurrected identification will survive only if the unavailability to me of Morgan's yacht is no restriction on my economic liberty. I can think of only one reason for saying so. It is that I am not here restricted with respect to whether I may sell something I own, or buy something in exchange for what I own.[11] If that is economic liberty, then indeed Morgan does not restrict it.

A different definition of economic liberty would include in it liberty to use goods and services. But I have no wish to recommend any particular definition of the phrase 'economic liberty'. Unlike 'liberty', it is an expression whose meaning needs to be stipulated, and I have no favourite stipulation.

So I reply to the liberal as follows. Either economic liberty includes the liberty to use goods and services, or it does not. If it does, then capitalism withholds freedom wherever it grants it: the Morgan case proves that. If, on the other hand, economic liberty relates to buying and selling, then the case for identifying economic liberty and free enterprise looks better. But see how narrowly we have had to define 'economic liberty' to obtain this result. On a wide but plausible definition of 'economic liberty', capitalism offers a particular limited form of it. On a narrow definition, the limitations recede, but we are now talking about a narrow liberty.

Some may have found the preceding arguments boringly sound. But not everyone. For there is, understandably in our capitalist civilisation, a strong attachment in theory and in practice to the falsehood that capitalism by its very nature offers a rich and extensive freedom. I want to mention two sources of this ideological illusion.

First, there is a tendency to take as part of the structure of human existence in general any structure around which, merely as things are, much of our activity is organised. In capitalist society, the in-

[11] This is pretty well what Narveson means by economic liberty: see op. cit. (note 1 above), p. 3.

stitution of private property is such a structure. It is treated as so *given* that the obstacles it puts to freedom are not perceived, while any impingement on it is readily noticed. Yet private property pretty well *is* a distribution of freedom *and* unfreedom. It is necessarily associated with the liberty of private owners to do as they wish with what they own,[12] but it no less necessarily withdraws liberty from those who do not own it. To think of capitalism as a realm of economic freedom is to miss half of its nature.

The second source of the illusion that capitalism is an essentially free society is that certain capitalist societies have, to their credit, protected many important freedoms beyond that of buying and selling:[13] freedom of speech, assembly, worship, publication, movement, political participation, and so on.

Opinions differ on how accidental the connection between capitalism and those freedoms has been and is. Here I need contend only that they are not necessary concomitants of capitalism, however intelligible it may be that their advent accompanied, and was even a factor in, the bourgeois ascendancy.

Freedom to buy and sell belongs to capitalism's inmost nature. Other freedoms do not, though they feature significantly in its history. I speculate that these truths get fused in the ideological conviction that capitalism is by nature a comprehensively free society.

I have wanted to show that private property, and therefore capitalist society, limit liberty, but I have not said that they do so more than communal property and socialist society. Each form of society is by its nature congenial and hostile to various sorts of liberty, for variously placed people. And concrete societies exemplifying either form will offer and withhold additional liberties whose presence or absence may not be inferred from the nature of the form itself. Which form is better for liberty, all things considered, is a question which may have no answer in the abstract.[14] Which form is better for liberty may depend on the historical circumstances.

The two social forms promote liberties of various kinds, but not, I think it important to insist, liberty in two different senses of that term. To the claim that capitalism gives people freedom some

[12] Qualifications: sometimes there are freedom-reducing duties of care and upkeep attached to private property, but one is rarely, on balance, *less* free as a result of owning something.

[13] Though with various degrees of backsliding, depending on the balance of class forces and national tradition, when capitalism is under fundamental challenge.

[14] I think it has no answer in the abstract, but I am not sure. For an attempt at a general answer favouring socialism, see Ernest Loevinsohn, 'Liberty and the Redistribution of Property', *Philosophy and Public Affairs* 6 (1976–7), 226–39.

socialists respond that what they get is *merely* bourgeois freedom. Good things can be meant by that response: that there are important particular liberties which capitalism does not confer, and/or that I do not have liberty, but only a necessary condition of it, when a course of action (e.g. yachting) is, though not *itself* against the law, unavailable to me anyway, because other laws (e.g. of private property) forbid me the means to perform it. But when socialists suggest that there is no real liberty under capitalism, or that socialism promises liberty of a higher and unprecedented kind, then I think their line is theoretically incorrect and politically disastrous. For liberty under capitalism is, where it exists, just that, liberty; and if socialism will not give us plenty of it, we shall rightly be disappointed.

Narveson thinks socialists speak falsely when they claim that they seek to expand freedom. He also wonders why they should *want* to say so: 'Why insist on stating one's aims in such a way as to foster the illusion that one is agreeing [in respect of ultimate values] with the very people one is opposing?'[15] But much socialist commitment represents a judgement that capitalism does not live up to its own professions. The real socialist challenge to the libertarian is that pure capitalism does not protect liberty in general, but only those liberties built into private property, an institution which also limits liberty. The real socialist challenge to the liberal is that the modifications of modified capitalism modify not liberty but private property, often in the interests of liberty itself. Consequently, transformations far more revolutionary than a liberal would contemplate might be justified on the very same grounds as those which support liberal reform.

A homespun example shows how communal property can offer a differently shaped liberty, in no different sense of that term. Neighbours A and B own sets of household tools. Each has some tools which the other lacks. If A needs a tool of a kind which only B has, then, private property being what it is, he is not free to take B's one for a while, even if B does not need it during that while. Now imagine that the following rule is imposed, bringing the tools into partly common ownership: each may take and use a tool belonging to the other without permission provided that the other is not using it and that he returns it when he no longer needs it, or when the other needs it, whichever comes first. *Things being what they are* (an important qualification: we are talking, as often we should, about the real world, not about remote possibilities), the communising rule

[15] op. cit. (note 1 above), p. 5.

would, I contend, increase tool-using freedom, on any reasonable view. To be sure, some freedoms are removed by the new rule. Neither neighbour is as assured of the same easy access as before to the tools that were wholly his. Sometimes he has to go next door to retrieve one of them. Nor can either now charge the other for use of a tool he himself does not then require. But these restrictions will likely be less important than the increased range of tools available. No one is as sovereign as before over any tool, so the privateness of the property is reduced. But freedom is probably expanded. (Though of course, and irrelevantly, each would have more freedom still if he were the sovereign owner of *all* the tools.)

An opponent might reply: the rules of private property do not forbid neighbours to contract in favour of the stated arrangement. If both would gain from the change, and they are rational, they will agree to it. No communist property rule, laid down independently of contract, is needed.

This is a good reply with respect to the case at hand. My only counter is the weakish one that life under capitalism sometimes causes an irrationally strong adherence to purely private use of purely private property which can lead to neglect of mutually gainful options.

That small point aside, it must be granted that contracts often generate desirably communal structures, sometimes with transaction costs which communist rules would not impose, but also without the administrative costs which often attach to communal regulation.

But the stated method of achieving communism cannot be generalised. We could not by contract bring into fully mutual ownership those non-household tools and resources which Marxists call means of production. They will never be won for socialism by contract, since they belong to a small minority, to whom the rest can offer no *quid pro quo*.[16] Most of the rest must hire out their labour power to members of that minority, in exchange for the right to some of the proceeds of their labour on facilities in whose ownership they do not share.

So we reach, at length, the third item in the title of this paper, and an important charge, with respect to liberty, which Marxists lay

16 Unless the last act of this scenario qualifies as a contract: in the course of a general strike a united working class demands that private property in major means of production be socialised, as a condition of their return to work, and a demoralised capitalist class meets the demand. (How, by the way, could libertarians object to such a revolution? For hints, see Nozick's essay on 'Coercion', in P. Laslett, W. G. Runciman and Q. Skinner, *Philosophy, Politics and Society*, Fourth Series (Oxford, 1972).)

against capitalism. It is that in capitalist society the great majority of people are forced to sell their labour power, because they do not own any means of production.

Marxists call that great majority the proletariat, or anyway classical Marxists did. In original Marxism the proletariat is defined as those who own their labour power but not means of production. It is inferred from the definition that they are forced to sell their labour power, on pain of starvation.

Now if the definition is supposed to tell us who belongs to the working class in the real world (as opposed to some abstract model), then it is inadequate. For plenty who own no means of production are not commonly accounted working class, nor is there any reason of high theory or of revolutionary practice so to classify them. Well-salaried architects may own no means of production, but they are not proletarians. The classical Marxist definition is therefore too wide.

It is also too narrow, or so I have argued elsewhere.[17] Some genuine proletarians do own means of production. I gave examples from the history of the capitalist garment industry, where skilled workers have owned their means of cutting and sewing cloth.

Yet it is true of those workers, or, not to beg a question which we are about to examine, *as* true of them as of those who lack means of production, that they are forced to sell their labour power to capitalists. For they cannot live by producing with the means they own, except in capitalist employment. In all cases the capitalist's power over the worker comes from his favourable position within the network of market relations. Only in standard cases is that position a matter of his owning means of production which the worker cannot acquire.

The counter-examples motivate a revision of the classical definition, which brings us closer to the heart of things. Instead of saying that the workers are the owners of labour power who own no means of production, we say that the workers are those who are forced to sell their labour power. We take the inference from the classical definition, and we make it the definition itself. (The first clause of the old definition, that workers own their labour power, is still implied, since you can sell only what you own; but the second element, lack of means of production, is dropped.)

The new definition says that a man is a proletarian if and only if he is forced to sell his labour power. Is the stated condition necessary

[17] *Karl Marx's Theory of History* (Oxford/Princeton, 1978), chapter 3, section 4.

and sufficient? Certainly not all who sell their labour power are proletarians, but the condition is that one be *forced* to sell it. Still, it must be admitted that plenty of salaried non-proletarians are as much forced as many workers. So the condition is not sufficient, and I have nothing to add here in an attempt to make it so.

Let us now ask whether the condition is a necessary one: *are* proletarians forced to sell their labour power?

Robert Nozick answers negatively. He grants that many proletarians have no alternative but to sell their labour power, but he denies that having no alternative but to do A entails being forced to do A: to have no alternative means to be forced only if injustice helps to explain the lack of alternative. Property distributions reflecting a past history of acquisition and exchange may leave a worker with no other choice, but he is nevertheless not forced to sell his labour power, if the acquiring and exchanging were not unfair.

Nozick's objection to our condition rests upon a false because moralised account of what it is to be forced to do something. We therefore set it aside.[18]

There is, however, an objection to the condition (as necessary condition) which does not depend upon a moralised view of what being forced involves. Before we come to it, a comment on how I intend to take the predicate 'is forced to sell his labour power'. It is supposed to supply a definition of the proletariat which departs minimally from the traditional Marxian one. Now for traditional Marxism classes are defined by social relations of production,[19] and the new definition is supposed to meet that constraint: it purports to disclose the nature of the proletariat's insertion in capitalist relations of production. But relations of production are, for Marxism, *objective*: what relations of production a man is in does not turn on his consciousness. It follows that if the proletarian is forced to sell his labour power in the relevant Marxist sense, then this must be because of his objective situation, and not because of his attitude to himself, his level of self-confidence, his cultural attainment, and so on.

Being forced by one's objective situation is being forced by factors other than the subjective ones just listed. But what is the right positive characterisation of those factors? It would seem that they

[18] For fuller discussion, see the article cited in note 10 above. (Anyone who agrees with Nozick may read 'has no choice but to' for all occurrences of 'is forced to' in what follows. He can take it that we are investigating the proposal that proletarians have no choice but to sell their labour power.)

[19] On social relations of production, see *Karl Marx's Theory of History*, op. cit. (note 17 above), chapter 2, section 1, and chapter 3, *passim*.

must be actual and possible actions of other people. But that is perhaps not enough. For here objective constraint is supposed to be due to relations of production. We must therefore stipulate, in addition, some connection between the constraining actions of others and relations of production. Several alternatives suggest themselves: that the actions be rendered necessary by production relations, that they be rendered likely by them, and that they be rendered possible by them – these are some of the candidates. The alternatives raise deep questions about structure, action and consciousness, which there is no space to pursue here. Bracketing them off, I shall take it as necessary and sufficient for X's being objectively forced to sell his labour power that there is no other course for him which would not be blocked by actions of others.

Under this interpretation of 'is forced to sell his labour power', a serious problem arises. For if there are persons whose objective position is identical with that of proletarians, but who are not forced to sell their labour power, then proletarians are not relevantly so forced, and the condition fails. And there certainly are such persons.

They are those proletarians, who, initially possessed of no greater resources than most, secure positions in the petty bourgeoisie and elsewhere, thereby rising above the proletariat. Striking cases in Britain are members of certain immigrant groups, who arrive penniless, and without good connections, but who propel themselves up the class hierarchy, with effort, luck and skill. One thinks – it is a contemporary example – of those who are willing to work very long hours in shops bought from native British petty bourgeois, shops which used to close early. Their initial capital is typically an amalgam of petty savings which they accumulated, perhaps painfully, while still in the proletarian condition, and some form of external finance. *Objectively speaking* most[20] proletarians are in a position to obtain these. Therefore most proletarians are not forced to sell their labour power.

I now refute two natural objections to the above argument.

The first objection is that the recently mentioned persons were, *while they were proletarians*, forced to sell their labour power. The examples show not that proletarians are not forced to sell their labour, but that proletarians are not forced to remain proletarians.

This objection displays failure to appreciate an important truth

20 At least most: it could be argued that this is true of the overwhelming majority, or even of all, depending on how we refine the difficult phrase "objectively speaking", which has not been fully analysed here. For the rest of this paper I modestly stick with "most".

about freedom and constraint for my awareness of which I am indebted to an article by Alvin Goldman:[21] *fully explicit attributions of freedom and constraint contain at least two temporal references.* To illustrate: I may now be in a position truly to say that I am free to attend a concert tomorrow night. If so, I am *now* free to attend a concert *tomorrow night.* In similar fashion, the time when I am constrained to perform an action need not be identical with the time of the action: I might *now* be forced to attend a concert *tomorrow night* (since you might already have ensured that if I do not, I shall suffer some great loss).

When Marxists say that proletarians are those who are forced to sell their labour power, they do not mean: 'X is a proletarian at time t if and only if X is at time t forced to sell his labour power at time t', for that would be compatible with his being free not to at $t+n$, no matter how small n is. X might be forced on Tuesday to sell his labour power on Tuesday, but if he is not forced on Tuesday to sell his labour power on Wednesday, then, though still a proletarian on Tuesday, he is not forced to sell his labour power in the required Marxist sense. The manifest intent of the Marxist claim is that the proletarian is forced *to continue* to sell his labour power, and we may understand 'is forced to sell his labour power' as short for that. It follows that because there is a route to escape from the proletariat, which our counter-examples travelled, the proletarian is not forced to sell his labour power in the required sense.

Proletarians who have the option of upward class ascent are not forced to sell their labour power, just because they have that option. Most proletarians have that option as much as our counter-examples did. Therefore most proletarians are not forced to sell their labour power.

But now we face a second objection. It is that necessarily not more than a few proletarians can exercise the option of upward ascent. For capitalism, to be capitalism, requires a substantial hired labour force, which would not exist if more than just a few workers rose.[22]

[21] 'Power, Time and Cost', in *Philosophical Studies* 26 (1974), 263–70: see especially pp. 263–5.

[22] 'The truth is this, that in this bourgeois society every workman, if he is an exceedingly clever and shrewd fellow, and gifted with bourgeois instincts and favoured by an exceptional fortune, can possibly convert himself into an *exploiteur du travail d'autrui*. But if there were no *travail* to be *exploité*, there would be no capitalist nor capitalist production.' Karl Marx, 'Results of the Immediate Process of Production', in *Capital: Volume I*, trans. Ben Fowkes (Harmondsworth, 1976), p. 1079. For similar texts, and commentary, see my *Karl Marx's Theory of History*, op. cit. (note 17 above), p. 243.

Put differently, there are necessarily only enough petty bourgeois and other non-proletarian positions for a small number of the proletariat to leave that estate.

The premise is correct, but does it defeat the argument against which it is directed? Does it refute the claim that most proletarians are not forced to sell their labour power? I think not.

An analogy will indicate why. Ten men are placed in a room the only exit from which is a huge and heavy locked door. At various distances from each lies a single heavy key. Whoever picks up this key – and each is physically able, with varying degrees of effort, to do so – and takes it to the door will find, after considerable self-application, a way to open the door and leave the room. But if he does so he alone will be able to leave it. Photoelectric devices ensure that it will open only just enough to permit one exit. Then it will close, and no one inside the room will be able to open it again.

It follows that, whatever happens, at least nine men will remain in the room.

Now suppose that not one of the men is disposed to try to obtain the key and leave the room. Perhaps the room is no bad place, and they do not want to leave. Or perhaps it is pretty bad, but they are too lazy to undertake the effort needed to escape. Or perhaps no one believes he would be able to secure the key in face of the capacity of the others to intervene (though they would not in fact intervene, since they are similarly diffident). Suppose that whatever grounds the indisposition to leave it is so strong that if, counterfactually, one of the men were to try to leave, the others would not interfere. The men's inaction is relevant to my argument, but the explanation of it is not.

Then whomever we select, it is true of the other nine that not one of them is going to try to get the key. Therefore it is true of the selected man that he is free to obtain the key: no one will stop him. Therefore it is true of the selected man that he is not forced to remain in the room. But all this is true of whomever we select. Therefore it is true of each man that he is not forced to remain in the room, even though necessarily nine will remain in the room.

Consider now a slightly different example: the situation described above, with some modifications. In the new case there are two doors and two keys. Again there are ten men, but this time one of them does try to get out, and succeeds, while the rest behave as before. Now necessarily eight will remain in the room, but it is true of each of the nine who do stay that he is free to leave it. The pertinent general feature, present in both cases, is that there is at least one means of egress which none will attempt to use, and which each is free to use, since, *ex hypothesi*, no one would block his way.

By now the application of the analogy may be obvious. The number of exits from the proletariat is, as a matter of objective circumstance, small. But most proletarians are not trying to escape, and, as a result,[23] *it is false that each exit is being actively pursued by some proletarian.*[24] Therefore for most[25] proletarians there exists a means of escape. So even though necessarily most proletarians will remain proletarians, and will sell their labour power, at most a minority are forced to do so.

In reaching this conclusion, which is one about the proletariat's *objective* position, we used some facts of consciousness, regarding workers' aspirations and intentions. That is legitimate. For if the workers are objectively forced to sell their labour power, then they are forced to do so whatever their consciousness may be. But actual subjective data entail that they are not forced to sell their labour power. Hence they are not objectively forced to sell their labour power.

One could say, speaking rather broadly, that we have found more freedom in the proletariat's situation than classical Marxism asserts. But if we return to the basis on which we affirm that most proletarians are not forced to sell their labour power we shall arrive at a more refined description of the objective position with respect to force and freedom. What was said will not be withdrawn, but we shall add significantly to it.

That basis was the reasoning originally applied to the case of the men in the locked room. Each is free to seize the key and leave. But note the conditional nature of his freedom. He is free not only *because* none of the others attempts to get the key, but *on condition* that they do not (a condition which, in the story, is fulfilled). Then *each is free only on condition that the others do not exercise their similar freedom.* Not more than one can exercise the liberty they all have. If, moreover, anyone were to exercise, it, then, because of the structure of the situation, all the others would lose it.

Since the freedom of each is contingent on the others' not exercising their similarly contingent freedom, we can say that there is a

[23] This is not a necessary consequence, just an actual one.

[24] What if it were true? What if there were a perpetual mad scramble for all available transproletarian positions? The consequences for constraint and freedom would depend on the answers to questions about objective constraint which we bracketed off on p. 20.

[25] 'Most': see note 20 above.

great deal of unfreedom in the group. With respect to leaving, *these free individuals compose a severely constrained group.*

In defence of this description, let us reconsider the question why the men do not try to leave. Three reasons were suggested earlier: lack of desire, laziness and diffidence. All three relate to wholly self-regarding attitudes, what a man wants and fears for himself alone. But the annals of human motivation show that sometimes people care about the fate of others, and they sometimes have that concern when they share a common oppression. Suppose, then, not so wildly, that there is a sentiment of solidarity in that room. A fourth explanation of the absence of attempt to leave now suggests itself. It is that no one will be satisfied with a personal escape which is not part of a general liberation.

The new supposition does not disturb the claim that each is free to leave, for we may assume that it remains true of each man that he would suffer no interference if, counterfactually, he sought to use the key (assume the others would have contempt for him, but not try to stop him). Each remains free to leave. Yet we can envisage members of the group communicating to their gaoler (imagine there is one) a demand for freedom, to which he could hardly reply that they are free already (even though, individually, they are). The hypothesis of solidarity makes it evident that this is an imprisoned group. But unless we say, absurdly, that the solidarity creates the imprisonment, we must say that the group is imprisoned whether or not solidarity obtains.

Returning to the proletariat, we can conclude, by parity of reasoning, that although most proletarians are free to escape the proletariat, indeed even if all are, *the proletariat is an imprisoned class.*

It was part of our argument for the freedom of individual proletarians that not every exit from the proletariat is crowded with would-be escapees. Let us now ask – we did not earlier – why this should be so. Here are some of the reasons:

1. It is not easy to escape, just possible, and often people do not attempt what is possible but hard.

2. There is also what Marx called the 'dull compulsion of economic relations'.[26] Long occupancy, for example from birth, of a subordinate class position nurtures the illusion, as important for the stability of the system as the myth of easy escape, that one's class position is natural and inescapable.

[26] *Capital: Volume I*, op. cit. (note 22 above), p. 899.

3. Finally, there is the fact that not all workers would like to be petty or trans-petty bourgeois. Eugene Debs said, 'I do not want to rise above the working class, I want to rise with them', thereby evincing an attitude like the one lately attributed to the men in the locked room. It is sometimes true of the worker that, in Brecht's words,

> He wants no servants under him
> And no boss over his head.[27]

Those lines envisage a better liberation: not just from the working class, but from class society.

Addendum

I have argued that the proletariat is an enslaved class, forced, as a class, to sell its labour power, despite the freedom of many, probably most, of its members not to do so. But I have still not provided a definition of the proletariat. One could not say: it is that group which is such that necessarily most of its members sell their labour power. For there are many such groups, and not all of them are proletariats. There is, for example, the group consisting of whoever the proletarians are in Britain and Sir Keith Joseph. That group is such that necessarily most of its members sell their labour power, but it is not a proletariat.

It is an interesting question, which I have not investigated, whether one might define the proletariat *beginning* with the concept of *the working class*, rather than *member of the working class*, which is where traditional attempts at definition begin, in effect if not in form. (I italicise 'beginning' because it must remain a constraint on the definition that it yield criteria of inclusion and exclusion of individuals, even if not immediately or directly.)

For good criticism of mistakes and infelicities in an earlier version of this piece, I thank Marcus Gabb, Danny Goldstick, Keith Graham, Robin Halpin, Alan Haworth, Charles Langley, David Lloyd-Thomas, Ernie Loevinsohn, John McMurtry, Jan Narveson, Chris Provis, Adrienne Pyne, Bill Shaw, Hillel Steiner, Jerry Valberg and Richard Wollheim. I am most grateful to Arnold Zuboff, from discussions with whom I benefited enormously at every stage.

[27] From his 'Song of the United Front'.

PATRICK GARDINER

Freedom as an Aesthetic Idea

Schiller's *Letters on the Aesthetic Education of Man* is a complex and intricate work which can be interpreted in many ways and in which various themes are to be found interwoven and combined. Though rich in content and fluent in exposition, it does not follow the pattern of a rigorous or firmly structured argument, but rather pursues an open and serpentine course; ideas taken up at one point are allowed to recede into the background at others, only to be brought forward again – often in a transfigured form – at later stages of the discussion. At the same time, it can be said to reflect a host of different preoccupations, some deriving from the period of political and ideological crisis during which it was composed, and some from stresses in the author's own temperament and the problems that confronted him as a highly self-conscious and self-critical artist; while these contribute to the vitality and suggestiveness of the book, the multiplicity of issues to which they give rise does not always make for easy understanding. None the less, two concerns may be picked out as central to Schiller's project, both primarily philosophical in character, and both drawing inspiration from doctrines recently advanced by Kant. The first involved the concept of human freedom, the second the distinctive nature of aesthetic judgement and experience. Whereas, however, Kant had been largely content to consider these topics in relative independence and as raising quite separate questions, it was one of Schiller's prime objects in the *Aesthetic Letters* to relate them and to exhibit them as intimately connected.

At first sight this might seem a strange, even quixotic, enterprise. Freedom, it might be claimed, essentially has to do with action and the will and with the relation in which men stand to other human beings; as such, it can only properly be discussed and examined in a moral or social context where practical decisions and the possibility of implementing these are in question. What conceivable relevance can it have to the sphere of aesthetics, the realm of taste and feeling and of private enjoyment of beauty? Does not the latter, of its very essence, fall outside the domain of the practical?

Schiller himself was fully alive to such objections, as indeed he had good reason to be. For some of them could be said to follow directly from a consideration of Kant's own theory of freedom, in which the idea of will was given priority of place and to which the conception of man as a being capable of determining his conduct in certain morally desirable ways was fundamental. Human freedom was portrayed by Kant as involving a capacity to act independently of the promptings of desire or inclination. It was, moreover, closely tied to morality through the notion of autonomy: Kant implied that it was only in so far as a man chose to make his actions conform to principles which he himself prescribed as binding upon all rational beings that what he did could properly and in the full sense be described as free. Thus an account had been offered which seemed, not merely to treat freedom as a precondition of morally praiseworthy action, but to identify the former with the conception of an autonomous rationality that altogether transcended the sphere of natural feeling and desire: 'what else', Kant rhetorically asked at one point, ' . . . can freedom of will be but autonomy – that is, the property which will has of being a law to itself?'[1] The outcome was an ethic never perhaps surpassed in the uncompromising austerity of its demands, often giving the impression that the manifestation of any kind of spontaneous sentiment or sympathetic feeling necessarily detracted from the moral worth of behaviour. And the doctrine of freedom which it embodied as an integral part appeared to be hardly less severe in its ultimate implications. For it apparently involved the claim that freedom could only be truly or 'positively' achieved by overcoming the 'sensuous' elements that characterised man as a causally governed creature of nature, and by conforming instead to the self-imposed laws of pure reason. From this it was natural to conclude that its attainment entailed a continual inner struggle: Kant spoke with approval of the 'compulsion' (*Zwang*) exercised by the moral law and of the way in which, through its opposition to 'subjective inclinations', it struck down and humbled our 'self-conceit'. Such metaphors were revealing. For in a general way the picture Kant drew of moral experience was imbued with the ideas of conflict and division, man's sensuous passions and proclivities being presented as forces which it was incumbent upon him to master and subdue if he was to realise himself as a rational being.

It must be admitted that Kant's account of freedom was not without a certain ambiguity, having two aspects which he did not

[1] *Groundwork of the Metaphysic of Morals*, trans. H. J. Paton (New York, 1964), p. 114.

always sufficiently distinguish. It was one thing to argue that it was always within a man's power not to follow his natural impulses and inclinations and to act instead according to principles prescribed by his reason alone. It was another to claim that it was only when he so chose that his actions could legitimately be dignified as free. Yet, on Kant's own showing, it was presumably entirely possible for him to decide otherwise. Furthermore, if he took such a course, he could be described as having chosen to give free expression to his natural desires in a manner that would have been denied to them if he had opted for moral autonomy in Kant's sense: from this point of view (it might be contended) to reserve for the latter the title of 'true freedom' was tantamount to giving priority to one sort of freedom at the expense of another. Kant himself sometimes recognised the distinction in question through the contrast he drew between *Willkür* (free or 'arbitrary' will) and *Wille* (autonomous practical reason); he did not, however, always do so, and in any case it was the sense in which freedom was equated with rational self-determination that he tended to stress. Nevertheless the difference remains and is important, not least for its bearing upon Schiller's reaction to the Kantian theory.

Along with many of his contemporaries, Schiller was from the first profoundly impressed by Kant's conception of the human will as a 'vital power' capable of rising above the realm of natural necessitation, and it was one that continued to haunt him. As he wrote in an essay published towards the end of his life, when he was discussing the concept of the sublime: 'We are ravished by the terrifying because we are able to will that which our sensuous impulses are appalled by, and can reject what they desire . . . We gladly subordinate our well-being and our existence to physical necessity, for we are reminded thereby that it cannot command our principles. Man is in its hands, but man's will is in his own hands.'[2] Further, as some of Schiller's earlier essays on dramatic criticism make clear, this notion played a crucial role in his interpretation of tragedy. The tragic hero, he suggested, was most effectively represented by one who withstood or overcame the forces of nature, whether these took the form of powerful inner urges or whether they manifested themselves externally in the shape of seductive or threatening circumstances. The dramatist could thereby exhibit in the clearest light the capacity of human beings to assert their independence of the 'blind necessity' that governed the natural order, the suffering en-

[2] *Two Essays by Friedrich von Schiller: Naive and Sentimental Poetry and On the Sublime*, trans. J. A. Elias (New York, 1966), p. 199.

tailed thereby only serving to underline the sense of wonder appropriate to a vindication of the 'supersensible' element in man on which Kant had laid such stress. An example which Schiller considered particularly apposite from this point of view was Corneille's *Le Cid*; and he was correspondingly less enthusiastic about plays, such as *King Lear*, in which the misfortunes that befell the central figure were attributable to his own weaknesses and faults of character.[3]

Yet, while Schiller's regard for Kant as affording a fresh perspective upon problems relating to dramatic art was deep and lasting, it did not prevent him from adopting a markedly more sceptical attitude towards some of the wider implications of the Kantian doctrine of moral freedom. In so doing he was, moreover, also aware that at the hands of Kant's self-proclaimed follower, Fichte, his ideas were being developed in a fashion which had already had the effect of greatly extending the claims made on behalf of practical reason and which was eventually to lead to an inflation of the ethical and volitional aspects of the human personality so extreme as apparently to leave little room for any others. Schiller's doubts on this score achieved their most eloquent and forthright expression in the *Aesthetic Letters*; it was there, above all, that he was concerned to emphasise the dangers inherent in a too narrow and circumscribed identification of freedom with rationality.

Schiller's reservations stemmed from a comprehensive view of the human subject which recognised and sought to do justice to its 'mixed' nature, and his own conception of freedom as it finally emerged can only be understood in terms of this. Any alternative ideal, whose realisation depended upon blocking the growth of some of our capacities in the interest of others, was in the last analysis inadequate; while to accord exclusive priority to the development of a single aspect of the human character was necessarily inimical to its health and fulfilment as a whole. A rigid and inflexible insistence upon the demands of moral autonomy represented just such a threat to our possibilities as human beings; the requirements imposed by a strict conformity to the edicts of self-legislative reason would, if allowed unrestricted sway, be as destructive of the life and functioning of the individual as the pressures of unfettered instinct, and equally divisive in their effects upon his personality. As Schiller remarked in one place, it would be a case of our giving ourselves 'a master within, who not infrequently ends by suppressing the rest of

[3] For an illuminating account of Schiller's treatment of tragedy in this context, see R. D. Miller, *Schiller and the Ideal of Freedom* (Oxford, 1970), chapters 2 and 3.

our potentialities'.[4] Amongst other things, such a position reflected a failure to recognise the legitimacy of our sensuous propensities, and it was a cardinal though common error to suppose that these could be mutilated and abused without damaging the overall integrity of a person, his status as a unitary whole. Certainly it was important and salutary to draw the attention of a 'degraded century' to the sublimity of the moral law and to man's capacity as a rational being to realise it in his behaviour; it was quite another matter, however, to treat it as comprising all that was truly valuable in human life, elevating it to a position of supremacy from which it was entitled to invade and dominate every other domain of human activity and experience. Kant himself might not have altogether intended his words to carry a message of the latter kind, but Schiller suggested that it was scarcely surprising if some of his followers had extracted it from what he had written.

In any event, the consequences of such an approach could only be spiritual impoverishment and a sense of deprivation: the 'inner unity of human nature' would be broken. Schiller was ready enough to admit that a complete surrender to instinctual or emotional urges would entail, quite literally, the loss or 'suspension' of the individual's reality as a 'person'. For the very notion of personality implied a degree of continuity and organisation, a capacity for self-direction and control, that was incompatible with an exclusive preoccupation with sensory satisfaction and the gratification of transitory appetites; ordinary language partly reflected this point when it described people under the influence of violent passions and impulses as being 'beside themselves'.[5] But while that was so, it was also true that counterbalancing dangers, no less serious, lurked on the other side. For if man was not a purely sensuous being, wholly subject to the vicissitudes of feeling, neither was he a purely rational one whose true nature could be exhaustively characterised in terms of his capacity for abstract thought and active will. Both elements were integral to his constitution as a human individual, and it followed that to accord to rationality predominance at the cost of feeling was ultimately as ruinous as to allow feeling to overwhelm rationality. There was an 'egotism of reason' that matched the 'egotism of the senses', and alongside the 'savage', in whom 'feeling predominates over principle', Schiller set the 'barbarian', in whom 'principle destroys feeling'. The mentality of the latter was marked

[4] *On the Aesthetic Education of Man*, trans. E. M. Wilkinson and L. A. Willoughby (Oxford, 1967), p. 89.
[5] ibid., p. 79.

by a contraction of the heart and a blunting of natural sensibility; at the same time, because of the narrowness and stringency of the requirements reason imposed, it was constantly liable to lapse into hypocrisy and self-deception – 'the barbarian derides and dishonours nature, but, more contemptible than the savage, as often as not continues to be the slave of his slave'.[6] It was, indeed, typical of one who belonged to this category that he should be 'at odds with himself', engaged in a conflict that he could not hope to win, and paying lip-service to ideals which his own behaviour continually belied.

Although he was partly concerned, in the name of a more generous conception of the human mind, to criticise specific philosophical doctrines of freedom, Schiller at the same time regarded his strictures as having a far wider bearing and significance. For he believed (in a manner that often recalls Herder) that such theoretical attempts to isolate and give precedence to certain functions of the psyche at the cost of others no less worthy of respect were symptomatic of tendencies that prevailed at the level of actual political and social existence. 'The various faculties', he wrote, '. . . appear as separate in practice as they are distinguished by the psychologist in theory, and we see not merely individuals, but whole classes of men, developing but one part of their potentialities, while of the rest, as in stunted growths, only vestigial traces remain.'[7] This had not always been the case. In common with others of his period Schiller looked back nostalgically to the era of classical Greece, when man was not 'at odds with himself' and when no dissension between the intellect and the senses had as yet provoked them into 'hostile partition' and mutual antagonism. It was the process of modern civilisation that had been responsible for inflicting 'this wound', through the proliferation of specialised intellectual disciplines and the parallel rise of increasingly bureaucratic political structures. Schiller had no wish to deny the advances that had been made or the material benefits that had ensued; none the less, the price had been a high one. Modern governments, in pursuing their overall objectives, were prone to treat their subjects from a point of view exclusively determined by the contributions they made to these aims; they thereby helped to reinforce and institutionalise trends that had arisen independently under the pressure of economic and technical developments. 'When the community makes his office the measure

[6] ibid., p. 21. The character of Angelo in Shakespeare's *Measure for Measure* seems perfectly to illustrate what Schiller had in mind.

[7] ibid., p. 33.

of the man; when in one of its citizens it prizes nothing but memory, in another a mere tabularising intelligence, in a third only mechanical skill . . . can we wonder', Schiller asks, 'that the remaining aptitudes of the psyche are neglected in order to give undivided attention to the one which will bring honour and profit?'[8]

It was Schiller's contention that the full extent of such 'fragmentary specialisation' had not as yet been realised or its consequences properly appraised. The restriction and coordination of human activities in ways appropriate to the most effective attainment of social goals might be a prerequisite for the creation of a civilised order, but it remained at best no more than a necessary instrument, a means to an end. Whatever its historical significance, it was not a permanent condition of social existence, nor should it be allowed finally to obscure, in the name of some utilitarian standard of mechanical efficiency, the vision of a society to which each man would belong as a 'complete' individual, able to enjoy the unconstrained and frictionless fulfilment of his various powers. These were fertile notions. By suggesting that the problems confronting his age were primarily ones of cleavage and estrangement, by treating the tensions involved as from one standpoint representing the price that had to be paid in the interests of social progress and from another as being conditions that must be overcome in the pursuit of a healing all-embracing harmony, Schiller had touched on a theme that was to recur in German thought for more than fifty years after he wrote. Unlike some of his more metaphysically-minded successors, however, he interpreted the issues in purely human terms, seeking a solution based upon an appeal to the aesthetic consciousness and to the possibilities of liberation that it offered. In his own words, 'it must be open to us to restore by means of a higher Art the totality of our nature which the arts themselves have destroyed'.[9]

The sentence quoted may contain an allusion to Rousseau, and particularly to his *Discourse on the Moral Effects of the Arts and Sciences*, in which the deleterious influence of artistic activities upon the human character had been delineated with a vehemence almost unequalled since Plato. In any event, Schiller was certainly acquainted with this line of argument, and in the tenth of his *Letters* he makes various references to Rousseau's points and historical examples. Yet the question of whether art could justifiably be viewed as a source of corruption clearly depended upon a correct conception of its nature and of the role it played in our mental life; and for a

[8] ibid., p. 31.
[9] ibid., p. 43.

more fruitful account, suggestive of the ways in which an understanding of aesthetic experiences might be relevant to the matters that concerned him, Schiller turned, not to Rousseau, but once more to Kant.

In some respects Kant's *Critique of Judgement* can be seen as an attempt to soften the sharp contrast drawn in his two previous Critiques between the spheres of theoretical and practical thinking, qualifying his earlier claim that in the investigation of nature the only admissible modes of explanation were of a causal or 'mechanistic' kind. Thus, in the second part of the book, he embarks upon an extended analysis of purposive notions, arguing that it is with reference to these, rather than to mechanical ideas, that we find it possible to come to terms with the workings of living organisms. Some of the references to nature in Schiller's own writings echo this altered emphasis; even so, it was not Kant's treatment of natural teleology that chiefly impressed him, but rather the detailed discussion of aesthetic appreciation which occupied the first part of the work. And here the most significant points of contrast seemed to be, not with what Kant had written previously about the nature of scientific understanding, but with what he had said about freedom in the setting of his moral philosophy.

The differences partly showed themselves in Kant's characterisation of the kind of attitude we typically adopt in aesthetic contexts, an attitude he described as 'contemplative'. In situations requiring action and practical choice our approach to things was governed by 'interest': the interest in question might spring from natural inclination or, alternatively, it might be founded upon respect for the claims of morality; but, whichever was the case, it precluded a 'free judgement' of the objects concerned – the conception we formed of them, the satisfaction we took in them, were dictated by what we wanted or by what morality required. On the other hand, the aesthetic pleasure we obtained from things could be said to be a 'free delight', since here 'no interest, whether of sense or reason, extorts approval'.[10] Thus, while in his ethics Kant tended (as has been seen) to identify freedom with moral autonomy, in his aesthetics he represented both morality and natural inclination alike as being in a sense opposed to it, since each restricted our responses to the world in specific ways. This detachment from interest, typical of the aesthetic outlook, was moreover connected by Kant with further features which differentiated it from the moral point of view. In the

[10] *Critique of Judgement*, trans. J. C. Meredith (Oxford, 1952), p. 49.

case of the latter, as he never tired of repeating, the universal prescriptions of reason were liable to collide with and override the particular and variable impulses of our sensuous nature; in the appreciation of beauty, on the other hand, our intellectual and sensuous faculties were not in conflict, nor was there a subordination of one to the other of the sort that occurred when our concerns were of a cognitive or scientific nature. Instead, Kant spoke of the powers of the mind being engaged in a 'free play', a harmonious and satisfying interaction; the formative and organising understanding and the sensuously orientated imagination were affected in a fashion that 'quickened' both, while setting constraints upon neither. He also implied that this somewhat mysterious process was occasioned by what he conceived to be the distinctive characteristic of the things we call beautiful; they manifested an order, a design, which could not be captured by a determinate rule or concept and which impressed us as being in some manner internal to the material that exhibited it rather than as having been imposed upon it from without.

As we have already noticed, Kant himself – despite certain qualifications implicit in his treatment of the sublime – was generally disposed to regard ethics and aesthetics as belonging to distinct domains which should on no account be confused. To Schiller, however, it seemed that the categories of aesthetic experience were susceptible to a much broader interpretation. Ideas of the kind evolved by Kant in the setting of an inquiry into the conditions of aesthetic taste could be extended to cover aspects of man's psychological and social well-being; as such, they could be said to have a moral bearing, and furthermore one that impinged upon the assumptions underlying Kant's own ethical theory. In trying to show how this was possible, Schiller introduced the notion of *play*.

To see why Schiller attached such importance to this notion we must return to his conception of human nature as being essentially 'mixed' and to his emphasis upon the part played by both intellectual and sensuous elements in the composition of the personality. In the *Aesthetic Letters* he postulates two basic mental powers or 'drives' – one rational and legislative, the other receptive and sensory – and he writes of each as having a necessary function to perform: the first seeks to impose order and direction, the second responds to changing conditions and supplies the material 'filling' of experience. (It is noticeable that, in his references to mental activity, Schiller tended to conflate epistemological and practical concerns in a fashion of which Kant himself would hardly have approved.) The functions in question were in fact complementary to one another, nature having placed us under an obligation 'not to divide what she had united'. It was hence only by a 'wanton transgression of nature' that they had come to be experienced and conceived in a manner that engendered inner discord and a destructive struggle for ascendancy. A remedy, however, lay to hand in the shape of a further principle, whose role was one of reconciliation and of mediating between the two extremes of rational and physical domination to which the psyche stood exposed. Of it Schiller wrote: 'To the extent that it deprives feelings and passions of their dynamic power, it will bring them into harmony with the ideas of reason; and to the extent that it deprives the laws of reason of their moral compulsion, it will reconcile them with the interests of the senses.'[11] The drive to which he assigned these commendable qualities he called the 'play-drive' (*Spieltrieb*), and he linked it explicitly with artistic expression and the appreciation of beauty.

Schiller was not unaware that his reference to 'play' in such a connection might be misinterpreted, encouraging once again the old complaints that art was something essentially trivial and frivolous. But this was to take a superficial view of the matter. We should not allow ourselves to be influenced by forms of play and amusement currently in vogue, but should instead seek a deeper and more extensive understanding of the phenomenon as it existed in the context of human life as a whole. Comprehended in this light, it could be seen as involving a suspension of all those practical needs and demands which normally bear down upon us with the weight of a burden; such a 'distancing' of the mind from everyday preoccupations was intrinsic to the idea of play, endowing it with a capacity to release our various powers from the limits within which they tended to be habitually constricted. The different sides of our nature could thus 'unfold' and 'expand' without danger of conflict or mutual jarring; liberated from 'the fetters of ends and purposes' in an activity that was 'at once its own end and its own means', relieved of 'the shackles of circumstance', it was possible through play to occupy a 'happy medium' between the spheres of law and physical contingency: such a 'middle disposition', Schiller affirms at one point, 'in which the psyche is subject neither to physical nor to moral constraint, and yet is active in both these ways, pre-eminently deserves to be called a free disposition'.[12] Given his high regard for the aesthetic doctrines contained in the *Critique of Judgement*, it is not unexpected to discover Schiller treating play, so conceived, as achieving consummation in

[11] op. cit. (note 4 above), p. 99.
[12] ibid., p. 141.

artistic expression and experience, or to find him speaking of beauty as the true 'object of the play-drive', affording a supreme 'union and equilibrium of reality and form'; the creations of art resemble a 'free play of nature', gratifying the senses and imagination while at the same time displaying an inner coherence that appeals to and satisfies the intellect. What, on the other hand, was distinctive of his position, sharply differentiating it from the Kantian, was his preparedness to make the capacity for aesthetic play central to his concept of a fully realised humanity, essential to the development of man as a complete being. It was on this account that he could write, in a famous passage, that 'man only plays when he is in the fullest sense of the word a human being, and he is only fully a human being when he plays';[13] it was with this in mind, too, that he looked forward to a time when each individual in society would fulfil his potentialities, the 'totality of his powers', in accordance with 'the laws of beauty', instead of existing – as was man's present plight – 'only as a fragment', a 'mere imprint of his occupation or of his specialised knowledge'.[14] In Schiller's eyes, man was not a creature to whom the capacity for aesthetic activity and enjoyment belonged as a contingent and dispensable attribute; it was, on the contrary, a necessity of his nature.

By relating art to the broader concept of play, and by presenting the latter as a universal mode of expression which permitted human powers customarily harnessed to utilitarian or practical aims a scope normally denied them, Schiller believed that he had uncovered an aspect of our condition that had been largely overlooked by the social and ethical theorists of his day. These had tended, either to accord exclusive priority to man's material wants and needs, or else (like Kant in his moral philosophy) to give an equally uncompromising prominence to man's status as a rational being, whose true worth and fulfilment were held to lie in the transcendence of his 'animal' nature. Such over-simplified portrayals of the human make-up had, moreover, been reflected in correspondingly distorted conceptions of freedom and in the political and social recommendations associated with them. It must (I think) be allowed that Schiller himself, when outlining his own positive proposals, did not always make it transparently clear where he stood. Thus there are occasions in the *Letters* when he appears to treat them as being merely intended to prepare the way for a 'rational' order, subject to the 'general will', in which the moral law would wholly prevail; and this is a position not

[13] ibid., p. 107.
[14] ibid., p. 35.

easy to square with his general condemnation of one-sided or exclusive social ideals. Nevertheless, in the main it was the emergence of what he called an 'aesthetic State', founded upon a respect for man's *gemischte Natur*, which he seems to have regarded as ultimately desirable. Freed from servitude to desires for possession and consumption and able in consequence to take satisfaction in the pure appearance of things, the members of such a community would treat 'disinterested pleasure' as amongst the necessities of existence. Not only would their modes of expression and behaviour exhibit a natural spontaneity and grace of the kind typified in works of art; the aesthetic sensibility which informed their outlook would also constitute a bond between them and hence exercise, subtly and unobtrusively, a socially cohesive force. From this point of view, Schiller implied, the type of consciousness he had in mind might be contrasted with the proprietary and competitive attitudes that motivated men in the contemporary world; unlike those, with their disastrously divisive consequences, it promoted harmony within the individual and society alike. For to the aesthetic spectator the world presented itself, not as something to be used and exploited for his personal ends, but as something to be appreciated and enjoyed in its own right; far from being a source of private anxiety and public contention, it offered a continual stimulus to the powers of perception and imagination which were the common property of all human beings. Thus, where the influence of such an outlook was pervasive, men would no longer be subject to 'the compulsion to infringe the freedom of others in order to assert their own', since each would be a willing participant in a form of life and experience that was by its very nature open to all.

The hopes and aspirations with which Schiller concludes his essay are expressed with a noble eloquence that almost disarms criticism. Even so, they are apt to produce a wide variety of reactions amongst present-day readers. To some they have seemed too vague, too obscure and inexact, to be worth taking seriously: at best, they have been felt to amount to an idealised fantasy which, whatever its charm, neglects the coarse texture of reality and comes as something of an anti-climax after the earlier sections of the *Letters*, with their shrewd and pointed insights; at worst, they have been held to be the product of 'bourgeois-humanist hopes' – 'a utopian dream of a circle comprised of an intellectual and moral élite'.[15] At the other extreme, there have been those to whom Schiller's ideal of

[15] Georg Lukács, *Goethe and his Age*, trans. R. Anchor (London, 1968), p. 135.

an aesthetic society has appeared both prescient and profound: it has been seen as anticipating Freud in recognising the extent to which traditional culture depends upon a massive renunciation of instinctual gratification and pleasure; at the same time, it has been interpreted – in a manner that might have caused its author some surprise – as looking forward to the emergence of erotically orientated 'non-repressive' social forms of a wholly new kind. Yet, however his positive proposals may be viewed, it is the diagnosis Schiller provided of the ills of his age, rather than the cure for them he somewhat tentatively offered, that is perhaps more likely to find a responsive modern echo.

Like Herder before him, who had inveighed against a condition in which men had become 'half thinkers, half feelers' and 'no single member partakes of the whole any more', Schiller portrayed the central predicament of his period as consisting in man's being divided against himself, both as an individual and in his relations to his human and natural surroundings. And he likewise implied that current ideologies, far from helping to remedy this state of affairs, had in fact accentuated it. In the last analysis the atomistic hedonism and individualism of Enlightenment social theory and the polarisation of reason and natural inclination intrinsic to Kantian moral theory mirrored different aspects of what was fundamentally the same unacceptable situation. Both operated with models of human nature that were too crude, being insensitive to the complex and finely balanced structure of our intellectual, emotional and imaginative needs; in consequence, they were incapable of taking proper account of the forms of deprivation and frustration which the development of an increasingly specialised and scientifically minded civilisation brought in its train. Dazzled by our successes in dominating and manipulating our natural environment, we were in danger of losing contact with the natural order to which from one point of view we inescapably belonged. It was with such considerations in mind that Schiller, writing in another context, compared our feeling for nature with that of 'an invalid for health'. We had become a prey to artificial wants that had no basis in our original constitution and were cramped by mental attitudes which had become so general that we no longer experienced them as constraints. The suggestion that through aesthetic education we can liberate ourselves from oppressive habits of thought and restore connections between areas of our psychical life which have been lost or severed may have its limitations; it is not, however, an empty or an untimely one.

PETER GAY

Freud and Freedom

On a Fox in Hedgehog's Clothing

'. . . the greatest healer and psychological theorist of our time . . .'

Isaiah Berlin on Sigmund Freud

I

Sigmund Freud was a determinist, yet his psychology is a psychology of freedom. This may be an authentic paradox; Isaiah Berlin has insisted that any attempt to reconcile determinism with free will is nothing better than sleight-of-hand. Or the paradox may be merely apparent, ready to yield to analysis; some modern philosophers have argued, with A. J. Ayer, that 'from the fact that my action is causally determined' it 'does not follow that I am not free'.[1] But even if Freud's views on determinism and freedom should be contradictory beyond repair – Freud himself was, after all, ambivalent about his own philosophical intentions and capacities – it will be profitable to examine them not merely as an exercise in the history of ideas, but also as a way of clarifying the competing claims of constraints on action and opportunities for choice, and of defining the setting, both personal and social, in which freedom becomes meaningful.

II

That capacious and suitably vague philosophical word, *determinism*, has long been used in several senses and remains hotly controversial; after centuries of objections by Roman Catholic theologians, in recent decades it has been French existentialists and Anglo-American philosophers of action who have most seriously questioned the whole doctrine, however defined. It cannot be my purpose to rehearse, let alone my ambition to resolve, the debate here. Surely, Berlin is right to remind us that 'the problem of free will', which is only the prob-

[1] 'Freedom and Necessity', in *Philosophical Essays* (London, 1954), p. 278. I want to thank (without burdening them with any responsibility) Quentin Skinner, Harry G. Frankfurt and Ernst Prelinger for their thoughtful reading of this essay.

lem of determinism in another guise, 'is at least as old as the Stoics', has 'tormented ordinary men as well as professional philosophers', and remains far from 'a definitive solution'.[2] Freud followed his deterministic course of thinking without uneasiness, with no sense of its obscurities, its problematic nature. He understood it to mean, quite straightforwardly, that just as there is no event in the physical universe without its cause (or, better, its causes), so there is no mental event, or mental state, without its causes. And Freud treated this conviction as more than a necessary ground for his psychology; it served him as an immensely instructive clue to the mysteries of mind, as an instrument of discovery.

Freud demonstrated the heuristic value of psychic determinism through all his work, but nowhere more accessibly or attractively than in *The Psychopathology of Everyday Life,* the book on which he worked in the 1890s, concurrently with his masterpiece, *The Interpretation of Dreams.* As we know, *The Psychopathology of Everyday Life* is among Freud's most popular books, even though – or, rather, just because – its theoretical yield is modest. I cannot overstate its strategic value for the acceptance of his strange and shocking theories; in this sprawling, over-stocked treasury of mental mistakes and odd compulsions he leaped to comprehensive inferences from ordinary incidents, from slips of the tongue, the misreading of texts, the forgetting of names, to a theory of the mind. Here were mental aberrations that readers could recognise and, finding them unthreatening, freely acknowledge. It was with a shrewd appreciation of their explanatory and persuasive power, after all, that Freud, more than a decade later, opened his popular *Introductory Lectures on Psychoanalysis* with an expansive section on *Fehlleistungen*, on the mind making – which is to say actively generating – mistakes. Each homespun illustration was just one more argument in favour of the universal determinism that governs mental life. And the demonstration that all events have their causes was accompanied by Freud's demonstration that these events also had their meaning – and the causes revealed that meaning. The President of the Lower House of the Austrian Parliament who, ceremoniously opening a session, solemnly declared the sitting 'closed', was not the victim of some inexplicable aberration; his 'error' was not a bit of spontaneous verbal sport, but a meaningful and caused revelation of his unconscious feelings about the session he was about to inaugurate and from which he expected nothing but

[2] *F.E.L.*, Introduction, p. xi.

trouble.[3] Such instances are familiar, and their very familiarity guaranteed them a hearing, and testified to the ubiquity of cause and the pervasiveness of meaning in the life of the mind.

Another, equally impressive witness for Freud's scientific determinism is the so-called fundamental rule of the psychoanalytic situation: the analysand is told – one of the few things he *is* told – to hold back nothing that comes into his mind, no matter how absurd, trivial, inconsequent or obscene. This procedure, which the patient rarely carries out but persistently attempts to evade, is known as 'free association'. The term is, in an instructive way, misleading. It generates pictures of the mind playing freely over the materials that present themselves in informal, often startling sequences, and the patient reporting them without neatening up or censoring the succession of his associations. But, as Roy Schafer has recently pointed out, there is really nothing free about the analysand's 'free association'; on the contrary, the fundamental rule works precisely because the conscious mind is compelled to review a mass of thoughts, feelings, memories over which it has no control, and which are determined by unconscious, strict causes. 'From this perspective', Schafer writes, 'the point of the free-association method is to make it plain just how unfree the analysand is.'[4] Freud did not intend to deceive his readers into thinking his system to be a voluntaristic one; the free-association method actually liberates the patient, but only to recognise where his true obligations lie. 'The designation "free" ', to quote Schafer again, 'makes sense only as referring to one's freeing oneself from the usual self-imposed constraints of verbal

[3] *The Psychopathology of Everyday Life* (London, 1901) is in *The Standard Edition of the Complete Psychological Works of Sigmund Freud*, ed. and trans. James Strachey and others, 24 vols (London 1953–75) (henceforth *S.E.*), vol. 6, p. 59. Subsequent references to *S.E.* are given by volume and page, thus: VI 59. It would be useful not to confound meaning with cause, though Freud, deliberately it would seem, did not keep them apart. After all, a piece of mental behaviour – a neurotic symptom, or a dream – may be meaningless, literally nonsensical, and still have a cause; many nineteenth-century psychologists, anxious to discover somatic or constitutional roots for the baffling actions of madmen and the equally baffling reports of dreamers, interpreted these actions, and these reports, in just this way. Freud, in contrast, indissolubly linked meaning with cause; it was precisely because each instance of mental life, whether a slip or a symptom, could be traced to antecedent causes, that the psychologist could count on finding meaning for them. And conversely, it was because each such instance had a meaning that it must be sure to have a cause. Reviewing, in 1924, the fundamentals of the science he had founded, Freud included among them 'the thorough-going meaningfulness and determination of even the apparently most obscure and arbitrary mental phenomena'. See Ernest Jones, *The Life and Work of Sigmund Freud*, vol. 1 (London, 1953), p. 366.

[4] Roy Schafer, *Language and Insight* (London, 1978), p. 40.

reasonableness, coherence, and verbal decorum.'[5] The psychoanalytic situation demonstrates, as do slips of the tongue, that man's mind cannot escape its laws.

III

Deterministic systems are, by and large, closed systems. In the defender of free will, they induce claustrophobia. He sees them as making man into the helpless victim of uncontrollable and often unknown forces, as reducing him to a mere puppet slavishly obeying an invisible and omnipotent puppeteer. The movements man is allowed to perform in such a system, the advocate of free will is bound to say, are never autonomous, let alone spontaneous. They are (he will say if he wants to vary his metaphor) steps in a ballet rigidly choreographed in advance. Choices, alternatives, the whole panoply of mental freedom are, in determinism, discredited as childish fictions; the determinist treats them with disdain as the last survivals of *naïveté*, as flowers (to speak with Isaiah Berlin) decking men's chains – and, I might add, artificial flowers at that. No sense of responsibility can flourish, or even survive, in such a system.

Freud's determinism is different. His structure is open to the world, hospitable to change and to possibilities; it makes room for the exercise of mental and moral effort. In the 1920s, in some reflections on his theory of dreams, Freud comments, 'Obviously one must hold oneself responsible for the evil impulses of one's dreams. What else is one to do with them?'[6] The confident tone of this observation makes it only the more decisive. Men are responsible for what they do, even for what they dream – 'obviously'. But how can they assume responsibility for their thoughts, and their dreams, if these are merely the last links in a chain of causes? Freud's commitment to chance, or 'accident', is the first step to a resolution of this difficulty.

IV

Central as Freud's conceptions of chance, or accident, were to his way of thinking, we must tease them out from casual asides, no less weighty for being embedded in texts dealing with other matters. Freud had firm but largely implicit views on many philosophical

[5] ibid.
[6] 'Some Additional Notes on Dream-Interpretation as a Whole' (1925), *S.E.* XIX 133.

issues, including those involving problems of scientific procedure. Disdainful of philosophers, Freud thought much philosophy to be either nonsensical or self-evident. And it was self-evident, to him, that all in life is chance, in one sense, while in another, nothing in life is chance.

It should surprise no one that Freud took the position that there is less chance in the world than most people believe. What often seems spontaneous is actually symptomatic. Instancing 'many apparently accidental injuries' happening to his patients, Freud found himself persuaded that they were 'really instances of self-injury', caused by 'an impulse to self-punishment'.[7] If this is not a surprising posture for a determinist to adopt, it *is* surprising that Freud can also insist that 'everything to do with our life is chance, from our origin out of the meeting of spermatozoon and ovum onwards'. He scarcely clarifies the matter by adding, 'chance which nevertheless has a share in the law and necessity of nature'.[8]

Plainly, by 'accident', or 'chance', Freud does not mean consequences without causes. He seems to visualise a mental event, or state, as much resembling a frequently flooded pond that is fed by many streams and canals, each with its own source, its own tributaries, and its own geological past; these streams and canals intersect and interweave, they run dry at times, and they can be dammed up at their mouths, so that which of these will contribute waters to the pond and cause it to overflow is not wholly predictable, though it is traceable after the event. Since there are always more accesses of water than necessary to flood the pond, there are always more possibilities than the actuality needs. 'Everything to do with our life is chance' – not in the sense, once again, that a person's mental history is wholly or even partly random; he comes into the world, after all, with a certain constitutional endowment, in a certain place, at a certain time, amidst a certain family. Freud's patient seduced by a maid might not have had that particular adult to perform this act of sexual enlightenment for him, if, say, the mother who engaged this maid had failed to attend a certain club meeting at which she had first heard the woman highly recommended. But her little boy might have been seduced by another maid (it is almost certain, at all events, that there would have been such a servant in his household), especially if he was a sensitive child. And even if he had not been seduced, some other events would probably have produced a similar neurosis in him, so that eventually he would have ended up

[7] *The Psychopathology of Everday Life*, *S.E.* VI 178–9.
[8] 'Leonardo da Vinci and a Memory of His Childhood' (1910), *S.E.* XI 137.

in Freud's consulting room after all, if perhaps with slightly different presenting symptoms.

Not all chances are equally remote or equally certain; the network of experiences in which personal life is enmeshed makes room alike for improbable contingencies and (though, of course, far more often) for highly probably occurrences. Consider 'Dora', one of Freud's most instructive early cases. One of Dora's symptoms, a difficulty in walking, that is dragging her leg, had emerged after a high fever; her puzzled physician had attributed the fever to a mild appendicitis but failed to diagnose the foot-dragging. Freud took the whole syndrome to be a 'true hysterical symptom', born from the way that Dora's neurosis had seized on an attack of influenza, a 'chance event', which it had then used 'for an utterance of its own'.[9] The bout of influenza was one of those bits of reality which, while impinging on Dora's life, might well have passed her by; had it not invaded her existence, Dora's neurosis would certainly have utilised another bit of reality. But then Dora would have been a slightly different kind of neurotic, changed, however subtly, from the neurotic-having-used-influenza-for-psychological-ends. There is room for play in Freud's world, and it is the task of accident to provide that play. As Freud put it in one of his last papers, it is difficult to distinguish between 'what is rigidly fixed by biological laws and what is open to movement and change under the influence of accidental experience'. It may be difficult to distinguish, but Freud saw irresistible invasions of the fortuitous in everyone's life, including the fact and character of infantile seduction, as well as 'the date at which the child's brothers and sisters are born or the time when it discovers the difference between the sexes, or again its direct observations of sexual intercourse or its parents' behaviour in encouraging or repelling it'.[10] How decisively or trivially such chance events shape the child's future depends on the event, its place – and the child. In any event, the power of accident over individual lives is no accident.

For Freud, his conception of chance had more than explanatory, it had polemical import. Thus, in a brief preface to the third edition of his *Three Essays on the Theory of Sexuality*, he notes that he has, throughout the book, given 'preference' to the 'accidental factors' determining sexual life, leaving 'disposition in the background'; for it is, after all, 'the accidental factors that play the principal part in analysis'.[11] What Freud is doing here is to stress the power of nur-

9 'Fragments of an Analysis of a Case of Hysteria' (1905), *S.E.* VII 102.
10 'Female Sexuality' (1931), *S.E.* XXI 242.
11 (1914), *S.E.* VII 131.

ture – at least, in psychoanalysis. This is rather ironic; after all, Freud has often been accused of 'biological determinism'. Actually, for the psychologists of his day, he was not biological enough. As early as 1912 he found it necessary to defend himself, a little irritably, against the charge that he had 'denied the importance of innate (constitutional) factors because I have stressed that of infantile impressions'. Rather, he argued, there are 'two sets of aetiological factors' that regularly 'determine a man's fate', namely '*Daimon* and *Tyche*' – endowment and chance.[12] While his contemporaries placed heavy emphasis on unchanging characteristics, popularised by such unscientific and dangerous clichés as 'national character', or 'blood', Freud, with his somewhat idiosyncratic use of 'accident', instead emphasised the pervasive play of experience in the shaping of the mind.

That experience is very rich indeed. The stark simplicity of Freud's dualism of instincts, his conviction that the Oedipus complex is universal, and those massive granite blocks from which the structure of psychoanalysis is built – conflict, defence, regression – have invited many of his readers to see in Freud a scientist who knows one big thing, a propounder of essentially simple laws, in short, a hedgehog. Nothing could be further from the real Freud. Freud was a fox, if a fox who at times affected hedgehog's clothing. He had an uncanny gift for detecting parallels and discovering relationships, and found fertile uses for this talent by exploring the resemblance of dreams to psychoses, children to neurotics, anxiety symptoms to erotic excitement. This was Freud, the finder of laws, the maker of patterns.

But there is another Freud, equally characteristic, though less visible: the celebrant of variety. Freud was not a psychological reductionist; he was not, for one thing, a pan-sexualist – an epithet against which he protested vigorously, justly, and in vain. To call his view of human nature monotonous is equivalent to calling the game of chess monotonous because it has few pieces and rests on few rules; just as in chess, so in human life, a handful of ingredients produces never-ending, ever-surprising variations. Uniformity and variety cooperate and alternate in Freud's view of man, to point both to recurrent patterns and unduplicable individuality.

Freud's splendid case histories are tributes to his perception and cheerful acceptance of this immense, inexhaustible variety of human types and human experience. They offer a bouquet of mental suffer-

[12] 'The Dynamics of Transference' (1912), *S.E.* XII 99n.

ing: obsessions, phobias, delusions, homosexuality, fetishism, anxiety attacks, hysterical pains, each characteristic of a group of syndromes, yet each unique. And Freud drew his observations from a widely assorted cast of characters: precocious small boys, spoiled Russian aristocrats, nubile Austrian adolescents, experienced physicians in search of psychoanalytic training, classic paranoiacs whom Freud knew only from books, and writers he came to value as friends. He was puzzled all his life by how these analysands had come to 'choose' the particular neurosis that brought them to his couch, but he was sure of two things: that while each patient could teach him much about other patients, each was irreplaceably himself; and that while the process of neurotic choice was obscure, it must be traced back to the unconscious, to early wishes and traumatic irruptions. Even if the act of choosing had been forgotten, had, for that matter, never been conscious, it had taken place. Man, for Freud, is the choosing animal.

V

Choice occupies a place of honour in Freud's psychology of freedom. And on the question of choice, philosophers aware of modern psychology have been at one with psychoanalysts; so much so, indeed, that their position has acquired the status of a commonplace in the scientific literature. They agree that the true range of choice is far narrower than choosers might think, or feel, it to be.[13] Choosers are hedged in by concealed constraints everywhere.

An obvious, perhaps too obvious, example of such constraints is the young man who falls in love over and over again, convinced that he is choosing his love objects freely, from a sizeable pool of eligible girls. On analysis, his presumably untrammelled serial infatuations turn out to be re-enactments of unresolved Oedipal conflicts; his women strikingly resemble one another – and his mother.

The analysis of choice is particularly vexed because the very persons most intimately involved in the process of choosing often sub-

[13] Thus Alasdair MacIntyre, throwing Freud into company with John Bowlby and (a little less felicitously) with learning theorists, writes: 'One can hardly doubt that more and more of behaviour will be included in accounts which show such behaviour to be causally dependent on antecedent conditions.' 'Determinism', *Mind* 66 (1957), 29. And see Isaiah Berlin: 'it is plainly a good thing that we should be reminded by social scientists that the scope of human choice is a good deal more limited than we used to suppose . . . And this certainly alters our ideas about the limits of freedom and responsibility.' 'Historical Inevitability' (1954), *F.E.L.*, p. 73.

mit contradictory testimony. They feel free, yet are unfree; they feel under compulsion, but for reasons different from those they advance. A good part of this confusion stems from what Freud once called 'the strange behaviour of patients', behaviour in which they combine 'a conscious knowing with not knowing'.[14] A patient may 'know' that he is performing compulsive ceremonies, and he may 'know', too, that they are neurotic symptoms; still, he does not feel capable of stopping his repetitive conduct: 'knowing' the truth has not made him free. A poignant example of such ineffectual knowledge is the sufferer from anorexia nervosa, who may starve herself literally to death knowing that she must eat to live, but cannot persuade herself to take the steps that will ensure her survival. One patient, reported in the *New York Times* in the spring of 1978, an intelligent college student, perceptively and pathetically remarked: 'It's like there are two of me. There's the intelligent Rochelle, who knows all about nutrition and what the proper things to eat are. But then there's the emotional Rochelle, who's dominating and won't let me take the upper hand and do the proper things.' And she goes on facing her future in fear and impotence: 'Of course, the possibility of death terrifies me. I'm not suicidal! I'm terrified of catching a cold because the doctors have said that I'd get pneumonia and it would kill me. But that doesn't make me eat more. It just doesn't seep in.'[15]

It just doesn't seep in. Rochelle seems to possess all the requisite instruments of freedom: she knows her condition, charts her loss of weight with growing anxiety, predicts the outcome of her crazy diet with terrible lucidity. Yet she cannot bring herself to eat. She knows and she does not know. She seems to be choosing her starvation and yet is not free to choose otherwise.

Not all illusory free choices are necessarily the consequence of such deep private pathology. They may be rooted less in the remote unconscious, which preserves infantile wishes and anxieties intact, than in the preconscious, which stores cultural ideals or prohibitions of which the individual has only intermittent inklings, and which sober introspection short of psychoanalytic probing can propel into the centre of awareness. One good instance is fashion, which for centuries cultural critics have liked to call a tyranny. Fashion, a pendant to private pathology, is a kind of social pathology. Consider a young couple setting out to buy their first furniture. They think they have defined the boundaries of their freedom: the size of their house is

[14] 'On Beginning the Treatment' (1913), *S.E.* XII 142.
[15] 11 May 1978, p. B9.

one limit for them, the amount of money available is another. Apart from this, they will insist, sincerely, that they, and their choice, are free: as long as the pieces are not too large or too expensive, they will buy what they like. After they have completed their purchases, they will continue to argue that they were guided by their taste alone. Did they not visit show-room after show-room, until they found lamps and tables and chairs that 'spoke to them'?

Nothing is easier than to demolish this feeble claim to personal autonomy, and to demonstrate that the taste of this couple was moulded firmly, exclusively, by outside agencies. They bought what was popular in their set or with their families. To be sure, psychological forces deeper, more cunningly hidden than the imperative, but relatively superficial commands of fashion are likely to have influenced the young couple, and hence fenced them in even more closely: I am thinking of the survival of identifications with parents' tastes or desires, which may show themselves in the struggle for dominance between husband and wife. Just as the child develops its superego, in Freud's words, not on the model of its parents, but on that of its parents' superego, so the wishes of the young couple will probably reflect not the possessions of their elders so much as their longings. Whatever the forces at work here, we seem entitled to amend the old adage that beggars can't be choosers and say that choosers apparently can't be choosers either.

Does it follow, as some strict determinists have argued, that all choice is merely the automatic fulfilment of antecedent, and unalterable, conditions? Freud would refuse to adopt this drastic position. All acts – or symptoms, or anxiety attacks – have causes, but their shape, their time, their strength, their very meaning are not wholly programmed in advance.

I want to illustrate the issues involved in Freud's version of determinism with a fictitious but not implausible tale, in which an individual finds himself placed before incompatible alternatives, but in which abstention is in the long run impossible. I am thinking of a gifted acoustical engineer, popular with his colleagues, highly paid, and with sufficient time for his private research. Then this engineer, who lives and works in the Midwest, receives an offer from a firm in Southern California, which seductively promises him a still higher salary and even more time for his 'own' work. He is tempted indeed. His wife, with whom, in good American fashion, he discusses his dilemma, declares herself neutral: she is happy in her native Michigan, but professes that she will be happy in Los Angeles as well; it is up to him to make the decision.

Thrown on his own resources, the engineer is, by all the evidence, torn one way and the other. He wants to go and he wants to stay. As day follows day, in his ruminations and his fantasies, he makes up his mind more than once; at times he sees himself moving, at other times he sees himself staying. In his perplexity, he has dictated two letters which his secretary keeps locked away in her desk, one accepting and the other rejecting the offer. There they both are, signed but not sealed. His friends are so puzzled that they hesitate to make even small bets about the outcome – so balanced does he seem on the knife-edge of choice. The clues point, with equal persuasiveness, in either direction. The engineer feels troubled, but he also feels free, and may really *be* free.

Then he makes his decision. He will stay. His secretary tears up the letter of acceptance, his friends give him a party, and the chief of his division informs him, privately, that he can expect a sizeable rise before the year is out.

As we anatomise this act of choice, we need not concentrate on the engineer's unconscious alone. The drama of decision played itself out across his mind, including his conscious ego; he had made sure to inform his superiors of the offer and of his state of mind, and had shrewdly negotiated for a rise before he made his final decision. Still, his unconscious had played a far from negligible part in his agonising appraisals. His ambivalence had been real enough and had run deep: all through his happy ordeal, he had reasons, including unconscious ones, that he could use to support either course of action. His father had long disdained his present position as unworthy of him, a fact of his life which did not enter into his conscious calculations at all; as he had constructed his parallel lists, 'staying' on the left and 'moving' on the right, he had not entered his father's preference on either side, though it might be legitimately on either list – or on both. Two aspects of his surviving Oedipal problems, powerful if suppressed negative and positive feelings toward his father, struggled for supremacy without his being aware of that conflict at all. And there were other, equally submerged struggles at work, pushing and pulling on him. Among these were his over-protective impulses towards his wife (who, he sensed, for all her strenuous neutrality, was sending him messages begging him to stay); these impulses, of which he had no inkling, concealed strong hostile feelings, as unconscious as his gestures of over-protection. And there were others still, which it would take a psychoanalyst to detect and unravel.

How free, then, was the engineer at that decisive moment that he told his secretary, 'Mail the letter to L.A. that says "No", and tear up the one that says "Yes"'? The engineer himself, as I have said, felt in control of his destiny, yet wholly undecided. 'I swear', he told a friend later, 'that half an hour before I told my secretary which letter to send, I had no idea which way I would jump.' Is freedom, then, essentially a state of inner confusion? Or is that confusion merely one of its symptoms?

VI

This vignette is not a real test, certainly not the one that would interest the student of Freud's deterministic psychology of freedom. It becomes an instructive test in the following variant: suppose that the California firm, shrewdly anticipating an impending rejection and imagining that its pressing hard had actually proved counterproductive, invites the engineer to take as long as a year, or even two, to make up his mind. And the engineer, appalled at his indecisiveness and his bouts of anxiety, resolves to enter psychoanalysis. In the course of that analysis he begins to confront some of the conflicts that had bedevilled him, though outside his sphere of awareness: his Oedipal ambivalence – that unconscious identification with an equally unconscious rebellion against his father – as well as his defensive conduct toward his wife. As he grows more introspective, more self-aware, these irrational survivals recede; they become less active, less relevant to his reconsideration. A year or so later, he can reflect about the offer with most, if not all, of the elements entering choice on the table; he can depend, far more than before, on practical considerations, and pay attention to his emotions without being flooded by them. Is he free now, or, at least, freer than before? Freud would say that he is.

Earlier, I noted that psychoanalysis acts to circumscribe the area of freedom in which men fancy they live. But psychoanalysis also acts in the opposite way: as a therapy, its precise intention is to *enlarge* the area of freedom. Philosophers, and those who echo them, like to say that freedom is the recognition of necessity, or (a little more subtly) that freedom is obedience to a law that one has made oneself.[16] But freedom is neither the one nor the other,

[16] See, for just one instance, the paper by Robert P. Knight, a distinguished psychoanalyst, on 'Determinism, "Freedom", and Psychotherapy' (1946), which quotes (with approval) Kant, Hegel and Engels to this effect, and an unattributed epigram, 'That man is free who is conscious of being the author of the law that he obeys.' *Clinician and Therapist: Selected Papers of Robert P. Knight*, ed. Stuart C. Miller (New York, 1972), pp. 140–1.

however valuable the recognition of necessity may turn out to be. One may reasonably argue that it is better to know realities than not to know them, and those realities include the boundaries of one's freedom. This was certainly Freud's view, as exemplified by his insistence on being told the truth, however unpalatable, even about his painful and ultimately fatal cancer: 'I . . . do not like to be deceived', he wrote bravely, perfectly in character, to Princess Marie Bonaparte late in April 1939, when he was very old and close to death. The deception he disliked was his doctors' mendacious reassurances that his cancer was actually receding.[17] He resented such bedside talk as an invasion of his dignity – and of his freedom.

The recognition of necessity, then, can be a precondition for freedom, and in two ways: first, it may point the way, however obliquely, to regions of autonomy that had been invisible, or indistinct, as long as the boundaries of compulsion's kingdom had not been firmly mapped. Moreover, such recognition may relieve the sort of anxiety that uncertainty is bound to induce, and thus increase one's capacity for making choices. But the Freudian therapy is only in part aimed at the calm and candid acceptance of one's powerlessness. In two celebrated summaries of therapeutic action, Freud suggests, clearly enough, that psychoanalysis aims to reduce, as much as to recognise, constraints. Freud said, in a number of ways, that the purpose of psychoanalysis is to make conscious what is unconscious; and he said, just once, in a much-quoted epigram, 'Where id was, there ego shall be.'[18]

One short text, buried in a footnote in *The Ego and the Id*, clarifies what Freud thought to be at stake in these two formulations: 'Analysis does not set out to abolish the possibility of morbid reactions, but to give the patient's ego *freedom* to choose one way or the other.'[19] Psychoanalysis has no power, but also no intention, to force its patients to be free; it does not guarantee, nor does it teach,

[17] *Sigmund Freud, Briefe 1873–1939*, selected and edited by Ernst L. Freud (London, 1960), p. 451; see Peter Gay, 'Sigmund Freud: A German and his Discontents', in *Freud, Jews and Other Germans: Masters and Victims in Modernist Culture* (Oxford, 1978), p. 81.

[18] *New Introductory Lectures on Psycho-Analysis* (1933), *S.E.* XXII 80.

[19] (1923), *S.E.* XIX 50n. I first called attention to this text in an early article, 'The Enlightenment in the History of Political Theory', *Political Science Quarterly* 69 (1954), 374–89; my quotation from Freud, whom I connect to the Enlightenment, is on p. 379n. (The article is reprinted, in a slightly revised version, in my *The Party of Humanity: Essays in the French Enlightenment* (New York, 1964).) It was only last year that I discovered that Robert Knight had employed the same sentence in his paper on 'Determinism, "Freedom", and Psychotherapy', first published eight years before mine. See Knight, op. cit. (note 16 above), p. 136.

wisdom. Freedom, in Freud's precise formulation, must embrace the option to make bad choices.

This much is plain. As long as mental forces that significantly affect human decisions – wishes, anxieties, conflicts – are unconscious, they act as determinants that the person making the decision cannot take into account, cannot weigh or measure, let alone discard. And even if they enter consciousness, one's awareness of them must reach down to their roots, the very lair of repression. To make the unconscious conscious is to do more than to provide intellectual food for thought; to put ego in place of id is, in Freud's metaphor, 'a work of culture – not unlike the draining of the Zuider Zee'.[20] It involves the shifting of mental energies to permit the patient not merely to assent to an abstract proposition but to understand with his whole mind. Unconscious elements in choice act, in both the technical and non-technical senses of that word alike, as compulsions; neurosis is a form of slavery. Symptoms may be compromises, but they are not compromises the neurotic has been free to negotiate. Lady Macbeth is not at liberty to take in, and act on, the information provided by her senses that her hands are clean. And the symptoms of obsessive neurotics are only the most palpable instances of the unconscious as the source of compulsion; the symptoms of other mental disorders share the same quality. The Don Juan is the servant of appetites that he falsely believes serve him; the agoraphobic is not only compelled to stay at home, but to lead his crippled life under the sway of passions he does not know, and will refuse to recognise when he is first presented to them.

I have called neurosis a form of slavery, but this strong characterisation defines other conditions as well. Infancy and childhood are slavery no less, more tolerable than neurosis only in that they include, in principle, realistic prospects for manumission; as Freud's scheme of human maturation sees growth as a laborious, often disrupted, and never complete attempt to escape from bondage. The glorious scenarios of omnipotence that small children enact in their fantasies are a precise measure of their impotence; it is only when they learn, from reality, to reduce their claims to power that their real power increases. Each stage of physical and mental development has its appropriate experience of bondage and its appropriate experiments in overcoming it. The word 'choice' in the technical psychoanalytic term 'object choice' is as Pickwickian as the word 'free' in 'free association'. The child is not merely compelled to

20 *New Introductory Lectures on Psycho-Analysis* (1933), *S.E.* XXII 80.

'choose' its love objects from a severely circumscribed field; what is more, it cannot refuse to choose. Only later, if it is fortunate, will it make choices which, rather than reflecting unconscious early memories and unappeased infantile desires, will be a play among possibilities.

Freud did not propagate the illusion that complete freedom is ever realistically in men's grasp. He accepted Moebius's wry remark that 'we are all to some extent hysterics'.[21] We must therefore excise Freud's name from Berlin's list of those who have dreamt of total self-determination.

> From Zeno to Spinoza [he has written], from the Gnostics to Leibniz, from Thomas Hobbes to Lenin and Freud, the battle-cry has been essentially the same; the object of knowledge and the methods of discovery have often been violently opposed, but that reality is knowable, and that knowledge and only knowledge liberates, and absolute knowledge liberates absolutely – that is common to many doctrines which are so large and valuable a part of Western civilization.[22]

That the truth will make men free is one of the few convictions that Freud has in common with Jesus, but that absolute knowledge liberates absolutely is a proposition that Freud would have rejected in some bewilderment, and with much disdain. It would have smacked too much of consolation, that commodity which, Freud said, was desired by 'the wildest revolutionaries no less passionately than the most virtuous pious believers'.[23] All men are fenced in by their individual psychological endowment and by the general conditions of life that nature has imposed on them, conditions that include man's long dependence and his conflict-ridden emotional development. All men – not just neurotics – must live with ambivalence, with the unslakeable thirst of eros and the immortal rage of aggression. The unconscious is a permanent part of human nature, and remains, in the healthiest of humans, a repository of irrational forces; it is at once the great agent of, and the strongest fetter on, human freedom. The wholly free man is even more of a myth than the psychoanalyst's ideal, the fully analysed patient.

I must add that Freud did not have psychological constraints alone in mind when he thought of man as being, at best, partially free. He knew that man's range of action is cabined and confined by the state of his health, the condition of his purse, the wishes of others, the

[21] *Three Essays on the Theory of Sexuality* (1905), *S.E.* VII 171.
[22] 'Historical Inevitability' (1954), *F.E.L.*, p. 80.
[23] *Civilization and Its Discontents* (1930), *S.E.* XXI 145.

scarcity of resources, to say nothing of the law's delay and the proud man's contumely. It is within such boundaries that psychological freedom can manoeuvre to make choices real.

VII

There is yet one more question to which the student of Sigmund Freud celebrating Isaiah Berlin may address himself. Does Freud's psychology of freedom place him among those who cherish 'negative' or those who cherish 'positive' freedom? In his important inaugural lecture, 'Two Concepts of Liberty', Berlin explicitly distinguished between these two versions of freedom. Reflecting on this lecture late, he disclaimed any 'intolerant monism' that offers 'a blank endorsement of the "negative" concept as opposed to its "positive" twin brother'.[24] But he does not – and could not – conceal that he strongly prefers the first to the second:

> Pluralism, with the measure of 'negative' liberty that it entails, seems to me a truer and more humane ideal than the goals of those who seek in the great, disciplined, authoritarian structures the ideal of 'positive' self-mastery by classes, or peoples, or the whole of mankind. It is truer, because it does, at least, recognize the fact that human goals are many, not all of them commensurable, and in perpetual rivalry with one another.[25]

Negative freedom, in short, is the goal of the fox. *Human goals are many, in perpetual rivalry*: 'not all good things are compatible'.[26] Sigmund Freud, who, far from minimising, consistently stressed the conflicting aims inherent within, and among, the institutions of the mind – the id, the ego, and the superego – did not put it very differently.

The distinction between negative and positive freedom amounts to far more than a squabble among metaphysicians; their partisans embrace fundamentally divergent views of politics, incompatible philosophies of life. Negative freedom, to put it economically, aims at the removal of obstructions; positive freedom, at the realisation of ideals. I shall call the proponents of negative freedom, the Liberals; and those of positive freedom, the Idealists.[27]

24 *F.E.L.*, Introduction, p. lviiin.

25 'Two Concepts of Liberty' (1958), *F.E.L.*, p. 171.

26 ibid., p. 167.

27 The distinction has sometimes been drawn, familiarly, as the distinction between 'freedom from' and 'freedom to', or 'freedom for'. (See, for a psychoanalyst's use of this pairing, Joseph H. Smith, 'The Psychoanalytic Understanding of Human Freedom: Freedom From and Freedom For', *Journal of the American Psychoanalytic*

It should surprise no one that the Idealists, the hedgehogs, proud of their distinguished intellectual ancestry and enamoured of their exalted vision of human destiny, are often rather scathing of what they consider the 'cynical' or 'formalist' position of their opponents. They are likely to remind the Liberals of the sardonic quip about the law in its august majesty leaving the poor free to sleep under the bridges, or of the implication running through Jean-Jacques Rousseau's *Contrat social*, that a man poor enough to sell his vote is not a free man, no matter what his formal constitutional rights. Political freedom in conditions of economic slavery, they will say, is a mockery; it is not freedom at all.[28]

The Idealists disdain negative freedom not merely as shallow and self-deceptive, but as low in aspiration as well. As Berlin has put it, they make much of the idea of the split self: the 'dominant' self, which liberates men from 'spiritual slavery', and the 'natural' self, which the dominant self must subdue.

> This dominant self is . . . variously identified with reason, with my 'higher nature', with the self which calculates and aims at what will satisfy it in the long run, with my 'real', or 'ideal', or 'autonomous' self, or with my self 'at its best'; which is then contrasted with irrational impulse, uncontrolled desires, my 'lower' nature, the pursuit of immediate pleasures, my 'empirical' or 'heteronomous' self, swept by every gust of desire and passion, needing to be rigidly disciplined if it is ever to rise to the full height of its 'real' nature.[29]

The aversion implicit in this description is heartfelt; such lofty thinking about the 'higher self' only too rapidly propels the proud

Association 26 (1978), 87–107. For an earlier use, see also the paper by Robert Waelder, 'Das Freiheitsproblem in der Psychoanalyse und das Problem der Realitätsprüfung', *Imago* 20 (1934); its English version, 'The Problem of Freedom in Psychoanalysis and the Problem of Reality Testing', can be found in the *International Journal of Psycho-Analysis* 17 (1936). Isaiah Berlin has used this locution as well (see 'Two Concepts of Liberty', *F.E.L.*, p. 131). It is graphic and, if used with caution, clarifying. But much of the time it describes not conflicting but correlative matters, the same experience viewed from two vantage points. The schoolboy enjoying his summer vacation is *free from* the obligation to attend classes and therefore *free to* go fishing or to a soccer game. Conversely, a painter *free to* paint in any style he wishes is thus free only as he is *free from* censorship or political pressure.

28 While this argument has a measure of legitimacy and a great deal of plausibility, its proponents often push it beyond its proper bounds to equate the shackles imposed by economic deprivation with the tyranny exercised in one-party states. The unemployed man may one day find a job; then he will leave his open-air habitat and perhaps vote his convictions. The dissident in a totalitarian system can hope for such freedom only after the system itself has been overthrown.

29 'Two Concepts of Liberty' (1958), *F.E.L.*, p. 132.

possessor of its sacred truth into forcing his insight on others, to 'bully, oppress, torture them in the name, and on behalf, of their "real" selves'.[30] But even if the Idealist stops short of such totalitarian ego-mania, Berlin finds this doctrine dangerous.

The debate between the two parties of freedom deserves clarification, and Isaiah Berlin has done much to clarify it. He has suggested that some of the criticisms voiced by the Idealists are not without merit, and I would agree that economic constraints limit the exercise of choice as effectively as do neurotic constraints. 'Liberty', he writes, 'is not the only goal of men.'[31] The partisan of negative freedom will acknowledge that there is every reason to work energetically towards social justice. 'To avoid glaring inequality or widespread misery I am ready to sacrifice some, or all, of my freedom.' But 'nothing is gained by a confusion of terms'.[32] There are values other than freedom, such as charity, justice, self-realisation, and it is to obstruct, indeed subvert, the task of moral valuation and intelligent political action to subsume all of these indisputable goods under that single rubric, freedom. Surely, this is right: the good of freedom can best be served by seeing it sharply for what it is: the absence, or removal, of restraints on choice.

Where does psychoanalysis fit into this debate? Superficially, there are resemblances between the Freudian system and the philosophy of positive freedom. Psychoanalytic theory – and therapy – are dominated by split selves. The exigent id confronts the calculating ego; id and ego confront the punishing superego. What is more, a psychoanalysis will produce, or rather foster, a split in the ego: the experiencing ego feels and effectively reports what it is going through in the analytic hour, while the observing ego listens to these outpourings and comments on them, at times and at best anticipating the interpretations of the psychoanalyst. And does Freud not perceive, or place, the institutions of the mind on a hierarchy of esteem? 'Where id was, there ego shall be' implies that Freud preferred the 'higher self' of rational calculations and disciplined thought to the 'empirical self' of irrational impulse and uncontrolled desire. One might see psychoanalysis, then, as an effort to assist the ideal self by subduing the sensual self, thus making Freud into an improbable and unwitting ally of Idealism.

The jargon of mental-health technicians and assorted publicists lends some plausibility to this interpretation. But it wholly

30 ibid., p. 133.
31 ibid., p. 125.
32 ibid.

misconceives the temperamental and intellectual direction of Freud's psychology. It may be that the well-analysed person has learned to 'master' his impulses, and is 'realising his potentialities'. But this mastery and this realisation are only the correlates of the negative freedoms that psychoanalysis has placed at his disposal. In removing inhibitions, undoing repressions, correcting distortions, reducing anxieties, analysis has, if I may so put it, struck mental shackles from the analysand's wrists. But it does not dictate to him how to use his hands; it will not compel him to live a full life or force him to fall in love; it will not prescribe ideals, but simply offer him an opportunity to determine for himself what he wants to do next. More than once Freud cautioned psychoanalysts against the ambition to become moral teachers or to fancy themselves models of maturity, a caution that Freudian psychoanalysts have, on the whole, heeded attentively.[33] And in issuing his warning, Freud acted as a philosophical Liberal, turning his back on the prescriptive pretensions of positive freedom. He saw the task of analysis, as we know, as being 'to give the patient's ego freedom to choose one way or the other'.

Some time ago, I had occasion to read an application for psychoanalytic treatment in which the applicant, unschooled in the jargon of the schools, put the matter with affecting simplicity: 'If I undertake psychoanalysis now I think I will be able to make – although perhaps not immediately – some important decisions concerning my marriage, work, and future. And know why I make such decisions. I hope to achieve freedom from my own past.' He was being overly sanguine: Freud never promised anyone – nor would his thought permit him to promise anyone – total freedom from the past. But the direction of this statement is in the spirit of Freud, concentrating, in true Liberal fashion, on the removal of obstructions, and of ignorance, in the service of freedom – in the spirit of Sigmund Freud, and of Isaiah Berlin.

33 See Heinz Hartmann's masterly treatment of the place of ethics, and of 'hidden' preaching, in psychoanalysis, in his *Psychoanalysis and Moral Values* (New York, 1960).

STUART HAMPSHIRE

Freedom and Explanation

or Seeing Double

I

History as an inquiry is not to be assimilated to the natural sciences, and historians should not seriously claim to be scientific. The events and trends that compose human history do not illustrate ascertainable general laws governing all human history, as the events in physical systems illustrate general laws governing all physical systems. Thirdly, the actions and sentiments of individuals in history, and also of social groups, have to be understood in a way that is distinctive and characteristic of historical understanding; it is different particularly in bringing out, as vividly as possible, the peculiar and transient idiosyncrasy of the individual or social group under study. This is the precision aimed at, and not the precision of scientific generality. These three propositions, expressed in my words, and not his, have certainly been prominent in Isaiah Berlin's published works and in his lectures, or at least propositions very near to them have been. I shall describe and advocate a philosophical position from which the truth of these three propositions could be inferred. But this is not the philosophical theory ordinarily associated with these three propositions, and I have no reason to believe that the theory which I shall describe and defend is accepted by Isaiah Berlin.

II

If I press my eyeballs while standing in front of a lighted candle, I shall usually see two lighted candles where previously I had seen one. I would know that I had interfered with the bodily mechanism which enables me to identify the objects before me and that enables me to handle them successfully. If I had been instructed in the physiology of perception, I would also know why the pressing of my eyeballs had precisely this effect of making me see double; I would be able to describe in some detail the mechanisms at work, and I would be able to specify the causes of the distortion. I would not for a moment believe that there were two candles before me, because I have had sufficient experience of the working of my eye to make allowances for the physical effect; and if I were asked to explain my beliefs about the identity of the objects before me, I would reply with further relevant beliefs and items of knowledge about my observing self and about the appearance of relevant things around me, which, taken together, explain my present judgement; and this kind of explanation could be called giving the grounds of my belief, at least when the explanation is offered under these conditions. The mechanisms of my body, including the brain and central nervous system, are used by me both in exploring objects external to me and in making changes in them, and also in investigating and changing the accessible mechanisms of my body. I use the complex instrument which functions according to the universal laws of physics and of chemistry, forming my perceptual beliefs in association with the instrument's interactions with the physical environment.

This is how we are placed in the world as observers of it. In order to explore and to observe the world we have to move, and to move parts of the body, eyes, hands, legs, and also to touch and move objects. We so act with specific intentions, resolved to notice precisely what happens as the effect of our actions. About such intentional actions yet another question 'Why?' can be asked, and this calls for an answer by reference to the beliefs and desires which, taken together, move us to take the action that we did.

The reasons that moved me to action, like the reasons that made me believe that there was only one candle, may be far from explicitly rehearsed. I may know that I have good reasons for the belief and also good reasons for the action, while I may have great difficulty in disentangling and making explicit what the reasons are. There may be a number of considerations of unequal weight and influence, stored and compressed in my mind, which need to be quoted in giving any sufficient explanation of my belief and of my action. But there are occasions of difficulty and uncertainty when I must explicitly review the considerations for and against a suggested belief and a suggested action, and also situations where, confronting a variety of conflicting evidence or a variety of conflicting reasons for action, I must formulate some definite conclusion. These are occasions on which I must brood on considerations for and against, and on which salient reasons become fully explicit and present to the subject's mind, or as fully explicit as reasons ever become. I shall dwell first on these brooding situations, when a man has to assume the pose represented by Rodin in his statue *Le Penseur*. I am alluding to Gilbert Ryle's article on 'Thinking and Reflecting'[1] in his collected papers. Ryle does not deny that there are such situations of brooding and that the occasional existence of the explicit and self-conscious thinker, in Rodin's sense, is essential to our concept of thought, both practical thought and theoretical thought, even though he rightly insists that Rodin's thinker is not the normal case of a thinker and not the normal case of a thoughtful man.

III

There are two standpoints from which the relation between reasons and conclusion in the brooding situation can be examined, whether the conclusion is a practical intention or a belief; from the standpoint of the subject who is making clear to himself what his reasons are at the time of drawing his conclusions, and from the standpoint of the subject looking back on a past conclusion and explaining to himself why he decided as he did. To these two standpoints another must be added: the standpoint of an observer, who is not the thinking subject, and who is not in a position to know directly, or to recall directly, what the reasons were which were explicitly present to the subject's mind and which led him, or seem to have led him, to his conclusion. Both for knowledge of the reasons that led to a conclusion in a contemporary case of brooding, and for retrospective explanation, the observer must rely on the subject's testimony and on other external evidence. The question 'Why?' is asked in the first person singular of the present tense about a belief and an intention, or course of action, when a man needs to clear his mind about what he believes on a particular topic and about what he will do in a particular situation. This posing of the question in the first person of the present tense is certainly not marginal and exceptional. If action alone is considered, the first person of the present form of the question 'Why?' might even be called central rather than the retrospective question, or the question 'Why?' asked by an observer.

In the Nicomachean Ethics Aristotle represents the process of brooding on the proper target of one's conduct as the first and fundamental form of practical reasoning. The clarification of one's intentions and purposes, and of the ends of action, is reasonably represented as both necessary and difficult. Men are frequently confused in their own minds both about what they want and about what

[1] *Collected Papers* (London, 1971), vol. 2, pp. 465–79.

they intend to achieve, and they give incorrect descriptions to themselves of the ends that they are pursuing. For example, they tell themselves that before all things they want to be rich, when in fact they want before all things some of the anticipated consequences of being rich. Observation of their behaviour or further questioning may show that money is for them only a means to an end; but they do not realise this, and in consequence they are apt to act in ways which defeat their own ends. In consequence their life, taken as a whole, is one of unhappiness and of unfulfilled potentialities.

It is a natural error, often supported by false philosophies of mind, that men must know what they want, and if they have formed intentions, they must always know, beyond the possibility of error, what their own intentions are. Even without the complexities of self-deception, sheer misconception of the objects of propositional attitudes, including desire, is a familiar kind of failure in self-knowledge. The errors to which we are liable here are typically not trivial, a mere mismatching of names, but substantial. We mistake the objects of our fears, and misunderstand the reasons for our own passions. We find it difficult to pick out the elements or features in a situation which explain our sadness and gloom, and skill and discipline are needed if we are to be clear about what we are enjoying, or what gives us deep satisfaction, in some scene in which we are involved, or in something that we are reading or hearing. 'What do I want to achieve?', 'What do I fear here?', 'What do I dislike about this?', 'What do I really enjoy, as opposed to those things which I persuade myself that I like?', 'What do I respect?', 'What do I admire?', 'What do I really intend to do about this, as opposed to merely wishing or hoping?' – these are all questions about which a man may think carefully. In answering them in any difficult case, he has to rehearse causal, or quasi-causal, hypotheses about what would be the case if one or other feature of the object or situation before him were changed. He has to review possibilities and alternatives, and he cannot avoid counterfactual speculations if he is to find accurate, and sufficiently complete, answers to these questions, and the questions are directly relevant to conduct.

IV

Some years ago, in 'Subjunctive Conditionals',[2] confronting the problem of singular counterfactuals as an epistemological problem,

[2] *Analysis* 9 (1949), 9–14.

I suggested that they had an ineliminable place in practical deliberation, which is a process of reviewing possible future worlds. Therefore some account of the normal conditions of their verification or falsification has to be given, even if the normal conditions of their verification precludes them from being acceptable in scientific theory. Partly because they are not regularly testable by experiment and observation, they were not a part of the unified language of science as reconstructed by W. V. Quine and other philosophical logicians. Their truth conditions are not uniformly and clearly specified, and vary with the context in which they are employed. But they have an indispensable part not only in practical calculations and causal judgements prior to action and non-causal judgements that impute responsibility in a rational way, but also in the formation of sentiments and attitudes and in reflections on them. In making clear and explicit the reasons for his hopes, fears, wishes, admirations, regrets, sadness, happiness and so forth, a man reflects on the conditions under which his sentiments and attitudes would change. He is then thinking counterfactually.

Aristotle represented rationality in the conduct of life as partly consisting in being clear about the objects of one's own desires, sentiments and attitudes, and in being clear also about the reasons why one feels as one does. Because he thought that explicitness was normally a part of rationality, knowing the reason why, and being able to give an account of why, was an essential part of the intelligence that a satisfactory life requires. In the control and direction of his desires and sentiments, no less than in deliberation about policies of action, a man has to reason counterfactually when he tries to make clear to himself why he has the feelings, attitudes and desires that he does. Practical deliberation on alternative courses of action is just one form of counterfactual reasoning, which calls into play the elementary notion of cause on which commonsense thinking depends.

In the brooding situation, in which a man considers the reasons for his contemporary desires, beliefs, intentions and attitudes, the reasons that explain his state of mind are both grounds and causes. When he recalls later what made him have the desires, beliefs, intentions and sentiments which were explicitly his at the time, and the weight that he gave to reasons in his explicit thinking, he can separate the normative question of whether they were good grounds from the historical question of whether he has accurately specified the considerations that were at work in his thinking, and whether his explicit reasoning masked other considerations present to his mind, and whether he was self-deceived. He is asking himself whether, if the situation had been different in such-and-such respects, his desires, beliefs, intentions and sentiments would have been different in such-and-such other respects; he is looking for a connection, or connections, between features of his previous thought and the features of the desire, belief or intention which is to be explained. That the notions of ground and cause should be confounded, or brought together, has often been a criticism of the rationalist philosophy brought forward by empiricists. But the elementary notion of cause, employed in calculations and ordinary manipulations and in most practical reasoning, unavoidably brings together ground and cause, as a man shifts from the standpoint of initiating subject and agent to that of objective explanation of observed change.

V

When the dogmas of empiricist philosophy are put on one side, it is not difficult to see what kind of connection between reason and conclusion is in question and how the counterfactual propositions are supported. We are constantly familiar with conditional intentions, and also with conditional beliefs and desires. We resolve to do something provided that such-and-such conditions are satisfied, and we will believe something if such-and-such evidence comes in, and we want something if it has such-and-such a feature and not otherwise. The singular counterfactual propositions are explicitly supported by conditional intentions in cases where the intention (or desire or belief) has been formed as the outcome of explicit reasoning, that is, in the brooding situation; for then the subject knows, or is in a position to know, that he formed the intention because of such-and-such considerations. The question 'What supports the singular counterfactual proposition?' is answered by 'The original intention itself, which at its formation was in this respect conditional.' One naturally thinks of counterfactual judgements as requiring support, in the sense that there should be an indirect means of satisfying oneself of their truth or falsity, since a direct means of testing them is normally excluded. When a person is speculating about the connection between his own intentions and attitudes, and when he is citing these connections as explanations, he is often in the exceptional position of knowing directly what conditions surrounded his original intentions and attitudes, while other persons, observing him, can only know from his testimony and by inference from parallel cases. Unless he has forgotten, the subject usually knows about the surrounding context of calculation in which his intention was on a particular occasion formed, and he can therefore explain why his intention assumed the particular form that it did, and under what conditions it would have been in certain respects different. He would be in a specially good position to know this if his intention or attitude had emerged from a situation of brooding.

Evidently a person explaining his own actions, intentions and attitudes is still explaining the actions and attitudes of an observed natural object, whose intentions and attitudes conform to natural tendencies; and he knows this. He is not infallible in his counterfactual judgements and in his explanations of himself, and he knows that he is liable on occasion to be self-deceived. It is sometimes difficult for him to be sure that what he thinks was his reason was in fact his reason, and difficult to be sure that he would have reacted with such-and-such a change of attitude under certain other conditions. The contrasting and controlling source of knowledge is observation, and particularly observation of uniform, or nearly uniform, connections between activating reasons and resulting intentions, attitudes and sentiments. These uniformities constitute supporting grounds for counterfactual judgements alongside the counterfactual judgements which emerge directly from processes of deliberation; and evidently the two sources of knowledge will sometimes be in conflict, pointing to contrary counterfactual judgements. Sometimes it will seem that a person's belief, desire or intention is to be explained by considerations present to his mind which are altogether exceptional and which are peculiar to this occasion. The counterfactual judgement is supported by a clear conditional intention, which on this occasion is taken to outweigh the observed uniformities of past behaviour in parallel cases. At other times it will seem undeniable, in view of the record, that the reasons that a man is offering to himself and to others to explain his intentions are mere rationalisations; he would not have changed his attitude if the circumstances had been different in the one respect which he picks out as the determining one.

VI

The alteration and balance between the two kinds of support for counterfactual judgements is an aspect of the conjugation of the psychological verbs which pick out propositional attitudes such as 'I want', 'I believe', 'I fear', 'I hope', and which move from first-person to second or third. It is open to everyone to think of himself or to observe himself, from the standpoint of a detached observer of his actual behaviour and from the records of the past: just as anyone may pause to reflect on his desires, beliefs and intentions, and on his fears and hopes, as he does in the brooding situation. When a man forms his plans for the future and firmly fixes his intentions, he needs to assure himself that, in all likelihood, he will actually do what he now says to himself that he will do; he needs to be sure that his intention really is an intention and not just a vague aspiration or wish. If the publicly accessible record showed that he had repeatedly formed similar intentions which never issued in action, because he subsequently changed his mind, or because he lost his nerve, there would be reason to doubt that his present intention was more than a mere wish; and this is a reason which should cause the subject to doubt also, because he can be an observer of himself, as others can. He who tells others that he will come to the meeting tomorrow, and that they can be sure of this because he is sure, still has no magical certainty about the future; his subjective assurance is checkable against the probabilities established by induction from his past performances.

The whole vocabulary of propositional attitudes – of desire, belief, fear, hope, anger, regret and so forth – has this same characteristic, and for the same reasons: there is always an interplay between the direct assurance of the subject and the external criteria applied by observers, including the subject himself. This is the epistemological reflection of the 'being in the world' of persons, who are both language-using, and therefore reflective, agents, and also observers of the other medium-sized objects, including other persons, whom they try to understand and to control for practical purposes. When a man speaks, he knows in advance what he will say, and this knowledge is not acquired by observation but comes to him from his intention. The words that he actually utters and that he hears may diverge from his intention, and the explanation may be a slip of the tongue, a quasi-mechanical fault in the execution of his intention. He might discover that he is unable to pronounce a word as he should and as he intended; his body does not follow his intention. Alternatively he may change his mind at the last moment of utterance and the word that then issues from his lips is different from the originally intended word. The borderline that divides the two divergences from the original intention may sometimes be very hard to discern, if we are trying to give an ordinary, pre-theoretical, causal explanation of the previously unintended word being uttered.

The subject himself may not know, on some occasions, whether it was a case of a mere physical malfunctioning or a change of mind at the last moment. He may be uncertain precisely because most intentions are not fully explicit and articulated, and the change of mind might have occurred without being brought into full consciousness. There is no guarantee that on all occasions a clear and reasonably certain account of what occurred can be obtained.

The only certainty is that there is a network of beliefs and desires which entered into a man's intentions on any particular occasion, whether or not the agent can on this occasion pick out the salient beliefs and desires which might properly be quoted in a normal causal explanation of his behaviour. The vocabulary that distinguishes the various propositional attitudes, including beliefs, desires and intentions, requires that the reasons taken by the subject to explain a specific attitude should be of a kind that is compatible with that specific attitude. If there is not the required connection between the explaining cause and reason and the resulting attitude, as the subject conceives them, he will begin to doubt his identification of the attitude. There is nothing mysterious about this lack of the prescribed Humean disconnection between the explaining cause and the explained effect, if one recalls the use of the psychological vocabulary in the first person singular of the present tense alongside its other use. The cause that explains the propositional attitude, if the cause is a belief or desire or another propositional attitude, must be of a kind that fits into a sequence of thought which the subject might follow. It may be true that I believe something, or that I want something, because I have been hypnotised with this effect, or, less probably, because an operation on my brain is having this effect. Then there is not the required connection between the cause and the effect; but in these circumstances it still will not be true that I, the subject, believe that this is the best explanation of my belief, or, in the case of hypnotism, that I believe that this is the best explanation of my desire. There will be another explanation, which I wrongly believe to be the correct explanation in terms of other beliefs and desires which are mine. This will be a rationalisation of my belief or desire, which I will think of as fitting into the system of my beliefs and desires. The connection between the brain operation and the desire or belief, and the hypnotism and the desire or belief, is not an intelligible connection, in the implied sense, precisely because it satisfies the requirement of Humean disconnection, and because it is not a conceivable part of a process of deliberation. The causal connection can be described as 'mechanical', and the implied hypothetical propositions – 'If it had not been for the brain operation, my attitude would have been different' – must be supported by testable general propositions if they are to be acceptable. The hypothetical propositions cannot occur in the first person as statements of conditional intentions; they would be unintelligible in this guise, because they do not form part of a conceivable thought-process ending with this conditional attitude.

We may think that we know why we have the beliefs and desires that we do, but we are sometimes wrong or partly wrong. But there is good reason to believe, first, that men in general are in the majority of cases not in error when they state the causes of their intentions, desires and attitudes, and, secondly, that any particular man is in general not in error when he states the causes of his intentions, desires and beliefs; and that this holds true for other propositional attitudes also. To recur to the original example: there is the situation in which I wrongly believe that I am seeing two candles, when this belief is the effect of a physical cause of which I am ignorant. But if and when I become aware of this causal connection, the propositional attitude is to some degree and in some way modified because of this awareness. The belief is checked by reflection on the unrespectable character of its apparent cause.

There is a rough balance between the causes of desires or beliefs, or other propositional attitudes, which are also fully explicit reasons actuating the subject, and those causes which are external to the subject's conscious and explicit thought. The rough balance arises from the fact that we all do explicitly review our beliefs and desires, and deliberate about them, and at the same time we are liable to be partly ignorant of causes external to our thought which are determining our desires and beliefs. Our knowledge or belief about each kind of cause is restricted and qualified by our knowledge or belief about the other. There is always a potential conflict between the reasons present to our mind as causing a belief or desire and the apparent causes external to our conscious, or unconscious, thinking; therefore there is always a potential conflict between the hypothetical propositions supported by the subject's intentions and the hypothetical propositions supported by general propositions. It is a recurrent philosophical error to take either side as permanently dominant, the subjective or the objective. The error may take the form of interpreting statements of intention as incorrigible, or alternatively of supposing that all specifications of reasons for attitudes or actions might be interpreted as rationalisations, because the real causes are to be found elsewhere and in conditions external to the subject's thought. Both theories cut across the entrenched uses of the psychological vocabulary, which is characterised by the conjugations of psychological verbs in Latin and Greek, and principally by pronouns in English. The shift from the first person to the second and third persons is the syntactical expression of changes of standpoint from which a state of mind can be attributed, and, taken together with changes of tense, the conjugation indicates the kind of support that the attribution may be expected to claim, if challenged. We each sometimes have the standpoint of the subject who forms, and reflects on, his own desires and beliefs, and sometimes have the standpoint of an observer or historian of his own past, relying either on probable inference or on direct testimony and memory. The alternation between the standpoints is not only a check on claims to incorrigibility for one kind of knowledge or the other; it is also a reflection of the fact, so easily obscured, that we each exist as natural objects, observably conforming to natural laws, and also as natural objects which have the peculiar gift of reflecting on our states of mind, and of applying any knowledge of causes that we acquire to modify our states of mind. The conjugation of psychological verbs, and the shift of standpoint, reflect the fact that mental powers and dispositions are embodied in bodily structures as the power of vision is embodied in the eye. The power of reflection includes the power not to yield to the inclination to think that there are two candles when the eyeballs are pressed, and it also includes the power to move one's eyes intentionally.

VII

This feedback of knowledge through the loop of reflective thinking introduces a complexity into the description of mental states which has no parallel in the description of physical states, that is, of states known only by observation and experiment. Our recognition of this added complexity, and of its peculiarity, is sometimes called an awareness of freedom, in a sense in which only thinking beings are free. The consequence of the added complexity of reflection is that the very same observable state of two persons, when classified from the observer's standpoint, will constitute different states of mind from the standpoint of the subjects; for their knowledge or belief about the nature and causes of the observable state will in part determine what their states of mind are. This is just another aspect of the familiar fact that actions by two persons may be identical when seen from the observer's standpoint, but different when the agents' understanding of their situations, and their intentions, are different. The distinction between the same publicly observable action, performed on two occasions or by two persons, and the different thoughts or intentions animating it, is one instance of a more general relation between the subject's reflections on his observable state and his observable state. The contrast between the thought about the action or sentiment, and the observable action or manifestation of the sentiment, constitutes, and creates, that sense of freedom which men take to be peculiar to themselves.

VIII

This contrast has been stated in different ways by philosophers, and one aspect of the contrast is precisely that distinction between human culture and language, vastly various in history and in geography, and a common biological inheritance. This is the distinction which provides one ground for viewing historical method as autonomous and as entirely different from the methods of natural science: a position which Isaiah Berlin has developed and commented upon, particularly in his important study of Vico. The claim has been that historians aim to recapture and reproduce the thought of particular people and periods in the past with all their idiosyncrasies and distinguishing marks, and that they both are, and should be, interested in particularities and nuances of styles and manners and local customs, and not at all in abstract generalisations about human affairs. Humanistic studies are essentially concerned with the varieties of languages in which men have cast their thought, each of them with its distinctive idioms and imagery, formed by the pressure of the particular memories and transmitted customs of one social order.

My argument is intended to show that the distinction between the methods and aims of history, as a humanistic study, and the methods and aims of the natural sciences rests on a more fundamental distinction: namely, that between reflexive, or intentional knowledge, which is not knowledge by observation, and knowledge by observation. This distinction in turn has its foundation in the natural powers of men as capable, because of the power of speech, of reflecting on their actions and feelings, and of planning their future actions and attitudes. But in the evolution of intelligence in the species the power of speech has for some reason been developed as a divisive power, which splits the species into comparatively uncommunicative groups. It seems to be essential to the power of speech that natural languages should hold groups together by exclusion, and that they should thereby contribute to a 'false speciation', in Erik Erikson's words. Whatever the advantage to the species of this splitting into many exclusive groups by language and culture, the effect has been to intensify the contrast between the observed and scientifically testable dispositions and states of the organism and the dispositions and states of the organism whose nature is in part dependent on the subject's recognition of them. Both the particular vocabulary used in the discrimination of emotions and attitudes, and the vocabulary used to discriminate customary forms of behaviour, may substantially modify the subject's conception of his emotions and of his actions. Modifying his conceptions, and modifying the way that he represents to himself and to others his actions and reactions, the idiosyncrasies of his language must enter into his direct experience; and a full allowance has to be made for these idiosyncrasies if an adequate description is to be given of his feelings and motives and conduct.

Adequacy of description has to be relative to some interest in view. The interest that demands an intentional description, taking account of the subject's representation of himself to himself, is not a contingent and dispensable interest, as if it just happened that men are interested in history as well as in natural science. The interest arises from the very existence of practical reasoning, from the mere fact that men make considered decisions, and also reflect on the decisions that they have made, and on the reasons for them. This is a fact, so elementary as to be scarcely noticeable, which has no regular place in textbooks of logic and of scientific method or in most standard accounts of causal reasoning. That explanations of desires and beliefs, and of the decisions that issue from them and that are explained by them, fit into a rational framework is often acknowledged; but acknowledged often with the wrong implication: that the rational explanation is not any kind of causal explanation, because causal explanations require the support of a presumed natural law. The older uses of the word 'cause', present in Descartes, Spinoza and Leibniz, allow that explanations in the context of practical reasoning are still causal explanations, because the counterfactual implications are still open to challenge from the evidence of parallel instances. A historian who constructs a narrative that shows the consequences of his protagonists' actions is employing a notion of cause which leaves him open to challenge from parallel instances in history. But he is not aiming at a precision in his counterfactual speculations, or a testability, which would satisfy a scientist, who is interested in building a theory that will yield precise measurements.

Experiment is the prerequisite of the discovery of natural laws, and of the precision which the discovery of natural laws makes possible. There is a set of arguments, which I have set out elsewhere, designed to show that experiment on intentional states, such as desires and beliefs, is, and always will be, confined within very narrow limits. Here I will mention the basis of just one of these arguments: the power of reflexive thinking, the power that gives us our sense of freedom, has the effect that the experimental inputs will have modified consequences when the experimental subject knows that he is the victim of the experiment. Reflexive thought sets a limit to the possibilities of manipulating desires and beliefs, as normal intentional states, whether the manipulation is for the sake of scientific theory or for other ends. Our sense of freedom is an awareness that we have this power to perceive, and to discount, manipulation, and that in this sense we are not helpless in the face of external causes, in respect at least of our beliefs and desires and similar propositional attitudes. Coming to understand what makes me want something which at the same time I think bad and which I therefore wish that I did not want, I shall often be in a better position to satisfy my second-order desire in virtue of my knowledge of the cause of the first-order desire.

Strict, or scientific, determinism is the framework within which all observed objects having a particular position are to be placed. Among the objects observed are human beings with a full range of observable characteristics, including characteristics of their behaviour and of bodily movement. When we wish to have a strictly deterministic account of human behaviour, and of bodily movements and changes, we can abstract from all intentional descriptions of human behaviour and look for experimentally testable correlations that are reasonably precise and that mention only observable characteristics. The experiments will be repeatable and some of the correlations discovered will after test be acceptable as laws of nature; and therefore they will be accepted as equally reliable among Amazonian tribes as they are in Stockholm or Cambridge, Mass. The correlations of physiology, and of those parts of cognitive and clinical psychology that use only the concepts of physiology, are of this character. But the social sciences are not of this character, in so far as they mention beliefs and sentiments and specify the content of beliefs independently of their observable manifestations.

Therefore either the social sciences have to be abstract and scientific or a social scientist must be content with the unscientific character of historical analysis and of interpretative anthropology and of other humanistic studies, such as linguistics and jurisprudence. They must be content with these Vichian studies, which Vico called, comprehensively, philology, if they are to study the diverse social structures and systems of belief which men have formed and are still forming. In spite of the dreams of empiricist philosophers from Hume and Mill onwards, there will not be a social science which is an extension of the true natural sciences into the domain of belief and custom. This prophesy of mine does not rest on a metaphysical claim that there is some division in reality, on an ontological dualism. It rests on an observation about human knowledge, and the forms which it naturally takes, because we happen to have the peculiar and limited powers of perception and of thoughtful behaviour that we do have. The framework of determinism embraces the objects of observation, and intentional knowledge, the outcome of reflection, has a different framework. The power of reflection, and the power to learn a language which is part of it, are natural endowments embodied in some still largely unknown structures of the brain, as the power of visual discrimination is embodied in the eye. It is this power to which men are referring, whether they know it or not, when they speak of the kind of freedom which only men, among the known species of animal, enjoy, and which they can still develop and exploit.

H. L. A. HART

Between Utility and Rights

I

I do not think that anyone familiar with what has been published in the last ten years, in England and the United States, on the philosophy of government can doubt that this subject, which is the meeting point of moral, political and legal philosophy, is undergoing a major change. We are currently witnessing, I think, the progress of a transition from a once widely accepted old faith that some form of utilitarianism, if only we could discover the right form, *must* capture the essence of political morality. The new faith is that the truth must lie not with a doctrine that takes the maximisation of aggregate or average general welfare for its goal, but with a doctrine of basic human rights, protecting specific basic liberties and interests of individuals, if only we could find some sufficiently firm foundation for such rights to meet some long familiar objections. Whereas not so long ago great energy and much ingenuity of many philosophers were devoted to making some form of utilitarianism work, latterly such energies and ingenuity have been devoted to the articulation of theories of basic rights.

As often with such changes of faith or redirection of philosophical energies and attention, the new insights which are currently offered us seem to dazzle at least as much as they illuminate. Certainly, as I shall try to show by reference to the work of two now influential contemporary writers, the new faith has been presented in forms which are, in spite of much brilliance, in the end unconvincing. My two examples, both American, are taken respectively from the Conservative Right and the Liberal Left of the political spectrum; and while the former, the Conservative, builds a theory of rights on the moral importance of the *separateness* or *distinctness* of human persons which utilitarianism is said to ignore, the latter, the Liberal Left, seeks to erect such a theory on their moral title to equal concern and respect which, it is said, unreconstructed utilitarianism implicitly denies. So while the first theory is dominated by the duty of governments to respect the separateness of persons, the second is dominated by the duty of governments to treat their subjects as equals, with equal concern and respect.

II

For a just appraisal of the first of these two theories it is necessary to gain a clear conception of what precisely is meant by the criticism found in different forms in very many different modern writers that unqualified utilitarianism fails to recognise, or abstracts from, the separateness of persons when, as a political philosophy, it calls on governments to maximise the total or the average net happiness or welfare of their subjects. Though this accusation of ignoring the separateness of persons can be seen as a version of the Kantian principle that human beings are ends in themselves it is none the less the distinctively modern criticism of utilitarianism. In England Bernard Williams[1] and in America John Rawls[2] have been the most eloquent expositors of this form of criticism; and John Rawls's claim that 'utilitarianism does not take seriously the distinction between persons' plays a very important role in his *A Theory of Justice.* Only faint hints of this particular criticism flickered through the many different attacks made in the past on utilitarian doctrine, ever since Jeremy Bentham in 1776 announced to the world that both government and the limits of government were to be justified by reference to the greatest happiness of the greatest number, and not by reference to any doctrine of natural rights: such doctrines he thought so much 'bawling upon paper',[3] and he first denounced them in 1776 in a brief rude reply[4] to the American Declaration of Independence.

What then does this distinctively modern criticism of utilitarianism, that it ignores the moral importance of the separateness of individuals, mean? I think its meaning is to be summed up in four main points, though not all the writers who make this criticism would endorse all of them.

The first point is this. In the perspective of classical maximising utilitarianism separate individuals are of no intrinsic importance but only important as the points at which fragments of what *is* important, i.e. the total aggregate of pleasure or happiness, are located. Individual persons for it are therefore merely the channels or locations where what is of value is to be found. It is for this reason that as long

[1] 'A Critique of Utilitarianism', in J. J. C. Smart and Bernard Williams, *Utilitarianism, For and Against* (Cambridge, 1973), pp. 108–18, and 'Persons, Character and Morality', in A. Rorty (ed.), *The Identity of Persons* (Berkeley, 1977).

[2] *A Theory of Justice* (Oxford, 1972), pp. 22–4, 27, 181, 183, 187.

[3] 'Anarchical Fallacies', in *The Works of Jeremy Bentham*, ed. John Bowring (Edinburgh, 1843) (hereafter *Works*), vol. 2, p. 494.

[4] For an account of this reply included in *An Answer to the Declaration of the American Congress* (London, 1776) by Bentham's friend John Lind, see my 'Bentham and the United States of America', *Journal of Law and Economics* 19 (1976), 555–6.

as the totals are thereby increased there is nothing, if no independent principles of distribution are introduced, to limit permissible trade-offs between the satisfactions of different persons. Hence one individual's happiness or pleasure, however innocent he may be, may be sacrificed to procure a greater happiness or pleasure located in other persons, and such replacements of one person by another are not only allowed but required by unqualified utilitarianism when unrestrained by distinct distributive principles.

Secondly, utilitarianism is not, as sometimes it is said to be, an individualistic and egalitarian doctrine, although in a sense it treats persons as equals, or of equal worth. For it does this only by in effect treating individual persons as of *no* worth; since not persons for the utilitarian but the experiences of pleasure or satisfaction or happiness which persons have are the sole items of worth or elements of value. It is of course true and very important that, according to the utilitarian maxim, 'everybody [is] to count for one, nobody for more than one'[5] in the sense that in any application of the greatest happiness calculus the equal pains or pleasures, satisfactions or dissatisfactions or preferences of different persons are given the same weight whether they be Brahmins or Untouchables, Jews or Christians, black or white. But since utilitarianism has no direct or intrinsic concern but only an instrumental concern with the relative *levels* of total well-being enjoyed by different persons, its form of equal concern and respect for persons embodied in the maxim 'everybody to count for one, nobody for more than one' may license the grossest form of inequality in the actual treatment of individuals, if that is required in order to maximise aggregate or average welfare. So long as that condition is satisfied, the situation in which a few enjoy great happiness while many suffer is as good as one in which happiness is more equally distributed.

Of course in comparing the aggregate economic welfare produced by equal and unequal distribution of resources account must be taken of factors such as diminishing marginal utility and also envy. These factors favour an equal distribution of resources but by no means always favour it conclusively. For there are also factors pointing the other way, such as administrative and transaction costs, loss of incentives and failure of the standard assumption that all individuals are equally good pleasure or satisfaction machines, and derive the same utility from the same amount of wealth.

[5] J. S. Mill, *Utilitarianism*, chapter 5, in *Collected Works of John Stuart Mill*, ed. J. M. Robson (Toronto/London, 1963–), vol. 10 (1969), p. 257, and Bentham, 'Plan of Parliamentary Reform', in *Works*, vol. 3, p. 459.

Thirdly, the modern critique of utilitarianism asserts that there is nothing self-evidently valuable or authoritative as a moral goal in the mere increase in totals of pleasure or happiness abstracted from all questions of distribution. The collective sum of different persons' pleasures, or the net balance of total happiness of different persons (supposing it makes sense to talk of adding them), is not in itself a pleasure or happiness which anybody experiences. Society is not an individual experiencing the aggregate collected pleasures or pains of its members; no person experiences such an aggregate.

Fourthly, according to this critique, maximising utilitarianism, if it is not restrained by distinct distributive principles, proceeds on a false analogy between the way in which it is rational for a single prudent individual to order his life and the way in which it is rational for a whole community to order its life through government. The analogy is this: it is rational for one man as a single individual to sacrifice a present satisfaction or pleasure for a greater satisfaction later, even if we discount somewhat the value of the later satisfaction because of its uncertainty. Such sacrifices are amongst the most elementary requirements of prudence and are commonly accepted as a virtue, and indeed a paradigm of practical rationality, and, of course, any form of saving is an example of this form of rationality. In its misleading analogy with an individual's prudence, maximising utilitarianism not merely treats one person's pleasure as replaceable by some greater pleasure of that same person, as prudence requires, but it also treats the pleasure or happiness of one individual as similarly replaceable without limit by the greater pleasure of other individuals. So in these ways it treats the division between persons as of no more moral significance than the division between times which separates one individual's earlier pleasure from his later pleasure, as if individuals were mere parts of a single persisting entity.

III

The modern insight that it is the arch-sin of unqualified utilitarianism to ignore in the ways I have mentioned the moral importance of the separateness of persons is, I think, in the main a profound and penetrating criticism. It holds good when utilitarianism is restated in terms of maximum want or preference satisfaction and minimum want or preference frustration rather than in the Benthamite form of the balances of pleasure and pain as psychological states, and it holds good when the maximand is taken to be average rather than total general welfare. But it is capable of being abused to discredit all attempts to diminish inequalities and all arguments that one man's loss may be compensated by another's gain such as have inspired policies of social welfare; all these are discredited as if all necessarily committed the cardinal sin committed by maximising utilitarianism of ignoring the separateness of individuals. This is I think the basis of the libertarian, strongly anti-utilitarian political theory developed by Robert Nozick in his influential book *Anarchy, State and Utopia.*[6] For Nozick a strictly limited set of near absolute individual rights constitute the foundation of morality. Such rights for him 'express the inviolability of persons'[7] and 'reflect the fact of our separate existences'.[8] The rights are these: each individual, so long as he does not violate the same rights of others, has the right not to be killed or assaulted, to be free from all forms of coercion or limitation of freedom, and the right not to have property legitimately acquired, taken, or the use of it limited. He has also the secondary right to punish and exact compensation for violation of his rights, to defend himself and others against such violation. He has the positive right to acquire property by making or finding things and by transfer or inheritance from others and he has the right to make such transfers and binding contracts.

The moral landscape which Nozick explicitly presents contains only rights and is empty of everything else except possibly the moral permissibility of avoiding what he terms catastrophe. Hence moral wrongdoing has only one form: the violation of rights, perpetrating a wrong to the holder of a right. So long as rights are not violated it matters not for morality, short of catastrophe, how a social system actually works, how individuals fare under it, what needs it fails to meet or what misery or inequalities it produces. In this scheme of things the basic rights which fill the moral landscape and express the inviolability of persons are few in number but are all equally stringent. The only legitimate State is one to which individuals have transferred their right to punish or exact compensation from others, and the State may not go beyond the night-watchman functions of using the transferred rights to protect persons against force, fraud, and theft or breaches of contract. In particular the State may not impose burdens on the wealth or income or restraints on the liberty of some citizens to relieve the needs or suffering, however great, of others. So a State may only tax its citizens to provide the police, the law courts and the armed forces necessary for defence and the per-

6 *Anarchy, State and Utopia* (Oxford, 1974).

7 ibid., p. 32.

8 ibid., p. 33.

formance of the night-watchman functions. Taxing earnings or profits for the relief of poverty or destitution, however dire the need, or for the general welfare such as public education is on this view morally indefensible; it is said to be 'on a par with' forced labour[9] or making the government imposing such taxes into 'part owners' of the persons taxed.[10]

Nozick's development of this extreme libertarian position is wide-ranging. It is full of original and ingenious argument splendidly designed to shake up any complacent interventionist into painful self-scrutiny. But it rests on the slenderest foundation. Indeed many critics have complained of the lack of any argument to show that human beings have the few and only the few but very stringent rights which Nozick assigns to them to support his conclusion that a morally legitimate government cannot have any more extensive functions than the night-watchman's. But the critics are wrong: there is argument of a sort, though it is woefully deficient. Careful scrutiny of his book shows that the argument consists of the assertion that if the functions of government are not limited to the protection of the basic stringent rights, then that arch-sin of ignoring the separateness of persons which modern critics impute to utilitarianism will have been committed. To sustain this argument Nozick at the start of his book envelops in metaphors all policies imposing burdens or restraints going beyond the functions of the night-watchman State, and the metaphors are in fact all drawn from a description of the arch-sin imputed to utilitarianism. Thus, not only is taxation said to be the equivalent of forced labour but every limitation of property rights, every restriction of liberty for the benefit of others going beyond the constraints imposed by the basic rights, is described as *violating* a person,[11] as a *sacrifice* of that person,[12] or as an outweighing of *one life* by others,[13] or a treatment of a distinct individual as *a resource*[14] for others. So conceptions of justice permitting a graduated income tax to provide for basic needs or to diminish social or economic inequalities are all said to neglect the basic truth 'that each individual is a separate person, that his is the only life he has'.[15] To hold that a person should bear costs that benefit others more is represented as a '*sacrifice*' of that person and as implying

[9] ibid., p. 169.
[10] ibid., p. 172.
[11] ibid., p. 32.
[12] ibid., p. 33.
[13] ibid.
[14] ibid.
[15] ibid.

what is false: namely that there is a single social entity with a life of which individual lives are merely part just as one individual's desires sacrificed for the sake of his other desires are only part of his life.[16] This imputation of the arch-sin committed by utilitarianism to any political philosophy which assigns functions to the State more extensive than the night-watchman's constitutes I think the foundation which Nozick offers for his system.

It is a paradoxical feature of Nozick's argument, hostile though it is to any form of utilitarianism, that it yields a result identical with one of the least acceptable conclusions of an unqualified maximising utilitarianism, namely that given certain conditions there is nothing to choose between a society where few enjoy great happiness and very many very little, and a society where happiness is more equally spread. For the utilitarian the condition is that in both societies either aggregate or average welfare is the same. For Nozick the condition is a historical one: that the patterns of distribution of wealth which exist at any time in a society should have come about through exercise of the rights and powers of acquisition and voluntary transfer included in ownership and without any violation of the few basic rights. Given the satisfaction of this historical condition, how people fare under the resulting patterns of distribution, whether grossly inegalitarian or egalitarian, is of no moral significance. The only virtue of social institutions on this view is that they protect the few basic rights, and their only vice is failure to do this. Any consequence of the exercise of such rights is unobjectionable. It is as if the model for Nozick's basic moral rights were a legal one. Just as there can be no legal objection to the exercise of a legal right, so in a morality empty as Nozick's is of everything except rights there can be no moral objection to the exercise of a moral right.

Why should a critic of society thus assume that there is only one form of moral wrong, namely violation of individual rights? Why should he turn his gaze away from the consequences in terms of human happiness or misery produced by the working of a system of such rights? The only answer apparent in Nozick's work is that to treat this misery as a matter of moral concern and to require some persons to contribute to the assistance of others only makes sense if one is prepared like the maximising utilitarian to disregard the separateness of individuals and share the superstition that those required to make such contributions are merely part of the life of a single persisting social entity which both makes the contributions

[16] ibid., pp. 32–3.

and experiences the balance of good that comes from such contributions. This of course simply assumes that utilitarianism is only intelligible if the satisfactions it seeks to maximise are regarded as those of a single social entity. It also assumes that the only alternative to the Nozickian philosophy of right is an unrestricted maximising utilitarianism which respects not persons but only experiences of pleasure or satisfaction; and this is of course a false dilemma. The impression that we are faced with these two unpalatable alternatives dissolves if we undertake the no doubt unexciting but indispensable chore of confronting Nozick's misleading descriptive terms such as 'sacrifice of one individual for others', 'treating one individual as a resource for others', 'making others a part owner of a man', 'forced labour' with the realities which these expressions are misused to describe. We must also substitute for the blindingly general use of concepts like 'interference with liberty' a discriminating catalogue which will enable us to distinguish those restrictions on liberties which can be imposed only at that intolerable cost of sacrificing an individual's life or depriving it of meaning which according to Nozick is the cost of any restriction of liberty except the restriction on the violation of basic rights. How can it be right to lump together, and ban as equally illegitimate, things so different in their impact on individual life as taking some of a man's income to save others from some great suffering and killing him or taking one of his vital organs for the same purpose? If we are to construct a tenable theory of rights for use in the criticism of law and society we must I fear ask such boring questions as: Is taxing a man's earnings or income which leaves him free to choose whether to work and to choose what work to do not altogether different in terms of the burden it imposes from forcing him to labour? Does it really sacrifice him or make him or his body just a resource for others? Does the admitted moral impermissibility of wounding or maiming others or the existence of an absolute moral right not to have one's vital organs taken for the benefit of others in any way support a conclusion that there exists an absolute moral right to retain untaxed all one's earnings or all the income accrued from inherited property except for taxes to support the army and the police? Can one man's great gain or relief from great suffering not outweigh a small loss of income imposed on another to provide it? Do such outweighings only make sense if the gain and the loss are of the same person or a single 'social entity'? Once we shake off that assumption and once we distinguish between the gravity of the different restrictions on different specific liberties and their importance for the conduct of a meaningful life or the development of the personality, the idea that they all, like unqualified maximising utilitarianism, ignore the moral importance of the division of humanity into separate individuals and threaten the proper inviolability of persons disappears into the mist.

There is of course much of value to be learnt from Nozick's ingenious and diverting pages, but there are also many quite different criticisms to be made of its foundations apart from the one which I have urged. But since other critics have been busy with many such criticisms I will here mention only one. Even if a social philosophy can draw its morality as Nozick assumes only from a single source; even if that source is individual rights, so that the only moral wrongdoing consists in wrongs done to individuals that violate their rights, and even if the foundation for such rights is respect for the separateness of persons, why should rights be limited as they are by Nozick to what Bentham called the negative services of others, that is to abstention from such things as murder, assault, theft and breach of contract? Why should there not be included a basic right to the positive service of the relief of great needs or suffering or the provision of basic education and skills when the cost of these is small compared with both the need to be met and with the financial resources of those taxed to provide them? Why should property rights, to be morally legitimate, have an absolute, permanent, exclusive, inheritable and unmodifiable character which leaves no room for this? Nozick is I think in particular called upon to answer this question because he is clear that though rights for him constitute the only source of constraint on action, they are not ends to be maximised;[17] the obligations they impose are as Nozick insists 'side constraints', so the rights form a protective bastion enabling an individual to achieve his own ends in a life he shapes himself; and *that*, Nozick thinks, is the individual's way of giving meaning to life.[18]

But it is of course an ancient insight that for a meaningful life not only the protection of freedom from deliberate restriction but opportunities and resources for its exercise are needed. Except for a few privileged and lucky persons, the ability to shape life for oneself and lead a meaningful life is something to be constructed by positive marshalling of social and economic resources. It is not something automatically guaranteed by a structure of negative rights. Nothing is more likely to bring freedom into contempt and so endanger it than failure to support those who lack, through no fault of their

[17] ibid., pp. 28–9.
[18] ibid., pp. 48–50.

own, the material and social conditions and opportunities which are needed if a man's freedom is to contribute to his welfare.

IV

My second example of contemporary right-based social philosophy is that put forward with very different political implications as one ground for rights in the original, fascinating, but very complex web of theory spun by Ronald Dworkin in his book *Taking Rights Seriously.*[19] Dworkin's theory at first sight seems to be, like Nozick's, implacably opposed to any form of utilitarianism; so much so that the concept of a right which he is concerned to vindicate is expressly described by him as 'an anti-utilitarian concept'. It is so described because for Dworkin 'if someone has a right to something then it is wrong for the government to deny it to him even though it would be in the general interest to do so'.[20]

In fact the two writers, in spite of this surface similarity, differ on almost every important issue except over the conviction that it is a morality of individual rights which both imposes moral limits on the coercive powers of governments, and in the last resort justifies the use of that power.

Before I turn to examine in detail Dworkin's main thesis I shall summarise the major differences between these two modern philosophers of Right. For Nozick the supreme value is freedom – the unimpeded individual will; for Dworkin it is equality of concern and respect, which as he warns us does not always entail equality of treatment. That governments must treat all their citizens with equal concern and respect is for Dworkin 'a postulate of political morality',[21] and, he presumes, everyone accepts it. Consequently these two thinkers' lists of basic rights are very different, the chief difference being that for Dworkin there is no general or residual right to liberty as there is for Nozick. Indeed though he recognises that many, if not most, liberal thinkers have believed in such a right as Jefferson did, Dworkin calls the idea 'absurd'.[22] There are only rights to specific liberties such as freedom of speech, worship, association, personal and sexual relationships. Since there is no general right to liberty there is no general conflict between liberty and equality, though the reconcilation of these two values is generally regarded as the main

[19] *Taking Rights Seriously* (London, 1977) (hereafter *T.R.S.*).
[20] ibid., p. 269.
[21] ibid., p. 272.
[22] ibid., p. 267.

problem of liberalism; nor, since there is no general right to liberty, is there any inconsistency, as Conservatives often claim, in the liberal's willingness to accept restriction on economic but not on personal freedom. This is why the political thrust of these two right-based theories is in opposite directions. So far from thinking that the State must be confined to the night-watchman's functions of protecting a few basic negative rights but not otherwise restricting freedom, Dworkin is clear that the State may exercise wide interventionist functions; so if overall social welfare fairly assessed would be thereby advanced, the State may restrict the use of property or freedom of contract, it may enforce desegregation, provide through taxation for public education and culture; it may both prohibit discrimination on grounds of sex or colour where these are taken to be badges of inferiority, and allow schemes of reverse racial discrimination, if required in the general interest, even in the form which the Supreme Court has recently refused to uphold in Bakke's case.[23] But there is no general right to liberty: so the freedom from legal restriction to drive both ways on Lexington Avenue and the freedom later regretted, but upheld in Lochner's case[24] against State legislation, to enter into labour contracts requiring more than ten hours work a day were, as long as they were left unrestricted, legal rights of a sort; but they were not and cannot constitute moral or political rights in Dworkin's strong 'anti-utilitarian' sense, just because restriction or abolition of these liberties might properly be imposed if it advanced general welfare. Finally, notwithstanding the general impression of hostility to utilitarianism suggested by his stress on the 'anti-utilitarian' character of the concept of a right, Dworkin does not reject it wholly as Nozick does but, as in the Lexington Avenue and labour contract examples, actually endorses a form of utilitarianism. Indeed he says 'the vast bulk of the laws which diminish my liberty are justified on utilitarian grounds'.[25] But the utilitarianism which Dworkin endorses is a purified or refined form of it in which a 'corrupting'[26] element which he finds in vulgar Benthamite utilitarianism is not allowed to weigh in determining decisions. Where the corrupting element does weigh it destroys according to Dworkin the fair egalitarian character 'everybody to

[23] ibid., chapter 9, pp. 223–39, and *New York Review of Books*, 10 November 1977, pp. 111–15.

[24] *T.R.S.*, pp. 191, 269, 278, and 198 U.S. 45 (1905) (decision of the U.S. Supreme Court).

[25] ibid., p. 269. It is clear that this means 'adequately justified', not merely 'said to be justified'.

[26] ibid., p. 235.

count for one, nobody for more than one' which utilitarian arguments otherwise have. This corrupting element causes their use or the use of a majority democratic vote (which he regards as the nearest practical political representation of utilitarianism) to violate, in the case of certain issues, the fundamental right of all to equal concern and respect.

Before we consider what this 'corrupting' element is and how it corrupts I wish to stress the following major point. Dworkin interestingly differs from most philosophers of the liberal tradition. He not merely seeks to draw a vital distinction between mere liberties which may be restricted in the general interest like freedom of contract to work more than a ten hour day, and those preferred liberties which are rights which may not be restricted, but he attempts to do this without entering into some familiar controversial matters. He does not make any appeal to the important role played in the conduct of individual life by such things as freedom of speech or of worship or of personal relations, to show that they are too precious to be allowed to be subordinated to general welfare. So he does not appeal to any theory of human nature designed to show that these liberties are, as John Stuart Mill claimed, among 'the essentials of human well-being',[27] 'the very ground work of our existence'[28] or to any substantive ideal of the good life or individual welfare. Instead Dworkin temptingly offers something which he believes to be uncontroversial by which to distinguish liberties which are to rank as moral rights like freedom of speech or worship from other freedoms, like freedom of contract or in the use of property, which are not moral rights and may be overridden if they conflict with general welfare. What distinguishes these former liberties is not their greater substantive value but rather a relational or comparative matter, in a sense a procedural matter: the mere consideration that there is an 'antecedent likelihood'[29] that if it were left to an unrestricted utilitarian calculation of the general interest of a majority vote to determine whether or not these should be restricted, the balance would be tipped in favour of restriction by that element which, as Dworkin believes, corrupts utilitarian arguments or a majority vote as a decision procedure, and causes it to fail to treat all as equals with equal concern and respect. So anti-utilitarian rights essentially are a response to a defect – a species of unfairness – likely to corrupt some utilitarian arguments or a majority vote as decision pro-

[27] op. cit. (note 5 above), p. 255.
[28] ibid., p. 251.
[29] *T.R.S.*, p. 278.

cedures. Hence the preferred liberties are those such as freedom of speech or sexual relations, which are to rank as rights when we know 'from our general knowledge of society'[30] that they are in danger of being overridden by the corrupting element in such a decision procedure.

What then is this element which may corrupt utilitarian argument or a democratic vote? Dworkin identifies it by a distinction between the personal and external preferences[31] or satisfaction of individuals, both of which vulgar utilitarianism counts in assessments of general welfare and both of which may be represented in a majority vote. An individual's personal preferences (or satisfactions) are for (or arise from) the assignment of goods or advantages including liberties to himself; his external preferences are for such assignments to others. A utilitarianism refined or purified in the sense that it counted only personal preferences in assessing the balance of social welfare would for Dworkin be 'the only defensible form of utilitarianism'[32] and indeed it is that which justifies the 'vast bulk of our laws diminishing liberty'.[33] It would he thinks genuinely treat persons as equals, even if the upshot was not their equal treatment. So where the balance of personal self-interested preferences supported some restriction on freedom (as it did according to Dworkin in the labour contract cases) or reverse discrimination (as in Bakke's case), the restriction or discrimination may be justified, and the freedom restricted or the claim not to be discriminated against is not a moral or constitutional right.[34] But the vulgar corrupt form of utilitarianism counts both external and personal preferences and is not an acceptable decision procedure since (so Dworkin argues) by counting in external preferences it fails to treat individuals with equal concern and respect or as equals.[35]

Dworkin's ambitious strategy in this argument is to derive rights to specific liberties from nothing more controversial than the duty of governments to treat their subjects with equal concern and respect. His argument here has a certain Byzantine complexity and it is important in assessing it not to be misled by an ambiguity in the way in which a right may be an 'anti-utilitarian right'. There is a natural interpretation of this expression which is not Dworkin's sense; it may

30 ibid., p. 277.
31 ibid., pp. 234–8, 275–8.
32 ibid., p. 276.
33 ibid., p. 269.
34 ibid., p. 236.
35 ibid., pp. 237, 275.

naturally be taken merely to mean that there are some liberties so precious for individual human life that they must not be overridden even in order to secure an advance in general welfare, because they are of greater value than any such increase of general welfare to be got by their denial, however fair the *procedure* for assessing the general welfare is and however genuinely as a procedure it treats persons as equals. Dworkin's sense is *not* that; his argument is not that these liberties must be safeguarded as rights because their value has been compared with that of the increase in general welfare and found to be greater than it, but because such liberties are likely to be defeated by an unfair form of utilitarian argument which by counting on external preferences fails to treat men as equals. So on this view the very identification of the liberties which are to rank as rights is dependent on the anticipated result of a majority vote or a utilitarian argument; whereas on the natural interpretation of an 'anti-utilitarian right' the liberties which are to rank as rights and prevail over general welfare are quite independently identified.

Dworkin's actual argument is more complicated than this already complex story, but I do not think what is omitted is needed for its just assessment. I think both the general form of the argument and its detail are vulnerable to many different objections. The most general objection is the following. What moral rights we have will, on this view, depend on what external preferences or prejudices are current and likely at any given time in any given society to dominate in a utilitarian decision procedure or majority vote. So as far as this argument for rights is concerned, with the progressive liberalisation of a society from which prejudices against, say, homosexual behaviour or the expression of heterodox opinions have faded away, rights to these liberties will (like the State in Karl Marx) wither away. So the more tolerant a society is, the fewer rights there will be; there will not merely be fewer occasions for asserting rights. This is surely paradoxical even if we take Dworkin only to be concerned with rights against the State. But this paradox is compounded by another. Since Dworkin's theory is a response specifically to an alleged defect of utilitarian argument it only establishes rights against the outcome of utilitarian arguments concerning general welfare or a majority democratic vote in which external preferences are likely to tip the balance. This theory as it stands cannot provide support for rights against a tyranny or authoritarian government which does not base its coercive legislation on considerations of general welfare or a majority vote. So this particular argument for rights helps to establish individual rights at neither extreme: neither in an extremely tolerant democracy nor in an extremely repressive tyranny. This of course narrows the scope of Dworkin's argument in ways which may surprise readers of his essay 'What Rights Do We Have?'. But of course he is entitled to reply that, narrow though it is, the reach of this particular argument extends to contemporary Western democracies in which the allegedly corrupting 'external preferences' hostile to certain liberties are rife as prejudices. He may say that *that* is good enough – for the time being.[36]

However, even if we accept this reply, a close examination of the detail of the argument shows it to be defective even within its limited scope; and the ways in which it is defective show an important general failing. In constructing his anti-utilitarian right-based theory Dworkin has sought to derive too much from the idea of equal concern and respect for persons, just as Nozick in constructing his theory sought to derive too much from the idea of the separateness of persons. Both of course appear to offer something comfortably firm and uncontroversial as a foundation for a theory of basic rights. But this appearance is deceptive: that it is so becomes clear if we press the question why, as Dworkin argues, does a utilitarian decision procedure or democratic vote which counts both personal and external preferences *for that reason* fail to treat persons as equals, so that when as he says it is 'antecedently likely' that external preferences may tip the balance against some individual's specific liberty, that liberty becomes clothed with the status of a moral right not to be overridden by such procedures. Dworkin's argument is that counting external preferences corrupts the utilitarian argument or a majority vote as a decision procedure, and this of course must be distinguished from any further independent moral objection there may be to the actual decision resulting from the procedure. An obvious example of such a vice in utilitarian argument or in a majority vote procedure would of course be double counting, e.g. counting one individual's (a Brahmin's or a white man's) vote or preference twice while counting another's (an Untouchable's or a black man's) only once. This is, of course, the very vice excluded by the maxim 'everybody to count for one, nobody for more than one' which Mill thought made utilitarianism so splendid. Of course an Untouchable

[36] This argument from the defect of unreconstructed utilitarianism in counting external preferences is said to be 'only one possible ground of rights' (ibid., p. 272, and (2nd impression) p. 356), and is stated to be applicable only in communities where the general collective justification of political decisions is the general welfare. Though it is indicated that different arguments would be needed where collective justification is not utilitarian (ibid. (2nd impression), p. 365), there is no indication how in such a case the liberties to be preferred as rights are to be identified.

denied some liberty, say liberty to worship, or a black student denied access to higher education as a result of such double counting would not have been treated as an equal, but the right needed to protect him against this is not a right to any specific liberty but simply a right to have his vote or preference count equally with the Brahmin's. And of course the decision to deprive him of the liberty in question might also be morally objectionable for reasons quite independent of the unfairness in the procedure by which it was reached: if freedom of religion or access to education is something of which no one should be deprived whatever decision procedure, fair or unfair, is used, then a right to that freedom would be necessary for its protection. But it is vital to distinguish the specific alleged vice of unrefined utilitarianism or a democratic vote in failing, e.g. through double counting, to treat persons as equals, from any independent objection to a particular decision reached through such arguments. It is necessary to bear this in mind in considering Dworkin's argument.

So, finally, why is counting external preferences thought to be, like the double counting of the Brahmin's or white man's preference, a vice of utilitarian argument or a majority vote? Dworkin actually says that the inclusion of external preference *is* a 'form of double counting'.[37] To understand this we must distinguish cases where the external preference is *favourable* to, and so supports, some personal preference or want for some good or advantage or liberty from cases where the external preference is hostile. Dworkin's simple example of the former is where one person wants the construction of a swimming-pool[38] for his use and other non-swimmers support this. But why is this a 'form of double counting'? No one's preference is counted twice as the Brahmin's is; it is only the case that the proposal for the allocation of some good to the swimmer is supported by the preferences both of the swimmer and (say) his disinterested non-swimmer neighbour. Each of the two preferences is counted only as one; and surely *not* to count the neighbour's disinterested preference on this issue would be to fail to treat the two as equals. It would be 'undercounting' and presumably as bad as double counting. Suppose – to widen the illustration – the issue is freedom for homosexual relationships, and suppose that (as may well have been the case at least in England when the old law was reformed in 1967)[39] it was the disinterested external preferences of liberal heterosexual persons that homosexuals should have this freedom that tipped the balance

[37] ibid., p. 235.
[38] ibid.
[39] Sexual Offences Act 1967.

against the external preferences of other heterosexuals who would deny this freedom. How in this situation could the defeated opponents of freedom or any one else complain that the procedure, through counting external preferences (both those supporting the freedom for others and those denying it) as well as the personal preferences of homosexuals wanting it for themselves, had failed to treat persons as equals?

It is clear that where the external preferences are hostile to the assignment of some liberty wanted by others, the phenomenon of one person's preferences being supported by those of another, which, as I think, Dworkin misdescribes as a 'form of double counting', is altogether absent. Why then, since the charge of double counting is irrelevant, does counting such hostile external preferences mean that the procedure does not treat persons as equals? Dworkin's answer seems to be that if, as a result of such preferences tipping the balance, persons are denied some liberty, say to form certain sexual relations, those so deprived suffer because by this result their conception of a proper or desirable form of life is despised by others, and this is tantamount to treating them as inferior to or of less worth than others, or not deserving equal concern or respect. So every denial of freedom on the basis of external preferences implies that those denied are not entitled to equal concern and respect, are not to be considered as equals. But even if we allow this most questionable interpretation of denials of freedom, still for Dworkin to argue in this way is altogether to change the argument. The objection is no longer that the utilitarian argument or a majority vote is, like double counting, unfair as a procedure because it counts in 'external preference', but that a particular *upshot* of the procedure where the balance is tipped by a *particular kind* of external preference, one which denies liberty and is assumed to express contempt, fails to treat persons as equals. But this is a vice not of the mere externality of the preferences that have tipped the balance but of their content: that is, their liberty-denying and respect-denying content. Yet this is no longer to assign certain liberties the status of ('anti-utilitarian') rights simply as a response to the specific defects of utilitarianism as Dworkin claims to do. But that is not the main weakness in his ingenious argument. What is fundamentally wrong is the suggested interpretation of denials of freedom as denials of equal concern or respect. This surely is mistaken. It is indeed least credible where the denial of the liberty is the upshot of a utilitarian decision procedure or majority vote in which the defeated minority's preference or vote for the liberty has been weighed equally with others and outweighed by numbers. Then the message need not be, as Dworkin interprets it, 'You and your views are inferior, not entitled to equal consideration, concern or respect', but 'You and your supporters are too few. You, like everyone else, are counted as one but no more than one. Increase your numbers and then your views may win out.' Where those who are denied by a majority vote the liberty they seek are able, as they are in a fairly working democracy, to continue to press their views in public argument and to attempt to change their opponents' minds, as they in fact with success did after several defeats when the law relating to homosexuality was changed in England, it seems quite impossible to construe every denial of liberty by a majority vote based on external preferences as a judgement that the minority whom it defeats are of inferior worth, not entitled to be treated as equals or with equal concern and respect. What is true is something different and quite familiar but no support for Dworkin's argument: namely that the procedural fairness of a voting system or utilitarian argument which weighs votes and preferences equally is no guarantee that all the requirements of fairness will be met in the actual working of the system in given social conditions. This is so because majority views may be, though they are not always, ill-informed and impervious to argument: a majority of theoretically independent voters may be consolidated by prejudice into a self-deafened or self-perpetuating block which affords no fair opportunities to a despised minority to publicise and argue its case. All that is possible and has sometimes been actual. But the moral unacceptability of the results in such cases is not traceable to the inherent vice of the decision procedure in counting external preferences, as if this was analogous to double counting. That, of course, would mean that every denial of liberty secured by the doubly counted votes or preferences would necessarily not only be a denial of liberty but also an instance of failing to treat those denied as equals.

I do not expect, however, that Dworkin would concede the point that the triumph of the external preference of a majority over a minority is not as such a denial of equal concern and respect for the defeated minority, even if in the face of my criticism he were to abandon the analogy which he uses to support the argument between such a triumph and the procedural vice of double counting, which vice in the plainest and most literal sense of these not very clear phrases certainly does fail to treat all 'as equals' or with 'equal concern and respect'. He would, I think, simply fall back on the idea that any imposition of external preferences is tantamount to a judgement that those on whom they are imposed are of inferior worth, not to be treated as equals or with equal concern and respect. But is this true? Of course that governments should as far as possible be neutral between all schemes of values and impose no external preferences may be an admirable ideal, and it may be the true centre of liberalism, as Dworkin argues, but I cannot see that this ideal is explained or justified or strengthened by its description as a form of or a derivative from the duty of governments to show equal concern and respect for its citizens. It is not clear why the rejection of his ideal and allowing a majority's external preferences denying a liberty to prevail is tantamount to an affirmation of the inferior worth of the minority. The majority imposing such external preferences may regard the minority's views as mistaken or sinful; but overriding them, for those reasons (however objectionable on other grounds), seems quite compatible with recognising the equal worth of the holders of such views and may even be inspired by concern for them. In any event both the liberal prescription for governments, 'impose no scheme of values on any one', and its opposite, 'impose this particular conception of the good life on all', though they are universal prescriptions, seem to have nothing specifically to do with equality or the value of equal concern and respect any more than have the prescriptions 'kill no one' and 'kill everyone', though of course conformity with such universal prescriptions will involve treating all alike in the relevant respect. My suspicions that the ideas of 'equal concern and respect' and treatment 'as equals' are either too indeterminate to play the fundamental role which they do in Dworkin's theory or that a vacuous use is being made of the notion of equality are heightened by his latest observations on this subject.[40] Here he argues that in addition to the liberal conception of equal concern and respect there is another conservative conception which far from requiring governments to be as neutral as possible between values or theories of the good life requires them to treat all men as a 'good man would wish to be treated' according to some particular preferred theory of the good life. On this view, denials of certain forms of sexual liberty as well as the maintenance of social and economic inequalities, if required by the preferred moral theory, would be the conservative form of treating all as equals and with equal concern and respect. But a notion of equal concern and respect hospitable to such violently opposed interpretations (or 'conceptions

[40] See Stuart Hampshire (ed.), *Liberalism in Public and Private Morality* (Cambridge, 1978), pp. 127–8, 136–40.

of the concept') does not seem to me to be a single concept at all, and it is far from clear why either of these two conceptions should be thought of as forms of equal concern and respect. Though the claim that liberal rights are derived from the duty of governments to treat all its citizens with equal concern and respect has a comforting appearance of resting them on something uncontroversial ('a postulate of political morality' which all are 'presumed to accept'),[41] this appearance dissolves when it is revealed that there is an alternative interpretation of this fundamental duty from which most liberal rights could not be derived but negations of many liberal rights could.

Though the points urged in the last paragraphs destroy the argument that any denial of liberty on this basis of external preferences is a denial of equal concern and respect and the attempted derivation of rights from equality, this does not mean that such denials of freedom are unobjectionable or that there is no right to it: it means rather that the freedom must be defended on other grounds than equality. Utilitarian arguments, even purified by the exclusion of external preferences, can produce illiberal and grossly inegalitarian results. Some liberties, because of the role they play in human life, are too precious to be put at the mercy of numbers even if in favourable circumstances they may win out. So to protect such precious liberties we need rights which are indeed 'anti-utilitarian rights' and 'anti-' much else, but so far as they are 'anti-utilitarian' they are so in the common, not the Dworkinian, sense of that expression, and they are needed as a shield not only against a preponderance of external preferences but against personal preferences also.[42] Freedom of speech, for example, may need to be defended against those who would abridge or suppress it as dangerous to their prosperity, security, or other personal interests. We cannot escape, as Dworkin's purported derivation of such rights from equality seeks to do, the assertions of the value of such liberties as compared with advances in general welfare, however fairly assessed.

[41] *T.R.S.*, p. 272.

[42] Dworkin certainly seems to endorse utilitarian arguments purified of external preferences, yet he states (ibid. (2nd impression), p. 357) that his arguments, though against an unrestricted utilitarianism, are not in favour of a restricted one. The contrary impression is given by earlier statements such as (ibid., p. 269) that the vast bulk of laws which diminish our liberty are justified on utilitarian grounds, and the following comment on the right to liberty of contract claimed in Lochner's case: 'I cannot think of any argument that a political decision to limit such a right . . . is antecedently likely to give effect to external preferences and *in that way* offend the right of those whose liberty is curtailed to equal concern and respect. If as I think no such argument can be made out then the alleged right does not exist' (ibid., p. 278, emphasis added).

It is in any case surely fantastic to suppose that what, for example, those denied freedom of worship, or homosexuals denied freedom to form sexual relations, have chiefly to complain about is not the restriction of their liberty with all its grave impact on personal life or development and happiness, but that they are not accorded *equal* concern and respect: that others are accorded a concern and respect denied to them. When it is argued that the denial to some of a certain freedom, say to some form of religious worship or to some form of sexual relations, is essentially a denial of equal concern and respect, the word 'equal' is playing an empty but misleading role. The vice of the denial of such freedom is not its inequality or unequal impact; if that *were* the vice the prohibition by a tyrant of all forms of religious worship or sexual activity would not increase the scale of the evil as in fact it surely would, and the evil would vanish if all were converted to the banned faith or to the prohibited form of sexual relationship. The evil is the denial of liberty or respect; not *equal* liberty or *equal* respect: and what is deplorable is the ill-treatment of the victims and not the relational matter of the unfairness of their treatment compared with others. This becomes clear if we contrast with this spurious invocation of equality a genuine case of a failure to treat men as equals in the literal sense of these words: namely literal double counting, giving the Brahmin or the white man two votes to the Untouchable's or the black man's single vote. Here the single vote given to the latter is indeed bad just because the others are given two: it is, unlike the denial of a religious or sexual freedom, a genuine denial of *equality* of concern and respect, and this evil *would* vanish and *not* increase if the restriction to a single vote were made universal.

V

I conclude that neither Nozick's nor Dworkin's attempt to derive rights from the seemingly uncontroversial ideas of the separateness of persons or from their title to equal concern and respect succeeds. So in the rough seas which the philosophy of political morality is presently crossing between the old faith in utilitarianism and the new faith in rights, perhaps these writers' chief and very considerable service is to have shown, by running up against them, some of the rocks and shoals to be avoided, but not where the safe channels lie for a prosperous voyage. That still awaits discovery. Much valuable work has been done, especially by these and other American philosophers, but there is much still to be done to identify the peculiar features of the dimension of morality constituted by the conception of basic moral rights and the way in which that dimension of morality relates to other values pursued through government; but I do not think a satisfactory foundation for a theory of rights will be found as long as the search is conducted in the shadow of utilitarianism, as both Nozick's and Dworkin's in their different ways are. For it is unlikely that the truth will be in a doctrine mainly defined by its freedom from utilitarianism's chief defect – neglecting the separateness of persons – or in a doctrine resting, like Dworkin's, everything on 'equal concern and respect' as a barrier against an allegedly corrupt form of utilitarianism.

A shorter version of this essay was delivered as the John Dewey Memorial Lecture at the Law School of Columbia University on 14 November 1978. I am indebted to Derek Parfit for many useful suggestions and criticisms both of the style and of the substance of the present version.

JAMES JOLL

Politicians and the Freedom to Choose

The Case of July 1914

Statesmen are widely held to have some freedom of choice in making their decisions; or at least this is what is presumably implied in all democratic political theory with its emphasis on 'responsible government' and the 'accountability' of ministers, as well as in democratic political practice, with its repeated attacks on 'guilty men', who often merely turn out to be people who at the time took a wrong decision. The victorious allied governments in 1919 were operating on this principle when they inserted the notorious 'war guilt' clause into the Treaty of Versailles, by which Germany accepted responsibility 'for causing all the loss and damage to the Allied governments and their nationals imposed upon them by the aggression of Germany'.

The historiographical discussion of this question, as far as the crisis of 1914 is concerned, has taken the form of arguing as to whether the German government was or was not in fact responsible for the outbreak of war, and if it was not, whether some other government was; or else it has been argued that no one was to blame – 'The nations slithered over the brink into the boiling cauldron of war without any trace of apprehension or dismay'[1] as Lloyd George put it – and that the cause of the catastrophe was the inadequacy of the international system rather than the fault of any particular government. The argument that it was the system rather than any individual or group of individuals that was to blame takes many forms, ranging from the general Marxist belief that wars are inherent in the nature of capitalism, and will only cease when the capitalist economy is abolished, to more specific attacks on armament manufacturers and other pressure groups who are alleged to have created in their own interest a situation which made war inevitable.

However, even the most fervent believers in historical inevitability generally admit that rulers have some freedom of action in the short term, that they do take decisions which have consequences, even

[1] David Lloyd George, *War Memoirs*, 2 vols. (London, 1938), vol. 1, p. 32.

though those consequences may not affect the pattern of long-term historical development. If we look at some of the limitations on the freedom of choice of the politicians and others taking crucial decisions in the crisis of July 1914, and try to find out how much they were aware of the restrictions on their freedom to choose, perhaps we may learn something both about the problem of freedom and inevitability in history and about the nature and limits of political responsibility.

The great Lord Salisbury when he was Foreign Secretary once said that he had been embarrassed by guests at Hatfield who condoled with him in an acute international crisis on the burden of responsibility under which he must be labouring.

> 'They would have been so terribly shocked if I had told them the truth – which was that I didn't understand what they were talking about.' . . . He was about to start upon a walk and was standing at the moment at the open door, looking out upon the threatening clouds of an autumn afternoon. 'I don't understand', he repeated, 'what people mean when they talk of the burden of responsibility. I should understand if they spoke of the burden of decision – I feel it now, trying to make up my mind whether or not to take a greatcoat with me. I feel it in exactly the same way, but no more, when I am writing a despatch upon which peace or war may depend. Its degree depends on the materials for decision available and not in the least upon the magnitude of the results which may follow.' Then, after a moment's pause and in a lower tone, he added, 'With the results I have nothing to do.'[2]

Can a statesman in fact do more than survey the weather and decide whether or not to take such refuge as he can find from a storm he cannot avert? Some of the participants in the international crisis of July 1914 felt, both at the time and subsequently, that their freedom of action had been seriously limited, that the storm which threatened was inescapable. The German Chancellor remarked helplessly that he saw 'a doom greater than human power hanging over Europe and over our country'.[3] And Sir Edward Grey subsequently claimed that the goals which he thought he was aiming at in July 1914 turned out to be different from those he actually achieved. 'I used to hope that I was meant to keep the country out of war. But perhaps my real business was to bring her into it unitedly.'[4] Indeed, one of the unresolved historical problems of the crisis is to determine just at what moment Grey came to believe that war was inevitable and so

[2] Lady Gwendolen Cecil, *Life of Robert Marquess of Salisbury*, vol. 1 (London, 1921), pp. 118–19.

[3] Kurt Riezler, *Tagebücher, Aufsätze, Dokumente* (Göttingen, 1972), p. 192.

[4] G. M. Trevelyan, *Grey of Fallodon* (London, 1937), p. 254.

began to pursue a policy aimed at carrying his party with him into war rather than one aimed at keeping out of war.

Political actions have consequences which the men who made them could not have predicted. In 1914, for example, hardly any of those in responsible positions had any idea of what the length and nature of the war would be. Would their decisions have been different if they had not been victims of what one scholar has called 'the short war illusion'?[5] Or were their conceptions of the 'vital national interests' involved in the crisis such that the necessity of preserving them outweighed all utilitarian calculations of profit and loss which might have suggested that the decision for war was not justified? Some of the choices taken in 1914 were not taken on the rational grounds of what might be achieved by embarking on a war whose nature could not be foreseen. In many cases the decision for war was a negative one and, rather than being an attempt to pursue attainable goals by means of war, was a desperate attempt to escape from insuperable domestic pressures regardless of the consequences.

Political leaders in 1914 were also limited by their own conception of how people behave. For an English liberal like Sir Edward Grey or Mr Asquith, as indeed for Mr Chamberlain in 1938, it was literally unthinkable that anyone actually wanted war, that they might be planning for a particular war at a particular time rather than stumbling into war because of some misunderstanding, some breakdown in the system of international communications. In 1914 Grey especially was a victim of this kind of limitation on his freedom of action. Two years earlier, during the crisis provoked by the Balkan Wars, he had, he believed, avoided a general war by convening in London a conference to work out diplomatic formulas which would enable the Great Powers to find respectable excuses for not intervening in support of any of the Balkan contestants, and to produce an agreed settlement which the smaller nations could then be obliged to accept. He saw no reason to think that a similar diplomatic technique might not solve the problem in 1914: 'I would continue the same policy as I had pursued throughout the Balkan crisis . . . the greater the risk of war the more closely would I adhere to this policy.'[6] By deciding that a course of action which had once

[5] L. L. Farrar Jr., *The Short War Illusion* (Santa Barbara, 1973). I am also much indebted to Dr Farrar for his article 'The Limits of Choice: July 1914 Reconsidered', *Conflict Resolution* 15 no 1 (March 1972), pp. 1–23.

[6] *British Documents on the Origins of the War* [hereafter *BD*], vol. 11 (London, 1926), no 41. See also Zara S. Steiner, *Britain and the Origins of the First World War* (London, 1977). I have learnt much from Dr Steiner's work and from discussions with her.

produced the results he intended would again produce similar results on a different occasion, he was limiting the possibilities open to him – a classic example of the inadequacies of induction based on too limited a number of examples.

But if the desire to repeat a success can have the psychological effect of limiting freedom of choice, so can fear of repeating a failure. In 1913 the Russian government had failed to give Serbia the backing she needed in order to secure an Adriatic port; and in 1914 the limits of the Russian government's choice seemed to be determined by the feeling that to fail to support Serbia again would lead to the complete loss of Russian credibility and influence in the Balkans. Freedom to choose is affected both by past successes and by past failures; and the firm desire to repeat a success or avoid a failure often blinds statesmen to the alternative courses which might be open to them. Often, however, a politician labours under even more weighty prejudices which restrict his freedom of action, prejudices which go unquestioned and unanalysed. These are the prejudices produced by the concept, often elaborated over centuries, of a 'vital national interest'.

The restrictions imposed on a government's freedom of action by what it regards as a national interest too important to be sacrificed under any circumstances are more complicated than may at first appear. Very often a traditional formula masks something different, and the actual interest involved may be obscured by the formulas which are used to express it. The obvious example in 1914 is the question of British policy towards Belgium. It had been taken as an axiom of British foreign policy for more than two hundred years that the possession of the coast of Flanders and the mouths of the Scheldt by a hostile power would be a direct and serious threat to Britain, and it has been widely believed both at the time and subsequently that it was the German invasion of Belgium which was directly responsible for Britain's entry into the war in 1914. In fact the case for war was argued in the British cabinet on other grounds, and it was pointed out that the terms of the 1839 treaty of guarantee of Belgian neutrality did not in fact oblige Britain to take unilateral action if the other guarantor powers did not join in. Bismarck once said that all treaties contained the unwritten clause 'rebus sic stantibus'; and other great powers have tended to take a similar view of their treaty obligations if these conflicted with their interests. It is not treaties which limit freedom of action but the strategic and political realities which underlie them; and these change with changing international and domestic circumstances. Governments can always find plausible excuses for evading their treaty obligations if compelling reasons of State demand it. On the other hand, and this is the case of Britain in 1914, a treaty obligation such as that to uphold the neutrality of Belgium provides a valuable cloak of respectability to justify a decision taken on other grounds. The British cabinet had taken its decision for war before the Germans invaded Belgium, but that invasion provided the government with the moral grounds for calling on their liberal followers to support the war.[7]

In 1914 the British concept of national interest was more flexible than that involved in the guarantee of Belgian neutrality. To the direct strategic interest in the Belgian coast was added the more metaphysical concept of the Balance of Power. 'It has become almost a historical truism', Sir Eyre Crowe, in 1914 the Assistant Under-Secretary at the Foreign Office, had written in his famous memorandum of 1 January 1907, 'to identify England's secular policy with the maintenance of this balance by throwing her weight now in this scale and now in that, but ever on the side opposed to the political dictatorship of the strongest single State or group at a given time.'[8] The strongest arguments for British intervention in 1914 were based on the assessment of what might happen if Britain stayed out, and were not far from the minds of those members of the Cabinet who were trying to convince themselves and their reluctant colleagues of the necessity of British intervention. The point was put baldly to them by the leaders of the Conservative opposition when they wrote in an attempt to stiffen the government's resolve: 'Any hesitation in now supporting France and Russia would be fatal to the honour and to the future security of the United Kingdom.'[9] Or as Eyre Crowe from within the Foreign Office put it, 'The theory that England cannot engage in a big war means her abdication as an independent state.'[10] It was this generalised conception of what constituted a great power and of what would be fatal to the independence of a State within the prevailing international system which determined the limits of choice of each of the belligerents. For Austria-Hungary her survival as a multi-national dynastic State seemed to depend on crushing Serbia in order to break Serbian influence among the southern Slav inhabitants of the Monarchy: but

[7] See K. M. Wilson, 'The British Cabinet's Decision for War, 2 August 1914', *British Journal of International Studies* 1 (1975), 148–9, and Cameron Hazlehurst, *Politicians at War* (London, 1971).

[8] *BD* vol. 3, Appendix A, pp. 397–420.

[9] Quoted by Cameron Hazlehurst, op. cit. (note 7 above), p. 41.

[10] *BD* vol. 11, no 369.

such action against Serbia was as much for its own sake as to achieve an immediate political goal: 'The monarchy must take an energetic decision to show its power of survival [*Lebenskraft*] and to put an end to the intolerable conditions in the south-east', the Hungarian Prime Minister told the German Ambassador on 14 July.[11] The German government, as Bethmann-Hollweg the Imperial Chancellor expressed it later, believed that it would have been *Selbstentmannung* (self-castration) for Germany to have failed to support Austria-Hungary.[12] Any system of belief, if strongly held, rules out in advance certain courses of action: but the prevalent social Darwinism of the generation before 1914 was particularly dangerous because of the policies which were implicit in it and which governments felt obliged to pursue.

Past experience and general systems of belief limit the freedom of action of statesmen just as much as they do that of anyone else, but politicians are also inhibited in their liberty of choice by purely political situations, by considerations, that is to say, which are peculiar to their profession. In recent historical discussions about the origins of the First World War there has been, for reasons which perhaps tell us as much about the 1960s and 1970s as they do about the years before 1914, a tendency to argue that the decisions in the July crisis were largely determined by domestic social and political pressures and that it was these as much as, if not more than, conceptions of *Weltpolitik* or the Balance of Power which made war inevitable. This view has become almost a new orthodoxy among many German historians and it has been developed in America by Professor Arno J. Mayer. There is room for differences in interpretation of this approach: did the German government opt for war because it was the only way the ruling class could see of avoiding revolution; or was the war the inevitable result of a general crisis in European society? 'The decision for war and the design for warfare', Arno Mayer has written, 'were forged in what was a crisis in the politics and policy of Europe's ruling and governing classes.'[13]

It is at this point that the classical Marxist view that war is inevitable because of the contradictions of capitalism needs, if it is to be at all convincing, to be supported by some detailed evidence of what the factors actually were which influenced the political and

[11] Imanuel Geiss (ed.), *Juli 1914* (Munich, 1965), p. 93.

[12] Fritz Stern, 'Bethmann-Hollweg and the War', in L. Krieger and F. Stern (eds.), *The Responsibility of Power* (New York, 1967), p. 267.

[13] Arno J. Mayer, 'Internal Crises and War since 1870', in Charles L. Bertrand (ed.), *Revolutionary Situations in Europe* (Montreal, 1977), p. 231.

military leaders in their vital decisions in July 1914. If we are to accept the analysis based on the idea of the overriding importance of domestic political factors in determining foreign policy, we need to be shown the exact points of interaction between domestic and foreign policy, the precise moments at which decisions were taken under the influence of fear of revolution or pressure from economic interest groups. This may well be an impossible task for the historian: as I have argued elsewhere, in moments of crisis political leaders fall back on unspoken assumptions, direct evidence for which is rarely to be found in the documents available to political historians.[14] There is nearly always a gap between our description of the factors which make up the general intellectual and emotional climate of an age and our description of the precise acts of individual politicians.

Here one is tempted to follow the view that politicians do not in fact have anything in mind when they take vital decisions other than the most immediate consequences in the short run – the resolution of a temporary political difficulty or the scoring of a small point off their opponents. There are undoubtedly occasions when this is so, as anyone in England during the second half of the 1970s hardly needs reminding, but it does not provide an adequate explanation of the decisions taken in 1914. In the case of most democracies and even some dictatorships statesmen are limited by the political system within which they are working. They may of course be able to ignore some of the obvious expressions of public opinion – the press, for example: as Grey wrote to a friend who was concerned about his reaction to newspaper criticism, 'Well really, I haven't time to read any papers except Times, Westminster Gazette and Spectator, and I have seen very little of the abuse. I get the drift of it from what is told me and from extracts sent me, but I have too much to do to mind.'[15] On the other hand, if ministers are to achieve anything at all, they have to persuade their political colleagues and their immediate political supporters to go along with them, and this necessarily places limitations on their freedom of action. (It also sometimes involves them in lying to their followers, as Grey did in June 1914 when he denied in Parliament that there had been any talks between the British and Russian naval authorities.)

[14] James Joll, *1914, The Unspoken Assumptions – An Inaugural Lecture* (London, 1968).

[15] Grey to Mrs L. Creighton, 4 February 1912, quoted by K. G. Robbins, 'Public Opinion, Press and Pressure Groups', in F. H. Hinsley (ed.), *British Foreign Policy under Sir Edward Grey* (Cambridge, 1977), p. 82.

In France, too, the workings of the democratic system imposed limitations on what in practice governments could choose to do. In 1914 the government – and especially Poincaré, the President of the Republic, who was personally committed to strengthening the alliance with Russia and to the eventual recovery of Alsace-Lorraine – were worried about the strength of anti-militarist feeling in France, and it was with relief that because the war started with the actual invasion of French soil the *Union Sacrée* could, for the time at least, become a reality, so that the question of alternative choices did not present itself. It was by no means clear earlier in the year that this would be the case: although in 1913 a majority of the Chamber had passed the law extending the period of compulsory military service from two to three years, the parliamentary situation was unstable (there were seven different governments and six prime ministers between January 1912 and June 1914), and the elections in the spring of 1914 had shown a marked swing to the left and notable gains by the socialist party, who were committed in principle to a general strike against war, a commitment reaffirmed at their party congress in July 1914, though doubtless with many mental reservations on the part of their leader, Jean Jaurès. Early in June the new chamber had overthrown the President's nominee as prime minister after only three days; and the new government's existence depended on not taking any controversial measures of any kind. The limitations on the freedom of choice of the government were here, as in England, imposed by the political divisions of the country at large. These limitations in fact led the French government in the last days of July to act in a devious and disingenuous way. In theory, the terms of the French alliance with Russia imposed on Russia the duty of consulting France before ordering general mobilisation, so that, again in theory, the French government could have exercised influence on the Russian government at a decisive moment. In practice, however, President Poincaré and the prime minister, Viviani, seem to have gone out of their way to pretend ignorance of the Russian mobilisation as long as possible, presumably so as to free themselves from the criticism that they could have done more to restrain the Russians from a step that would almost certainly lead to war. It was important that the emphasis should be laid on the German mobilisation and not on the Russian mobilisation which preceded it, so as to demonstrate publicly Germany's responsibility; and it was as essential for the French government to be able to assert this as it was for the German government to show that the war was the result of Russian aggression.

The rulers of autocratic States clearly have a greater choice of alternative courses of action than those of democracies, but even they have to take into consideration possible opposition which may limit their freedom of action. In Germany, for example, the ruling classes were shaken by the Social Democrats' success in the Reichstag elections of 1912, when they secured one-third of the votes and became the largest single party in the Imperial Parliament. In extreme conservative circles there was talk of a right-wing coup to abolish universal suffrage and ban the socialist party, and thus restore uninhibited freedom of action to the government. And even a comparatively moderate political leader such as the Chancellor, Bethmann-Hollweg, while seeking ways to integrate the socialists into the German State, was afraid that their much-publicised anti-militarism might make them an effective brake on German policy in the event of war. He thus made it one of the chief aims of his diplomacy to engineer a situation in which war when it did come would appear to be the result of Russian aggression, since the Social Democrats from the days of Marx and Engels had always recognised the legitimacy of a war against 'tsarist autocracy'. It is however ironical that, just as Bethmann felt constrained in his diplomacy to pursue policies which would carry the socialists with him (though he of course also hoped that if Russia could be branded as an aggressor there was a good chance that England would remain neutral), many of the socialist leaders themselves believed that, for all their protestations of international solidarity at the congresses of the Second International, the option of actively opposing a war was not in fact one which was open to them. They feared that the passionate anti-militarist campaign of Karl Liebknecht would only be an embarrassment and might lead to a confrontation with the whole strength of the Prussian military establishment; and we also now know that their venerable leader, August Bebel, in the last years of his life, was telling the British Consul in Zurich that only the British navy could curb German militarism, since the Social Democrats were powerless to do so.[16]

Even the Serbian government was not wholly free from considerations of internal politics in taking its decisions. It has been suggested that they might have gone as far as total acceptance of the Austro-Hungarian ultimatum if this choice had not been ruled out for them by the fact that the participation of Austrian officials in the

[16] See Helmut Bley, *Bebel und die Strategie der Kriegsverhütung 1904–1913* (Göttingen, 1975), and R. J. Crampton, 'August Bebel and the British Foreign Office', *History* 58 (1973).

inquiry into the assassination of the Archduke Francis Ferdinand might have revealed the extent to which the government was under the influence of the Black Hand, the secret nationalist society. Perhaps they feared a revelation which would have had serious repercussions both internally and internationally as much as they feared what they claimed to be an intolerable infringement of their sovereignty.

When the crisis came in July 1914, all the governments of Europe were already in a situation in which, for the reasons I have suggested, their choice of action was limited and certain courses were closed to them. Their own domestic political situation, the immediate pressures to which they were subjected, their general beliefs about the world and about the nature of international society all combined to determine the course of action on which they finally decided. But there is also another way in which the actions of governments in a crisis are less free than they might at first appear. If one looks at the details of the July crisis, one is often struck by how irrelevant the decisions taken are to the actual situation as we now know it to have developed. Again and again during the last days of peace we have the impression that those responsible were taking decisions about situations which had already changed without their knowing it. It is this which gives in the light of our subsequent knowledge an unreal air to the discussions in the British cabinet during the critical days. It is, for example, clear that by the time Sir Edward Grey realised the full gravity of the situation and had some inkling of what the Austro-Hungarian government intended to do, the Austrian ultimatum to Serbia had already been despatched so that the possibility of influencing the Austrian government as he hoped to do had already passed. Again, on 29 July, when Grey was still hoping that the German government might persuade the Austrians to accept the conciliatory reply which the Serbian government had returned to their ultimatum, he had to face the fact that, as the German Chancellor told the British Ambassador, 'The Austro-Hungarian government had answered that it was too late . . . as events had marched too rapidly.'[17]

Again, on 31 July, the Tsar noted on the bottom of a telegram from Paris which recommended delay in mobilisation for fear of offering Germany the pretext to mobilise, 'This telegram has come too late'; as indeed it had, since the Tsar only received it after he had

[17] *BD* vol. 11, no 264.

reluctantly agreed to issue the orders for the Russian mobilisation.[18] Perhaps it would have made no difference: but perhaps a delay in the Russian mobilisation might have delayed the final intensification of the crisis and given substance to Grey's hopes that there were still chances to save the peace and that certain choices, which were in fact already closed, were still open to him.

It is a widespread psychological trait that people are reluctant to give up hope and to abandon the belief that there is still something they can do to influence events. If Grey and many members of the Liberal Party and indeed Sazonov, the Russian foreign minister, whose vacillating moods contributed to the general diplomatic confusion, continued to believe that something could be done to avert catastrophe, the socialist members of the Second International, although forced to recognise their powerlessness to influence events, were also unwilling to accept the worst or to realise that events were moving too fast to be controlled. 'Les choses ne peuvent ne pas s'arranger' the French socialist leader Jean Jaurès remarked on the day before he was assassinated.[19] Actually the International Socialist Bureau which met in Brussels on 29 July had been less concerned with ways of preventing war than with the administrative problems of changing the place of the forthcoming International Socialist Congress from Vienna to Paris on the assumption that it was still possible to go ahead with plans for a meeting there in a fortnight's time. Like the members of many of the governments involved in the crisis – and like many military commanders in both World Wars – they had simply got the time scale within which they were operating wrong.

For the politicians the belief that there was still something they could do alternated with the feeling that they were helpless, that things were moving too fast for them. Bethmann-Hollweg, a man of true conservative temperament who tended to believe that everything was bound to be for the worst and whose hour-by-hour changes of mood were recorded in the recently published diary of his personal assistant Kurt Riezler, finally admitted on 31 July that the situation had got out of control – though it may well be argued that this was largely his fault: 'All the governments – including that of Russia – and the great majority of the peoples are pacific, but the situation has got out of hand [*es sei die Direktion verloren*] and the

[18] Quoted by Luigi Albertini, *The Origins of the War of 1914*, trans. Isabella M. Massey, vol. 2 (London, 1953), p. 6†1.

[19] E. Vandervelde, *Jaurès* (Paris, 1919), p. 6.

stone has started rolling.'[20] What this meant was that his own freedom of action had finally gone, that it was the plans of the generals which had now taken over, and that the consequences of their earlier decisions had now become irreversible. A. J. P. Taylor has analysed the crisis in terms of 'war by timetable', of plans which cannot be abandoned once they have been set in motion. It was a situation which the civilian politicians were at the time reluctant to recognise; and the moment when they realised that their options were closed was when they were confronted with the practical consequences of the order to mobilise. After the war it became a commonplace to say 'Mobilisation means war', but at the time this was by no means obvious to many of the protagonists. Sazonov had genuinely believed that the Tsar had a choice of changing the military plans at the last minute so as to mobilise on the Austro-Hungarian frontier without mobilising against Germany. He failed to see what the consequences of any sort of mobilisation were likely to be: 'Surely mobilisation is not equivalent to war with you either. Is it?' Sazonov asked the German ambassador, who replied 'Perhaps not in theory. But . . . once the button is pressed and the machinery of mobilisation is set in motion, there is no stopping it.'[21] Certainly, the German military leaders were under no illusions about what the results of mobilisation were likely to be, and even Moltke, the Chief of the General Staff and one of the German leaders most convinced that now was the most favourable time to fight a war he had long believed to be inevitable, seems to have had some hesitations before taking the irrevocable step. Once the decision was taken, even the Kaiser himself, the *Allerhöchster Kriegsherr*, could not reverse it. On 1 August, the Kaiser, misunderstanding a telegram from London, thought that war might still be averted, called for champagne and asked the Chief of Staff whether it would be possible to limit the military action to the eastern front without mobilising against France. To do this would have meant dismantling the entire plan for the opening stages of the war as it had been laid down by Schlieffen years before; and although the Kaiser was very annoyed when Moltke told him that a last minute change of plan was logistically impossible, there was in fact nothing he could do. Freedom of action had in practice been surrendered in 1905 with the adoption of Schlieffen's plan for a simultaneous war on both fronts, to be opened by a knock-out blow at France.

[20] *Die deutsche Dokumente zum Kriegsausbruch* (Berlin, 1919), vol. 2, p. 307. See also Luigi Albertini, op. cit. (note 18 above), vol. 3, p. 15.

[21] Quoted by Albertini, ibid., vol. 2, p. 481.

So far I have suggested that, in a crisis such as that of July 1914, those responsible for deciding policy already have some courses of action in practice closed to them, and their freedom to choose is less than they themselves suppose. Moreover in many cases the consequences of their decisions are very different from what they expect. In 1914 even those people who wanted a war of some kind – some of the German and Austrian leaders, for instance – did not want the kind of war they actually got. But to say that men deceive themselves or that their plans go wrong or that events move too fast for them to control is a long way from regarding their actions as determined by long-term historical forces against which they or anyone else are powerless. 'What can and what cannot be done by particular agents in specific circumstances is an empirical question, properly settled, like all such questions, by an appeal to experience', Isaiah Berlin has written.[22] The vast amount of work done by sociologists and political scientists on the subject of decision-making has suggested new kinds of evidence which have to be considered in assessing the factors which make a particular decision probable or improbable. In general, however, the range of what in practice cannot be done is perhaps wider than is generally supposed both by participants and by subsequent historians, as an analysis of the events of July 1914 seems to show. But in determining what courses of action are ruled out in advance and what the results of the decisions actually taken are likely to be, can we go beyond the analysis of short-term decisions and their immediate consequences? What kind of demonstration would we need to show that in fact political leaders – and for that matter, all of us – are not only the victims of circumstances, as we say, but also the agents of larger social and historical forces which the intelligent recognise and the foolish try to defy? What evidence would we need to be able to accept a view such as that which maintains that the decision for war in 1914 was the result of 'a crisis in the politics and policy of Europe's ruling and governing classes' or a product of the contradictions of capitalism, and how can we keep such an inquiry within the limits of a legitimate empirical research?

Many political and social theorists – and they range from Lenin to Hannah Arendt – would be content with establishing what they think is the general pattern of development and would be uninterested in the precise details of a specific historical situation or in those facts which do not fit their model. As Lenin wrote in *Imperialism, The Highest Stage of Capitalism*, 'In order to depict

[22] *F.E.L.*, p. 71, note 1.

the objective position one must not take examples or isolated data . . . but the *whole* of the data concerning the *basis* of economic life in . . . the *whole* world.'[23] The charting of broad trends can be a perfectly valid form of historical activity. It is the basic aim of many quantitative historians and has produced such important though not uncontroversial works as Shorter and Tilly's study *Strikes in France 1830–1968* or Fogel and Engerman's account of slavery in America, *Time on the Cross*. Yet these studies, which discard as of little interest those individual cases which do not fit the broad statistical pattern, seem rather unsatisfactory to many other historians, and may have contributed to the insistence of writers such as Richard Cobb or, in a different way, Theodore Zeldin that no historical generalisations are possible, that there is no proper historical study except the study of individual lives or at most of small groups of people, and that the number of exceptions to any general law of historical change is so great as to be bound to make the law invalid.

Yet, when we study a detailed historical episode such as the July crisis in 1914, our analysis of the specific choices and decisions made suggests the need for some more general theoretical framework, or at least a broader frame of reference, if we are to understand what the political and military leaders of 1914 could do and what they could not do. Men are the prisoners not only of their own earlier decisions but of other people's earlier decisions. Thus both the Tsar and the Kaiser, for all their autocratic pretensions, found that they were bound by plans that their general staffs had made several years before: but to understand those plans we need some general picture, not only of the development of strategic thought, but also of the reasons why, in their particular societies, the general staffs had come to hold a position of such importance. We need to know why the Germans believed they were bound to fight a war on two fronts and why the recovery of Alsace-Lorraine was a goal which no French government felt able to renounce. To understand the hesitations of the British government in 1914 we need to know – quite apart from studying the Irish question and the part it played in their thinking – a great deal about the presuppositions of British liberalism: and to understand the way in which the necessity for war was taken for granted by so many people, we need to understand the nature of the influence of social Darwinian thinking and above all the nature of the multifarious phenomenon we label 'imperialism'.

The attraction of a Marxist theory of history is that it appears to

[23] V. I. Lenin, *Imperialism, the Highest Stage of Capitalism*, new edition (London, 1948), p. 12.

offer an explanation for all these phenomena in terms of a comparatively small number of basic factors. (This of course is to say nothing of the attraction it has as a 'philosophy of praxis' which guarantees victory to those whose class situation or intellectual astuteness has given them insight into the way history is going.) The importance of Marxism for non-Marxist historians is obvious, and it has changed fundamentally and irreversibly the kind of questions which historians ask. What it does not always do is to supply the answers. When, for example, we come to look at which economic interest groups in 1914 were in favour of war and which against, we are struck not only by the difficulty mentioned earlier of determining the exact points at which these groups actually influence governments but also by the complexity and divergence of interests within the capitalist world, a divergence which by no means corresponds to the divisions between national States. Even if it were accepted that war was inherent in the nature of capitalism, because capitalism developed the spirit of competition and the conditions for an armed struggle for the maintenance of profits by a few financiers and other capitalists, there is still a gap between this type of explanation and the explanation which an analysis of, say, July 1914 demands in terms of specific decisions by particular individuals. While Rosa Luxemburg's argument that imperialism colours the whole range of moral as well as economic values of a society draws attention to the connections between imperialism, protectionism and militarism, it still leaves many stages to be filled in between deciding in what precise way Wilhelmine Germany or Edwardian England was an imperialist society and explaining the particular decisions of 1914.

One solution of this particular historiographical dilemma is to reject all attempts at any long-term, wide-ranging explanation in terms of general social, economic or intellectual factors. Maurice Cowling is an extreme exponent of a view, which A. J. P. Taylor seems sometimes to share, that all one can hope to find out as a historian is the immediate short-term actions of politicians and the immediate short-term reasons for them. To look for anything else is to try to impose a pattern on events or intentions for which there is no evidence. But many of us are sufficiently Hegelian, if not Marxist, to want to try to bring into our explanations the moral values of a society, the *Zeitgeist* as well as the economic interests of the participants both as individuals and as members of a class. Perhaps this means resigning ourselves to a kind of two-tier history. On the one hand there are the broad lines of social and economic development, of demographic change or of the even longer-term effects of differences in the climate and other aspects of the environment. Some of these can be analysed in terms of scientific laws and so form the basis for predictions of the future. In this kind of development even so revolutionary a historical experience as the First World War is only a minor episode, a small irregularity on the graph. On the other hand, there is the world in which the decisions of an individual leader, however they are conditioned, can affect the lives and happiness of millions and change the course of history for decades. It is in this latter category that the study of the origins of the First World War belongs. And if the choices open to the political leaders at the time were more limited than they themselves perhaps supposed and their freedom of action constrained by an infinite number of earlier decisions by themselves and others, they were in a situation no different from that of most of us; and they still had to make choices, even if the options were limited. Where there was a difference between those in positions of political responsibility and the rest was in the scale of the consequences of their decisions. These decisions made a difference to the lives of several generations in a way that the decisions of a private individual would not have done. For this reason the question of the inevitability of the war, or of that particular war at that particular date, is not one which can be answered except in terms of individual responsibility. In spite of all the forces making for war and in spite of all the evidence we now have about the will to war of certain sections of the European ruling class, and about the domestic pressures to which they were subjected, we still feel that things might have turned out differently, and that a war a few years later might have taken a different form and had a different result. This is the justification for political history and even for historical biography. 'A week is a long time in politics,' Sir Harold Wilson once remarked. A greater socialist leader put it more philosophically in a famous passage from *Left-Wing Communism, an Infantile Disorder*: 'World history reckons in decades. Ten or twenty years sooner or later makes no difference when measured by the scale of world history . . . But precisely for that reason it is a howling theoretical blunder to apply the scale of world history to practical politics.'[24] The details of that ten or twenty years' difference are a legitimate field of inquiry for a historian, and he will continue to try to bring the scale of world history into direct relation with the particular decisions and the range of choices available to individuals who are responsible for taking them.

[24] V. I. Lenin, *Left-Wing Communism, an Infantile Disorder* (Peking, 1970), p. 50.

ROBIN MILNER-GULLAND

Heroes of their Time?

Form and Idea in Büchner's *Danton's Death* and Lermontov's *Hero of our Time*

The 1830s – a tense, ambiguous, unclassifiable period in European literary and cultural history – saw the precocious flowering of genius in two young writers who, despite their wide differences of origin, circumstances and indeed literary method, have a strange and perhaps instructive kinship. Georg Büchner was born near Darmstadt in Hesse in October 1813, Mikhail Lermontov almost a year later in Moscow. Büchner died of typhus at 23, Lermontov was killed in a duel at 27; but the best work of each has startling maturity. Each left complete one full-length prose masterpiece; Büchner, the play *Danton's Death* (*Dantons Tod*); Lermontov, the novel *Hero of our Time* (*Geroy nashego vremeni*). Though neither nowadays could be said to suffer from neglect at the hands of literary historians,[1] it does not really seem that either has been fully or properly 'placed' in the general picture of European culture. Büchner,

[1] There are many editions and critical studies of Büchner in German, and (since the Second World War) in English. However, some textual problems concerning *Dantons Tod* remain: the once-standard *Inselverlag* edition (by F. Bergemann) has been superseded by the more accurate text prepared by W. Lehmann: *Sämtliche Werke und Briefe*, vol. 1 (Hamburg, 1967). Unfortunately the long-awaited third volume of the Hamburg edition, with promised variant readings and critical apparatus, has not appeared at the time of writing. There is a useful edition for English readers: M. Jacobs (ed.), *Dantons Tod and Woyzeck*, 2nd ed. (Manchester, 1968). A good recent study with full bibliography is D. G. Richards, *Georg Büchner and the Birth of Modern Drama* (New York, 1977).

Dantons Tod has been the despair of translators. The reader must be warned against the only version currently in print in England (by J. Maxwell) – an 'acting edition' that takes vast liberties with the text and is full of errors. The best translation so far is by C. R. Mueller: *Georg Büchner – Complete Plays and Prose* (New York, 1963). [Since this was written, the good version by V. Price, *The Plays of Georg Büchner*, has been republished (Oxford, 1979; 1st ed. 1971).]

Geroy nashego vremeni is available in a Bradda Books edition with English notes, ed. D. J. Richards (London, 1962). A good Soviet edition with an important critical afterword by B. M. Eykhenbaum was published by ANSSR (Moscow, 1962); note also V. A. Manuilov, *Geroy nashego vremeni – kommentariy*, with bibliography (Moscow/Leningrad, 1966). The only serious critical study in English is J. Mersereau,

totally forgotten until the late nineteenth century, became something of a cult-figure in Germany (though scarcely outside) during the twentieth, yet tends to be taken as an anachronistic oddity, his legacy manipulated to legitimise various modern German cultural trends. Lermontov's dazzling achievement as a late-Romantic poet has tended to outshine his far more innovative prose work; even historians of the Russian novel, while paying lip-service to his importance, tend to bypass him, while many a non-Russian reader to whom Tolstoy, Dostoevsky or Chekhov are entirely familiar will scarcely so much as recognise his name.

The commentators' uneasiness is understandable: Büchner's and Lermontov's major works are truly experimental, like nothing that had been known before (perhaps, indeed, since). Yet they *are* still figures of their own period; their works belong not only to its literature but to its world of ideas, which they both illumine and enrich. Any reader of *Danton's Death* and *Hero of our Time* is likely to feel that these are designedly 'thinkers' works', inviting interpretation, while both writers' known opinions confirm this impression: Büchner himself 'had no taste for dilettante literature [*Unterhaltungslektüre*]; when reading he had to be made to think'; Lermontov, in his author's preface to *Hero of our Time*, castigates a reading public 'so naïve and immature that it cannot understand a fable unless the moral is given at the end'. So it is not surprising that these works are seldom treated as 'purely' literary: witness habitual classifications of *Danton's Death* as 'political drama' or of *Hero of our Time* as a 'psychological novel'. The reader's desire to find a social, political, historical, psychological or philosophical 'message' in them is legitimate and normal; but it cannot be expected to be a simple task. As works of imaginative literature they do not state any explicit conclusion, argue any case, or even indeed make clear the authors' standpoint in relation to the events and problems presented. Both works can easily – too easily – be mined for sparkling aphorisms or memorable turns of phrase that can support some

---

Mikhail Lermontov (Illinois, 1962): note also the long chapter in R. Freeborn, *The Rise of the Russian Novel* (Cambridge, 1973).

There are several adequate translations: recommended is P. Foote's Penguin Classics version, *A Hero of our Time* (Harmondsworth, 1966). The title of Lermontov's work is probably best rendered *Hero of our Time*, since there is no definite or indefinite article in Russian; 'of our times' or 'of our own times' are dubious.

Quotations in this article are from the Mueller and Foote translations, occasionally slightly amended in the interests of precision.

preconceived but partial opinion of their significance; Büchner and Lermontov are thereby diminished.

This paper is written in the strong conviction that the search for meaning in a work of the imagination – even meaning of a non-aesthetic order – can lead to satisfactory results only if its starting-point is a close examination of the work as an artistic totality: that such meaning proceeds from – or rather, inheres in – such qualities as genre, diction, narrative viewpoint, articulation of parts, overall structure, and is not something separable from them, let alone pre-existent. Further, an understanding of the literary-historical circumstances of composition, the specific problems of genre and tradition of a given period, enhances rather than diminishes our awareness of true originality and urgency in the expression of ideas through literature. It is my intention, then, to enter Büchner's and Lermontov's world of ideas by way of a critical consideration of the aesthetic form and nature of their works. In a short paper it will naturally be impossible to emulate the efforts of previous investigators who have produced detailed, in some cases book-length analyses of the works in question: interesting aspects will have to be ignored, important problems mentioned only in passing. Yet I trust that it will prove worthwhile to sketch at least the main landmarks in the intellectual world of two coeval writers who have not, so far as I know, been more than fleetingly compared by critics.[2] By counterpointing major themes in two apparently very different works we may hope for an enriched understanding both of the extent to which they are voices of their age and of the further resonances their originality may have today.

What happens in *Danton's Death*?

In a remarkable letter to his fiancée – written no later than March 1834, perhaps several months earlier – Büchner wrote:

I have been studying the history of the Revolution. I have felt as though crushed beneath the fatalism of history . . . The individual [is] no more than foam on the wave, greatness mere chance, the mastery of genius a puppet

[2] M. Lindenberger in his study *Georg Büchner* (Illinois, 1964), pp. 142–4, brings Büchner, Stendhal and Lermontov together as ironists who overcame their Romantic roots. Stendhal, though of an older generation (b. 1783) belongs as a novelist to the 1830s; he too was interested in the figure of Danton (see epigraph to *Le Rouge et le noir*).

play . . . I am no guillotine blade. The word *Must* is one of the curses with which mankind is baptised. The saying: 'It must needs be that offences come; but woe to him by whom the offence cometh' is terrifying. What is it in us that lies, murders, steals? I no longer care to pursue this thought.

The thought, however, continued to pursue *him*. Many months later, at twenty-one, already well on the way to becoming a professional scientist,[3] Büchner suddenly launched on a literary career[4] that was destined to last only two years; in *Danton's Death* (which he finished within five weeks, concealing his writing from his parents) he not only picked up and developed precisely these themes, but remembered his own words so well that he put some of them, scarcely changed, into the mouth of his main character. In the interim Büchner himself had become an active revolutionary in his own small German state, largely writing and clandestinely publishing *Der Hessische Landbote* (*The Hessian Courier*), a powerful appeal for the overthrow of monarchy and aristocracy. When *Danton's Death* was written Büchner knew himself to be in imminent danger of arrest, and desperately hoped (successfully, as it turned out) for publication in order to finance his escape abroad.

Knowing the bizarre background to its composition, critics have often been tempted to read into *Danton's Death* the direct influence of Büchner's biography and state of mind: some (from its first reviewers to, inevitably, Lukács) have seen it as a revolutionary propaganda-tract, others (particularly in recent decades) as the product of profound personal disillusion with the efficacy of political activity. The variety of these incompatible points of view at least bears witness to Büchner's success in sinking his own personality into the historical material, as he explicitly wished: '[The dramatist's] highest task is to come as close as possible to history as it really was [*wie sie sich wirklich begeben*]' – a formulation strikingly reminiscent of Ranke's famous 'wie es eigentlich gewesen', though doubtless arrived at independently. The challenge represented by the selfless attempt to recreate the elusive stuff of the past was evidently fascinating in an age when 'the pastness of the past' (John Rosselli's

[3] Büchner's scientific career was rather successful; he ended his life as lecturer in biology at the University of Zürich (and was preparing to lecture also in philosophy). His younger brother Ludwig became immensely famous as author of the popular materialist treatise *Kraft und Stoff* (reading recommended by the 'nihilist' Bazarov in Turgenev's *Fathers and Children*).

[4] After *Danton's Death* Büchner wrote *Leonce und Lena*, a wry comedy; *Woyzeck*, left uncompleted, the tragedy of a humble and incoherent man; a lost play, *Pietro Aretino*; and the prose fragment *Lenz*, a remarkable study of mental derangement.

phrase) was felt more keenly than ever before; Pushkin, whose *Boris Godunov* (1825) is arguably the other great historical drama of Büchner's lifetime, similarly believed that 'a dramatist can fully renounce his own line of thought in order to transfer completely into the period he is describing'.[5] Neither Pushkin nor Büchner, of course, denied the dramatist's passionate involvement with events he had chosen to represent; but both felt that the claims of historical truthfulness came before any idealistic, moralistic or capriciously personal shaping of material (and were quite aware of the profound conceptual problems that the quest for such 'truthfulness' involves). Büchner's subject 'chose' him, as we saw from his words quoted above, well before he became an active revolutionary or a dramatist: he had no wish to manipulate it for propagandistic purposes (despite the fact that his main sources – Thiers, Mignet, Strahlheim – might be regarded as distinctly anti-revolutionary). It is only indirectly, from the *manner* of his presentation, that we can deduce the important messages that the bare facts of history hold for him and which he wishes to pass on to us.

Maurice Benn has well indicated the audacity ('worthy of Danton himself') of Büchner's choice of theme for his first play: the French Revolution, the 'great subject' even a Goethe could never get to grips with.[6] For Büchner the forty-year-old events must have seemed near enough to retain immediacy, remote enough to be enigmatic. He approaches them, however, not in the panoramic vein characteristic of his contemporary Grabbe, not by parading the scenes of high drama or conflict with which the revolutionary years were filled, but through the single close-knit action of the few days that led up to the execution of Danton and his party on 5 April 1794. Büchner neither shows us Danton in the days of his greatness, nor does he (like Saint-Georges de Bouhélier in *Le sang de Danton*, 1931) follow the events through to their natural retributive climax with the downfall of Robespierre soon afterwards. There are few 'theatrical' effects: even in the meeting of Danton and Robespierre Büchner avoids the conventionally-dramatic confrontation of a Richard with a Bolingbroke. Before the curtain has gone up, or the book has been opened, we know from the play's title what it is leading up to, and there are few if any surprises on the way.

If that were all, *Danton's Death* would be tedious and long forgotten; but such of course is not the case, and there are several reasons

[5] T. Wolff, *Pushkin on Literature* (London, 1971), p. 22–3.
[6] M. Benn, *The Drama of Revolt* (Cambridge, 1976), pp. 103–4.

why we are gripped by it throughout its length. One is that Büchner, while imposing stringent limitations on his stage-action, continually beckons our minds outwards, beyond the temporal confines of his plot, to the whole savage course of revolutionary history. We need to have done our homework – for there is no standard 'exposition' to give us a frame of reference – and to remain alert for crucial allusions to events beyond the play's compass. And as the letter to his fiancée already quoted suggests, examination of the Revolution leads Büchner into considerations about the whole nature of history and of human destiny within it (we shall have more to say about the consequences of the highly deterministic philosophy he formulates in this connection). A second reason is that, more than half a century before Chekhov gave the concept wide currency, *Danton's Death* clearly reveals itself as a drama of 'interior' rather than 'exterior' action, where (surprisingly, given the violent setting) words, moods and personal interrelationshps move the plot forward more effectively than confrontations, pistol-shots or embraces. A third lies in the extraordinary iridescence of the play's texture, the kaleidoscopic scene-changes, the gallery of personnel from demagogues to *demimondaines*, from dispossessed aristocrats to sansculottes, from epicureans to executioners – presented not chaotically (once we have found our bearings among them) but almost balletically, tellingly juxtaposed and contrasted in their appearances.

Perhaps the play's greatest shock and most enduring fascination, however, reside in its language. In part this is again a matter of variegation: Büchner evidently revels in, for example, the strange 'Roman-Republican' diction affected by citizens of the revolutionary period, the rhetoric of the rabble-rousing orators which in many cases he reproduced from his sources verbatim, the colloquial chatter of the plebeians, the outrageous coarseness of Danton's friends (for which he felt the need to excuse himself on grounds of historical verisimilitude in a letter to his family after the play's publication). This wide linguistic range, like the frequent scene-changes, was an evident legacy from Shakespeare – the only writer of the past for whom Büchner frequently expressed his unconditional admiration. But the variety of language employed for straightforward purposes of characterisation or situation does not represent the truly remarkable aspect of Büchner's handling of words. What astonishes us from the first scene of the play to the last is the quite 'unrealistic' (or is it supra-realistic?) way in which characters' – almost any characters' – language is capable of taking off into extraordinary flights of imagery: sometimes evidently beautiful, more often grotesque, visionary or apocalyptic, straining at the outer limits of metaphor. At these moments normal categories of being tend to break down: the abstract is concretised, the concrete disembodied, while weird reversals between the animate and the inanimate can spawn esoteric, even (when taken in isolation) scarcely comprehensible metaphysical dicta ('Creation has spread itself so wide that there is nothing empty any more, multitudes everywhere. This is the suicide of nothingness, creation is its wound, we are its drops of blood, the world is the grave in which it rots').

The effect of these flights of metaphorism, immediately impressive to reader or listener but strangely disregarded by many commentators, is profound. They poeticise (which does not mean 'prettify') what might otherwise have been the grossly naturalistic texture of the play. Such passages scarcely even bother to imitate normal dialogue, though occasionally they are counterpointed to produce a remarkable 'chorus' effect (most notably among Danton and his friends during their last moments before being summoned to execution). They provide instead an externalisation of the characters' inner imaginings, nightmares and speculations, and taken together cast a sort of transcendental skein over the play's careful reconstruction of historical actuality. It is remarkable that in the great pan-European Shakespearean revival of the late eighteenth and early nineteenth centuries poets as considerable as Goéthe, Pushkin and Hugo, whose dramas show their intoxication with Shakespeare's anti-classical directness, vividness and variegation of texture, never seem to have grasped what English ears would consider the essential poetry of Shakespeare – and that Büchner alone seems to have absorbed its essence and found a modern equivalent. This is a truer 'Shakespeareanism' than the situational and linguistic reminiscences (most evidently of *Hamlet*, but also of *King Lear*, *Julius Caesar*, *Othello*, some of the chronicle plays, etc.) that the play more obviously presents. It is interesting that *Danton's Death*, coming towards the end of the European 'neo-Shakespearean' tradition, both marks its literary culmination and looks far beyond it (e.g. to the montage effects of cinema and television).

It is often considered that *Danton's Death* is a 'static' play; we know what it is leading up to, and there is little dramatic conflict on the way. Büchner's technique, however, allows no slackening of tension: with virtually every scene (even the meeting of Danton and Robespierre) we are plunged, as befits montage, *in medias res*, walking in as it were upon conversations that began before we arrived and will go on after we leave – a device that heightens the immediacy of past events in a way 'straight' history cannot emulate. Consciousness of the power of such a technique may lie behind the words in which (with mixed pride and humility) Büchner defined the playwright's aim: 'The dramatic poet is, in my eyes, nothing but a writer of history, except that he stands above the latter in that he creates history for the second time; he transplants us directly into the time, instead of giving a dry account of it . . .'. The formulation is reminiscent of Aristotle ('Poetry, therefore, is a more philosophical and higher thing than history . . .'),[7] and there is much else in the play that evokes Aristotelian tragedy. This may sound astonishing in view of Büchner's conscious and wholesale rejection of the neo-Aristotelian 'rules' associated particularly with the French so-called classical drama of the seventeenth and eighteenth centuries (a rejection characteristic of 'Shakespeareanism' from the 1770s onwards); several reputable modern critics (particularly Lindenberger) make Büchner almost into a standard-bearer of anti-Aristotelianism, while Jacobs roundly states 'Büchner's first play is not a tragedy.'[8] The rule-bound neo-Aristotelianism of the Baroque age, however, is neither here nor there: more perceptive and persuasive is Leo Aylen's characterisation of *Danton's Death* as 'the only play that makes me wonder whether there could have been tragedy in the nineteenth century . . . in some sense a play of myth'.[9] The question is a complicated one, and space does not permit it to be fully argued here: the chief points to be made in favour of viewing *Danton's Death* in the light of (ultimately) Greek tragedy are its taut and logical construction, giving a 'unified' feel to the whole conception (jeopardised, by contrast, in *Boris Godunov* – another play with tragic elements – by, for example, a five-year gap between the fourth and fifth scenes); the 'poetic' diction discussed earlier, that stands above individual characterisation and turns our minds constantly to the universal issues that emerge from particular situations; the sense that human events are not chaotically random (despite the professed atheism of all characters except Philippeau) but controlled in a scarcely graspable way by shadowy, far from benign powers; above all by the transmutation of the course of the French Revolution into a great mythic action of tragic force. Of course our apprehension of the tragic qualities of *Danton's Death* will affect, and be affected by, our interpretation of the commanding figure of Danton himself, and

[7] Aristotle, *Poetics*, IX (S. H. Butcher's translation).
[8] M. Jacobs, op. cit. (note 1 above), p. xix.
[9] L. Aylen, *Greek Tragedy and the Modern World* (London, 1964), p. 236.

to him we shall return in due course. However, it is worth noting that Aristotle repeatedly affirms that it is not the hero that makes the tragedy, but the quality of the action represented ('serious, complete and of a certain magnitude'). We noted earlier that it would be in vain to look for conventional 'exterior' action; the subtle 'interior' dynamic of the play, however, gives the lie to any 'static' concept of its structure, such as was evidently held by its first publisher in gratuitously subtitling it *Dramatic Scenes from the French Reign of Terror* – much to Büchner's annoyance.

In *Danton's Death* the main thread of 'exterior' action is the series of steps by which Danton and his allies have their liberty and lives curtailed: in the first act the plan to liquidate them is hatched, in the second we see them on the point of arrest, in the third on trial, in the fourth executed. Since Danton takes no serious measures to resist this process it presents itself as uncomplicated and inexorable. The 'interior' action by contrast is multi-faceted and impossible to reduce to a précis. Through it a wide range of characters, not only the Dantonists, discover, discuss and attempt to come to terms with their destiny. The heady possibilities, the tormenting compulsions and ultimate limits of political activity are explored. The convolutions of human nature are revealed: the base and the sordid, the ridiculous and the cynical, the hedonistic and the fastidious, the contemplative and the energetic, the magnanimous and the deranged, the fanatical and the noble. Above all, the constraints, both socially and naturally imposed, upon human happiness, freedom and general well-being gradually manifest themselves, and are accepted or resisted in the most various ways. The final such constraint is mortality, and death stalks the play in a great variety of forms (all violent) from the alarming opening moments (where Danton at a social gathering tells his wife Julie he loves her 'like the grave') to the final defiant self-immolation of the 'mad' (but who is mad in an insane world?) Lucile – and indeed beyond, for Robespierre's and Saint-Just's execution, which both Danton and Robespierre guess to be imminent, marks the play's 'horizon'. Lucile, deranged by the loss of Camille Desmoulins, ends her life and the play by her cry of 'Long live the King!', having previously shouted aimlessly into the void of the Place de la Révolution without result. There are no monarchistic implications in this either for the unpolitical Lucile or (of course) for Büchner himself: but we sense that the appalling series of blood-lettings that began with the royal executions, reaching its climax in Danton's and its epilogue in Robespierre's, forms a single tragic and unified action that has already taken on the power of modern myth.

What happens in *Hero of our Time*?

Danton's Death is an experimental literary work in its bold theme, its disregard of polite taboos, its language (above all the almost autonomous role of metaphor), its 'montage' effects and its stress on interior rather than exterior action. Its overall structure is more conventional – that of a four-act 'well made play' – and its generic impulse has roots in ancient tragedy. In complete contrast *Hero of our Time* is written in the smooth, flexible, easy-going language of 'international' prose fiction of the early nineteenth century; its themes may be in some respects shocking, but no more so than might have been expected in the generation of Poe, Hoffmann or Byron – and on a personal rather than broadly historical level; its obvious models are in the literature of its own, and the immediately preceding, period; we recognise in it well-worn elements of society tale, love intrigue, adventure story and traveller's notebook. Its experimentalism – perhaps even more radical than that of *Danton's Death* – resides primarily in its form and articulation. The two works, at first sight so different, approach each other not in the manner, but in the fact of their experimental nature; their kinship will begin to manifest itself only when we examine the hero-figures of each and the world of ideas within which they move.

I earlier referred to *Hero of our Time* as a 'novel', and this is normal usage; 'novel' is after all a capacious concept. But it is worth noting that Lermontov did not characterise it so, using only the words 'book' or 'composition'; within the work his narrator refers to 'notes' and at one point to his 'chain of tales'. The latter expression indicates the feature of the work that every reader will notice at once: that it is composed of five – or rather, counting two brief but important prefaces, seven – separate sections, each with its own title, each more or less self-contained yet linked with all the others in one way, and one way only: through the figure of Pechorin, the young officer who is gradually revealed as the eponymous 'hero of our time'. These sections are neither chapters, nor parts (the book is actually presented in two parts, the second containing only the last two sections), nor short stories (though several of them have often been extracted and treated as such). They scarcely form a 'cycle', since they are quite unlike each other: in length (from two to around eighty pages); in kind (two are 'prefaces', albeit different from each other, one is set out as a diary, one is an anecdote, one a double anecdote, one an adventure tale interwoven with traveller's notes, one a traveller's reminiscence with only 'linking' significance); in narrative manner (a wide spectrum, from the rhetorical through the romantic, the introspective, the sardonic to the matter-of-fact, from story-telling to diary confidences); in narrative viewpoint (there are three main narrators: the author figure – to be distinguished from the real author, who also appears; a simple old officer, Maksim Maksimych; and Pechorin himself). The arrangement of the sections does not correspond to their relative chronology – which is indeed quite hard to work out, since there is no main narrative thread to which to relate 'flashbacks', save in the first main section, 'Bela' (itself of rather complex construction), with its 'pendant' 'Maksim Maksimych'. Not only is the order of episodes 'shuffled': some are supposed to follow directly on from each other, between some there is an unspecified time-gap, while two overlap. A third of the way through the book the narrator suddenly kills off his hero with an insouciance that must surely be unique in literature ('Not long ago I heard that Pechorin had died on his way back from Persia. This news made me very pleased . . .'), before resurrecting him for the last three sections – the heart of the book – which are presented as extracts from his diary (yet themselves differ considerably from each other). All this extraordinary formal juggling takes place in a book well under two hundred pages in length.

What does it all add up to? Do Lermontov's strange manipulations of genre, narration and time-sequence, without parallel in the no-nonsense world of nineteenth-century fiction, merely disconcert or puzzle us? Do we perhaps look for the book's core of meaning in its digressive and parodistic elements (as in *Tristram Shandy* or *Eugene Onegin*), or, as with some modernistic works, in the display of technical trickery for its own sake? Few readers in fact find themselves irritated by Lermontov's formal devices; the work grips us as any well told story might, and we hardly notice that our perceptions are being directed towards a different kind of action and a different world of problems from those that the orthodox novel has led us to expect in a work of prose fiction. The experimental aspect of *Hero of our Time* is magnificently successful in its very unobtrusiveness; but it is no mere 'dressing-up' of the work's content: the content manifests itself entirely and necessarily through its eccentric and ultimately (as Lermontov must have intended) thought-provoking form.

The genesis of this most original work remains mysterious: no rough notes or recorded conversations survive to let us guess whether Lermontov planned it as a whole from the outset, or whether it slowly grew out of travel notes or independent short stories (three sections were in fact published separately in advance of the book). Its inception is usually associated with Lermontov's own travels in the area of the Caucasus in 1837 (he had been posted there as a punishment for his poem criticising the Court on the occasion of the death of Pushkin); the first edition appeared in 1840, the second shortly before Lermontov's death in 1841, with the addition of the important opening preface ('the first and at the same time the last thing in any book', as it tells us), which should certainly be treated as an integral part of the work. It is here that he begins the teasing of his readership that in more subtle ways is to pervade much of the text, castigating those of his public who took the Hero of our Time as exemplary, or (quite understandably) 'remarked that the author had portrayed himself and his acquaintances'[10] – though he does not unequivocally deny the latter possibility. He then purports to reveal that the Hero of our Time is a portrait, not of a single person, but 'of the vices of our whole generation in their ultimate development': a phrase calculated to rouse lurid expectations of scathing social satire that the book makes no attempt to fulfil. In four short paragraphs the preface manages also to suggest that the book will be variously a fable, a joke, a 'keen weapon', a fairy-tale, a diagnosis, and a 'picture of contemporary man' (drawn for amusement without any 'dream of correcting human vices'). The reader is not simply teased, but being prepared for the multiple ambiguities of message with which *Hero of our Time* will eventually face him.

With the transition from the preface to the first three sections of the main body of the book the narration passes from the author himself to the 'author figure', an itinerant writer of travel-sketches (or 'rapturous story-teller' as he describes himself); though his footnotes lead us at first to believe he is to be identified with Lermontov, we eventually come to realise that he is a fictional figure, and not an entirely serious one: irredeemably middle-brow, rather arch, prone to grasp the wrong end of the stick. He falls greedily upon Maksim Maksimych (his chance companion on the Georgian Military Highway) in the hope, eventually of course realised, that the old warrior will share his exotic reminiscences with him. The figure of Pechorin, evoked at third hand, begins to obtrude upon the cosy world we share with the narrator and Maksim Maksimych; the latter recounts the violent and ill-fated story of Pechorin's abduction of a local chieftain's daughter, Bela. In the next section (by the sort of

[10] Speculation about the autobiographical content (undoubtedly considerable) of *Hero of our Time* is never-ending. For balanced assessments see Eykhenbaum and Manuilov (see note 1 above).

coincidence which a proper novelist might find objectionable, but here seems perfectly in order) they briefly encounter Pechorin himself, setting out for the travels from which he will not return. The snub he seems to deliver to Maksim Maksimych somehow jolts the reader more than his ill-treatment of Bela. Pechorin shows no interest in the notebooks that Maksim Maksimych had zealously guarded for him; the author acquires them, and on learning of Pechorin's death is delighted to be able to publish them. Extracts from Pechorin's journal form the last three sections of the book – two-thirds of the entire text.

The figure of Pechorin, then, emerges as the centre of the work, and we soon guess that what we have in our hands is a 'personal novel' in the long tradition that has led from *Werther*, through *René* and *Adolphe*, affected perhaps by *Childe Harold* and *Eugene Onegin*, to the most recent (1836) in the series, Musset's *La confession d'un enfant de siècle* – the more so since Pechorin clearly displays the unsociability, the rootlessness, the hauteur, the over-refined sensibilities, the penchant for unhappy emotional entanglement and above all the susceptibility to crushing boredom that his predecessors brought into literature. Maksim Maksimych and the travelling author indeed discuss this cast of mind as if it were 'fashion' or (significantly) a 'vice'; Lermontov himself, the 'Russian Byron', knew this Romantic tradition well, and felt its lure. His attitude towards it, however, is equivocal and ironical: Eykhenbaum has ingeniously argued that *Hero of our Time* is in part a conscious polemic against Musset. Any expectations we might have harboured of a coherently novelistic account of the life and 'personal' vicissitudes of an *enfant de siècle* dissolve as we become aware of the multiple narrative viewpoint and splintered chronology of Lermontov's work. Not only does the report of Pechorin's death bring the expected terminal point of the action forward into the first half of the book: the author fails to give us any information about it save that it was 'on the way back from Persia' (imagine what a conventional novelist would have made of such a death by suicide, or in battle, or in a duel!), so letting us understand that we should not look for a normal 'chain of events' in the book's account of Pechorin.

If then we are not going to follow Pechorin's life story, is *Hero of our Time* simply a series of static 'scenes', much as its first publisher considered *Danton's Death* to be? What pulls our interest forward through the book? Will we close it with a feeling of anticlimax, of having got nowhere in particular? Even though the book's ending is problematic (we shall return to it later), most readers would agree that there *is* a continual sense of progression through its successive sections – one very different from any novelistic chain of cause and effect. The book represents a journey not through Pechorin's life, but into the interior of his soul: its episodes mark successive stages of our investigation (which later coincides with *his* investigation) of what makes him tick. First we have Maksim Maksimych's recollection of events of several years ago, themselves retold; next the narrator's brief (and uncomprehending) glimpse of Pechorin in the flesh; then (in the 'Preface to Pechorin's Journal') we share the narrator's awakening to the real Pechorin; finally we proceed to the journal itself, in which Pechorin pitilessly records his own worst actions and digs into his deeper motivations.

Lermontov's choice of diary form was a master-stroke: only in this way could Pechorin's self-investigation carry the stamp of authenticity and (despite the pettiness of some of his adventures) the seriousness that would give the later part of his work its necessary weight. The author's remarks in the preface to the journal (and here we are surely listening to Lermontov himself speaking through his fictional narrator) are very important if we are to understand his aims and methods: 'The history of a human soul, even the most trivial soul, is almost more interesting and useful than the history of a whole people, especially when it is the consequence of the observation of a mature mind on itself, and when it is written without the vain desire to arouse sympathy or astonishment.' With true Lermontovian sharpness he goes on to indicate and simultaneously criticise his work's only real ancestor: 'Rousseau's *Confessions* have one fault, that he used to read them to his friends.' We are therefore urged to accept Pechorin's sincerity and take his testimony at face value: in doing so we realise the inadequacies of the well-meaning but limited narrators of the earlier sections. The journal in fact counterbalances them, or rather outweighs them; like the itinerant author, Pechorin writes 'travel notes' of a kind, but although the journal is full of outward incident, it is Pechorin's journey to the 'interior' that counts; the author journeys over the Krestovy Pass, but Pechorin is (in Rilke's phrase) 'ausgesetzt auf den Bergen des Herzens' ('exposed on the mountains of the heart'). Where the itinerant author's responses (to scenery, people or events) are those of literature, Pechorin's are those of life.

Far the greater part of the journal – indeed around half the book's total length – is taken up by 'Princess Mary', the only section presented in a day-to-day diary format. Set in the spa town of Pyatigorsk, it has an eventful plot: love intrigues (all disastrous), venomous plotting, a duel in which Pechorin kills his opponent, the riding of a horse to death, the sundering of friends. Here the outward action and inner meditation are in continuous counterpoint: 'There are two men within me – one lives in the full sense of the word, the other reflects and judges him.' Chances of reconciliation between the two halves of his personality seem nil, and Pechorin is bleakly forced to contemplate all his own cantankerousness, coldness and self-destructiveness without so much as the consolations of exculpating or blaming himself. 'Pity and malice', indeed, are beside the point, whether towards himself or towards others; for is he not a plaything of destiny, an 'axe in the hands of fate'? Such questionings, present but hardly noticed earlier in the book, become more and more insistent during 'Princess Mary', their sinister background note lending wider resonance to what might have been merely a narcissistic introspection. If the deterministic philosophy of life that is forcing itself upon him at least relieves him of responsibility, it also deprives him of the liberty that he values above life and even honour.

'Princess Mary' is flanked by two brief anecdotal sections, 'Taman' and 'The Fatalist', that have often been presented as independent short stories: the reader may well wonder why, save for purposes of comparatively light relief, they stand where they do, or indeed come into the book at all. Yet on closer examination both are seen to play an essential role in the book's construction: partly because they provide a prelude and coda to the intensities of 'Princess Mary', more importantly because they show new facets of the theme of fate and because in each Pechorin shows himself from a new angle and in a new milieu. With 'Taman', the first episode from the journal, we have (as Richard Peace observes) 'Pechorin, as it were, seeing himself from the outside';[11] the voyage into his soul has not yet begun, but he establishes his bona fides with us by recounting an incident in which (most unusually!) he makes a fool of himself. Having involuntarily through inquisitiveness wrecked the lives of three poor people, and almost been drowned by them for his pains, he asks: 'Why did fate toss me into the peaceful midst of these *honest smugglers*? I had shattered their calm, like a stone thrown into a still pool – and like a stone, too, I had nearly gone to the bottom.' Whereas in other episodes Pechorin generally wrecks people's lives by choice, or at least with awareness of what is going on, 'Taman' demonstrates to him that he is destined to bring havoc in his train whether he wishes it or not.

[11] R. A. Peace, 'The Role of *Taman*' in Lermontov's *Geroy nashego vremeni*', *Slavonic and East European Review* 45 (1967), 28.

In 'The Fatalist' Pechorin and a fellow-officer, Vulich, resolve to test the Moslem belief in predestination, by discovering whether the hour of death is predetermined. Vulich plays a sort of 'Russian roulette' and survives, but Pechorin fancies he has seen the mark of death on his face; Vulich is subsequently killed by a drunken Cossack whom Pechorin then single-handedly disarms. 'How could one not be a fatalist after this?' he asks himself; yet he still 'prefers to doubt everything'. On the last page of the book, we are shown Pechorin addressing the question of predestination not to a fellow intellectual, but to a simple honest man: none other than Maksim Maksimych (for we are in the same outpost where the events retold in 'Bela' took place). When he finally comprehends the question, he gives a rambling response, of which the first part is 'anti-deterministic', the second 'deterministic' in drift; the last sentence of the book is 'That's all I could get out of him – he's not at all keen on metaphysical discussions.' It is a splendid and thought-provoking touch of irony to have Pechorin turn to the apparently despised Maksim Maksimych for an answer to the fundamental question of his life, and to tie the end of the book so aptly to its beginning.

Danton and Pechorin as heroes

The works we have been considering are each dominated by a central character; memorable but enigmatic figures, whose personalities trouble and mystify the reader, but are clearly at the heart of the work's meaning. Neither is obviously admirable, both specifically repudiate ordinary notions of good or evil, lead irregular lives, have caused suffering and death, are morbidly introspective and prone to debilitating *taedium vitae*. Each is presented by his author 'inconclusively'; there is no great moment of illumination, repentance or regeneration that will neatly turn our sympathies in his favour. Each is fighting an unending, private, philosophical battle whose circumstances are enmeshed with the experiences of his life. In each case their creators seem to set out to present them clinically as 'case studies', but finish, I believe, by giving us heroes for a post-heroic world.

Some of Danton's commentators have been tempted to regard him as 'anti-hero' rather than hero. Lazy, pleasure-loving, uxorious, dissolute, smug in his former glory, he is fonder of words than actions, but does not even deploy these in time to save himself or the friends who are dragged down with him. Such a picture, certainly, can be gleaned from his enemies – supported perhaps by such a friend of Danton's as Lacroix (who never seems properly to understand him). Yet Büchner seldom if ever ironises at Danton's expense, and few readers or spectators doubt by the end that the play indeed has a hero, and that he is Danton. The historical Danton doubtless fascinated Büchner as a 'difficult' character, mysterious to the historians, an extempore orator few of whose speeches are preserved – but it is noteworthy that in the play Büchner never suggests that Danton had actually demeaned himself through being financially compromised by enemies of the Revolution, as historians have continued to suppose.

Seeking the heroic in Danton, critics have tended to concentrate on what he is *not*: in other words, to contrast his rather indefinite programme with Robespierre's alarming mix of Virtue and Terror; in the process Robespierre has to be seen as a hypocritical villain (Benn goes so far as to turn him into a Stalin). But Büchner makes no such facile black-and-white contrasts. He presents Robespierre too as a tragic figure, a self-appointed prophet doomed to martyrdom, courageous and self-tormented, betrayed by his oldest friend, and one suspects he dropped him from the play after the second act lest he grow into a figure to rival the main character (Pushkin behaves similarly towards the Pretender Dmitri in *Boris Godunov*). Behind Robespierre stands the thoroughly terrifying figure of Saint-Just, the inhuman bureaucrat (behind Danton, likewise, stand the flighty and unbalanced figures of Camille Desmoulins and other 'Dantonists'), but the real villains of the play are the minor sadists, opportunists, hypocrites and hatchet-men – Billaud, Collot, Barère, Fouquier, Dumas, Laflotte etc.

Again it would seem over-simple to make Danton into a Shakespearean hero (as Richards and other commentators do) by loading him, Macbeth-like, with tragic guilt. True, a remarkable scene shows him haunted by the September massacres – yet he and Julie are sincere in their conviction that these were unavoidable, and were, indeed, Danton's greatest revolutionary master-stroke.[12] To the end he remains true to his old principles: 'The flood of the Revolution can toss up our bodies where it likes, but they'll still be

[12] Aylen, op. cit (note 9 above), finds it a weakness of the play that we are not shown Danton's process of decision in September: yet it is scarcely to be imagined that Danton agonised over imperative political necessity. His (and Pechorin's) awareness of guilt might be best expressed in the words of Goethe's Harper, addressing the heavenly powers: 'Ihr führt ins Leben uns hinein,/Ihr lasst den Armen schuldig werden,/Dann überlasst ihr ihn der Pein:/Denn alle Schuld rächt sich auf Erden.'

able to pick up our fossilised bones and smash in the heads of kings with them.' Like Pechorin, Danton feels regret but not repentance. What has happened is part of politics, and politicians get their hands dirty (echoes again of *Boris*!); this is the clue to why Danton's 'inactivity', really a renunciation of politics – thus a renunciation of his chances of life – is an important aspect of his heroic quality (the more so since it was bound to be misunderstood as 'laziness'). It is interesting that quasi-heroic renunciation of action (as the prime cause of suffering) is also the philosophical mainspring of that most unusual (though far from tragic) novel *Oblomov* by Goncharov, a contemporary by birth of Büchner. Neither of course knew the other; more remarkably, there is no evidence that Büchner (who wrote philosophical papers) was so much as aware of the existence of Schopenhauer, to whose world-view he gives flesh and blood. When Philippeau in the last act of the play asks Danton what he wishes for, he answers with the single word 'Ruhe' (for which neither 'peace' nor 'rest' seem adequate translations). He remains a 'powerful nature', as he puts it to the Tribunal (whom he can still cause to tremble when he unleashes his rhetoric); but it takes a great will to renounce its own power as Danton does.

Early in the play Danton 'flirts with death', as he himself admits; with growing intimacy he comes to understand its reality and help others to do so (his example leads Julie to choose a 'beautiful' death, by suicide, that will counterbalance in the scales of eternity his 'ugly' one). Danton however does not really affect the sentimental 'death wish' that appealed to certain Romantics and to another of Büchner's coevals, Wagner; perhaps surprisingly, he emerges as a staunch affirmer of life. His commerce with the *grisettes*, for all the bawdiness of language, seems metaphysical rather than lascivious; he flirts with them, as he does with death, the better to understand life in all its teeming spontaneity. Observing the raw life of the street, Danton says to Camille: 'I don't understand why people don't just plant themselves in the street and laugh in one another's faces. I should think they would have to be laughing from their windows and from their graves, and that heaven itself would burst and the earth roll over in laughter.' Consolation and wholeness come with great moments when reason and emotion are no longer fragmented – in laughter, love-making, shouting; by the end only the last is left to Danton and his friends, and as the play progresses the shout or scream becomes one of its key symbols. His ultimate ability to make his death part of his life, and to reach out to others as he does so, is the play's main action; not for nothing does the title suggest that of all the varied deaths in the play it is Danton's that is to be taken as exemplary.

Pechorin appears to differ from Danton not merely in the outward circumstances of his life but in an important quality of character: where Danton is big-hearted and surrounded by admirers, Pechorin is misanthropic and proclaims himself incapable of friendship. Yet the distinction is not so great, for from the startling first scene we see that under Danton's *bonhomie* runs a current of despair at his own and everyone's isolation, to be transcended only in the confines of prison. Pechorin too can be a lion of society when he wishes; isolation is his choice, not out of a sense of superiority so much as from despair at the emptiness of his life, which will play itself out in solitary travels. His isolation is symbolic: whatever false trail the opening preface leaves regarding his typicality, the book is clearly concerned to show Pechorin's exceptional qualities.

Lermontov's title (devised after he had perhaps fortunately rejected the wording *One of the Heroes of the Beginning of the Century*) poses, but scarcely solves, the problem of Pechorin's 'heroism'. The opening preface, with its equivocations, bluffs and double-bluffs, leaves the reader, by design it would seem, to make his own readjustments once the tale is under way. The narrator's 'Preface to Pechorin's Journal', however, takes a different tone: 'Some readers might like to know my own opinion of Pechorin's character. My answer is given in the title of his book. "But that's malicious irony!" they'll retort. I don't know.' By the end of the journal the reader is likely, despite everything, to sympathise with and probably admire Pechorin. Though throughout the book he has been shown as displaying conventional audacity, it is only in the last episode of 'The Fatalist' that we get the laconic account of a selfless and courageous exploit he has performed. It may scarcely seem to compensate for the deaths, enmities and broken hearts that he has so freely scattered behind him, yet it may clinch our impression of a certain wayward nobility, and show us why he can twist almost anybody (save the 'honest smugglers'!) round his little finger.

If Pechorin is a hero, however, it is not primarily in his dealings (often most unheroic) with the outer world that his heroism resides. Rather it is in his approach to himself: solipsistically doubtful that anyone else in the world has autonomous existence, he needs all the more courage to descend into the depths of his own soul, and to do so for no eyes but his own. The voyage of self-analysis completed, he abandons his record of it – his notebooks – for reasons which we can only guess at, but which can scarcely be cheerful ones:

presumably as a gesture of self-renunciation that is almost a symbolic suicide.

We are left to ponder in what sense Pechorin may be not only a hero, but 'of our time'. Again we must be alert for bluffing or ambiguity on the author's part. Since the book's appearance readers have eagerly sought references to the current events of the 1820s and 30s in it, the more so since (as Turgenev, in particular, was soon to find) critics in Russia were keen to unravel socio-political messages from works of the imagination. But habitual attempts to make Pechorin into, say, a frustrated 'Decembrist' revolutionary can rest on only the vaguest grounds (his fatalistic philosophy has something in common with the historical views of the leading Decembrist theoreticians). It is hard to believe that a good job, or even a good cause, would have been Pechorin's salvation any more than a good woman could have been: his malaise is too fundamental and all-commanding. He is of his own time above all in his intense and subtle psychologising, inconceivable before the early nineteenth century; *Hero of our Time* is probably the first psychological work – the first work in which the examination of the intricate perversities of human motive and conduct is the mainspring of the action – in European fiction. And Pechorin, as a strange but recognisable 'case', belongs not so much to Lermontov's, as to any epoch. Lermontov's cajoling complicity with us readers – whenever we live – makes *Hero of our Time* eternally 'modern', and the 'our' of the title seems to refer as much to ourselves as to its readers of a hundred and forty years ago.

Time, fate and freedom

There can scarcely have been a period in the history of European culture when philosophers were so involved with artistic considerations, or artists so responsive at the world of ideas, as that of the mid-eighteenth to mid-nineteenth centuries. From Rousseau and Diderot to Lessing, Kant, Hegel, Schopenhauer, Schelling and a host of lesser figures, philosophers sought to bring problems of aesthetic expression into their world-view, and were often indeed notable literary figures in their own right (Marx was to stand aside from this tradition, Nietszche was to take it up again). In the arts the colossal figure of Goethe stands as the greatest modern 'philosophical poet', while the whole Romantic movement is as much a philosophical quest as a period of aesthetic innovation. Nowadays, when the interpenetration of philosophy and literature is often regarded as a most questionable business,[13] the achievements of that epoch deserve all the more to be taken to heart.

The works of Büchner and Lermontov clearly belong to such a tradition, and mark, indeed, a culmination of it. The world of ideas in which they move is hardly a comfortable one. Where Büchner's exact contemporary Hebbel could write 'Hegelian', progressivist and thus fundamentally optimistic tragedies, Büchner's Danton and Lermontov's Pechorin move in a world to which utter pessimism is the only reasonable response – though reason is itself suspect as a means by which to plumb its depths. The more reflective the hero, the more he will be aware of the fragmentation of his own personality; the stronger his will, the more frustration and suffering it will entail; the more he beats against its walls, the more intolerable the prison-house of life becomes.[14] This, as has been hinted, is a Schopenhauerian rather than a Hegelian world; our two authors share Schopenhauer's wry lucidity and strong apprehension of beauty (perhaps the creation of a work of art is the only convincing answer to the miseries of existence). Yet in their presentation of a world where old ethical certainties had slipped away, where selfishness is the root of behaviour, Büchner and Lermontov seem to look ahead of their time: Knight quotes words of Danton whose psychology 'appears to belong to the age of Taine';[15] the intuitive kill-or-be-killed ethic of Pechorin seems almost post-Darwinian; their apprehension of cosmic chaos in an age that is moving 'beyond good and evil' belongs with the philosophy of Nietzsche. Even the oldest certainty, that of regular temporal sequence (the cornerstone of the nineteenth-century novel) has deserted Danton and Pechorin: the former complains time 'is losing' him, the latter that he is incapable of distancing himself from the past; the strange chronological sequence of *Hero of our Time* is perhaps a reflection of Pechorin's disordered temporal perceptions. For both Danton and Pechorin the world is a sort of monstrous theatrical performance. Pechorin sees himself as 'the indispensable figure of the fifth act, thrust into the painful role of executioner or betrayer', while the

[13] Note particularly the 1978 B.B.C. discussion between Iris Murdoch and Bryan Magee in the philosophical series *Men of Ideas* (in book form: London, 1978).

[14] I am indebted to Henry Gifford for pointing out to me the ramifications of prison symbolism, so potently developed in *Danton's Death*, in nineteenth-century literature. For illuminating comments on the theme (particularly in connection with Dickens, yet another contemporary of Büchner and Lermontov) see L. Trilling, *The Opposing Self* (New York, 1950).

[15] A. H. J. Knight, *Georg Büchner* (Oxford, 1951), P. 75.

background to *Danton's Death* is a terrifying carnival of blood, where the victims of the guillotine are judged as actors: ('When I saw him [Hérault] standing at the Arc de Triomphe, I said to myself: "Now there's one who'd look good up on the guillotine . . . It's a good thing that dying's become so public." ') Clearly such a world is 'unnatural', yet there is no way out through a Rousseauesque appeal to the 'natural': on the one hand the sympathetic *grisette* Marion, on the other Saint-Just in his most frightening speech, both appeal to 'the way things are', the natural law, to justify their actions.

What comforts can be found in a disordered, amoral, incomprehensible world, where our apparently independent activities are puppet-motions, controlled by forces beyond our will or reason? Neither Büchner nor Lermontov as it happens is ready to give in to bleak determinism without a fight; and one reason why their works continue to live is that they hint at how, despite the worst that destiny can throw at us, we can subvert, if not overthrow its power. At the end of *Danton's Death* the mad Lucile summons up the shreds of sanity to shout her deliberately absurd challenge (that has the ring of existentialism about it) to the world,[16] while Danton has discovered that certain of the simplest human values retain their power when the futile rigmarole of ordinary life is stripped away. As for Pechorin, his remarkably comprehensive scepticism about our powers to know even our own minds ('who really knows if he believes a thing or not?') turns into something like a programme of hope: 'I prefer to doubt everything. Such an attitude makes no difference to a man's determination – on the contrary, as far as I am concerned, I always go more boldly forward when I don't know what lies ahead.' At the end of *Hero of our Time* we can see him (inspired possibly by Maksim Maksimych?) turning 'from metaphysical speculations to attend to the ground under my feet'; the symbolic contrast of firm ground and unstable water has run through the whole book. He ceases, presumably, to prod other people into cries of pain to prove his independent will; gives up indeed the whole of life as he has known it in defence of the freedom that he 'will never sell', and to which he clings despite the rational absurdity of even conceiving of its possibility. Without sentimentality, in the teeth of their characters' expressed philosophies, both Büchner and Lermon-

[16] Most editions give the following stage-direction immediately before Lucile's last cry: [*Reflecting, and then as if making a decision, suddenly*]. The Hamburg edition (see note 1 above) omits this, and until the variant readings are published its status must remain doubtful. If authentic, the stage-direction adds to the 'existentialist' effect of Lucile's action.

tov retain a stubborn intuition of independent and worthwhile human action, an irrational faith in the value of the individual that their coeval Kierkegaard would have applauded, and to which we continue to respond today.

ARNALDO MOMIGLIANO

Persian Empire and Greek Freedom

I

There is a feature common to Greek and Jewish history which allows a direct comparison of the two nations even before their cultural contacts become recognisable by ordinary criteria. Both Greeks and Jews defined themselves in relation to Persia. But Greek religious, political and social life had already reached its classical form before the Greeks fought against the Persians. Their victory against the Persians added much to their self-consciousness and no doubt contributed to the specific developments of the fifth century B.C. in Athens and elsewhere. Yet, fundamentally, the Greeks were right in feeling that they were what they were before the Persians entered upon the scene. The Jews, on the other hand, shaped their theocracy *inside* the Persian Empire and were aware of their permanent debt to the founder of the Persian Empire. A paradoxical consequence was that the Greeks came to notice certain basic points of similarity between their own political predicaments and those of the Persians, whereas the Jews, while calling Cyrus a Messiah, never dreamt of being like the Persians or of finding acceptable models of behaviour in Persia. A more precise analysis of this aspect of the difference between Greeks and Jews may be worth the effort.

I offer here to Isaiah Berlin an attempt to define the Greek attitude (or attitudes) towards the Persians, reserving the comparison with the Jewish attitude (or attitudes) for a little volume which I am writing at present. Isaiah Berlin is, in any case, the last man to need to be reminded of this side of our common Jewish heritage.

II

The rise of the Persian Empire was not only dangerous to the Greeks: it had placed them in an ambiguous position. The Persian State was pulled in two directions: one ended in the Mediterranean; the other, if pursued fully, would have led the Persian kings towards India, as it did their successor Alexander the Great. What at best contributed to coordinating the expansion in the two directions (and at worst prevented the Empire from falling to pieces) was the careful organisation of internal communication and the constant search for new river and sea lanes. We know comparatively very little of the efforts of the Persian kings to control the whole of the Iranian plateau and to create a barrier against the nomadic tribes on the north-east of their State. Persian control there meant the introduction of a system of taxation and military vassalage among people in conditions of natural economy. In the east the Persian kings had their most difficult work to do and therefore looked with special relish in the opposite direction – where power could be organised on the basis of pre-existing institutions, glory was obtained against a background of monumental cities and respected temples, and collaborators could be won from old-established urban aristocracies.

Persian interest in Greek collaboration went beyond the field of Greek mercenaries and artisans, whose reputation among the Persians was undisputed. The Persians attracted intellectuals, especially doctors, from Greece and turned for political and military advice to Greek exiles. We know perhaps about 300 names of Greeks who served the Persians in the two centuries before Alexander (ordinary mercenaries and artisans are by definition excluded as their names would be known only exceptionally). An ex-king of Sparta, Demaratus, and one of the leaders of Athens, Themistocles, belong to this company; and of course the two historians, Ctesias and Xenophon, are in it, the first as a court doctor, the second as a leader of mercenaries. If a large part of Greece – including the Thebans and, *de facto*, the Argives – sided with the Persians during Xerxes' invasion of 480–479 B.C., if even the oracle of Delphi 'medised' on that occasion, this must be accounted for by more than sheer fright before what appeared to be the overwhelming power of the Achaemenids. There must have been an element of attraction towards a stable international order which seemd to ensure protection for the wealthy class and furnished shelter from restless neighbours like the Athenians or the Spartans. Even in Athens public opinion was by no means unanimously against Persia. The tyrants had left friends behind. And Sparta, like Delphi, had not forgotten her failure to defend Croesus of Lydia against the Persians – with consequent loss of prestige. The Persians had acquired the reputation of being wealthy, generous and easy-going masters; they had been seen at close quarters to be civilised, god-fearing, 'truth-telling' aristocrats, good at riding and hunting just as Greek aristocrats liked to be.

We shall never know for certain, but a little story told by Herodotus must be authentic. Before the battle of Plataea a wealthy citizen of Thebes gave a banquet to which he invited the Persian commander Mardonius, fifty of the noblest Persians, and fifty of the most distinguished Boeotians. One of the Greek guests (from Orchomenos, not from Thebes) was Thersander, who lived long enough to entrust his recollections of the evening to Herodotus. A Persian and a Greek sat side by side on each couch, and the Persian who shared Thersander's couch addressed him in the Greek tongue and 'inquired from him from what city he came'. After these formalities the Persian frankly expressed his fears of a Persian (and therefore Theban) defeat and added: 'Many of us Persians know our danger, but we are constrained by necessity to do as our leader bids us. Verily it is the sorest of all human sorrows, to abound in knowledge and yet have no power' (9.16). Here we learn of a Persian who could speak Greek, and even more of the very human anxiety he could express to his Greek comrade on the eve of the decisive battle.

And yet, at any given moment, the Greek world was only of peripheral importance to the Persian State. Even in Asia Minor the Greeks were after all a small minority. The commercial groups prospering under Persia were centred in Mesopotamia, like the Murašu family, and in the Phoenician towns rather than in the Greek cities. Aramaic letters and neo-Babylonian tablets have told us much about the affairs of Aršam (Arsames to the Greeks), who was a satrap of Egypt in the second part of the fifth century.[1] A member of the royal family, he had wealth in Babylonian real estate and close connections with the Murašu family. Carthage, a Phoenician colony which was involved in continuous struggles with Greek competition and remained influential among the Phoenicians of the motherland, certainly encouraged the latter to side with the Persians rather than with the Greeks. Ancient tales and modern speculations about the alleged alliance between Persians and Carthaginians against the Greeks in 480 can be discounted. But the fact remains that in 480 both the Persians and the Carthaginians made war against the Greeks. It is another fact that for many Greeks – and more specifically for the citizens of Sparta and Athens – the attractions of Persia and the solid merits of life in a Greek polis were incompatible. They were developing a style of political discussion, judicial decision and intellectual debate which they knew to be peculiar to themselves. They thought that by obeying their own laws they avoided human masters and could truly be considered free. As Phocylides said of Assyria, and his reference could easily be extended to Persia: 'an orderly city,

[1] G. R. Driver, *Aramaic Documents of the Fifth Century B.C.* (Oxford, 1965), pp. 88–96. For Hellenised aristocracy cf. L. Robert, *Journal des Savants* (1978), 5.

though small and set on a rock, outranks senseless Niniveh'. We do not know where and by whom freedom was first associated with democracy, freedom of speech thus becoming one of the most important aspects of democracy. Whether or not those Ionian citizens who passed from Croesus' control to Cyrus' rule regarded democratic freedom as the antithesis of Persian despotism, the antithesis was clear to Spartans and Athenians – and to those who fought with them. There are clear indications that as soon as the Persians replaced the Lydians as rulers of Asia Minor many of the Greeks felt that the whole fabric of their life was in danger. There were projects, duly reported by Herodotus, of abandoning Asiatic Ionia for distant and barbaric Sardinia, and at least the citizens of Phocaea and Teos actually emigrated to other countries and faced unpleasant adventures in their search for new homes. Internal social conflicts in the Greek cities helped to identify the anti-Persian groups with the enemies of tyranny. Though the connection between the internal social conflicts of the Greek cities of Asia and the presence of the Persians was ambivalent in contemporary eyes, there was no doubt about the support which the Persians gave to the exiled tyrant of Athens, Hippias. In Athens Phrynichus depressed the Athenians by his tragedy, *The Capture of Miletus*, which he composed before 480 B.C. in a very different mood from that of *The Phoenician Women*, which is later than 480. Nor were the Greeks alone in finding the Persians less accommodating than they had wished or hoped. The story of Pythius, the Lydian magnate who entertained Xerxes and his whole army in a most lavish fashion, offering at the same time to give him a sum of money for the war, is too good not to be enjoyed in its Herodotean context, 7. 27–8. But the second instalment of the story, in chapters 38–9, must be spelt out because it shows that collaboration with the kings of Persia had its dangers: the king expected not only lavish entertainment and money from his protégés, but presence on the battlefield. Pythius, who tried to get his eldest son excused from service, doomed him to death.

III

It was only to be expected that the Greeks during and after the wars with Persia should look with attention at the Persian constitution, history and customs. Herodotus had both predecessors and successors, though probably none with his brilliance and intellectual generosity. Empedocles composed a poem, *Persika*, about the expedition of Xerxes. The story reported by Diogenes Laertius (8.2.57) is that either his sister or his daughter destroyed it. The Hellenised Lydian Xanthus informed the Greeks about the Persian Magi. One Greek at least really learned Persian: Themistocles. But he did so out of necessity. In the late fifth century, however, the Athenians and the Spartans must have had some experts to interpret Aramaic texts. An Aramaic letter (Thucydides says 'a letter written in Assyrian characters') was sent by the Persians to the Spartans. It was intercepted by the Athenians and duly translated (4.50).

We must immediately add that neither the linguistic nor the religious situation of the Persian Empire was likely to impress the Greeks deeply, at least in the fifth century. The fact that imperial Persian texts were also available in Elamite, Accadian, Egyptian and Aramaic translations, though not necessarily all of them together, only made the inferior status of the Greek language in the Persian Empire more obvious. No doubt official letters to Greek States and individuals were often drawn up in Greek by the Persian chancellery, and there were displays of bilingual texts in Persian (or Aramaic) and Greek when they could be of special relevance to Greek speakers (Herodotus 4.87). But Greek was not one of the privileged languages of the Empire. And – with the exceptions noted above – what was not in Greek was usually not read by the Greeks. Darius' stelae celebrating the reopening of the old Suez Canal in Persian, Elamite, Accadian and Egyptian – or the statue of Darius, which turned up in Susa in 1972 with inscriptions in the same four languages[2] – are symbolic of the invisible barrier separating the monolingual Greeks from the multilingual Empire.

The linguistic barrier was enough to prevent any Greek from appreciating the subtleties of Persian religious thought, even if the *Gathas* had already been written down by the fifth century B.C. and had been known in the imperial circles of Persia – which is of course very doubtful. But perhaps we ought not to mention the *Gathas* because we risk being asked how much of them we can understand ourselves. Linguistic incompetence alone would make it impossible for any Greek to appreciate the religious policy of the Persian kings in its real terms and in its local and temporal variations. Even Herodotus was compelled to be, to say the least, one-sided in his report of the persecution of the Egyptian priests by Cambyses because the epigraphical evidence was inaccessible to him (3.28–9). Cyrus' respect for Yahweh and for Marduk made all the difference to the Jews and to the Babylonians. As it happens we do

[2] J. Perrot, *Journal of Persian Studies* 12 (1974), 217.

not even know of any step taken by Cyrus in favour of Greek cults. What is usually put on a par with Cyrus' policy towards Jews and Babylonians is a letter from Darius to his satrap Gadatas for the purpose of confirming privileges to a wealthy temple of Apollo in Magnesia.[3] The text, which I for one consider authentic, provides excellent comparative evidence for the Persian legal terminology used in edicts reported in the Bible in favour of the Temple of Jerusalem. But the benefits which the Greeks of Asia Minor in general could derive from privileges granted to one of their temples were almost negligible. Outside Asia Minor Darius' letter to Gadatas probably remained unknown. In any case, after the Ionian rebellion and Xerxes' invasion of Greece, there was another side. The Persians had shown the Greeks how they could treat the temples belonging to their enemies. They had sacked the temple-oracle of Branchidae (Herodotus 6.19) and had burned down the sanctuary on the acropolis of Athens while killing those who had sought refuge in it as suppliants (8.53).

A last misapprehension to be cleared up concerning the attitude of the Greeks to the Persian Empire is that about Greek influences in Persian art. In 1929 archaeologists were alerted by the discovery of the Susa foundation text which stated: 'The stone cutters who worked the stone they were Ionians and Sardians.'[4] Later the influence of Greek artistic techniques and styles was established at Pasargadae and Persepolis just as much as at Susa. A well known inscription in a quarry of Persepolis tells us that the Greek Pytharchos was its superintendent, if not the owner.[5] Although today nobody would repeat what Gisela Richter stated as a fact in 1946, that Persian art was peripheric Greek art,[6] the impression seems still to prevail that the architecture and the sculpture of the capitals of the Persian Empire must have looked familiar and understandable to the Greeks because the Greeks contributed so much, in workers and techniques, to their creation. This is probably an illusion. Persepolis remained almost unknown to the Greek world until Alexander burned it down. Even Susa, where Greek ambassadors used to go, was visited by few Greeks, and there is no telling what they felt about Achaemenid imperial buildings. There is no sign that the Persians liked Athenian pottery (as the Etruscans did), and there is no sign that the Greeks liked the emphasis of Persian art on the majesty of

[3] Meiggs-Lewis, *Greek Historical Inscriptions*, 12.
[4] R. G. Kent, *Old Persian*, 2nd ed. (New Haven, 1953), p. 144.
[5] G. Pugliese Carratelli, *East and West* 16 (1966), 31-2.
[6] *American Journal of Archaeology* 50 (1946), 15–30.

the King of Kings. There is not even clear evidence that they noticed it.[7]

IV

What defined the reaction of the Greeks to the Persians was of course political evaluation. They were reconfirmed in their faith in law and freedom and consequently in their dislike of tyrants. Their experience of tyranny was after all very recent, and the wars with Persia had indicated that it was by no means a foregone conclusion that the word 'tyrant' should for ever be confined to the memories of the past. What emerges from Aeschylus and from Herodotus, who knew his Aeschylus well (2.156), is trust in freedom. Democritus said that 'poverty in democracy is better than wealth in serfdom' (Fragment 251); he must have thought of the Persians who had generally the reputation of being rich. According to Herodotus, Demaratus made the same point about the Spartans in one of his alleged conversations with the King of Persia: 'Law is the master whom the Spartans have; and this master they fear more than thy subjects fear thee.' When the Spartan commander Pausanias, who had previously despised Persian luxury (Herodotus 9.82), adopted Persian dress, he was discredited (Thucydides 1.130). In Greek eyes there was little to choose between Greek tyrants and Persian kings.

In its turn the trust in freedom was rooted in the awareness that Greek tyrants or Persian kings go beyond the natural limits of humanity and try to acquire divine attributes. Dislike of the Persian monarchy consequently crystallised round the notion of *proskynesis* – the act of homage to the Persian kings. It was considered unworthy of a Greek. The prevailing opinion of the Greeks appears to have been that *proskynesis* meant falling prostrate before the master (this must be Aeschylus' meaning in *Persians* 588). Plutarch has the curious story of how the Theban Ismenias avoided the indignity by a subterfuge: 'he threw his ring down on the ground in front of him and then stooped and picked it up, thus giving the impression that he was making the *proskynesis*' (*Artaxerxes* 22). The symbolism of *proskynesis* was apparently a troubling one when Alexander tried to have himself recognised as the Persian King of Kings.[8] What precise acts and gestures the different categories of subjects were supposed to perform in front of the King of Persia is another

[7] M. Root, *The King and Kingship in Achaemenid Art* [*Acta Iranica* 19] (Tehran/Liège, 1978).

[8] E. Bickerman, *La Parola del Passato* 91 (1963), 243–55.

matter. It would appear that a Persian dignitary kissed his own hand and bowed in the presence of the king,[9] but this is irrelevant to what the Greeks thought and felt. In any case, both bringing one's hand to one's mouth and prostration were, for the Greeks, acts of cult: extending them to mortals was sacrilege. Love of freedom and respect for the true gods here coalesced.

It was also to be expected that after the defeats at Salamis, Plataea and Mycale the Greeks would conclude that the Persians were bad soldiers. Neither Aeschylus nor Herodotus had a high opinion of their military attitudes. The Hippocratic author of the treatise on *Airs, Waters and Places* (written perhaps about 440 B.C.) emphasises the non-martial character of the Persians. In the fourth century B.C. the same evaluation was strongly expressed by Xenophon. It is Xenophon who transmits to us the report of a Greek ambassador that he had found in Persia many cooks, but no man fit to fight the Greeks (*Hellenica* 7.1.38). Stories circulated both in the fifth and in the fourth century that Persian soldiers had to be driven by the lash into battle (Herodotus 7.56 and 223; Xenophon, *Anabasis* 3.4.26). It was said, in conflict with other statements, that the Persians were corrupt, cruel, soft, faithless, incestuous and generally pleasure-loving: their many wives and concubines and their harem intrigues (all evidently upper-class phenomena) were contrasted with Greek sexual and family life. These facile and contemptuous judgements are most frequent in the fourth century.

The Greek reaction to the Persians might easily have terminated at this low point. If it had, we should have been deprived of its more thoughtful suggestions. Some Greeks realised that there was a difference between a king like Darius, who repressed the rebellion of his own subjects and tried to punish the Athenians as supporters of rebels, and a king like Xerxes who aimed at conquering the whole of Greece. What is more, this distinction, once introduced, led to some questions on the nature of Persian ambitions which were bound to emphasise the similarities, rather than the differences, between Greeks and Persians. At a superficial level victory encouraged the Greeks to consider themselves different from, and superior to, the Persians. At a deeper level the differences became blurred. Neither statement would have made sense to the Jews under Persian rule or after it.

Granted the improbability of the Greeks' going beyond the most overt aspects of Persian life because of lack of linguistic equipment,

[9] R. N. Frye, *Iranica Antica* 9 (1972), 102–7.

it was inevitable that some Persian kings should be found more guilty than others of overweening pride, *hybris*. Pride, to the Greeks, was an individual, not an institutional, characteristic. Attention was therefore diverted from Persian institutions to the individual attitudes of the Persian kings. Xerxes became one of the worst examples of oriental tyranny, whereas Darius – not to speak of Cyrus the Great – got away with little criticism and much sympathy. In Aeschylus' *Persians*, performed eight years after the battle of Salamis, Xerxes' superhuman attitudes are condemned by the ghost of his father Darius. Xerxes, in his father's judgement, had not respected the limits imposed by the gods on the Persian Empire, he had wanted too much. Thus the Persians were the first to suffer from the transgressions of their kings: as subjects they were not held responsible for the deeds of their masters. The tragedy as seen by Aeschylus was the tragedy of a nation let down by its leader; it explained the Greek victory with reference to what the Persian King had done to his own people. However alien the customs of the Persians could seem to the Greeks (and Aeschylus was certainly ready to underline their slightly comic peculiarities), the Athenian spectators were asked to give their sympathy to the Persians.

Herodotus is even more restrained in his judgement of the Persian defeat. There is no need here to recapitulate the initial chapters of his seventh book, which must surely be reckoned among the most penetrating pages ever written about human temptations. Xerxes himself, however avid for glory, is on the point of being persuaded by his uncle and adviser Artabanus that he must give up the ambition of conquering Greece. As Artabanus forcefully puts it, when the choice is between counsel tending to increase pride and counsel tending to its abatement, the latter must be preferred. Yet some demon repeatedly appearing in dreams coerces not only Xerxes, but Artabanus too, to follow the worse counsel. The doom of Xerxes and his armies is willed by the gods. Xerxes' arrogance is not so much a sin as an indication of divine disfavour. This conclusion is bound to affect the whole question of Graeco-Persian relations. It puts other statements by Herodotus into proper perspective.

Herodotus is not certain that the conflict between Persians and Greeks was inevitable. He has no sympathy for the instigators of the Ionian rebellion against Persia. He says in so many words that by involving themselves in this rebellion the Athenians were 'the beginning of many evils for Greeks and Barbarians' (5.97). He had already said in the first chapters of his history that according to the Persians the Greeks were greatly to be blamed because in the Trojan

War they had invaded Asia before the Persians had attacked Europe (1.4). Quite pointedly Herodotus remarked that after the repression of the Ionian rebellion Darius eliminated the tyrants from the Greek cities against all expectations. This proved according to Herodotus that the Persian government was not essentially incompatible with democracy (6.43). In its turn this Persian understanding for democratic institutions shows, always in the eyes of Herodotus, that at a certain moment of their history the Persians had genuinely faced the choice between monarchy, aristocracy and democracy and had preferred the first after debate (3.80–2). Herodotus obviously enjoyed reporting the story that Cyrus the Great rebuked the Spartan ambassador with the words: 'I never yet feared men who have a place set apart in the midst of their city where they deceive each other by committing perjury' (1.153). This is backed by the remark presented as Herodotus' own that in allowing themselves to be persuaded to help the Ionian rebels (whereas King Cleomenes of Sparta had refused to do so) the Athenians proved that it was easier to deceive thirty thousand men than one (5.97). In other chapters Herodotus amuses himself by comparing the powers of the Spartan kings with those of the Persian and Egyptian kings (6.59).

Herodotus does not see any contradiction in extolling the courage and love of liberty of Spartans and Athenians while recognising that Athens at least had been guilty of gratuitous provocation towards Persia and was vulnerable in its institutions. He does indeed announce what he declares to be an unpopular truth in his day: that the Athenians had been the saviours of Greece. 'Having chosen to keep Greece free, they [the Athenians] raised up that portion of the Greek nation which had not gone over to the Medes and so, next to the gods, they repulsed the invader . . . They had the courage to remain faithful to their land and await the coming of the enemy' (7.139).

Herodotus is obviously careful not to give himself away by commenting on anything that happened after 479. He mentions Pericles, but only in the context of a dream which his mother had a few days before giving birth to him: 'She fancied she had delivered a lion' (6.131). To call a man a lion is not, in Greek imagery, a safe compliment. We shall not try to guess what Herodotus had in mind. He was obviously aware of criticisms against Athens in general and Pericles in particular. He lived to recognise what Thucydides was to express in so many words, that the Athenians had gained the reputation of being tyrants of unwilling subjects. But whereas Thucydides concentrates on the inner logic of the development of power in Greece, Herodotus regarded results as being beyond human calculation. All that human beings can do is not to forget what is good because badness is mixed with it. The last words of Herodotus' history are of suspense and warning. The lesson is attributed to Cyrus the Great. No one can mistake the importance of what Herodotus is saying, or the meaning of the choice of speaker. When they were already the masters of Asia, the Persians asked Cyrus to give them a better land. Cyrus answered that a more comfortable climate would make them weaker, less capable of ruling an empire. 'And the Persians [concludes Herodotus] departed with altered minds, admitted that Cyrus was wiser than they, and chose rather to dwell in a barren land and be rulers than to cultivate plains and be slaves of others' (9.122). The names of Cyrus and the Persians are interchangeable with those of Pericles and the Athenians. The anti-Persian league founded by the Athenians in 478 had soon turned into an instrument of Athenian power. The Athenians created their own empire and pointedly imitated the Persians by imposing a tribute on their subjects and by repressing any rebellion. In Athens, as in Persia, freedom required power, because power is a condition of freedom, but power proved in fact unobtainable without ruling others. We have been ushered by Herodotus into the age of Greek imperialism via Persian imperialism. Herodotus clearly did not intend to obliterate the difference between the two nations. His sympathetic characterisation of the Persians, who teach their sons three things only – to ride, to draw the bow, and to tell the truth (1.136) – is also an indication of the limits he saw in their minds. This is confirmed not so much by some specific statements on the Greeks, which may even be suspected of being tinged with irony (especially 1.60), but by the picture of Greek life as it emerges as a whole from his history. What, however, Herodotus proclaims at the end of his long search, his long *historia*, is the common predicament of Greeks and Persians in their acquisition of power. For Greeks or for Persians, the choice is between ruling or being ruled.

Nobody after Herodotus expressed the same view with similar depth and shrewdness. His rival Ctesias, who had lived inside the Persian court for many years, rather developed that analysis of dynastic conflicts and harem intrigues which makes him such a useful counterpart to the Book of Esther; and this usefulness would be greater if his text were preserved in its entirety. But the interpretation of the character of the Persians, and more specifically of Cyrus the Great, which we find in Xenophon – the many-sided student of Persian affairs – is based on presuppositions comparable with those of Herodotus. In Xenophon the Persians act according to political principles which are intelligible to the Greeks, owe much to Greek collaboration and, in the specific case of Cyrus the Great, are inspired by a type of education in which the Greeks can mirror themselves. Two major assumptions of Xenophon are the legitimacy of imperialism – that is, of unlimited rule and economic exploitation of conquered enemies – and the pre-eminence of the political and military institutions capable of supporting imperialism.

The difference between Herodotus and Xenophon is of course that Xenophon reaches the point at which idealisation of the past (Cyrus the Great and, to a lesser extent, the younger Cyrus) conceals reality and becomes a factor in misunderstanding the present, and therefore a weakness. In the same way there is a disturbing element of mere imagination in the vague and idealised notions which begin to circulate in the circles of Plato and Pythagoras about the figure of Zoroaster and the teaching of the Magi. After all, in the fifth century the Greeks had been the masters of their own destiny and had alone taken the decision to fight the Persians. In the fourth century they were led to conquer the Persians by the Macedonians. There is a lack of self-control in what the Greeks say about the Persians in the fourth century: their judgements oscillate between the extremes of contempt and idealisation. Xenophon is even half-conscious of his own contradictions, which became more acute in old age when he wrote the pamphlet on the 'Revenues' – an essentially pacifist pamphlet. But one thing the Greeks continued seriously to believe before and after the conquest of Alexander the Great. The Persian Empire was an aggregate of subject territories held together by a central force. No religious link, no common language or literature, no common art helped to make the Empire what it was. It was basically a question of the relation of strength between the centre and the periphery. The personality of the King contributed to this relation in the Greek terms of greater or lesser wisdom: it contributed so much that after Herodotus no one in Greece asked himself (to the best of my knowledge) whether there could be an alternative to monarchy in Persia. But there was no effort to see what kept the Empire together behind the administrative façade; and – most significantly – there was no attempt to understand how people lived under Persian rule. If the Egyptians were an exception, it was because the Egyptians had been well known to the Greeks before the Persian conquest and managed to regain independence from the Persians with Greek help for long periods between Cambyses and Alexander.

When the Greeks provided the Macedonians with the necessary technological and ideological apparatus to govern what had been the

Empire of the Achaemenids, they transmitted their conclusions to their new Macedonian sovereigns. These conclusions determined the policy of the heirs of Alexander. We know now what these conclusions were. The superiority of the Greek way of life had once again been proved on the battlefield, and nobody was there to make sophistic distinctions between Greek hoplites and Macedonian phalangists. Conquest was self-justifying. Monarchy was necessary in the East, if not elsewhere. And therefore a monarch had to exercise self-control – as Alexander's lack of control had just made evident. But there was not much one needed to know about the Persians, and even less about their subjects. No real acquaintance with their language or, indeed, with their religion was required, except at the most external points of contact between cults and government. An imperial climate singularly devoid of religious and ethical scruples characterises the first century of Graeco-Macedonian rule of Asia and Egypt. This did not exclude pleasant surprises in which intellectuals had every reason to indulge in discovering pockets of wisdom either in India or in Persia or in that most unfamiliar territory – Judaea. But the meaning and the consequences of these discoveries will have to be considered against the background of an aggressive feeling of superiority displayed by the Graeco-Macedonians. The Greeks settled in the countries they conquered to an extent which was unthinkable under the Persians. They made relations with the natives conditional on their acceptance of Greek language and customs. They offered the natives many more opportunities of employment and emigration than the Persians had probably ever done. If they cared little about what their subjects believed, even in so far as this might be relevant to the administration of their State, they nevertheless made Hellenisation the condition for favour and advancement. They adopted the imperialism of the Persians and rather incongruously added to it a policy of Hellenisation. The Jews who had been given two centuries by the Persians in which to think about themselves now found that they had to think about their new masters, too.

LARRY SIEDENTOP

Two Liberal Traditions

Nothing reduces the value of discussion about modern political thought more than the contrast commonly drawn between 'liberalism' and 'socialism'. That contrast has become *simpliste* and misleading. It rests on assumptions which do not stand up to examination. In particular, the contrast has come to be made in a way that neglects the richness of liberal thought in the nineteenth century, and ignores the extent to which modes of argument and themes which are usually assigned to 'socialism' formed an important part of liberal thought in that period. Indeed, some of these modes of argument and themes were *introduced* by liberal thinkers, and only later adopted by socialist writers. To that extent, it is fair to say that the conventional contrast between the two traditions is particularly unfair to liberalism – excluding from it some of its own progeny.

Even at first glance the contrast between liberalism and socialism seems inadequate. To say, as so many writers do, that the two traditions give priority to different concepts – liberty in the one case, equality in the other – fails to make clear the sense in which liberalism is itself rooted in the concept of 'natural' equality. The presumption in favour of equal treatment, built into the framework of ideas in Contract Theory, meant that no man had a moral obligation to obey another as such – that is, the right to command and the duty to obey were no longer written into hereditary social roles as in a caste society. Thus, the fundamental or root concept of liberalism is equality, and its commitment to liberty springs from that.

In the same way, the commonplace view that liberalism is sociologically naïve – that it is a priori and unhistorical in its mode of argument when compared to 'historical materialism' – is untenable. That commonplace view neglects two things. First, it neglects the sense in which socialism is itself a priori and parasitic on the norms of liberal theory, especially the Contract School of the seventeenth and early eighteenth century, for its commitment to human equality. (Rousseau's *Discourse on the Origins of Inequality* undoubtedly played an important role in that transmission.) Secondly, the view that liberalism is sociologically naïve neglects the fact that it was liberal thinkers of the later eighteenth and early nineteenth century who began to reject 'the state of nature' as the proper starting-point for political argument and developed instead the first systematic theories of social change. The narrowing or 'hardening' of the concept of law in Contract Theory – with the help of arguments about sovereignty and law as command – had made possible a much clearer distinction between *les lois* and *les moeurs*, between political and social structures. Liberals like Montesquieu and Turgot were the first to begin to use these concepts independently, and to draw attention to the importance of social change.

Why do these things go unrecognised today? What has given rise to the misleading contrast drawn between liberalism and socialism? One development especially, I think. One strand of the liberal tradition has been emphasised to the exclusion of another. Yet the other is in many ways the richer tradition. To oversimplify somewhat, these two traditions can be described as the English and French traditions. What I shall argue is that the standard picture of liberalism is derived almost entirely from English liberal thought, and neglects French liberal thought – with the result that our picture of the development of both liberalism and socialism is distorted.

Many of the criticisms commonly directed at 'liberalism' apply chiefly to the English liberal tradition. What are the most important of these criticisms? At least three must be considered. First, it is often alleged that liberalism involves an impoverished concept of the person; that it overlooks the social nature of man. This criticism is closely connected to recent discussion about methodological individualism – to criticism of a mode of argument which postulates an atomised, unhistorical individual who looks (to many socialist thinkers at least) suspiciously like an entrepreneurial type fostered by nascent capitalist society. In effect, the criticism is that liberal thought neglects to explore the influence of social conditions on the agent, that it neglects the socialising process.

The second, closely related criticism of liberalism is that it shirks the hard work of understanding how changing social relations and attitudes reflect or spring from changes in the mode of production. On this view, one of the constant features of liberal thought is its preoccupation with the political or legal sphere and its neglect of civil society. Finally, a third criticism of liberalism is that it has an inadequate concept of liberty or liberation. Here the argument is that in its concern to define criteria which will create and protect a sphere of private action (and *ipso facto* limit the sphere of legitimate state action), liberalism fails to appreciate the moralising role of political participation – that it fails to understand the fulfilment which the performance of civic duty brings.

The vulnerability of English liberal thought to these criticisms – which I do not deny – results largely from its close association with empiricist philosophy.[1] From Locke to J. S. Mill leading English liberals found their vocation as philosophers of mind and based their political arguments on the empiricist (or sensationalist) theory of knowledge. Now by far the most striking thing about empiricist epistemology during that period is that it was exercised by the problem of individual knowledge of the natural world. That is, the central questions posed were: how does the individual mind acquire knowledge of the external world, and how can we be sure that such knowledge is accurate? These questions had been stimulated by developments in seventeenth-century natural science, and their elucidation involved exploring the meaning of such ideas as 'causation' and 'law'. The criteria of reliable knowledge which came to be defined by Locke and Hume made observable regularities or uniformities of behaviour the test. True to its original inspiration – the natural sciences – empiricist philosophy insisted on verification as the test of 'true' knowledge.

But that empiricist test for knowledge created a wholly new problem of social explanation. In retrospect, we can see that what the first empiricists did was, in effect, to collapse the concept of 'rules' into that of empirical laws. Early empiricist philosophy – or the sensationalist model of the mind – did not offer a satisfactory account of the nature of rule-governed action. It did not explain the role of social norms in shaping individual intentions and making action possible. It did not explore the dependence of the concept of the 'self' on a social context. Rousseau was one of the first to notice this weakness, and struggled to remedy it, with mixed success. French social thinkers in the late eighteenth and early nineteenth century took far more seriously questions about the origin of language and the sense in which society is a normative or rule-governed (rather than merely causal) order. These questions preoccupied thinkers as different as Condillac, Rousseau, Bonald and Maistre. They explored *the conditions of social action* – that is, the sense in which it is only possible to speak of individual motives and intentions by placing them in a context of social rules. In effect, these French thinkers made the first real criticisms of methodological individualism in social studies.

[1] I recognise that important sociological insights emerged in eighteenth-century Anglo-Scottish historical writing, but they did not create a new programme for political theory.

French liberals of the early nineteenth century benefited from that critique of empiricist philosophy. They adapted values from earlier English liberals such as Locke to these new ideas about the social nature of man, concerning themselves much less with the question of how the individual mind acquires accurate knowledge of the external or natural world. Instead of being philosophers of mind, they tended to be historians or jurists. Instead of wrestling with the problem of verification or induction, they took a keen interest in the socialising process. Instead of seeing history in terms of the advance of science (here Comte and Mill were the true heirs of early empiricist philosophy), they were interested in the changing forms of property rights, the social classes which such property rights created, and the conflict between classes. Thus, where the early liberals moved from the problem of individual knowledge to a concern with individual rights and interests, the French liberals of the early nineteenth century moved from interest in the socialising process to concern with the *types* of social organisation. They began to develop models in order to identify and understand different types of society. And they began to relate particular versions of political concepts to different social structures – as in Benjamin Constant's essay on 'Ancient and Modern Liberty'.[2]

As a result French liberals – Mme de Stael, Benjamin Constant; a group called the *Doctrinaires* who included Royer-Collard, Barante and Guizot; and, above all, Alexis de Tocqueville – took a step which was decisive for the later development of political thought. In effect, they began to insist that political theory be founded on a theory of social change. No political theory, they argued, could be founded merely on assumptions about an unchanging or essential human nature or on assumptions about the contents of the human mind. In that sense, the French liberals rejected a deductive model and substituted an inductive model for political theory – changing economic and social structures established constraints within which political organisation had to work. 'Given' certain economic and social conditions, then only certain political options were open. If, for example, the subdivision of property, the spread of education and social mobility had undermined the caste system of feudal society, then aristocratic government on a quasi-feudal model was no longer possible.

That did not mean that economic and social conditions dictated one political outcome. The French liberals – especially the *Doc-*

[2] To be found in his *L'Esprit de conquête et de l'usurpation* (Paris, 1814).

trinaires and Tocqueville – insisted on the reality of political choice, but *within limits*. Those limits were imposed by 'social structure'. Thus, the *Doctrinaires* observed that the development of the state rested upon the weakening of the feudal hierarchy, the rise of towns and the growth of a market economy. But, within the larger pattern, they were also struck by the different forms of the state and of political ideas which emerged in England and France. They began to explore the sources of that difference.

It is not too much to claim that the *Doctrinaires* were the originators of a sociological approach to political theory. They were the first political thinkers who consistently rejected the classical term 'constitution' as inadequate for political and social analysis. By distinguishing between laws as commands (enforced by public power) and other social rules, they drew a distinction between political institutions and social structure, and developed criteria for applying the latter concept – criteria such as the distribution of property, education and social mobility. When referring to social structure, the *Doctrinaires* used terms such as *la condition sociale*, *l'état social*, etc.

By drawing attention to changes in *les moeurs* and social conditions, the *Doctrinaires* insisted, in effect, on the limited efficacy of law. Ultimately, they argued, law is less powerful than *les moeurs*; it cannot be used successfully if it is turned against the whole 'direction' of social change. Lawmakers become powerless if they seek to overturn or ignore the division of labour in a society, the distribution of property and popular expectations. In that sense, lawmakers must accept a foundation of economic and social facts as given – seeking merely to modify rather than overturn such a powerful concatenation of circumstances.

François Guizot spoke for the *Doctrinaires* when he wrote in his *Essays on the History of France* (1822):

> It is by the study of political institutions that most writers . . . have sought to understand the state of a society, the degree or type of its civilisation. It would have been wiser to study first the society itself in order to understand its political institutions. Before becoming a cause, political institutions are an effect; a society produces them before being modified by them. Thus, instead of looking to the system or forms of government in order to understand the state of the people, it is the state of the people that must be examined first in order to know what must have been, what could have been its government. . .
>
> Society, its composition, the manner of life of individuals according to their social position, the relations of the different classes, the condition

[*l'état*] of persons especially – that is the first question which demands attention from . . . the inquirer who seeks to understand how a people are governed.

Feudal institutions, Guizot argued, could only be understood in that way. The ownership of land carried with it the right to govern its inhabitants.

The study of the condition of lands must thus precede that of the condition of persons. In order to understand the political institutions, it is necessary to understand the different social conditions [classes] and their relations. In order to understand the different social conditions, it is necessary to understand the nature and relations of properties.

In view of the emphasis by French liberals on property relations and class conflict, it is hardly surprising that Marx derived not just historical information but social theory from Guizot and Tocqueville – those 'bourgeois historians' whom he went out of his way to praise in later years. The pity is that by describing them simply as historians he obscured the nature of his debt to them. Yet it was the *Doctrinaires*' concept of social structure and their emphasis on the priority of economic change that gradually created a new mode of political argument.

The role of the *Doctrinaires* in creating a sociological basis for political theory has gone unnoticed. In fact, the credit has been claimed for two other groups of thinkers – wrongly, I think. Marxists sometimes point to the theories of social change developed by eighteenth-century Scots such as Adam Ferguson and Adam Smith as the origin of sociological argument. And it *is* perfectly true that what has been called the 'Four Stages' theory – in which human development is traced through (*a*) hunting and gathering, (*b*) nomadic and pastoral, (*c*) agricultural, and (*d*) commercial stages – represented an enormous breakthrough in understanding.[3] For the mode of subsistence is used to identify each stage, and other practices are related 'functionally' to it. Yet the Scottish thinkers were not primarily interested in the problem of government. Their theories of social change are not designed to explore political issues or to contribute to the solution of pressing political problems of their own time. Hence the universal scope of their theories, which were not fashioned as a means of political reform. That is where the *Doc-*

[3] Ronald Meek, *Social Science and the Ignoble Savage* (Cambridge, 1976).

trinaires differ. They were faced with the problem of reconstructing French institutions – and especially government – after the Revolution.

Leading *Doctrinaires* such as Royer-Collard and Guizot held important political posts under the Restoration. Hence their accounts of social change were fashioned to throw light on the current predicament of France. In order to understand the new condition of French society, they narrowed their accounts of social change to Western Europe since the early feudal period. They no longer attempted to encompass the whole of human development. Rather, they sought to understand how changes in the form of French government 'sprang from' social and economic changes, and, *a fortiori*, to what extent the highly centralised state machine which the Restoration inherited from Napoleon was inevitable under modern social conditions, or whether decentralisation was possible. Thus, they sought to explore the structure of modern society – which they began to call 'democratic' – with that political problem – centralisation – constantly in mind.

Recently, still another group of thinkers has been given credit for creating modern sociological argument. In *The Sociological Tradition* Robert Nisbet has laid great emphasis on the contribution of counter-revolutionary writers such as Burke, Bonald and Maistre to the definition of the key differences between traditional and modern society.[4] It is certainly true that the counter-revolutionaries relentlessly criticised the methodological individualism (in the form of Natural Rights theory) of the Enlightenment, and contributed to a more holist approach to the study of society. In particular, they explored the factors making for social cohesion, and perhaps unwittingly helped to develop the concepts of social structure and function. But there is one great difficulty involved in making a strong claim for them as founders of sociological argument. They ruled out fundamental social change. That is, they assumed that only one type of society was possible – a hierarchical one on the model of the *ancien régime*. Any departure from that model was defined as degeneration or decay, rather than mere change; and the conservatives were forever tempted to attribute such developments to conspiracy and/or heresy. Thus, instead of attempting to develop models which would make it possible to understand the evolution of Western European society, their argument remained wholly normative. Departure from their preferred model of society threatened

[4] Robert Nisbet, *The Sociological Tradition* (London, 1967).

to produce not another type of society but 'non-society' – that is, anarchy and dissolution. That is the severe limitation on the conservatives' contribution to the origins of sociological argument.

Undoubtedly early nineteenth-century French liberals did learn from the writings of the conservatives. They learned, for example, to take far more seriously the problem of social order, the role of common beliefs in creating social authority. They also learned to take far more seriously the question of whether the atomisation of society merely paves the way for the reign of brute force – which was the conservatives' reworking of the argument from classical political thought that democracy leads first to anarchy and then to tyranny. But the liberals did *not* adopt the conservatives' general strategy in argument. They did not define authority in such a way that it entails a hierarchical society; they began to ask what *kind* of authority would be compatible with greater social equality. By accepting the possibility of 'democratic' authority, they ruled out a *simpliste* distinction between authority and power – with the growth of naked power seen as the inevitable consequence of the rejection of rightful (hierarchical) authority.

Thus, it was the French liberals who did the really hard work of analysis, and who created the first truly sociological idiom. For they rejected the wholly normative framework of the conservatives, and gradually defined concepts, such as social stratification and élites, which could be used for comparative analysis. The liberals gradually defined what seemed to them the major variables for the analysis of social change – the division of labour, the distribution of property, education, mobility and the level of expectation. Thus, it was the French liberals who invented the concept of a social – as distinct from a political – revolution. It is no accident that their greatest protégé, Alexis de Tocqueville, popularised the concept of a 'Democratic Revolution' spreading through the West.

In sum, the *Doctrinaires* came to accept that social change was irreversible and in that sense 'inevitable'. Any attempt to use positive law or the state machine to undo the new division of labour and the increasing subdivision of property would be futile. Positive law was too frail a weapon to counter the thrust of new social habits, customs and expectations. How did the *Doctrinaires* come to these conclusions? Here some knowledge of French political history from 1815 to 1830 is indispensable. In the 1820s what might be called 'The Great Debate' took place in Paris – a debate which dominated the Chamber of Deputies, the press and pamphleteering. That debate was sparked off by the end of the period of relatively liberal *Doc-*

trinaire government (1815–20), after the assassination of the heir to the throne, the Duc de Berri, in 1820. *Doctrinaire* government was succeeded by the ultra-royalist ministry of Villèle, which governed France – abetted by Charles X after 1824 – until the end of 1827.

The new ultra-royalist government of Villèle embarked on an ambitious programme of legislation – and its proposals over the next few years seemed to the *Doctrinaires* to amount to an attempt to restore the *ancien régime* in France. In rapid succession came bills to curtail press freedom, to restrict the suffrage, to restore primogeniture and entail, to make sacrilege a crime punishable by death, to indemnify the *noblesse* for their losses during the Revolution. Now the *Doctrinaires* – both those who remained in parliament, such as Royer-Collard, and those who had been dismissed from administrative posts, such as Barante and Guizot – set about showing that such proposals were incompatible with the new state of society in France. It was in doing so that they applied the terms 'aristocratic' and 'democratic' not merely to forms of government but to types of society. In their usage, an aristocratic society is defined by inequality of basic rights and conditions – the castes of feudal society being an extreme form – while democratic society is marked by relative equality of rights and conditions.

To combat the ultra-royalist legislative programme, the *Doctrinaires* found it necessary to point out the structural differences between 'aristocratic' society and 'democratic' society – to show how the former had given way irremediably to the latter in France. Oddly, the ultra-royalists' farouche proposals provided just the points of comparison which were needed. For they drew attention to the respects in which modern society differed *fundamentally* from medieval society. Thus, the *Doctrinaires* were able to define the structure of democratic society by way of contrast with the model of society implied by the ultras' proposals. They were able to show, in speeches and in writings, that the ultra model of society no longer corresponded to anything in the real world. France, in other words, had undergone a profound social revolution. Wealth, power and education had been redistributed to a crucial extent. From a caste society founded on inequality of rights and the concentration of property, France had become a society founded on equality of fundamental rights – with the subdivision and circulation of property and a more complex division of labour. The fixed social positions of an 'aristocratic' society had created a powerful, self-confident élite resting on a permanently subordinated class. The dislodging of individuals from fixed positions in a 'democratic' society (or atomisation, as the *Doctrinaires* began to call it) releases individual ambition and raises expectations; it creates anxiety, competition and social mobility. While the first type of society was associated with subsistence agriculture, the latter is associated with the growth of a market economy.

Clearly, the *Doctrinaires* offered a theory of social change rather than an account of social decay or degeneration as conservatives such as Maistre and Bonald had done. Their use of models in order to identify types of society was primarily analytical and neutral. Only after identifying the main features of each type did they discuss the advantages and disadvantages of the different types of social organisation. An excellent example of that is Guizot's discussion of feudalism in his lectures on the *History of Civilisation in Europe* (1828). Thus, while the *Doctrinaires* by no means did away with normative political theory – Guizot, for example, published several works on the nature of representative government – they did insist on a secure sociological basis for political theory. Ultra-royalist proposals to restore the *ancien régime* seemed to them to illustrate the dangers of political theory which lacked such a basis. It became irrelevant and obscurantist.

The mistaken premise of writers like Nisbet ought now to be clear. The major breakthrough in sociological argument – the attempt to found political argument on theories of social change – did not result from the debate generated by the French Revolution soon after 1789. Rather, it resulted from the debate *under the Restoration* generated by ultra-royalist proposals to restore the *ancien régime*. Liberals taking part in that debate created a new mode of argument. They rejected a wholly normative approach to political theory, developing models which made possible the analysis of social and economic change, and, *a fortiori*, the limits of political choice. Theirs was the really hard work in forging categories for sociological argument. The greatest work of nineteenth century French liberal thought, Tocqueville's *Democracy in America* (1835–40), exemplified and rested upon that new mode of argument which had emerged under the Restoration.

What was the consequence for political theory of that change in the mode of argument accomplished by the *Doctrinaires* and their protégé, Tocqueville? It was (*a*) a redefinition of the political problem, and (*b*) a more complex concept of liberty.

French liberals began to approach the problem of state power and authority in a very different way from their seventeenth- and eighteenth-century English predecessors. They were no longer wrestling with the problem of political obligation in its classical form. Nor were they seeking to define criteria which would permanently delimit the area of legitimate state action. Confronted by a far more powerful state machine than any known to the English liberals, they sought to understand what had contributed to the centralisation of power (in particular, the role of class struggle), and what the obstacles to decentralisation in an atomised or democratic society might be. Thus, the *Doctrinaires* began to ask new questions. What changes in social structure were bound up with the emergence of the state? In what ways did the structure of modern democratic society facilitate a concentration of power which might put both local self-government and individual rights at risk? To what extent is decentralisation compatible with political unity?

In order to explore these new questions, the *Doctrinaires* fixed their attention on developments in Western Europe since the early Middle Ages. In examining changes in social structure, they were struck by one thing especially – the rise of the bourgeoisie out of the original castes of feudal society. In examining changes in political structure, they were equally struck by one thing – the way the growth of the state paralleled the growth of this new intermediate social class. How, then, were the two related? In effect, the *Doctrinaires* explored the relationship in two ways: conceptually and historically. Conceptually, they pointed out that the state (and the correlated concept of sovereignty) is a necessary condition for a structure of equal fundamental rights. The idea of a *general* political society, in which *all* are subject to a centralised agency acknowledged to have the right to make and enforce rules of conduct binding on *all*, is part of what we mean by 'social equality'. A permanently classified society, on the other hand, does not entail such a centralised authority; for in it rights and duties are defined into hereditary social roles. Thus, making a distinction between the 'individual' and his social roles implies the role of the state, the concept of sovereignty. Political centralisation and social atomisation are different aspects of the same process. The gradual collapse of the two original feudal castes into the new intermediate social condition – in that sense the triumph of the bourgeoisie or social equality – implies the growth of the state.

But what kind of state? The second task undertaken by the *Doctrinaires* was to show how the different forms of the modern state must be understood as consequences of different patterns of class struggle. They identified two primary patterns – exemplified by the histories of England and France. The differences between the two derived from the weakness of central government in France in the early feudal period, and its relative strength in England after the Conquest. In France, the weakness of the Crown *vis-à-vis* the feudal nobility led the Crown to support the claims of the new boroughs, and thus created in time a tacit alliance between the Crown and the *tiers état* directed against the power of the feudal nobility. The *tiers état* acquiesced in the growth of royal power in order to destroy their local aristocratic oppressors. In England, on the other hand, a different pattern of alliance grew up. The Norman Conquest had involved the creation of a relatively strong central power. Faced by the threat of royal tyranny, the English aristocracy gradually formed an alliance with the new boroughs, and eventually called representatives of the commons to Parliament. Thus, the English aristocracy joined the commons in limiting the pretensions of the Crown, and fought to establish common rights. The result was the creation of the English constitution – in which the rights of the Crown were balanced by the rights of Parliament. In turn, the alliance between the aristocracy and the middle classes in England meant that the original caste society was gradually transformed – the feudal aristocracy based on birth and conquest fusing with a new aristocracy based on wealth. A more open social structure was the result.

Thus, different patterns of class conflict and alliance in the two countries had crucial political consequences. In France, the alliance of the *tiers état* and the Crown against the *noblesse* meant that government was centralised in the executive; whereas in England the alliance of the nobility and the commons led to the centralisation of government in the legislature. By the eighteenth-century, then, the French monarchy claimed a monopoly of political right, while in England Parliament claimed to be sovereign. That difference had important consequences for the structure of government in the two countries. It meant that in England political centralisation – the growth of the state – was not accompanied by administrative centralisation; the upper classes kept local affairs firmly in their own hands. In France, on the other hand, local autonomy had been sacrificed by the bourgeoisie in order to destroy their feudal oppressors. Thus, the French government had fallen completely into the hands of the King's agents, hierarchically organised over the country as a whole. In consequence, free *moeurs* (the habit of self-government and voluntary association) had died in France, while in England free *moeurs* were sustained by local autonomy.

This historical argument was not the work of any one *Doctrinaire*. It emerged gradually from 1815 to 1830 in the writings of Mme de

Stael, Royer-Collard, Barante and Guizot. In Guizot's lectures at the Sorbonne in the late 1820s the argument took its definitive historical form – the form which so impressed the young Alexis de Tocqueville, who attended Guizot's lectures assiduously from 1828 until the July Revolution in 1830. Tocqueville had the genius to see where the *Doctrinaires*' argument led, how it might be applied to political theory. In *Democracy in America* he generalised the *Doctrinaires*' analysis, basing his argument on the models of two types of society and drawing attention to the dangers which arise in the transition from an 'aristocratic' society to a 'democratic' society. The disappearance of intermediate institutions – of the hereditary corporations and great magnates of aristocratic society – threatens to leave society without autonomous local institutions.

> The people, at the moment when they begin to feel their power, finding that the nobles direct all local affairs, become discontented with provincial government, less as provincial than as aristocratic.[5]

They look to central government for support against their local oppressors. Thus, the struggle against social privilege proceeds by strengthening central government. As society is levelled or atomised, power and authority tend to go to the centre – to be concentrated in central government, which *alone* can claim to speak in the name of *all*.

> This natural tendency of a democratic people to centralise the business of government . . . has its most rapid growth in an epoch of struggle and transition, when the aristocratic and democratic principles are disputing with each other for ascendancy.[6]

The changes are not merely political. Economic and social interdependence develop as the fixed, unequal positions of the older society give way to greater equality of rights, which permits freedom of movement, exchange and an increasingly complex division of labour. These changes create *a new scale of social organisation*. They are made possible by the state, and, in turn, they reinforce the role of the state. Thus, the state grows rapidly at the expense of traditional associations such as the manor, commune, guild – and perhaps even the family.

[5] *Memoir, Letters, and Remains of Alexis de Tocqueville* (London, 1861), vol. 1, p. 243.

[6] ibid.

What is the outcome? Whereas power and authority had been localised by the hierarchy of aristocratic society, the dislodging of individuals from fixed social positions – growing equality or atomisation – paves the way for centralisation. A democratic social structure offers no 'natural' obstacle to the growth of centralised, bureaucratic power.

Tocqueville took over the image of an atomised society from the *Doctrinaires*, and he made it perhaps the most powerful of all sociological images. That image seemed to him to conjure up the central feature of democratic society – the change in the scale of social organisation, at the expense of local autonomy. That image made it possible to identify remote bureaucratic power as the new enemy. As early as 1822 Royer-Collard had used the image of *la société en poussière* to point out the centralisation which threatens a democratic society.

> We have seen the old society perish, and with it that crowd of domestic institutions and independent magistracies which it carried within it . . . true republics within the monarchy. These institutions did not, it is true, share sovereignty; but they opposed to it everywhere limits which were defended obstinately. Not one of them has survived. The revolution has only left individuals standing . . . It has dissolved even the (so to speak) physical association of the commune . . . This is a spectacle without precedent! Before now one had seen only in philosophers' books a nation so decomposed and reduced to its ultimate constituents.
>
> From an atomised society has emerged centralisation. There is no need to look elsewhere for its origin. Centralisation has not arrived with its head erect, with the authority of a principle; rather, it has developed modestly, as a consequence, a necessity. Indeed, there where there are only individuals, all business which is not theirs is necessarily public business, the business of the state. There where there are no independent magistrates, there are only the agents of central power. That is how we have become an *administered* people, under the hand of irresponsible civil servants, themselves centralised in the power of which they are agents.[7]

Thus, it became a premise of the *Doctrinaires* that the growth of state power was intrinsically connected with the atomisation of society, with the destruction of traditional intermediate bodies.

To the *Doctrinaires*, the inadequacy of Montesquieu's theory of the separation of powers suddenly seemed obvious. It rested on a hidden presupposition, the survival of an aristocratic social structure. For what limited the concentration of power in Montesquieu's theory? Montesquieu assumed that the legislature, in whole or in

[7] P. Royer-Collard, 'De la liberté de la presse', *Discours*, 2 January 1822.

part, would consist of representatives of a traditional superior class – which would keep local affairs in its own hands (on the English model), and thus prevent the growth of a despotic central administration. If the informal constraints on the growth of central power provided by an aristocratic social structure are removed, then no formal limitation on its authority – and, consequently, on the growth of its power – exists. In a democratic or atomised society, the separation of powers or functions in central government is not a sufficient safeguard against an excessive concentration of power legitimated by the concept of state 'sovereignty'. For when these agencies of central government act in concert, then there are no independent centres of resistance left in society, no legal means of opposition.

In a democratic society, how could a degree of local autonomy be reconciled with the growth of the state? How could a balance of power between the centre and periphery of society be established? That became *the political problem* as defined by the *Doctrinaires* in the 1820s. Under their influence, Tocqueville learned to see the problem in that way. In 1828 he wrote:

> There are two great drawbacks to avoid in organising a country. Either the whole strength of social organisation is centred on one point, or it is spread over the country. Either alternative has its advantages and its drawbacks. If all is tied into one bundle, and the bundle gets undone, everything falls apart and there is no nation left. Where power is dispersed, action is clearly hindered, but there is strength everywhere.[8]

Soon Tocqueville concluded that America, rather than England, offered a solution. England had avoided administrative centralisation because it remained to a crucial extent an aristocratic society. The United States provided the only successful example of decentralisation in a democratic or atomised society. Why? Federalism had prospered because there was no need to destroy an aristocratic society there. Thus, American federalism seemed to offer a paradigm for the decentralisation which ought to come in Europe when the transitional struggles against social privilege had been won. Tocqueville turned American federalism into an instructive myth, in order to demonstrate that local self-government is compatible with social equality and that those who argued that community is possible only within a fixed social hierarchy were mistaken. American federalism

[8] Alexis de Tocqueville, *Journeys to England and Ireland*, trans. G. Lawrence and J. P. Mayer (London, 1958), pp. 23–4.

provided Tocqueville with the means of criticising the unitary concept of the state and of sovereignty – by exploring different ways in which authority and power could be devolved within a political system. With the help of the federalist example, he was able to argue that the natural weakness of a democratic or atomised social structure – its tendency to centralise power and authority – could be corrected by means of political reform.

That new concern with the devolution of power and authority – with countering the trend towards centralisation – became the badge of the French liberals. It also shaped their discussions of the concept of liberty. Concerned with the changing structure of society, they found the empiricist concept of liberty – what Isaiah Berlin has called negative liberty – inadequate. In their view, that negative or physicalist concept of liberty (defined as the absence of impediment or constraint) was not very helpful in a social context – that is, a context of rule-governed action. It remained important as providing a final criterion for distinguishing between coerced and free action. But, apart from that, it did not help much to clarify the different types of liberty which might be available in a modern nation. It did not identify different forms of rule-governed action, or make any use of the distinction between *les lois* and *les moeurs* – between political and social structure – which they now regarded as one of the conquests of modern political thought. In that way, the negative or physicalist concept of liberty revealed its origins in early empiricism. It failed to establish that intentions and motives, indeed action itself, are only conceivable within a framework of social rules. For that reason it failed to distinguish between the 'absence of constraint' and the 'absence of obligation'.

The French liberals therefore tried to adapt the concept of liberty to a social or rule-governed context – relating different versions of the concept to changes in social structure. Nearest to the negative concept, they found, was the medieval notion of rights or liberties as personal privileges – that is, a sense of liberty or right resting not on general rules, but ultimately on the individual's will, his ability to resist encroachment and enforce his commands. In that sense, the negative concept of liberty, defined as the absence of impediment or constraint, might be shown to be more characteristic of hierarchical societies, where 'rights' are understood as personal privileges, than of egalitarian societies, where 'rights' are by definition general and imply duties to others. Thus, it could be argued that the notion of 'equal civil liberty' implies public duty and a kind of self-discipline in a way that the artistocratic notion of liberty as privilege does not.

In a society where rights were thus seen as *de facto* personal possessions, a fierce sense of individual independence was generated among the dominant class. That extreme sense of independence was necessarily weakened as social levelling and the emergence of the state created a new notion of rights and rules as by definition general and protected by public power. The emergence of political guarantees for rights and their generalisation implies a notion of reciprocity which would have been unintelligible in a caste society resting on the assumption of natural inequality.

Obviously, once rights are seen as rule-dependent and generally applicable, then the idea of 'civil liberty' becomes important in identifying areas of free or uncoerced action defined and protected by law. But civil liberty does not exhaust the meaning of liberty in the context of the modern state. The idea of 'political liberty' is necessary to identify the forms of participation which might be available to individuals to influence the law- or rule-making process in a society. A society in which the idea of rights was associated above all with personal will, with the ability to enforce commands and resist encroachments, was unlikely to conceive of liberty as essentially involving the right and duty to take part in the formulation of rules which would then bind all. Yet, by the same token, the individual will to resist, and in that sense negative liberty, may be weakened by a society in which participation provides an alternative conception of liberty.

Clearly, the 'self-imposition of rules' was the sense of liberty which Rousseau asserted in *Du contrat social.* But Rousseau had gone too far, in the view of the French liberals. Rousseau had removed participation from a context of civil liberties (and the negative freedom which they protect) and identified it instead with 'virtue' – thus collapsing the concept of liberty into that of morality. Benjamin Constant protested against Rousseau's strategy by making his famous contrast between ancient and modern liberty; the implication of his argument was that in modern society 'participation' would have to be reconciled with respect for civil liberties. To set up an ancient *polis* such as Sparta as a model was to ignore both the utterly different scale of modern society and the moral revolution which had issued in changed ideas about the proper relationship between the individual and the group. Thus, Constant and other French liberals insisted that emphasis on participation and civic duty should not jeopardise a sphere of fundamental individual rights against the group or the state. Only by recognising such rights was 'virtue' in a modern, individualist sense promoted; to emphasise participation or political liberty on the ancient model to the exclusion of individual freedom or choice was to hold up a concept of virtue which belonged to a totally different type of society – a society in which virtue consisted in solidarity or submergence in the group. Thus, the French liberals were at pains to distinguish and defend the roles of conscience and civil liberty on the one hand, political rights and civic virtue on the other.

Not only that. True to their consistent concern with social structures, the French liberals applied the concept of liberty to social structure, and identified another sense of 'liberty' – a sense which in many ways they found the most interesting and the most important to vindicate. That was the concept of 'free *moeurs*'. Free *moeurs* were understood to be a set of attitudes and habits fostered in individuals when civil liberty and political liberty (or participation) were joined together in a society, each reinforcing the other. The concept was used especially by Mme de Stael and Tocqueville. By free *moeurs* they meant a sense of personal capacity, which promoted both self-reliance and the habit of free association, and thus moulded all social relations. Free *moeurs* created an active citizenry attached to local freedom and joined together in numerous voluntary associations – the only real safeguard against excessive centralisation, which, in turn, destroys free *moeurs*.

It is fascinating to see how Tocqueville used these different senses of 'liberty' to develop his argument in *Democracy in America*. What was to be expected from the development of local freedom and flourishing voluntary associations? First of all, the multiplication of political rights would result. Citizens would no longer be passive spectators of the operations of government between periodic national elections. The right to influence the actions of government at all levels – local and regional as well as national – would gradually develop a sense of the citizen's duty to exercise such rights. Only in that way would representative government become a full reality. Representative institutions at the centre were not enough. They would always be precarious so long as they existed alone. Following the *Doctrinaires*, Tocqueville insisted that anything like the French attempt to combine representative institutions at the centre with a highly centralised administrative machine, an over-powerful executive, was fraught with danger for liberty (in all its senses).

The second advantage expected from the development of local freedom was an enhanced sense of individual independence from the state. That is, the exercise of political rights and participation in government would make people more aware of their civil rights and increase their determination to defend them against both administrative abuse and legislative encroachment. Indeed, participation (in a context of civil liberty) would be likely to lead to calls for new rights, for the extension of civil liberty. Developing a clearer and firmer sense of the meaning of rights, citizens would be less pliable, less likely to tolerate the infringement or contraction of civil liberties. Thus, Tocqueville did not believe that it was possible to define a timeless criterion which would settle once and for all the legitimate sphere of individual action. The improvement of government in the direction of greater participation would be a more effective motor of the growth of civil liberty.

The third and perhaps greatest advantage which Tocqueville and other French liberals expected to follow from the development of local freedom and participation was a sense of personal capacity. That is what they meant by the development of free *moeurs*. As we have seen, the liberals' concern with changes in social structure led them to apply the concept of liberty outside the sphere of political institutions. They became impressed by the advantages which an alert and active citizenry carried into all their social relations. That spirit could be satirised – and has been by later socialists – as the spirit of self-help, of Samuel Smiles. But that is a crude, reductionist account of what the French liberals had in mind. Like Rousseau, they were struck by *the moralising role of politics*. They did not take human wants or preferences as *given*, on the English utilitarian model. Rather, they pointed to the connection between wants and intentions and the structure of institutions. A despotic state administration, which subjected citizens to *la tutelle* on the French model, either undermines free *moeurs* (in a nation which has been free) or prevents them from developing. In such a society risk-taking and reliance on voluntary associations decline in favour of *place-seeking*. The immunities and security which state employment offers become the object of ambitions. The attitudes of the civil service become a kind of norm, and increasingly set the tone, even in the sphere of private or commercial activity.

Tocqueville and other French liberals were deeply impressed by the spirit of enterprise which underlay the growth of the British Empire and its prosperity. They traced it to the free *moeurs* – to the way the upper classes in Britain had retained the management of their own affairs, and had not been pushed aside by a centralised state machine. Yet Tocqueville saw that England, where social leveling had by no means reached the French condition, had yet to face the political hazards associated with a democratic social revolution.

He was constantly on the lookout for signs of administrative centralisation in England – and found them in various reforms of the 1830s and 40s such as the Poor Law Reform, the Factory Inspectorate, etc.

The new sociological mode of argument developed by the French liberals – their attempt to relate changes in social structure to changes in political institutions and ideas – amounted to a stunningly original breakthrough. The chief result was that these cautious liberals, almost despite themselves, became the first consistent champions of participation in modern political thought. At times that honour has been claimed for Rousseau. But his argument for participation in *Du contrat social* rests on assumptions and definitions which radically undermined its effectiveness. By assuming that 'real' self-government was possible only in a small community, Rousseau failed to develop an argument which could be applied to the reform of the nation-state. And by eroding the distinction between liberty and morality to the extent that he does, Rousseau blinded some later liberals – it might be argued – to the advantage of political participation. French liberals of the early nineteenth century avoided both these traps. They argued not so much for limited government as for the maximum possible sharing out of political power – so that devolution would in effect impose limits on the concentration of power and increase popular resistance to the infringement of civil liberties. Their interest in social structure led them to apply the concept of liberty to *moeurs* – in free *moeurs* – but *without* threatening the distinction between voluntary and coerced action as Rousseau had done. Tocqueville's didactic uses of the spirit of the New England township illustrates that.

This new mode of argument did not develop in English liberalism. Nothing illustrates that better than comparison of the writings of Tocqueville and his contemporary, J. S. Mill. Mill was brought up in a liberal tradition based on the primacy of the problem of knowledge (which led him to champion an inductivist programme), while the utilitarianism which provided the foundation of his political theory was methodologically individualist and unsociological. Thus, the liberalism of Mill's youth took little interest in tracing changing patterns of social and political organisation. Mill was himself struck by the difference on this point between French and English liberalism after he became acquainted with the Saint-Simonians and the writings of Guizot and Tocqueville. He came to admire their work greatly (as his reviews reveal), but he did not feel able to argue in the same fashion. Unable to argue in the new sociological mode, he was content to adopt some of the conclusions *without* the foundation of sociological argument which had given rise to them. Thus, in *On Liberty* and *Representative Government* we find Mill introducing themes from Tocqueville – the danger of centralisation, threats to local liberty and variety, the moralising role of politics.

None of these ideas had anything to do with the utiltarianism of Mill's youth. The utilitarian model for social policy was – as Tocqueville liked to point out – a highly centralising model. It laid emphasis exclusively on aggregation, on achieving the most 'rational' or desirable balance of satisfactions. Efficiency and rationality were its criteria for judging policy proposals. Utilitarianism, like classical economics, took wants as *given*. It was not interested in the ways in which different types of social organisation *shape* individual wants. Thus, it placed no obvious value on participation as such. Mill imported the themes of self-development and free *moeurs* from the more sociological tradition of French liberalism. He adapted them to the less historical mode of political argument he had been brought up in. Thus, Mill proceeds by putting forward general principles and deducing their consequences. But when he suddenly introduces threats to liberty such as uniformity or the tyranny of public opinion, the reader is rather puzzled. These threats seem to refer to particular social conditions, perhaps even a theory of social change. But what theory? What Mill has done is introduce some of the conclusions of the French liberals, without introducing their premises – the theory of social change on which they founded their political arguments.

Mill acknowledged his debt to Tocqueville. But he adapted themes from *Democracy in America* to a mode of argument unaffected by the new sociological mode of argument. Mill's way of arguing would not have been astonishing to, say, Locke, whereas Tocqueville's mode of argument might have seemed incomprehensible to the latter. By the early nineteenth century in France, the possibility of fundamental social change, of a social revolution so profound that the inherited hierarchy of European society was fragmented beyond recognition, had firmly established itself in the minds of French liberals. In England, on the other hand, the triumph of gradualism left the old structure of society largely intact. The early development of England beyond a caste society had long fascinated French liberals. But in the nineteenth century that very openness of English society helped to restrict the sphere of English liberal thought – preventing it from developing a systematic interest in social change, which became the badge of French liberalism. English liberals took the relatively open hierarchy of English society for granted. In that sense, it seems fair to say that much English liberal thought of the nineteenth and early twentieth century rested on a hidden sociological premise.

The contrast between Tocqueville and J. S. Mill is exceedingly instructive. Despite their friendship and influence on each other, Mill and Tocqueville represent two poles of liberal thought – two traditions which had diverged significantly by the mid-nineteenth century.

It is no accident that French liberals introduced the problem of mass society – of atomisation and centralisation – into the mainstream of modern political thought. By 1815 they were without illusions about the survival of an aristocratic society. Perhaps because the changes in French society were more sudden and violent, French liberal thought has since the early nineteenth century accepted that questions of political theory cannot be divorced from questions about social structure. The result has been a more historical, less a priori mode of argument from Tocqueville to Raymond Aron, with less attention paid to fine logical points and definitions, it is true, but with more concern to show how concepts are joined together in points of view or ideologies, and how these in turn spring out of particular social conditions and help to transform them. 'Change' is thus central to political theory for French liberals as for Marxists, and both offer a sharp contrast to the static model of argument which goes far back in the history of English liberalism.

CHARLES TAYLOR

What's Wrong with Negative Liberty

This is an attempt to resolve one of the issues that separate 'positive' and 'negative' theories of freedom, as these have been distinguished in Isaiah Berlin's seminal essay, 'Two Concepts of Liberty'.[1] Although one can discuss almost endlessly the detailed formulation of the distinction, I believe it is undeniable that there are two such families of conceptions of political freedom abroad in our civilisation.

Thus there clearly are theories, widely canvassed in liberal society, which want to define freedom exclusively in terms of the independence of the individual from interference by others, be these governments, corporations or private persons; and equally clearly these theories are challenged by those who believe that freedom resides at least in part in collective control over the common life. We unproblematically recognise theories descended from Rousseau and Marx as fitting in this category.

There is quite a gamut of views in each category. And this is worth bearing in mind, because it is too easy in the course of polemic to fix on the extreme, almost caricatural variants of each family. When people attack positive theories of freedom, they generally have some Left totalitarian theory in mind, according to which freedom resides exclusively in exercising collective control over one's destiny in a classless society, the kind of theory which underlies, for instance, official Communism. This view, in its caricaturally extreme form, refuses to recognise the freedoms guaranteed in other societies as genuine. The destruction of 'bourgeois freedoms' is no real loss of freedom, and coercion can be justified in the name of freedom if it is needed to bring into existence the classless society in which alone men are properly free. Men can, in short, be forced to be free.

Even as applied to official Communism, this portrait is a little extreme, although it undoubtedly expresses the inner logic of this kind of theory. But it is an absurd caricature if applied to the whole family of positive conceptions. This includes all those views of modern political life which owe something to the ancient republican tradition, according to which men's ruling themselves is seen as an acti-

[1] *F.E.L.*, pp. 118–72.

vity valuable in itself, and not only for instrumental reasons. It includes in its scope thinkers like Tocqueville, and even arguably the J. S. Mill of *On Representative Government*. It has no necessary connection with the view that freedom consists *purely and simply* in the collective control over the common life, or that there is no freedom worth the name outside a context of collective control. And it does not therefore generate necessarily a doctrine that men can be forced to be free.

On the other side, there is a corresponding caricatural version of negative freedom which tends to come to the fore. This is the tough-minded version, going back to Hobbes, or in another way to Bentham, which sees freedom simply as the absence of external physical or legal obstacles. This view will have no truck with other less immediately obvious obstacles to freedom, for instance, lack of awareness, or false consciousness, or repression, or other inner factors of this kind. It holds firmly to the view that to speak of such inner factors as relevant to the issue about freedom, to speak for instance of someone's being less free because of false consciousness, is to abuse words. The only clear meaning which can be given to freedom is that of the absence of external obstacles.

I call this view caricatural as a representative portrait of the negative view, because it rules out of court one of the most powerful motives behind the modern defence of freedom as individual independence, viz., the post-Romantic idea that each person's form of self-realisation is original to him/her, and can therefore only be worked out independently. This is one of the reasons for the defence of individual liberty by among others J. S. Mill (this time in his *On Liberty*). But if we think of freedom as including something like the freedom of self-fulfilment, or self-realisation according to our own pattern, then we plainly have something which can fail for inner reasons as well as because of external obstacles. We can fail to achieve our own self-realisation through inner fears, or false consciousness, as well as because of external coercion. Thus the modern notion of negative freedom which gives weight to the securing of each person's right to realise him/herself in his/her own way cannot make do with the Hobbes/Bentham notion of freedom. The moral psychology of these authors is too simple, or perhaps we should say too crude, for its purposes.

Now there is a strange asymmetry here. The extreme caricatural views tend to come to the fore in the polemic, as I mentioned above. But whereas the extreme 'forced-to-be-free' view is one which the opponents of positive liberty try to pin on them, as one would expect in the heat of argument, the proponents of negative liberty themselves often seem anxious to espouse their extreme, Hobbesian view. Thus even Isaiah Berlin, in his eloquent exposition of the two concepts of liberty, seems to quote Bentham[2] approvingly and Hobbes[3] as well. Why is this?

To see this we have to examine more closely what is at stake between the two views. The negative theories, as we saw, want to define freedom in terms of individual independence from others; the positive also want to identify freedom with collective self-government. But behind this lie some deeper differences of doctrines.

Isaiah Berlin points out that negative theories are concerned with the area in which the subject should be left without interference, whereas the positive doctrines are concerned with who or what controls. I should like to put the point behind this in a slightly different way. Doctrines of positive freedom are concerned with a view of freedom which involves essentially the exercising of control over one's life. On this view, one is free only to the extent that one has effectively determined oneself and the shape of one's life. The concept of freedom here is an exercise-concept.

By contrast, negative theories can rely simply on an opportunity-concept, where being free is a matter of what we can do, of what it is open to us to do, whether or not we do anything to exercise these options. This certainly is the case of the crude, original Hobbesian concept. Freedom consists just in there being no obstacle. It is a sufficient condition of one's being free that nothing stand in the way.

But we have to say that negative theories *can* rely on an opportunity-concept, rather than that they necessarily do so rely, for we have to allow for that part of the gamut of negative theories mentioned above which incorporates some notion of self-realisation. Plainly this kind of view can't rely simply on an opportunity-concept. We can't say that someone is free, on a self-realisation view, if he is totally unrealised, if for instance he is totally unaware of his potential, if fulfilling it has never even arisen as a question for him, or if he is paralysed by the fear of breaking with some norm which he has internalised but which does not authentically reflect him. Within this conceptual scheme, some degree of exercise is necessary for a man to be thought free. Or if we want to think of the internal bars to freedom as obstacles on all fours with the external ones, then being in a position to exercise freedom, having the oppor-

[2] *F.E.L.*, p. 148, note 1.
[3] ibid., p. 164.

tunity, involves removing the internal barriers; and this is not possible without having to some extent realised myself. So that with the freedom of self-realisation, having the opportunity to be free requires that I already be exercising freedom. A pure opportunity-concept is impossible here.

But if negative theories can be grounded on either an opportunity- or an exercise-concept, the same is not true of positive theories. The view that freedom involves at least partially collective self-rule is essentially grounded on an exercise-concept. For this view (at least partly) identifies freedom with self-direction, i.e., the actual exercise of directing control over one's life.

But this already gives us a hint towards illuminating the above paradox, that while the extreme variant of positive freedom is usually pinned on its protagonists by their opponents, negative theorists seem prone to embrace the crudest versions of their theory themselves. For if an opportunity-concept is incombinable with a positive theory, but either it or its alternative can suit a negative theory, then one way of ruling out positive theories in principle is by firmly espousing an opportunity-concept. One cuts off the positive theories by the root, as it were, even though one may also pay a price in the atrophy of a wide range of negative theories as well. At least by taking one's stand firmly on the crude side of the negative range, where only opportunity concepts are recognised, one leaves no place for a positive theory to grow.

Taking one's stand here has the advantage that one is holding the line around a very simple and basic issue of principle, and one where the negative view seems to have some backing in common sense. The basic intuition here is that freedom is a matter of being able to do something or other, of not having obstacles in one's way, rather than being a capacity that we have to realise. It naturally seems more prudent to fight the Totalitarian Menace at this last-ditch position, digging in behind the natural frontier of this simple issue, rather than engaging the enemy on the open terrain of exercise-concepts, where one will have to fight to discriminate the good from the bad among such concepts; fight, for instance, for a view of individual self-realisation against various notions of collective self-realisation, of a nation, or a class. It seems easier and safer to cut all the nonsense off at the start by declaring all self-realisation views to be metaphysical hog-wash. Freedom should just be tough-mindedly defined as the absence of external obstacles.

Of course, there are independent reasons for wanting to define freedom tough-mindedly. In particular there is the immense influence of the anti-metaphysical, materialist, natural-science-oriented temper of thought in our civilisation. Something of this spirit at its inception induced Hobbes to take the line that he did, and the same spirit goes marching on today. Indeed, it is because of the prevalence of ths spirit that the line is so easy to defend, forensically speaking, in our society.

Nevertheless, I think that one of the strongest motives for defending the crude Hobbes-Bentham concept, that freedom is the absence of external obstacles, physical or legal, is the strategic one above. For most of those who take this line thereby abandon many of their own intuitions, sharing as they do with the rest of us in a post-Romantic civilisation which puts great value on self-realisation, and values freedom largely because of this. It is fear of the Totalitarian Menace, I would argue, which has led them to abandon this terrain to the enemy.

I want to argue that this not only robs their eventual forensic victory of much of its value, since they become incapable of defending liberalism in the form we in fact value it, but I want to make the stronger claim that this Maginot Line mentality actually ensures defeat, as is often the case with Maginot Line mentalities. The Hobbes-Bentham view, I want to argue, is indefensible as a view of freedom.

To see this, let's examine the line more closely, and the temptation to stand on it. The advantage of the view that freedom is the absence of external obstacles is its simplicity. It allows us to say that freedom is being able to do what you want, where what you want is unproblematically understood as what the agent can identify as his desires. By contrast an exercise-concept of freedom requires that we discriminate among motivations. If we are free in the exercise of certain capacities, then we are not free, or less free, when these capacities are in some way unfulfilled or blocked. But the obstacles can be internal as well as external. And this must be so, for the capacities relevant to freedom must involve some self-awareness, self-understanding, moral discrimination and self-control, otherwise their exercise couldn't amount to freedom in the sense of self-direction; and this being so, we can fail to be free because these internal conditions are not realised. But where this happens, where, for example, we are quite self-deceived, or utterly fail to discriminate properly the ends we seek, or have lost self-control, we can quite easily be doing what we want in the sense of what we can identify as our wants, without being free; indeed, we can be further entrenching our unfreedom.

Once one adopts a self-realisation view, or indeed, any exercise-concept of freedom, then being able to do what one wants can no longer be accepted as a sufficient condition of being free. For this view puts certain conditions on one's motivation. You are not free if you are motivated, through fear, inauthentically internalised standards, or false consciousness, to thwart your self-realisation. This is sometimes put by saying that for a self-realisation view, you have to be able to do what you really want, or to follow your real will, or to fulfil the desires of your own true self. But these formulas, particularly the last, may mislead, by making us think that exercise concepts of freedom are tied to some particular metaphysic, in particular that of a higher and lower self. We shall see below that this is far from being the case, and that there is a much wider range of bases for discriminating authentic and inauthentic desires.

In any case, the point for our discussion here is that for an exercise-concept of freedom, being free can't just be a question of doing what you want in the unproblematic sense. It must also be that what you want doesn't run against the grain of your basic purposes, or your self-realisation. Or to put the issue in another way, which converges on the same point, the subject himself can't be the final authority on the question whether he is free; for he cannot be the final authority on the question whether his desires are authentic, whether they do or do not frustrate his purposes.

To put the issue in this second way is to make more palpable the temptation for defenders of the negative view to hold their Maginot Line. For once we admit that the agent himself is not the final authority on his own freedom, do we not open the way to totalitarian manipulation? Do we not legitimate others, supposedly wiser about his purposes than himself, redirecting his feet on the right path, perhaps even by force, and all this in the name of freedom?

The answer is that of course we don't. Not by this concession alone. For there may also be good reasons for holding that others are not likely to be in a better position to understand his real purposes. This indeed plausibly follows from the post-Romantic view above that each person has his/her own original form of realisation. Some others, who know us intimately, and who surpass us in wisdom, are undoubtedly in a position to advise us, but no official body can possess a doctrine or a technique whereby they could know how to put us on the rails, because such a doctrine or technique cannot in principle exist if human beings really differ in their self-realisation.

Or again, we may hold a self-realisation view of freedom, and hence believe that there are certain conditions on my motivation necessary to my being free, but also believe that there are other necessary conditions which rule out my being forcibly led towards some definition of my self-realisation by external authority. Indeed, in these last two paragraphs I have given a portrait of what I think is a very widely held view in liberal society, a view which values self-realisation, and accepts that it can fail for internal reasons, but which believes that no valid guidance can be provided in principle by social authority, because of human diversity and originality, and holds that the attempt to impose such guidance will destroy other necessary conditions of freedom.

It is however true that totalitarian theories of positive freedom do build on a conception which involves discriminating between motivations. Indeed, one can represent the path from the negative to the positive conceptions of freedom as consisting of two steps: the first moves us from a notion of freedom as doing what one wants to a notion which discriminates motivations and equates freedom with doing what we really want, or obeying our real will, or truly directing our lives. The second step introduces some doctrine purporting to show that we cannot do what we really want, or follow our real will, outside of a society of a certain canonical form, incorporating true self-government. It follows that we can only be free in such a society, and that being free *is* governing ourselves collectively according to this canonical form.

We might see an example of this second step in Rousseau's view that only a social contract society in which all give themselves totally to the whole preserves us from other-dependence and ensures that we obey only ourselves; or in Marx's doctrine of man as a species-being who realises his potential in a mode of social production, and who must thus take control of this mode collectively.

Faced with this two-step process, it seems safer and easier to stop it at the first step, to insist firmly that freedom is just a matter of the absence of external obstacles, that it therefore involves no discrimination of motivation and permits in principle no second-guessing of the subject by any one else. This is the essence of the Maginot Line strategy. It is very tempting. But I want to claim that it is wrong. I want to argue that we cannot defend a view of freedom which doesn't involve at least some qualitative discrimination as to motive, i.e., which doesn't put some restrictions on motivation among the necessary conditions of freedom, and hence which could rule out second-guessing in principle.

There are some considerations one can put forward straight off to show that the pure Hobbesian concept won't work, that there are some discriminations among motivations which are essential to the concept of freedom as we use it. Even where we think of freedom as the absence of external obstacles, it is not the absence of such obstacles *simpliciter*. For we make discriminations between obstacles as representing more or less serious infringements of freedom. And we do this, because we deploy the concept against a background understanding that certain goals and activities are more significant than others.

Thus we could say that my freedom is restricted if the local authority puts up a new traffic light at an intersection close to my home; so that where previously I could cross as I liked, consistently with avoiding collision with other cars, now I have to wait until the light is green. In a philosophical argument, we might call this a restriction of freedom, but not in a serious political debate. The reason is that it is too trivial, the activity and purposes inhibited here are not really significant. It is not just a matter of our having made a trade-off, and considered that a small loss of liberty was worth fewer traffic accidents, or less danger for the children; we are reluctant to speak here of a loss of liberty at all; what we feel we are trading off is convenience against safety.

By contrast a law which forbids me from worshipping according to the form I believe in is a serious blow to liberty; even a law which tried to restrict this to certain times (as the traffic light restricts my crossing of the intersection to certain times) would be seen as a serious restriction. Why this difference between the two cases? Because we have a background understanding, too obvious to spell out, of some activities and goals as highly significant for human beings and others as less so. One's religious belief is recognised, even by atheists, as supremely important, because it is that by which the believer defines himself as a moral being. By contrast my rhythm of movement through the city traffic is trivial. We don't want to speak of these two in the same breath. We don't even readily admit that liberty is at stake in the traffic light case. For *de minimis non curat libertas*.

But this recourse to significance takes us beyond a Hobbesian scheme. Freedom is no longer just the absence of external obstacle *tout court*, but the absence of external obstacle to significant action, to what is important to man. There are discriminations to be made; some restrictions are more serious than others, some are utterly trivial. About many, there is of course controversy. But what the judgement turns on is some sense of what is significant for human life. Restricting the expression of people's religious and ethical convictions is more significant than restricting their movement around uninhabited parts of the country; and both are more significant than the trivia of traffic control.

But the Hobbesian scheme has no place for the notion of significance. It will allow only for purely quantitative judgements. On the toughest-minded version of his conception, where Hobbes seems to be about to define liberty in terms of the absence of physical obstacles, one is presented with the vertiginous prospect of human freedom being measurable in the same way as the degrees of freedom of some physical object, say a lever. Later we see that this won't do, because we have to take account of legal obstacles to my action. But in any case, such a quantitative conception of freedom is a non-starter.

Consider the following diabolical defence of Albania as a free country. We recognise that religion has been abolished in Albania, whereas it hasn't been in Britain. But on the other hand there are probably far fewer traffic lights per head in Tirana than in London. (I haven't checked for myself, but this is a very plausible assumption.) Suppose an apologist for Albanian Socialism were nevertheless to claim that this country was freer than Britain, because the number of acts restricted was far smaller. After all, only a minority of Londoners practise some religion in public places, but all have to negotiate their way through traffic. Those who do practise a religion generally do so on one day of the week, while they are held up at traffic lights every day. In sheer quantitative terms, the number of acts restricted by traffic lights must be greater than that restricted by a ban on public religious practice. So if Britain is considered a free society, why not Albania?

So the application even of our negative notion of freedom requires a background conception of what is significant, according to which some restrictions are seen to be without relevance for freedom altogether, and others are judged as being of greater and lesser importance. So some discrimination among motivations seems essential to our concept of freedom. A minute's reflection shows why this must be so. Freedom is important to us because we are purposive beings. But then there must be distinctions in the significance of different kinds of freedom based on the distinction in the significance of different purposes.

But of course, this still doesn't involve the kind of discrimination mentioned above, the kind which would allow us to say that someone who was doing what he wanted (in the unproblematic sense) wasn't really free, the kind of discrimination which allows us to put conditions on people's motivations necessary to their being free, and hence to second-guess them. All we have shown is that we make discriminations between more or less significant freedoms, based on discriminations among the purposes people have.

This creates some embarrassment for the crude negative theory, but it can cope with it by simply adding a recognition that we make judgements of significance. Its central claim that freedom just is the absence of external obstacles seems untouched, as also its view of freedom as an opportunity-concept. It is just that we now have to admit that not all opportunities are equal.

But there is more trouble in store for the crude view when we examine further what these qualitative discriminations are based on. What lies behind our judging certain purposes/feelings as more significant than others? One might think that there was room here again for another quantitative theory; that the more significant purposes are those we want more. But this account is either vacuous or false.

It is true but vacuous if we take wanting more just to mean being more significant. It is false as soon as we try to give wanting more an independent criterion, such as, for instance, the urgency or force of a desire, or the prevalence of one desire over another, because it is a matter of the most banal experience that the purposes we know to be more significant are not always those which we desire with the greatest urgency to encompass, nor the ones that actually always win out in cases of conflict of desires.

When we reflect on this kind of significance, we come up against what I have called elsewhere the fact of strong evaluation, the fact that we human subjects are not only subjects of first-order desires, but of second-order desires, desires about desires. We experience our desires and purposes as qualitatively discriminated, as higher or lower, noble or base, integrated or fragmented, significant or trivial, good and bad. This means that we experience some of our desires and goals as intrinsically more significant than others: some passing comfort is less important than the fulfilment of our lifetime vocation, our *amour propre* less important than a love relationship; while we experience some others as bad, not just comparatively, but absolutely: we desire not to be moved by spite, or some childish desire to impress at all costs. And these judgements of significance are quite independent of the strength of the respective desires: the craving for comfort may be overwhelming at this moment, we may be obsessed with our *amour propre*, but the judgement of significance stands.

But then the question arises whether this fact of strong evaluation doesn't have other consequences for our notion of freedom, than just that it permits us to rank freedoms in importance. Is freedom not at stake when we find ourselves carried away by a less significant goal to override a highly significant one? Or when we are led to act out of a motive we consider bad or despicable?

The answer is that we sometimes do speak in this way. Suppose I have some irrational fear, which is preventing me from doing something I very much want to do. Say the fear of public speaking is preventing me from taking up a career that I should find very fulfilling, and that I should be quite good at, if I could just get over this 'hang-up'. It is clear that we experience this fear as an obstacle, and that we feel we are less than we would be if we could overcome it.

Or again, consider the case where I am very attached to comfort. To go on short rations, and to miss my creature comforts for a time, makes me very depressed. I find myself making a big thing of this. Because of this reaction I can't do certain things that I should like very much to do, such as going on an expedition over the Andes, or a canoe trip in the Yukon. Once again, it is quite understandable if I experience this attachment as an obstacle, and feel that I should be freer without it.

Or I could find that my spiteful feelings and reactions which I almost can't inhibit are undermining a relationship which is terribly important to me. At times, I feel as though I am almost assisting as a helpless witness at my own destructive behaviour, as I lash out again with my unbridled tongue at her. I long to be able not to feel this spite. As long as I feel it, even control is not an option, because it just builds up inside until it either bursts out, or else the feeling somehow communicates itself, and queers things between us. I long to be free of this feeling.

These are quite understandable cases, where we can speak of freedom or its absence without strain. What I have called strong evaluation is essentially involved here. For these are not just cases of conflict, even cases of painful conflict. If the conflict is between two desires with which I have no trouble identifying, there can be no talk of lesser freedom, no matter how painful or fateful. Thus if what is breaking up my relationship is my finding fulfilment in a job which, say, takes me away from home a lot, I have indeed a terrible conflict, but I would have no temptation to speak of myself as less free.

Even seeing a great difference in the significance of the two terms doesn't seem to be a sufficient condition of my wanting to speak of freedom and its absence. Thus my marriage may be breaking up because I like going to the pub and playing cards on Saturday nights with the boys. I may feel quite unequivocally that my marriage is much more important than the release and comradeship of the Saturday night bash. But nevertheless I wouldn't want to talk of my being freer if I could slough off this desire.

The difference seems to be that in this case, unlike the ones above, I still identify with the less important desire, I still see it as expressive of myself, so that I couldn't lose it without altering who I am, losing something of my personality. Whereas my irrational fear, my being quite distressed by discomfort, my spite – these are all things which I can easily see myself losing without any loss whatsoever to what I am. This is why I can see them as obstacles to my purposes, and hence to my freedom, even though they are in a sense unquestionably desires and feelings of mine.

Before exploring further what's involved in this, let's go back and keep score. It would seem that these cases make a bigger breach in the crude negative theory. For they seem to be cases in which the obstacles to freedom are internal; and if this is so, then freedom can't simply be interpreted as the absence of *external* obstacles; and the fact that I'm doing what I want, in the sense of following my strongest desire, isn't sufficient to establish that I'm free. On the contrary, we have to make discriminations among motivations, and accept that acting out of some motivations, for example irrational fear or spite, or this too great need for comfort, is not freedom, is even a negation of freedom.

But although the crude negative theory can't be sustained in the face of these examples, perhaps something which springs from the same concerns can be reconstructed. For although we have to admit that there are internal, motivational, necessary conditions for freedom, we can perhaps still avoid any legitimation of what I called above the second-guessing of the subject. If our negative theory allows for strong evaluation, allows that some goals are really important to us, and that other desires are seen as not fully ours, then can it not retain the thesis that freedom is being able to do what I want, that is, what I can identify myself as wanting, where this means not just what I identify as my strongest desire, but what I identify as my true, authentic desire or purpose? The subject would still be the final arbiter of his being free/unfree, as indeed he is clearly capable of discerning this in the examples above, where I relied precisely on the subject's own experience of constraint, of motives with which he can't identify. We should have sloughed off the untenable Hobbesian reductive-materialist metaphysics, according to which only external obstacles count, as though action were just movement, and there could be no internal, motivational obstacles to our deeper purposes. But we would be retaining the basic concern of the negative theory, that the subject is still the final authority as to what his freedom consists in, and cannot be second-guessed by external authority. Freedom would be modified to read: the absence of internal or external obstacle to what I truly or authentically want. But we would still be holding the Maginot Line. Or would we?

I think not, in fact. I think that this hybrid or middle position is untenable, where we are willing to admit that we can speak of what we truly want, as against what we most strongly desire, and of some desires as obstacles to our freedom, while we still will not allow for second-guessing. For to rule this out in principle is to rule out in principle that the subject can ever be wrong about what he truly wants. And how can he never, in principle, be wrong, unless there is nothing to be right or wrong about in this matter?

That in fact is the thesis our negative theorist will have to defend. And it is a plausible one for the same intellectual (reductive-empiricist) tradition from which the crude negative theory springs. On this view, our feelings are brute facts about us; that is, it is a fact about us that we are affected in such and such a way, but our feelings can't themselves be understood as involving some perception or sense of what they relate to, and hence as potentially veridical or illusory, authentic or inauthentic. On this scheme, the fact that a certain desire represented one of our fundamental purposes, and another a mere force with which we cannot identify, would concern merely the brute quality of the affect in both cases. It would be a matter of the raw feel of these two desires that this was their respective status.

In such circumstances, the subject's own classification would be incorrigible. There is no such thing as an imperceptible raw feel. If the subject failed to experience a certain desire as fundamental, and if what we meant by 'fundamental' applied to desire was that the felt experience of it has a certain quality, then the desire couldn't be fundamental. We can see this if we look at those feelings which we can agree are brute in this sense: for instance, the stab of pain I feel when the dentist jabs into my tooth, or the crawling unease when someone runs his fingernail along the blackboard. There can be no question of misperception here. If I fail to 'perceive' the pain, I am not in pain. Might it not be so with our fundamental desires, and those which we repudiate?

The answer is clearly no. For first of all, many of our feelings and desires, including the relevant ones for these kinds of conflicts, are not brute. By contrast with pain and the fingernail-on-blackboard sensation, shame and fear, for instance, are emotions which involve our experiencing the situation as bearing a certain import for us, as being dangerous or shameful. This is why shame and fear can be inappropriate, or even irrational, where pain and a frisson cannot. Thus we can be in error in feeling shame or fear. We can even be consciously aware of the unfounded nature of our feelings, and this is when we castigate them as irrational.

Thus the notion that we can understand all our feelings and desires as brute, in the above sense, is not on. But more, the idea that we could discriminate our fundamental desires, or those which we want to repudiate, by the quality of brute affect is grotesque. When I am convinced that some career, or an expedition in the Andes, or a love relationship, is of fundamental importance to me (to recur to the above examples), it cannot be just because of the throbs, *élans* or tremors I feel; I must also have some sense that these are of great significance for me, meet important, long-lasting needs, represent a fulfilment of something central to me, will bring me closer to what I really am, or something of the sort. The whole notion of our identity, whereby we recognise that some goals, desires, allegiances are central to what we are, while others are not or are less so, can make sense only against a background of desires and feelings which are not brute, but what I shall call import-attributing, to invent a term of art for the occasion.

Thus we have to see our emotional life as made up largely of import-attributing desires and feelings, that is, desires and feelings which we can experience mistakenly. And not only can we be mistaken in this, we clearly must accept, in cases like the above where we want to repudiate certain desires, that we are mistaken.

For let us consider the distinction mentioned above between conflicts where we feel fettered by one desire, and those where we do not, where, for instance, in the example mentioned above, a man is torn between his career and his marriage. What made the difference was that in the case of genuine conflict both desires are the agent's, whereas in the cases where he feels fettered by one, this desire is one he wants to repudiate.

But what is it to feel that a desire is not truly mine? Presumably, I feel that I should be better off without it, that I don't lose anything in getting rid of it, I remain quite complete without it. What could lie behind this sense?

Well, one could imagine feeling this about a brute desire. I may feel this about my addiction to smoking, for instance – wish I could get rid of it, experience it as a fetter, and believe that I should be well rid of it. But addictions are a special case; we understand them to be unnatural, externally-induced desires. We couldn't say in general that we are ready to envisage losing our brute desires without a sense of diminution. On the contrary, to lose my desire for, and hence delectation in, oysters, mushroom pizza, or Peking duck would be a terrible deprivation. I should fight against such a change with all the strength at my disposal.

So being brute is not what makes desires repudiable. And besides, in the above examples the repudiated desires aren't brute. In the first case, I am chained by unreasoning fear, an import-attributing emotion, in which the fact of being mistaken is already recognised when I identify the fear as irrational or unreasoning. Spite, too, which moves me in the third case, is an import-attributing emotion. To feel spite is to see oneself and the target of one's resentment in a certain light; it is to feel in some way wounded, or damaged, by his success or good fortune, and the more hurt the more he is fortunate. To overcome feelings of spite, as against just holding them in, is to come to see self and other in a different light, in particular, to set aside self-pity, and the sense of being personally wounded by what the other does and is.

(I should also like to claim that the obstacle in the third example, the too great attachment to comfort, while not itself import-attributing, is also bound up with the way we see things. The problem is here not just that we dislike discomfort, but that we are too easily depressed by it; and this is something which we overcome only by sensing a different order of priorities, whereby small discomforts matter less. But if this is thought too dubious, we can concentrate on the other two examples.)

Now how can we feel that an import-attributing desire is not truly ours? We can do this only if we see it as mistaken, that is, the import or the good it supposedly gives us a sense of is not a genuine import or good. The irrational fear is a fetter, because it is irrational; spite is a fetter because it is rooted in a self-absorption which distorts our perspective on everything, and the pleasures of venting it preclude any genuine satisfaction. Losing these desires we lose nothing, because their loss deprives us of no genuine good or pleasure or satisfaction. In this they are quite different from my love of oysters, mushroom pizza and Peking duck.

It would appear from this that to see our desires as brute gives us no clue as to why some of them are repudiable. On the contrary it is precisely their not being brute which can explain this. It is because they are import-attributing desires which are mistaken that we can feel that we would lose nothing in sloughing them off. Everything which is truly important to us would be safeguarded. If they were just brute desires, we couldn't feel this unequivocally, as we certainly do not when it comes to the pleasures of the palate. True, we also feel that our desire to smoke is repudiable, but there is a special explanation here, which is not available in the case of spite.

Thus we can experience some desires as fetters, because we can experience them as not ours. And we can experience them as not ours because we see them as incorporating a quite erroneous appreciation of our situation and of what matters to us. We can see this again if we contrast the case of spite with that of another emotion which partly overlaps, and which is highly considered in some societies, the desire for revenge. In certain traditional societies this is far from being considered a despicable emotion. On the contrary, it is a duty of honour on a male relative to avenge a man's death. We might imagine that this too might give rise to conflict. It might conflict with the attempts of a new regime to bring some order to the land. The government would have to stop people taking vengeance, in the name of peace.

But short of a conversion to a new ethical outlook, this would be seen as a trade-off, the sacrifice of one legitimate goal for the sake of another. And it would seem monstrous were one to propose reconditioning people so that they no longer felt the desire to avenge their kin. This would be to unman them.[4]

Why do we feel so different about spite (and for that matter also revenge)? Because the desire for revenge for an ancient Icelander was his sense of a real obligation incumbent on him, something it would be dishonourable to repudiate; while for us, spite is the child of a distorted perspective on things.

We cannot therefore understand our desires and emotions as all brute, and in particular we cannot make sense of our discrimination of some desires as more important and fundamental, or of our repudiation of others, unless we understand our feelings to be import-attributing. This is essential to there being what we have called strong evaluation. Consequently the half-way position which admits strong evaluation, admits that our desires may frustrate our deeper purposes, admits therefore that there may be inner obstacles

[4] Compare the unease we feel at the reconditioning of the hero of Anthony Burgess's *A Clockwork Orange*.

to freedom, and yet will not admit that the subject may be wrong or mistaken about these purposes – this position doesn't seem tenable. For the only way to make the subject's assessment incorrigible in principle would be to claim that there was nothing to be right or wrong about here; and that could only be so if experiencing a given feeling were a matter of the qualities of brute feeling. But this it cannot be if we are to make sense of the whole background of strong evaluation, more significant goals, and aims that we repudiate. This whole scheme requires that we understand the emotions concerned as import-attributing, as, indeed, it is clear that we must do on other grounds as well.

But once we admit that our feelings are import-attributing, then we admit the possibility of error, or false appreciation. And indeed, we have to admit a kind of false appreciation which the agent himself detects in order to make sense of the cases where we experience our own desires as fetters. How can we exclude in principle that there may be other false appreciations which the agent does not detect? That he may be profoundly in error, that is, have a very distorted sense of his fundamental purposes? Who can say that such people can't exist? All cases are, of course, controversial; but I should nominate Charles Manson and Andreas Baader for this category, among others. I pick them out as people with a strong sense of some purposes and goals as incomparably more fundamental than others, or at least with a propensity to act the having such a sense so as to take in even themselves a good part of the time, but whose sense of fundamental purpose was shot through with confusion and error. And once we recognise such extreme cases, how avoid admitting that many of the rest of mankind can suffer to a lesser degree from the same disabilities?

What has this got to do with freedom? Well, to resume what we have seen: our attributions of freedom make sense against a background sense of more and less significant purposes, for the question of freedom/unfreedom is bound up with the frustration/fulfilment of our purposes. Further, our significant purposes can be frustrated by our own desires, and where these are sufficiently based on misappreciation, we consider them as not really ours, and experience them as fetters. A man's freedom can therefore be hemmed in by internal, motivational obstacles, as well as external ones. A man who is driven by spite to jeopardise his most important relationships, in spite of himself, as it were, or who is prevented by unreasoning fear from taking up the career he truly wants, is not really made more free if one lifts the external obstacles to his venting his spite or acting on his fear. Or at best he is liberated into a very impoverished freedom.

If through linguistic/ideological purism one wants to stick to the crude definition, and insist that men are equally freed from whom the same external obstacles are lifted, regardless of their motivational state, then one will just have to introduce some other term to mark the distinction, and say that one man is capable of taking proper advantage of his freedom, and the other (the one in the grip of spite, or fear) is not. This is because in the meaningful sense of 'free', that for which we value it, in the sense of being able to act on one's important purposes, the internally fettered man is not free. If we choose to give 'free' a special (Hobbesian) sense which avoids this issue, we'll just have to introduce another term to deal with it.

Moreover since we have already seen that we are always making judgements of degrees of freedom, based on the significance of the activities or purposes which are left unfettered, how can we deny that the man, externally free but still stymied by his repudiated desires, is less free than one who has no such inner obstacles?

But if this is so, then can we not say of the man with a highly distorted view of his fundamental purpose, the Manson or Baader of my discussion above, that he may not be significantly freer when we lift even the internal barriers to his doing what is in line with this purpose, or at best may be liberated into a very impoverished freedom? Should a Manson overcome his last remaining compunction against sending his minions to kill on caprice, so that he could act unchecked, would we consider him freer, as we should undoubtedly consider the man who had done away with spite or unreasoning fear? Hardly, and certainly not to the same degree. For what he sees as his purpose here partakes so much of the nature of spite and unreasoning fear in the other cases, that is, it is an aspiration largely shaped by confusion, illusion and distorted perspective.

Once we see that we make distinctions of degree and significance in freedoms depending on the significance of the purpose fettered/enabled, how can we deny that it makes a difference to the degree of freedom not only whether one of my basic purposes is frustrated by my own desires but also whether I have grievously misidentified this purpose? The only way to avoid this would be to hold that there is no such thing as getting it wrong, that your basic purpose is just what you feel it to be. But there is such a thing as getting it wrong, as we have seen, and the very distinctions of significance depend on this fact.

But if this is so, then the crude negative view of freedom, the

Hobbesian definition, is untenable. Freedom can't just be the absence of external obstacles, for there may also be internal ones. And nor may the internal obstacles be just confined to those that the subject identifies as such, so that he is the final arbiter; for he may be profoundly mistaken about his purposes and about what he wants to repudiate. And if so, he is less capable of freedom in the meaningful sense of the word. Hence we cannot maintain the incorrigibility of the subject's judgements about his freedom, or rule out second-guessing, as we put it above. And at the same time, we are forced to abandon the pure opportunity-concept of freedom.

For freedom now involves my being able to recognise adequately my more important purposes, and my being able to overcome or at least neutralise my motivational fetters, as well as my way being free of external obstacles. But clearly the first condition (and, I would argue, also the second) require me to have become something, to have achieved a certain condition of self-clairvoyance and self-understanding. I must be actually exercising self-understanding in order to be truly or fully free. I can no longer understand freedom just as an opportunity-concept.

In all these three formulations of the issue – opportunity- versus exercise-concept; whether freedom requires that we discriminate among motivations; whether it allows of second-guessing the subject – the extreme negative view shows up as wrong. The idea of holding the Maginot Line before this Hobbesian concept is misguided not only because it involves abandoning some of the most inspiring terrain of liberalism, which is concerned with individual self-realisation, but also because the line turns out to be untenable. The first step from the Hobbesian definition to a positive notion, to a view of freedom as the ability to fulfil my purposes, and as being greater the more significant the purposes, is one we cannot help taking. Whether we must also take the second step, to a view of freedom which sees it as realisable or fully realisable only within a certain form of society; and whether in taking a step of this kind one is necessarily committed to justifying the excesses of totalitarian oppression in the name of liberty; these are questions which must now be addressed. What is certain is that they cannot simply be evaded by a philistine definition of freedom which relegates them by fiat to the limbo of metaphysical pseudo-questions. This is altogether too quick a way with them.

FRANCO VENTURI

'Venise et, par occasion, de la liberté'

Translated from the Italian by David Robey

The publication in 1748 of the *Esprit des loix* reopened for European public opinion the problem, among many others, of Venice. The impressions, some interesting and some disappointing, which Montesquieu took back with him from his stay on the lagoon in 1728 were now superseded; the case of the Republic of St Mark was too important politically for him to let himself be dominated completely by the memory of the atmosphere of tiredness and abandon which had then struck him. 'No more strength, commerce, riches, laws; only debauchery there has the name of liberty', he had written to the Duke of Berwick on 15 September, just as he was leaving the *Dominante*. And yet, he had finally concluded, without Venice it was impossible to understand the 'nature of aristocracy', or to see how the fundamental concepts of equality and liberty operated in this form of government.

Indeed, in spite of the inequality everywhere to be seen between rich and poor, between the ruling city and its provinces, in spite of its clear lack of economic, social and political balance, Venice had still kept alive that urge towards equality which stood at the root of every republic, in contrast with what happened in despotic and monarchical regimes, where 'everyone aims for superiority'.[1] It was at Venice that one could observe closely what occurred when this egalitarian urge was implanted in a system that was not democratic but aristocratic. The result was a whole series of compromises, adaptations, cunning constitutional and legislative measures undertaken in order to keep alive the 'spirit of equality', but without placing in doubt or in danger the very basis of the State – the fact, that is, that power was limited to a restricted number of nobles. Ancient Rome and the republics of antiquity, in general, like those of the modern era, had made similar experiments; but the example of Venice was especially noteworthy. Venice had shown itself capable of obeying the fundamental imperative of such a regime, where 'the aristocratic

[1] *De l'esprit des lois*, book 5, chapter 4.

families must, as far as possible, become part of the people'. 'The closer an aristocracy comes to democracy, the more perfect it is; as it approaches monarchy, so it becomes less perfect.' It was sufficient to compare Venice with Poland, another aristocratic republic, in order to see that, however far the former was from perfection, it was not tainted by the latter's sin of joining social to political slavery, by making the peasants the serfs of the nobility.[2] Similarly the Venetians had acted 'very wisely' over the delicate problem of the relationship between the *Dominante*'s patricians and the mainland nobility. In this as well they had drawn on that 'spirit of moderation' which is an indispensable substitute in every aristocracy for the virtue and equality that operate in democracies, a spirit of moderation with which the ruling class's customs as well as laws must be permeated. 'Modesty and simplicity of manners are the strength of an aristocratic nobility . . . it merges with the people, it makes it share all its pleasures.' On the other hand the Venetians had succeeded in avoiding the two greatest dangers that threaten every republic: 'the extreme inequality of those that govern and those that are governed', as well as the 'same inequality between the different members of the governing body'. Nor, in order to escape these dangers, had they ever considered turning to forcible redistributions of wealth, to agrarian laws, etc., but had rightly limited themselves to abolishing rights of primogeniture or majorats, the privileges, that is, of the nobility.[3] No doubt the very fact that the aristocracy had become hereditary undermined the principle of republican equality, and made any authentic 'moderation' difficult, indeed risked transforming Venice into a 'despotic republic with a multiplicity of despots'. But it also had to be admitted that 'Venice is one of the republics that best compensated, through its laws, for the disadvantages of hereditary aristocracy.'[4]

Nevertheless, in spite of such clever adjustments, even there, in the heart of the Venetian republic, despotism reared its ugly head. One needed only to look at the 'mouth of stone', where anyone could place an accusation: 'you would say it is the mouth of tyranny'.[5] Behind it stood the Council of Ten and the State Inquisitors. These were also a political instrument whose purpose was to keep alive artificially the constantly threatened structure of the republic, to re-establish, with their 'exorbitant power', a balance that was ever in

2 ibid., book 2, chapter 3.
3 ibid., book 5, chapter 8.
4 ibid., book 8, chapter 5.
5 ibid., book 5, chapter 8.

danger. The Spartan Ephors and the Roman Dictators had had a similar function. But in Venice it was a matter, not of defending the aristocracy against the people, as had been the case in the republics of antiquity, but of preserving equality within the body of the nobility, of settling, that is, the struggles between families and groups. Hence the secret, occult character of this Venetian magistrature, 'because the crimes that it punishes are always deep, and always grow in secret and in silence'.[6]

The spirit of equality therefore survived in Venice, filtered and channelled through the most diverse expedients. Liberty, on the other hand, was in grave danger, permanently threatened by the power of the *inquisition générale* and by the restriction in numbers of the nobility. From this last point of view the comparison with monarchies was, in the end, unfavourable to republics. In the famous chapter on the British constitution, Montesquieu observed that in the republics of Italy a true division of powers was impossible; legislation, government and justice always finished up in the hands of the same persons or the same families. For this reason liberty dwelt there less easily than in monarchies. One only had to observe Venice to be persuaded of this; sometimes the means of government which it used were as violent as those of the government of Turkey. It had to be admitted, however, that the 'pure hereditary aristocracy of the Italian republics does not exactly correspond to Asian despotism'.[7] Their rule was tempered in many ways; nevertheless the Venetian Ephors were, in reality, just as despotic as their Spartan predecessors. As Montesquieu had written in a note, at Venice, in contrast to what happened under the Roman dictatorship, 'the Council of Ten stifles not only factions, but even disquiet'.[8]

Not many years after the publication of the *Esprit des loix* there appeared in Venice two large volumes in defence and illustration of the republican tradition, both of which seemed to offer a calm and solemn answer to the worries voiced by Montesquieu. In 1752 the large folio volume by Marco Foscarini, *Della letteratura veneziana*,[9] was published; in the same year there was circulated the *Prospetto* of Vettor Sandi's *Storia civile*, the first volume of which was to appear in 1755. The two authors were profoundly different. A *grand seigneur* of literature and politics, heir to one of the most illustrious

[6] ibid., book 2, chapter 3.

[7] ibid., book 11, chapter 6.

[8] *Mes pensées* 48 (1528), in *Oeuvres complètes de Montesquieu*, ed. A. Masson, vol. 2 (Paris, 1950), p. 19.

[9] *Della letteratura veneziana libri otto di Marco Foscarini cavaliere e procuratore* (Padua, 1752).

names in the Republic, ambassador to Vienna and Turin, *procuratore di San Marco* and doge, teacher and model to a whole generation, Marco Foscarini turned his eyes to the past, to find there the certainty that Venice, although now forced to follow a policy of prudent neutrality, was none the less great on account of the civilisation it had created – a civilisation which was not literary but technical, not rhetorical but active, and still alive in the political forms of its republican constitution. A modest lawyer at the Treasury, belonging to a family raised to the nobility only in 1685, and working all his life to ensure the 'legitimate interests of the Exchequer', Vettor Sandi looked for and found in the history of Venice the proof of the excellence of the nobility that had governed the city for centuries. In spite of all that divided them, both were united by a firm, deep link: the consciousness and pride of being citizens of Venice, members of the patriciate that not only ruled, but was the *Serenissima Repubblica.* At the centre of both works lay a single problem, that of the nature and functioning of the aristocratic form of government. In short, a sort of Whig interpretation, if we can put it that way, of Venetian history.

What Vettor Sandi intended to write, therefore, was not a history of the international life of Venice, and not even a strictly political or economic history. Nor was his aim to 'delight rhetoricians and grammarians' with fine speeches and descriptions, or even to construct a 'system', in the manner of scientists, of physicists. His was to be a 'civic', a constitutional history.[10] The civilisation which Foscarini had evoked had a firm foundation in public law.'The study of law must come before all other forms of study', he wrote, 'for it is on law that there rests the peace of civilised life, without which men's minds would lie inactive, nor would any of the better arts survive.'[11]

As often happens to constitutional histories, this work too tended to observe those facts above all that had contributed to the formation of present reality, neglecting past attempts to find new ways, to give birth to institutions not destined to survive. Its emphasis was on the continuity of the aristocratic republic. Even the first settlers, fugitives from barbarian raids, were far from being of 'ignoble or

[10] *Principi di storia civile della Repubblica di Venezia dalla sua fondazione sino all'anno di N.S. 1700, scritti da Vettor Sandi nobile veneto*, 6 vols (Venice, 1755–6), and *Principi di storia civile della Repubblica di Venezia, scritti da Vettor Sandi nobile veneto, dall'anno di N.S. 1700 sino all'anno 1767*, 3 vols (Venice, 1769–72). I am grateful to Mr Brendan Dooley, who, in a recent seminar which I held at the University of Chicago, emphasised the direct derivation from Giambattista Vico of the ideas on which Vettor Sandi's historiography rests.

[11] op. cit., part 1, vol. 1, p. 5.

beggarly condition'.[12] From the very beginning laws, not individuals, had governed the Venetians. The forms of government might have changed across the centuries, but the 'aristocratic essence' had always remained the same. Gasparo Contarini and Sebastiano Erizzo had been wrong to maintain that Venice was a mixed state, with elements of democracy, monarchy and aristocracy[13] – an abstract interpretation derived from Aristotelian principles, and not 'founded on the singular facts of this ancient Venetian polity',[14] a matter 'that should be left to academics'.[15] The study of Venetian history leads to different conclusions. To understand it one must follow step by step the birth and formation of the nobility, all of which is contained in its first seed. 'The doges were never kings.'[16] At the centre of the 'Venetian civic system' stood the principle that was to ensure its development and continuity: the multiplicity and rotation of magistracies, 'a device that not only produces the greatest vigilance, the most active execution of duty . . . but by employing them also involves many, and in the end, with the passage of time, almost all citizens in the care of the common fatherland'.[17] The institution of the Council of Ten had come by the fourteenth century (but the exact date, like all the power of this Tribunal, remained a mystery) to symbolise and guarantee the ripening, now complete, of aristocratic liberty – a 'most holy institution, since succeeding centuries and the present time show the great merit of this council in preserving the Republic by keeping its citizens without distinction equal and respectful of the law, both of these being sources of aristocratic liberty'.[18] It was enough to look at ancient Rome to be persuaded of its indispensability. If that ancient republic 'had instituted a magistrature similar in its nature and rules to this one, one may reasonably conjecture that it [the republic] would still survive

[12] ibid., p. 47.

[13] *Della repubblica et magistrati di Venetia libri V di M. Gasparo Contarini che fu poi cardinale. Con un ragionamento intorno alla medesima di M. Donato Giannotti fiorentino et i discorsi di M. Sebastiano Erizzo e di Bartolomeo Cavalcanti, aggiuntovi uno di nuovo dell'eccellenza delle repubbliche onde con molta dottrina si mostra quanto siano utili i governi pubblici e necessari i privati per conservazione del genere humano, con la deffinizione di tutte le qualità de gli stati* (Venice, 1591). Contarini often affirms that Venice is a 'mixture of royal, popular and noble states' (e.g. ibid., p. 58). Erizzo in his *Discorso dei governi civili* takes as his model republic that of Rome, where 'so well balanced' was the 'power of each party', that they were 'forced to conspire together and to help each other' (ibid., p. 248).

[14] Vettor Sandi, op. cit. (note 10 above), part 1, vol. 2, 372.

[15] ibid., p. 890.

[16] ibid., vol. 1, p. 231.

[17] ibid., vol. 2, p. 898.

[18] ibid., part 2, vol. 1, p. 33.

today'.[19] When the Council of Ten seemed in some way to harm or endanger the internal equilibrium of the Venetian aristocracy, as it did in 1458, 1582 and 1628, the Great Council (*Maggior Consiglio*) had shown itself 'most vigilant' and capable of effecting the necessary reforms.[20]

Thus the Council of Ten had always been the indispensable means of giving new stimulus, from time to time, to the complex mechanism of the Venetian magistratures. No one understood this necessity better than Vettor Sandi, who had described in volume after volume the labyrinth of the Venetian State. As he penetrated into this ancient forest his style had often become uncertain, and he had often found himself forced to excessive use of the word 'perhaps'. Indeed clear general criteria for the classification of the various types of magistrature were altogether lacking. As one proceeds with a reading of Sandi, it is impossible not to think of Montesquieu and his division of powers. Sandi was also forced by the very logic of things to establish a distinction between magistratures that were mainly jurisdictional, and those more directly concerned with legislation and administration. And since in Venice political power tended to be concentrated in the hands of the richer and older aristocracy, whereas the judiciary were often from the less prosperous and powerful nobility, this polarisation came in the end to serve as an essential, if not explicit, criterion for the understanding of the inner life of the city. At the base of the Republic's constitution lay the theoretical principle of the equality of all citizens, the idea that all the nobility should have access to office, and the much proclaimed intention of establishing a continuous circulation, an uninterrupted exchange inside the ruling class. In fact every magistrature represented a compromise, reached and preserved with some difficulty, between these principles and the social and political reality of Venice. The legal tradition, the juridical tastes that permeate Vettor Sandi's volumes, cannot hide, either from him or from his readers, the fact that, within the picture of an intangible and remote aristocracy, there is a constantly shifting kaleidoscope of the most diverse groups and interests.

The proof came in 1761, some six years after the publication of the *Storia civile*. In what Sandi had held to be the root of the Republic, the Council of Ten, a crisis occurred. For 133 years the question had appeared to be closed, and there had been no need to call upon the special committee of five *correttori* to discuss once again the fun-

[19] ibid., vol. 2, p. 719.
[20] ibid., part 3, vol. 1, p. 2.

damental problems of the constitution. Now discontent had become still more widespread; the aristocracy's typical sense of moderation was disappearing; disputes were becoming violent. Pietro Franceschi, later to be the secretary and official historian of this *correzione*, saw the root of the trouble in the concentration of wealth in the hands of a few, and in the poor nobility's envy of the rich, who in their turn repaid this envy with contempt. He added that the family nucleus of the old patriciate had dissolved; the young, both men and women, had become accustomed to living alone, in their *casini*. There 'secret cliques' had arisen of opponents of the Council of Ten, of those whose more or less secret aim was to limit or abolish its power. The head of this party was Angelo Querini, a young aristocrat profoundly imbued with the aristocratic tradition of his country, but also open to the spiritual influence of the European Enlightenment. After the hard experience of these political struggles he was to finish by turning his attention above all to Bacon and Voltaire. For him the power of the State Inquisitors was despotic. To oppose them he was ready to place himself at the head of the less rich and powerful nobles, to make himself the representative of the judicial magistratures against those that held greater executive power. Elected *avogador di Comun*, he came to feel himself invested with a sort of tribunicial power. Certainly he did not intend to follow ancient Roman models by appealing to the people; but within the framework of the aristocracy he called back into question the balance that had been achieved in the course of centuries. One need only think for a moment of France to understand the meaning of such a position as his. There the *parlements* also fought in the name of the monarchy's fundamental laws, presenting themselves as the representatives of the ancient constitution. In doing so they finished by shaking the very roots of the *ancien régime*, forcing Louis XV and Louis XVI to use up in the struggle with them much of the power and prestige of the monarchy. In Venice too a conflict of jurisdictions, a clash between magistratures finished by raising once again the problem of the 'despotic' character of the Council of Ten, and by provoking an attempt at the constitutional reorganisation of the Republic – an attempt which, however, failed to produce any real and profound transformation of the State. In Venice too the war was one of attrition, important but not decisive. Like the monarchical tradition in France, the Venetian republican tradition turned out once again to be too strong, in the minds of the reformers as in those of their adversaries, for any true break with the past to be possible.

On 12 August 1761 Angelo Querini was arrested by the Inquisitors and banished to the *castello* of Verona. 'The arrest', as Pietro Franceschi recounted, 'brought pallor and terror to every class of person.' Another chronicler, Nicolò Balbi, observed that 'even the mass of indifferent citizens was seized by the suspicion that an attempt was being made to shackle the liberty of the *patria*'. The government took steps to protect itself against this wave of distrust and fear. A secret meeting in the Doge's chamber decided to summon the *correttori.* Angelo Querini's supporters hoped in vain to have him elected one of the five members of this committee, thereby bringing about his liberation and political triumph. Even the boat that was to fetch him from Verona was made ready. But circumspection prevailed in the *Maggior Consiglio*; Querini remained in prison, and the committee was dominated by Marco Foscarini, the historian of Venetian civilisation, and an upholder of the Inquisitors' power, albeit subject to certain new controls and limitations. Pier Antonio Malipiero, one of Angelo Querini's supporters, maintained in vain that the Inquisitors operated 'more according to the practice of the courts of Turin and France than to that of a republic'. He also received the answer that the 'perfect aristocracy', the 'true form' of government by the 'optimates' which Venice enjoyed, required a strong power with an 'impenetrable procedure [*rito*]' in order to keep in check the 'insolence of the more powerful citizens'. Once again the idea of equality came into conflict with that of liberty. Alvise Zen and Pier Antonio Malipiero fought in vain against the Council of Ten, recalling among other things how the decemvirate had usurped all the power of ancient Rome and brought the city to ruin. In vain they maintained that it was precisely such arbitrary punishments as that inflicted on Angelo Querini that diminished the dignity, prestige and power of the nobility. In vain they spoke of the Bastille and the Tower of London, concluding that the 'dark dungeons, the *piombi* and pits used by the Ten are not to be found anywhere else in the civilised world, and are cruel remains of the ancient tyrants of Lombardy', that is, of a feudal world very different from that of the Venetian Republic. Against these observations their adversaries mobilised the whole of the Venetian past. As Franceschi, the secretary, said, Machiavelli's words should not be forgotten, that 'the Florentine republic fell into the most abhorrent servitude by dint of continually regulating the system in order to preserve liberty'.[21]

[21] Machiavelli had discussed the power of the 'ten citizens who can punish any citizen without appeal', comparing them to similar institutions in other Italian cities, and above all in Florence, 'which had been making changes for two hundred years, as our records reliably tell us, without ever being in a state that would allow us truly to call it a republic'. *Discourses*, book 1, chapter 59.

When, on 7 March 1762, the discussion reached the *Maggior Consiglio*, it could be seen how deeply the whole body of the nobility was concerned by the questions that had been raised. Alvise Zen began his speech shouting 'Libertà, libertà', then launched an all-out attack against the power of the Inquisitors. In him there still lived the aristocratic ideal rejected by Vettor Sandi: all power should reside solely in the *Maggior Consiglio*, thus ensuring for the 'marvellous aristocracy' of Venice a 'continual alternation of command and subjection among its citizens'. 'The Republic must put into effect its fundamental maxims, according to which liberty and equality among citizens must be joined with authority in the magistracies, and their subordination to the councils and colleges, in order to hold firm the old republican system, which requires that the power of decision [*potere risolutivo*] be held by the councils and not by the magistracies.' Thus he read a whole page of Gasparo Contarini, in his view far more authoritative, as far as Venice was concerned, than anything written by foreigners like Machiavelli and Giannotti. He called for all legislative power to be removed from the Ten, and for a permanent assurance that judgements would be delivered in public and that the freedom of speech would be preserved. All the inveterate habits rose against him, the ancient, traditional fears and terrors. The spectre appeared once again of Florence's submission to the Medici, while Venice had managed to avoid a similar misfortune. The relationship between the *Dominante* and the mainland seemed once again to be in danger; 'the implacable hatred of the subjects for the order of patricians' made another threatening appearance. In the mouth of Foscarini the whole of history, both ancient and modern, was mobilised against every attempt at radical reform. The 'new doctrines' could lead to nothing but disorder and indiscipline. The secrecy of the Inquisitors was an indispensable element of the constitution; 'other republics mostly perished because they lacked this active, secret force'. the superiority of Venice in this respect had been rightly acknowledged by 'Machiavelli among the Italians, Pufendorf among the Germans, and Montesquieu among the French'. He reminded his listeners that Montesquieu had 'died in our own day, and that his work on the *Spirit of the Laws* had passed through the hands of almost all men who have savoured, however little, the good taste of modern literature'. Translating from French, he read the passages cited above[22] from book 2, chapter 3. To which Alvise Zen replied that it should not be forgotten how Montesquieu had called the Ten a 'tyrannical tribunal'; and how Machiavelli had

[22] p. 195.

maintained that the 'principal reason for the fall of Sparta was its Ephors', that the fall of Rome had been caused by its Dictators. With a mixture of irony and solemnity Foscarini replied to Alvise Zen that when, in fulfilment of his duty as a nobleman, he had administered the Greek islands in the Adriatic, he ought to have made use of his free time to study the 'imaginary republic of Plato or any other of those ancient systems on the basis of which Lycurgus and Solon had once given laws to those peoples'. He would then have realised how 'badly constructed', fragile and short-lived such republics were. Let him then consider the case of Venice, and he would see how the city had succeeded in surviving across the centuries. In order to explain the kernel of his thought, Foscarini presented to the eyes of his listeners the picture of one of the old patrician *palazzi* of Venice, which it would be vain to try to modernise and make 'better lit and more comfortable' by building new corridors and passages. The result of that would be that 'it would become far less easy than before to go from the main rooms of the house [*stanze nobili*] to those destined to fulfil the lowest functions'. There was a firm and long-established link between the nobility and the people, and it should not be interfered with. Besides, every alteration to the building would have 'weakened its foundations, threatening sooner or later a sudden collapse'. And all this was to be done simply for the sake of 'making a little more light in the rooms'. But this light would have revealed nothing but ruins. How could one want to knock down, in the 'majestic palace' of the ruling aristocracy, that 'essential staircase' that was the Tribunal of State Inquisitors? No doubt the ancestral palace was 'a little dark'. But it was the product not of 'metaphysical architecture', but of the 'salutary maxims of government which we inherited from our ancestors, which were guarded by our fathers, and which we must hand down intact to our children'. Wise, solemn, conservative, empirical, Marco Foscarini seems almost the Edmund Burke of the Venetian nobility.

The discussion in the *Maggior Consiglio* became increasingly animated, nor did it lack its moments of drama. Angelo Querini's friends made a great show of punctilious reverence for the Republic's traditions, hoping thus to gain the votes of the more conservative nobility. Thus Malipiero launched a polemical attack against Foscarini, accusing him of giving too much weight to Montesquieu. He (Malipiero) had read the whole of the *Esprit des loix*, but only 'for entertainment, on holiday in the country', and certainly not in order to 'use it for the sake of vain display in the very different circumstances of the Republic'. Paolo Renier, one of the most important politicians of the day, and later Doge, intervened with an extraordinarily equivocal and ambiguous speech, trying to sow sufficient doubt in the minds of the nobility to induce them to abstain from the next vote, that is to cast votes which, as they said in Venice, were 'not sincere'. An essential element of the constitution had been violated, it seemed to him, by the *correzione* and by the subsequent discussions: the element of silence and mystery, on which the foundation of the Republic should rest. 'The secrets of government resemble those perpetual flames which the ancients buried in tombs, which were kept alight as long as they remained enclosed, but were extinguished as soon as they were uncovered and exposed to the air.' The vote reflected this fear which weighed increasingly heavily on the huge hall of the *Maggior Consiglio*, the fear that a deep crack had been made, almost unintentionally, in the ancient edifice of the Venetian aristocracy. The first vote was null, and the second produced only one or two votes' difference between the 'ayes' and the 'noes'. But Marco Foscarini was not stopped by procedural doubts: 'Raising his hands towards the sky, with a loud, clear voice and weeping copiously with emotion, he thanked the Lord God for granting his divine aid to the Republic.'[23]

There is little evidence of the defeated side's state of mind. On the other hand there is repeated proof of the huge sigh of relief that spread through Venice when it became known that nothing essential had been changed in the Republic's form of government. 'We have just seen Venice in terror at the thought of losing its Inquisitors . . . It is a case of tyranny overcoming itself and endeavouring to make itself more terrible than its chains', that acute observer Ange Goudar wrote later in his *Considerations on the Causes of the Weakness and the Power of the Russian Empire.*[24] The merchants apparently were especially happy, because they felt they had been defended against the aristocrats. The 'universal sense of relief spread even to the lowest levels of society', Nicolò Balbi noted. There were 'happy voices' and bonfires in all the streets. There was even an attempt, not perhaps without some provocation on the part of the Inquisitors themselves, to set fire to the houses of Zen and Renier. Poems in

[23] Cf. *Istoria dei correttori eletti nell'anno 1761, scritta da Pietro Franceschi, segretario delli stessi* (Venice, Museo Correr, MS. Cic. 1684) and *Rellazione delle cose occorse e delle dispute tenute in Maggior Consiglio per la correzione dell'Eccelso Consiglio di Dieci e delli suoi magistrati interni seguita l'anno 1762, estesa da N.B.P.V.* [Nicolò Balbi Patrizio Veneto] (Venice, Biblioteca Marciana, MS. Ital. Classe 7, 740 (7483)).

[24] p. 78.

Italian and Latin against Angelo Querini and his followers multiplied. I shall mention only those of the historian Vettor Sandi, who voiced his delight at seeing the *patria* 'summo civili periculo liberata', and proposed that a monument be erected to Foscarini and the majority of the *correttori* for bringing universal peace under the protection of the laws back to the Republic.[25]

When, on 19 May 1762, the Doge Francesco Loredan died, these anxieties had not yet disappeared. Thanks to his victory in the *correzione*, Marco Foscarini was elected. He immediately reaffirmed in a speech that majestic vision of Venetian continuity that was particularly close to his heart. 'We have learnt', he said, speaking to the people from the Hall of the Four Doors, 'better than ever before how strong the foundations of liberty are in that government which, after the passage of centuries, still retains in uncorrupted form the strict institutions of its ancestors'. He was hailed *Doge Serenissimo* by the professors of the University of Padua, to whom, he said, he felt particularly close. The Papal *nunzio* wished to recall the 'sublime station' he had attained in the 'history of literature and the fine arts'. It fell to the envoy of Great Britain, John Murray, to emphasise the political significance of these ceremonies: 'The ancient crown of this Republic which has been transmitted to Your Serenity has increased in splendour, and shows to other princes how pure and stable is that crown whose ornament is liberty.'[26] It seemed as if there was a moment, during the brief reign of Marco Foscarini (he died on 31 March 1763), when aristocratic equality and liberty, pride in the past and gradual transformation, enlightened conservatism and the spirit of reform, all succeeded in reaching a new equilibrium in Venice. But it was an illusion; with Foscarini's death there began a period of extraordinary fruitfulness, but dominated by harsh conflict between Church and State, as well as by strong economic and social pressure to change the archaic reality of the Republic. Then it was seen what a heavy obstacle that constitutional tradition was that Marco Foscarini had striven so intelligently and passionately to preserve and invigorate. The Council of Ten, the State Inquisitors, the conflicts between the various magistratures, the political monopoly of the nobility, all remained intact, and made any development difficult and slow.

[25] *Componimenti vari sattirici di diversi autori* (Venice, Museo Correr, cod. Cic. 1486), f. 104, *Per li noti strepiti della veneziana Repubblica.*

[26] *Memorie venete per la biblioteca di monsignor illustrissimo e reverendissimo Gasparo Negri* (Venice, Museo Correr, cod. Cic, 1538) and Emilio Morpurgo, *Marco Foscarini e Venezia nel secolo XVIII* (Florence, 1880), p. 356.

In a book published at the very moment when Foscarini was elected Doge, the *Contrat social*, the political life of Venice was once more brought into discussion. Rousseau knew the Republic of St Mark well, having stayed there for some time, and spoken of it in some detail in the dispatches he wrote during the War of the Austrian Succession in the name of the French ambassador. He had then described the most important patrician personalities, among other things, and had not failed to indicate the important role Marco Foscarini had assumed among them. 'A State long ago dissolved', he called Venice in the *Contrat social*.[27] And yet, like so many other European observers, he could not resign himself to its relegation to the class of concluded, dead experiments. He saw it too much with Montesquieu's eyes not to appreciate the means by which it had succeeded in surviving. He too observed with interest the 'moderation of the rich and the contentment of the poor' which it had successfully ensured.[28] It too had followed the general rule, according to which every State tended to pass from democracy to aristocracy and to monarchy. But it had progressed with extraordinary slowness, so much so that 'after twelve hundred years the Venetians still seem only to be at the second stage'. The *serrata* of the *Maggior Consiglio* in 1198 had marked their passage from democracy to aristocracy, but at that point they had managed to stop. It was untrue to say that their doges had ever been kings; and unlike that of Ancient Rome, their aristocracy had continued to be based on the entire class of nobles, not only on the Senate.[29] In reality, Rousseau concluded, the government of Venice was not a typical aristocracy. 'If the people has no share in the government, the nobility itself is part of the people.' The Venetian nobility was not made up only of the rich and powerful; 'a multitude of poor *barnabotes* has never come anywhere near a magistrature, all they gain from their nobility being the right to attend the *Maggior Consiglio* and a vain title of excellence'. The comparison with Geneva was instructive. Many Genevan nobles were no more privileged than ordinary Genevan citizens; 'it is certain that, leaving aside the extreme disparity between the two republics, the Genevan bourgeoisie corresponds exactly to the Venetian patriciate, our *natifs* and *habitans* to the citizens and people of Venice, and our peasants to the *terraferma* subjects: in short, however one considers this republic, aside from its greatness, its

[27] Book 3, chapter 5, note.
[28] Book 3, chapter 5.
[29] ibid., chapter 10, note.

government is no more aristocratic than ours'.[30] However paradoxical in appearance, these observations in fact cast a true light on the similar communal origins and republican element of Venice and Geneva. Equality among the governing class's members was the keystone of the constitution of both cities. Montesquieu had seen this equality as reconcilable with aristocracy. Now Rousseau emphasised the democratic element that it contained, always of course within the bounds of the governing class. Beneath this there stood the *natifs* of Geneva and the 'citizens' of Venice (the *citadins*, that is; not the noble *citoyens* but a special category with which Rousseau was perfectly familiar, and from which the Republic of St Mark drew the best of its secretaries, its minor officials and diplomats, such as Pietro Franceschi, for instance, who has often been referred to above). The real difference between Venice and Geneva was not therefore to be found in the social and political foundations of the two cities, but in the presence in one, and absence in the other, of a *chef à vie*, the doge, and in the modes of election to office.

This interpretation greatly irritated Voltaire. 'All of this is revoltingly false', he wrote in his *Idées républicaines*. 'This is the first time it has been said that the Venetian government was not entirely aristocratic', an 'extravagance' which would certainly have been 'severely punished' in Venice. It was not in the least true that those senators 'for whom our author uses the contemptuous term *barnabotes* have never been magistrates; I can cite more than fifty who have held the most important offices'. Nor could the Republic's *terraferma* domains be compared to the peasant subjects of the city of Geneva. 'Among these mainland subjects, in Verona, Vicenza, Brescia, and in many other cities, there are titled lords belonging to the most ancient nobility, many of whom have commanded armies.'[31] These words in Voltaire's *Idées républicaines* were written at one of the culminating moments of his complex series of interventions in the conflicts of the Genevan republic. As I believe Peter Gay has shown, the date is 1765, and Voltaire's polemic against Rousseau coincides with his attempt at supporting the bourgeois of the Great Council against the oligarchy of the *négatifs*, the members of the Council of Twenty-Five.[32] It was precisely the comparison with Geneva that led Voltaire to emphasise the aristocratic character of Venice – the basic equality, that is, of those who constituted the

[30] *Du contrat social*, book 4, chapter 3.

[31] *Idées républicaines* xxxv.

[32] Peter Gay, *Voltaire's Politics* (New York, 1965), pp. 185 ff. and 346 ff., appendix II, 'The date of Voltaire's *Idées républicaines*'.

Republic – to accept, in short, the interpretation codified by Vettor Sandi and reaffirmed in the *correzione* of 1761–2. Geneva, not Venice, could be considered a 'mixture of democracy and aristocracy';[33] 'we were born equal and we have remained so', he wrote in the name of the Genevans, 'and we have entrusted our dignities, that is our public offices, to those who seemed to us best suited to hold them'.[34] The democratic element that Rousseau had seen in Venice was, rather, an inherent feature of the 'municipal government' from which the Republic of Geneva had developed.[35] This consideration helped soon after to lead him beyond his defence of the *natifs*, of the General Council, to a defence of the entire population of the Genevan Republic, while Rousseau was to remain anchored to the tradition of his city. Thus Venice had become an important reference point in the dispute between the two *philosophes*.

Nor was it merely the desire to contradict Rousseau that impelled Voltaire later to take up once again the arguments he had expounded in his *Idées républicaines*, when he wrote his open letter to Hume on 24 October 1766.

> Rousseau apparently has no desire to seek asylum in Venice. He says that the nobility there is part of the people, that it is a multitude of *barnabotes*; that the Genevan bourgeoisie corresponds exactly to the Venetian patriciate, the Genevan peasantry to the *terraferma* subjects. He is ignorant of the fact that among the *terraferma* subjects, in Padua, Vicenza, Verona, Brescia, Bergamo, Cremona [which in reality was part of Austrian Lombardy] etc., there are a thousand families belonging to the most ancient nobility.

For Voltaire Venice remained a model admired and esteemed from a distance, one to which he liked to return every now and then, in the search for a successful experiment, though one now lacking in intrinsic vigour, in aristocratic liberty. Thus when he put together his *Questions sur l'encyclopédie*, he did not fail to pause and speak of 'Venise et, par occasion, de la liberté'. The entire history of Venice now seemed to him to be guided by the will to independence and liberty.[36] At its origins lay neither a revolt, nor a liberation, nor an act of usurpation: the Venetians were 'lords of Venice (if one may dare to use this bold comparison) as God is the lord of the earth, because he founded it'. His style takes wing when he speaks of the *Serenissima*'s beginnings. 'At that time of military and ecclesiastical

[33] ibid. xxx.
[34] ibid. x.
[35] ibid.
[36] *Questions sur l'Encyclopédie par des amateurs* (s.l., 1771), vol: 9, pp. 31 ff.

brigandage Attila swoops down like a vulture, and the Venetians take refuge in the sea like halcyons. Nothing protects them but themselves; they make their nest in the midst of the waters, they increase it, people it, defend it, enrich it.' Threatened at the same time by the corrupt and greedy Eastern Empire, and by that of the Germans in the West, it seemed to him like a 'flying fish pursued by a falcon and a shark together, and which escapes from one and the other'. Ancient Rome had lost the 'freedom acquired by Brutus' after five hundred years; 'Venice has kept hers for eleven centuries, and I flatter myself that she will keep it for ever.' Unlike Genoa, it had no need for any 'privilege of Berengar', the 'charter of a passing tyrant'; 'the true charter of liberty is independence sustained by strength'. Switzerland owed its liberty to its own courage and firmness, and to its mountains. The United States of Holland had acquired their liberty 'at the very moment of their union'. Over all these States, both ancient and modern, there loomed one question: 'Why is liberty so rare?'

'Because it is the greatest of goods.'

MORTON WHITE

Oughts and Cans

For more than twenty years, Isaiah Berlin and I have discussed – in and out of print – the relationship between a moral statement that a person ought to perform a certain action and the statement that the action is voluntary.[1] I have held that the relationship is not that of logical implication; and I have also held that the relationship is moral because I think it may be expressed by the moral statement 'No one should judge an action as obligatory (or as permissible) unless he thinks it is voluntary.' But one may see from Berlin's Introduction to his *Four Essays on Liberty* that he does not hold that the relationship is that of logical implication, though he does resist my idea that it is moral. And since he tries in some detail to tell us in that Introduction how he does view the relationship, I should like to examine what he says there on this difficult and important philosophical question.

We must remember that one of the main theses of Berlin's 'Historical Inevitability' is that a statement that an agent is under obligation and a statement that the agent's choice is determined or caused are *incompatible*; and that is why I had supposed at first that he was arguing in the following familiar way: 'Brutus ought to have killed Caesar' logically implies 'Brutus killed Caesar voluntarily'; 'Brutus killed Caesar voluntarily' logically implies 'Brutus's choosing to kill Caesar was uncaused'; 'Brutus's choosing to kill Caesar was uncaused' logically implies the denial of determinism; therefore, 'Brutus ought to have killed Caesar' logically implies the denial of determinism. And if this statement of obligation about Brutus logically implies the denial of determinism, then it is logically incompatible with it. Now I deny the first implication in this chain and I also deny that the statement that Brutus ought to have killed Caesar *logically implies* that Brutus could have made a different choice from the one he did make. But all of this seems to be beside the point in

[1] See my review of Isaiah Berlin, *Historical Inevitability* (London, 1954), in *Perspectives USA*, no 16 (Summer 1956), 191–6, reprinted in my *Religion, Politics, and the Higher Learning* (Cambridge, Massachusetts, 1959), pp. 75–84; my *Foundations of Historical Knowledge* (New York, 1965), chapter 7 *passim*; also *F.E.L.*, pp. xix–xxiii, xxxvi–xxxvii.

the light of what Berlin says in his Introduction. For there he writes the following about the incompatibility which he asserts:

> What kind of incompatibility this is, logical, conceptual, psychological, or of some other kind, is a question to which I do not volunteer an answer. The relations of factual beliefs to moral attitudes (or beliefs) – both the logic and psychology of this – seem to me to need further philosophical investigation. The thesis that no relevant logical relationship exists, e.g. the division between fact and value often attributed to Hume, seems to me to be unplausible, and to point to a problem, not to its solution.[2]

It would appear from the first two sentences of this passage that although Berlin does not volunteer an answer to the question whether the incompatibility in question is 'logical, conceptual, psychological, or of some other kind', and therefore seems to leave open the possibility that the incompatibility he asserts is ordinary logical incompatibility, later statements by him seem to close this door. Even though it seems to him implausible in the third sentence of the above passage that 'no relevant logical relationship' should exist between a moral statement of obligation and a factual statement about freedom of choice, we soon come to see that this unspecified logical relationship between obligation and the denial of determinism is not that of ordinary implication; and, by connected reasoning, the logical relationship of incompatibility he asserts between obligation and determinism is not that which holds between 'John is a bachelor' and 'John is married'. Rather, Berlin seems to assert that the *intelligibility* of statements of obligation implies the falsity of determinism and therefore that determinism implies the *unintelligibility* of those statements. We see this most clearly when Berlin advises us what to say to a person of another culture or, for that matter, to a person of our own culture – even to a Hobbes or a Hume – who accepts determinism and at the same time says that Brutus was (or was not) under a moral obligation to kill Caesar. According to Berlin, we should tell that person *not* that 'he was logically contradicting himself . . . but that he was being incoherent, that we could not see what reasons he could have for using such terms, that his language, if it was intended to apply to the real world, was no longer sufficiently intelligible to us'.[3] Here it is clear that the incompatibility asserted by Berlin is not that which exists between 'John is a bachelor' and 'John is married' (or between 'John is a

[2] *F.E.L.*, p. xii, note 1.
[3] ibid., p. xxii.

bachelor' and 'John is not a bachelor'). It is another 'logical relationship' that he specifies first by applying the words 'unreasonable' and 'incoherent' to those who would say that Brutus ought to have killed Caesar *and* that determinism is true; 'it is not rational', Berlin also says, 'both to believe that choices are caused, and to consider men as deserving of reproach or indignation (or their opposites) for choosing to act or refrain as they do'.[4]

In our effort to discover what this last sentence means, we are helped by the following passage, in which the connection between determinism and our moral discourse is made somewhat clearer:

> The supposition that, if determinism were shown to be valid, ethical language would have to be drastically revised is not a psychological or a physiological, still less an ethical, hypothesis. It is an assertion about what any system of thought that employs the basic concepts of our normal morality would permit or exclude. The proposition that it is unreasonable to condemn men whose choices are not free rests not on a particular set of moral values (which another culture might reject) but on the particular nexus between descriptive and evaluative concepts which governs the language we use and the thoughts we think. To say that you might as well morally blame a table as an ignorant barbarian or an incurable addict is not an ethical proposition, but one which emphasizes the conceptual truth that this kind of praise and blame makes sense only among persons capable of free choice.[5]

At least two questions are raised by Berlin's views as I have expounded them so far. What truth supposedly links the concept of a caused choice with the unintelligibility of moral terms of which he speaks? And what is the status of this truth?

The closest I can come to illustrating a clear singular truth of this kind is this: 'If Brutus's choosing to kill Caesar was caused, then the sentence "Brutus deserves praise (or reproach) for choosing to kill Caesar" is unintelligible.' Generalised, this truth would take something like the following form: 'Whenever a choice is caused, then a sentence used to assert that a person who makes that choice deserves praise (or reproach) is not intelligible.' This general truth links two predicates or, perhaps some would prefer to say, concepts. One is the relatively simple concept of being a caused choice, but the other is semantic and more complex, since it is the attribute of being a choice referred to in a moral sentence that is not intelligible. And if one wishes to speak of this general truth as implying an incompatibility, it is the incompatibility between being a caused choice and

[4] ibid.
[5] ibid., pp. xxii–xxiii.

being a choice that may be intelligibly praised or reproached. We may also say that it implies an incompatibility between the *truth* of a singular sentence asserting that a choice is caused and the *intelligibility* of a singular sentence that putatively asserts that this choice deserves praise (or reproach). In other words, if the first singular sentence is true, then the second is not intelligible. In still other words, the truth of the first singular sentence implies the incomprehensibility of the second.

What is the status of a general truth that asserts this incompatibility or a related implication? Leaving aside the first quoted passage, in which Berlin seems to shy away from answering this question, I think we may say on the basis of the second quoted passage that he regards it as what he calls a 'conceptual truth'. It is a conceptual truth which formulates what he refers to in the second passage as 'the particular nexus between descriptive and evaluative concepts which governs the language we use and the thoughts we think'. I assume that 'free choice' is a descriptive expression for him, that 'ought' is an evaluative expression, and that the general truth I have just formulated would present the 'particular nexus' between these expressions or the corresponding concepts.

In what sense is this a conceptual truth? Surely it is not a so-called analytic truth such as 'Every square is a rectangle' or 'Every bachelor is unmarried.' It would be hard to say that the concept of a caused choice 'contains' the concept of a choice which is said to deserve reproach (or blame) only in an unintelligible sentence. And if we define an analytic truth as one which is true by virtue of the meanings of its terms, it is hard to see that the conceptual truth in question is analytic by that definition. Its denial is not self-contradictory. I cannot believe, moreover, that Berlin would say that his conceptual truth is synthetic a priori or that it is a Wittgensteinian rule of a language game. Perhaps one may come a little closer to understanding the status of Berlin's conceptual truth if one thinks of examples used by those who speak of what Gilbert Ryle used to call 'category-mistakes'. Just as some philosophers would have us say that it is nonsense to say that cardinal numbers are edible (as opposed to addable), so Berlin might declare it nonsensical to say that a caused choice, as opposed to an uncaused choice, deserves praise (or reproach). The fact is, however, that even if one were not to question Ryle's questionable theory of category-mistakes, it is not evident that when we reproach a person for making a choice that is caused we do so in a sentence that is unintelligible in accordance with the theory of Ryle.

Berlin tells us that the moral judgement he has in mind is of the Kantian sort, and yet he also tells us that it is of the sort that ordinary people make. Yet it is hard to believe that ordinary people hold with Kant and Berlin that it is *nonsense* to say that a caused choice is one which ought (or ought not) to be made. In my opinion many ordinary people subscribe to some form of determinism; they think that nothing happens without a cause. Therefore, when they hold that only a choice which is free should be morally judged, they do not think of a free choice as an uncaused choice. On the contrary, it seems to me that they are likely to be attracted to a view, once suggested by G. E. Moore, according to which a choice may be free and yet caused. In the course of considering the possibility that a voluntary act is not only an act that the agent would not have performed if he had chosen not to perform it but also an act that the agent could have chosen not to perform, Moore proposes two possible interpretations of 'He could have chosen what in fact he did not choose' which logically permit the choice that the agent did in fact make to be caused, and hence do not exclude the truth of determinism. According to one interpretation, this sentence means that the agent would have chosen differently if he had chosen so to choose. According to another such interpretation, this sentence means that no man could know for certain that the agent would not have chosen differently from the way in which the agent did choose. Plainly, if either of these two interpretations is correct, then even Berlin would not say that it is nonsensical to say of a caused choice to perform a certain action that the choice or the action is obligatory (or permissible). The fact that the *choice* was caused in either of these cases would not prevent it or the action from being called free and hence subject to moral judgements of that sort.

Does Berlin say that no such view of a free choice is tenable? Does he insist that even if each is a correct interpretation of what it *sometimes* means to say that an agent could have chosen otherwise, neither of them gives '*the* meaning' of such a statement when it is asserted in order to justify the making of a moral judgement? Does he maintain that other interpretations of such a statement, like 'He was not coerced to choose as he in fact chose' – which will also not imply that the agent's choice was uncaused – *could not* be what ordinary men have in mind when they say that the agent's choice was free? If so, on what basis does Berlin do so? When he tries to explain why plenty of distinguished thinkers praise or reproach persons for making choices that these thinkers regard as caused, he says that this merely 'shows that some normally lucid and self-critical thinkers are at times liable to confusion'. But what do they *confuse* when they try to show that the principle of causality or determinism, which may be as commonly held among ordinary persons as any other so-called metaphysical principle, is compatible with the principle that only a free action or choice should be judged morally? On the contrary, such thinkers are often unusually clear about what the issues are when they try to do this by *seeking* an appropriate analysis of the concept of free *choice*. Whether they have been correct in their analyses is beside the point, for their effort is comprehensible and does not run foul of any logical or 'conceptual' truth that would import confusion or nonsense into the discussion.

I am aware that Berlin rejects the view that a free action is merely one that the agent would not have performed if he had chosen not to perform it – this being a view that is compatible with determinism because it does not require us to affirm that the agent could have chosen not to perform the act. But Berlin does not seriously consider the view that a free action is one that the agent would not have performed if he had chosen not to perform it and, in addition, one that the agent could have chosen not to perform in a sense of 'could have chosen' that is compatible with determinism. And this may be why he does not investigate interpretations of 'could have chosen otherwise' that are compatible with determinism. In any case, it seems to me that a philosopher who rests so heavily on what ordinary people say and think is bound to consider this effort to reconcile moral responsibility and determinism precisely because many ordinary people do believe in both of them while agreeing with Berlin that a morally judgeable action is one that the agent could have chosen not to perform.

Up to now, I have questioned two major claims made by Berlin: (*a*) his claim that it is a 'conceptual truth' that a caused choice is praised (or blamed) only in a nonsensical sentence; and (*b*) his claim that a free choice is analysable only as an uncaused choice. No plausible interpretation of the phrase 'conceptual truth' will link what Berlin wants such a truth to link in a clear 'logical relationship'. And claim (*b*) I have criticised by saying that Berlin has not proved that ordinary people, to whose habits of thought and language he so frequently appeals, believe that 'free choice' is synonymous with 'uncaused choice'. But let us suppose that he were persuaded to accept an interpretation of 'free choice' which would not logically force moral judges to reject determinism. And let us also suppose that he were then to claim that it was a 'conceptual truth' that a sentence in which we praised or blamed this sort of unfree choice was nonsense. Would I agree with him? I am afraid not, because I do not think that any plausible interpretation of the connection between moral judgement and free choice is conceptual, logical, analytic or logically necessary. Rather, as I have argued elsewhere, it is a connection which is asserted by saying that we should not pass moral judgement on a certain kind of choice or on a certain kind of act, that it would be morally objectionable to do so. Had Berlin consistently maintained the agnosticism he avows in one place about what sort of incompatibility he asserts between determinism and moral judgeability, he would have allowed that my position had a fighting chance, since it may be expressed by saying that determinism and moral judgeability are *morally* incompatible. But, as we have seen, soon after he had written that he would not volunteer an answer to the question: 'What kind of incompatibility this is, logical, conceptual, psychological, or of some other kind', he advanced a view of the incompatibility and proceeded to criticise mine.

Having said why I find it difficult to accept Berlin's view of the relationship between moral statements and statements of freedom, I want now to turn to what he has to say about my alternative view of the relationship.

He focuses on my contention that a person or a culture that does not accept the dictum that ' "Ought" implies "can" ' does not make a *logical* blunder and therefore that the person or culture may not be accused, in the language of older philosophers, of failing to perceive a truth of reason. For this reason, I think, he asks me rhetorically whether I would find it 'reasonable' to say to a kleptomaniac: 'You cannot, it is true, help choosing to steal, even though you may think it wrong to do so. Nevertheless you must not do it.' Here I must point out that, the word 'reasonable' being used as it is, I might well reply that I would *not* think it 'reasonable'. But such a reply would be compatible with my claim that ' "Ought" implies "can" ' is a moral principle and not a logical principle. Accepting that moral principle, I might well refrain, as Berlin thinks I should, from passing moral judgement on the action of the kleptomaniac; and, more to the point, I might well say that it would be unreasonable to pass moral judgement on it. We often say it is unreasonable to do what moral principles command us not to do in certain circumstances, without concluding that moral principles are like mathematical or logical principles in being analytic, necessary, a priori, self-evident or demonstrable; or that they are conceptual truths in Berlin's sense. And we often say it is reasonable to do what such moral principles command us to do in certain circumstances.

Berlin cannot, therefore, refute my view by asking me rhetorically, as he also does, how I could *defend* passing a moral judgement on an action which I admitted was unfree. For I made it clear that I would *not* pass such a moral judgement, because I *accepted* the dictum ' "Ought" implies "can" even though I regarded it as a moral dictum.

Berlin also criticises my view by remarking that I fail to recognise that blaming an incurable addict is like blaming a table, and therefore that I fail to see that the unintelligibility of such blame is based on a conceptual rather than an ethical truth.[6] Therefore, Berlin thinks that 'The addict ought not to have taken opium yesterday' is unintelligible for the same reason that 'The table ought not to have fallen yesterday' is unintelligible. He appears to think that these sentences are unintelligible because the addict's taking of the opium and the table's falling are both unfree in the same sense. But we know that although the table cannot *choose* to do *anything*, this is not true of the addict. Therefore, when the table fell, it did not choose to fall, whereas the addict did choose to take opium when he took it. However, Berlin holds that a free act must be such that the agent could have chosen differently from the way in which he did choose.[7] In that case he could hardly apply the adjectives 'free' and 'unfree' to the addict's act in the same sense as he would apply them to the table's falling. Since the table did *not* choose to fall and could not have chosen at all, how can we affirm or deny that it could have chosen differently from the way in which it *did choose*? By contrast, since the addict chose to take opium yesterday, we can affirm or deny that he could have chosen differently from the way he did choose. Therefore, when Berlin says that the addict's taking opium yesterday was *not* free, he must mean something different from what he means when he says that the table's falling was not free. If so, then the alleged unintelligibility of 'The addict ought not to have taken opium yesterday' and 'The table ought not to have fallen yesterday' cannot be based on the same considerations. The grounds for not blaming a table might be based on a 'conceptual truth' if that kind of truth could be characterised clearly, but that would not touch my claim that the grounds for not blaming an addict are ethical.

Under the circumstances, I am very sorry to say that Berlin and I are still far apart on two fundamental questions even though we understand each other far better than we did twenty-five years ago.

[6] ibid.

[7] *F.E.L.*, p. 64, note 1.

We disagree on the status of ' "Ought" implies "can" ', we disagree on the interpretation of 'can', and either one of these disagreements is enough to divide us on the question whether the acceptance of determinism makes nonsense of certain moral sentences. But is there, I keep asking myself, anything that we could do to bring our views closer together? And the answer I keep coming up with is that Berlin and I had better go on talking with each other for many more years about *oughts* and *cans* and their connections with each other.

BERNARD WILLIAMS

Conflicts of Values

Isaiah Berlin has always insisted that there is a plurality of values which can conflict with one another, and which are not reducible to one another; consequently, that we cannot conceive of a situation in which it was true both that all value-conflict had been eliminated, and that there had been no loss of value on the way. To have insisted on these truths is one of the conspicuous services that Berlin has rendered to a sound and humane conception of social thought.

In Berlin's own thought, these truths are associated with the foundations of liberalism.[1] The history of that movement itself shows that the consequences of these views need not be quietist or conservative. Yet while this has been so, there does remain a problem about the relation of this kind of pluralism to action, a problem at least for a modern, developed, and relatively liberal society. Even there, it is of course true that the business of reaffirming and defending the plurality of values is itself a political task, one to which Berlin's writings make a permanent contribution. But more is needed, if the pluralist is not to spend too much of his time as a rueful spectator of political change which is itself powered by forces which either have nothing to do with values at all, or else express value-claims more exclusive than the pluralist himself would admit.

There does not exist much adequate philosophy on the question of how a pluralistic theory of values might be combined with, indeed issue in, radical social action. The conditions of there being any such philosophy are certainly complex and at present unclear. But we shall be able to see how, if at all, they might be satisfied only if we understand better than we do now what it is for values to be plural, conflicting and irreducible. That means understanding, in particular, their conflicts, since it is precisely their conflicts which systematisers (at the limit, reductionists) seek to overcome, while pluralists of the Berlin spirit regard the conflicts as both ineliminable and not re-

[1] I have speculated about the form of that association in my introduction to Berlin's collection of philosophical papers, *Concepts and Categories* (London, 1978).

soluble without remainder. These remarks will be concerned with the subject of conflict.

It is in fact a large subject – larger than might be suggested by the literature, which has typically tended to regard value-conflict, except perhaps in the most contingent and superficial connections, as a pathology of social and moral thought, and as something to be overcome – whether by theorising, as in the tradition of analytical philosophy and its ancestors, or by a historical process, as in Hegelian and Marxist interpretations. It is my view, as it is Berlin's, that value-conflict is not necessarily pathological at all, but something necessarily involved in human values, and to be taken as central by any adequate understanding of them. I also think, though Berlin may not, that where conflict needs to be overcome, this 'need' is not of a purely logical character, nor a requirement of pure rationality, but rather a kind of social or personal need, the pressure of which will be felt in some historical circumstances rather than others. I shall not try to make good these claims here, but merely try to shed some light on them from one or two different directions.

The type of conflict which will concern us is one-party conflict; and we will take that as one-*person* conflict. (There are of course one-party conflicts where the party is not one person, as with policy disagreements within a firm or other such agency; but for present purposes these can be regarded as special cases of two- (or more) party conflict in the context of agreed procedures or objectives.) Philosophical inquiry which is primarily concerned with epistemological or semantic issues of objectivity naturally concentrates on two-party conflict, where the problem is that of resolving *disagreement*: it is generally assumed that the parties have each their own harmonious set of value-beliefs. Accompanying that, usually, is an assumption that, whatever may turn out to be the case with two-party conflicts, at any rate one-person conflict must be capable of being rationally resolved: at the very least, the theory of rational behaviour must make it an undisputed aim of the rational agent to reduce conflict in his personal set of values to the minimum. This assumption is characteristically made even by those who do not think that interpersonal conflicts of value necessarily admit of rational resolution.

The assumption is in fact unreasonable. For those, moreover, who combine it with scepticism about rationally resolving interpersonal conflict, it is doubly unreasonable: some one-person conflicts of values are expressions of a complex inheritance of values, from different social sources, and what we experience in ourselves as a conflict is something which could have been, and perhaps was, expressed as a conflict between two societies, or between two historical states of one society. The same point comes out the opposite way round, so to speak: a characteristic dispute about values in society, such as some issue of equality against freedom, is not one most typically enacted by a body of single-minded egalitarians confronting a body of equally single-minded libertarians, but is rather a conflict which one person, equipped with a more generous range of human values, could find enacted in himself.

It is worth taking first, if briefly, the type of one-person conflict which has in fact been most studied – the so-called conflict of obligations. This is the area of the conflict of values which is most directly linked to reasons for action. As such, it is not entirely typical, but it does present some useful considerations. In particular, it reveals some ways in which conflict is not necessarily pathological, even though it is real conflict and both the obligations which are parties to the conflict actually exist and actually apply to the situation.

Such cases are basically different from those others, themselves very familiar, in which conflict is only apparent, and there are not in fact two conflicting obligations at all. For example, suppose an agent promises his father to support, after the father's death, a certain charity, but he later finds himself short of money and cannot both support the charity and, let us say, make some provision for his own children which he feels he should make. One resolution of the problem which could be available is that he had reason in good faith to think that it was a tacit but understood condition on the promise that it applied only if there were enough money left after such things as providing for his children. Whether this thought was sound would of course be a matter of historical fact and judgement – it would not become sound just because it resolved the difficulty. But if it is sound, then there is no conflict at all. One of the obligations has evaporated.

There is a temptation, helped by the ambiguous terminology of 'prima facie obligations', to take this relatively painless kind of case as the pattern for the resolution of a conflict of obligations. The evident fact that there is at most one of the two things which, all things considered, I should do, is taken to be equivalent to the idea that, all things considered, there is only one obligation. But this is a mistake. There are certainly two obligations in a real case of this kind, though one may outweigh the other. The one that outweighs has greater stringency, but the one that is outweighed also possesses some stringency, and this is expressed in what, by way of compensation, I may have to do for the parties who are disadvantaged by its being outweighed; whether I have merely to explain and apologise, or whether I have to engage further in some more substantial reparatory action. (Those who rely heavily on '*ought* implies *can*' in these connections should consider why – particularly if the conflict of obligations was not my fault – I should have to do any of these things.) The fact, on the other hand, that one obligation was genuinely outweighed by the other is expressed in the consideration that the disadvantaged party has no justified complaint about what I chose to do. They may have some complaint about my compensatory activity, or lack of it, but if the obligation was indeed outweighed, then they have no justified complaint about my not having done what I was obliged to them to do: except perhaps to the extent that the conflict of obligations was my own fault.

In another, and more drastic, kind of case, however,[2] which might be called the 'tragic' kind, an agent can justifiably think that whatever he does will be wrong: that there are conflicting moral requirements, and that neither of them succeeds in overriding or outweighing the other. In this case, though it can actually emerge from deliberation that one of the courses of action is the one that, all things considered, one had better take, it is, and it remains, true that each of the courses of action is morally required, and at a level which means that, whatever he does, the agent will have reason to feel regret at the deepest level. If, in such a case, we do not necessarily say that the victims have a justified complaint, it is because such cases can lie beyond complaint, as they can lie also beyond any adequate compensatory action.

I shall not raise here any questions of detail about the logic of such situations.[3] The present point is just that it must be a mistake to suppose that what we have here is a case of logical inconsistency, such that the agent could not be justified or rational in thinking that each of these moral requirements applied to him. This is to misplace the source of the agent's trouble, in suggesting that what is wrong is his

[2] There are further cases: e.g. a political type of case, which is not exceptional, as the tragic case is, but where, unlike the situation of outweighing, the victim has a justified complaint. For some remarks on this, see Stuart Hampshire (ed.), *Public and Private Morality* (Cambridge, 1978), pp. 59–65.

[3] I have discussed some of them in 'Ethical Consistency', reprinted in *Problems of the Self* (Cambridge, 1973). On the central notion of agent-regret, there is some more in 'Moral Luck', *Proceedings of the Aristotelian Society*, supplementary vol. 50 (1976), 115–35.

thought about the moral situation, whereas what is wrong lies in his situation itself – something which may or may not be his fault. Someone might argue on larger metaphysical grounds of some kind that such situations could not arise, that it was impossible that any agent should meet such a situation; but, if there were such an argument, it would have to yield a metaphysical impossibility, or, in some way, a moral impossibility, and not a proof that the judgements involved in such a situation were contradictory. There is a substantial and interesting question: 'What would have to be true of the world and of an agent that it should be impossible for him to be in a situation where whatever he did was wrong?' I doubt in fact that there is anything that could produce such a guarantee short of the existence of a rather interventionist God, or else the total reduction of moral life to rules of efficient behaviour – two extremes which precisely leave out the actual location of moral experience. But it is at any rate a real question, which it would not be if the correct thing to say were: nothing has to be true of the agent or of the world for this to be so, it is guaranteed by the logic of moral expressions.

In this, as elsewhere in these areas, logical and semantic theory has to be responsive to experience, and to what a reflective agent feels that he needs to say. At the same time, it is of course true that such experiences need interpretation in terms of general ideas about the status of moral thought – for instance, with regard to issues of objectivity. I shall not try to pursue such questions here, but it is worth remarking that in so far as we are drawn towards the objectivity of ethics by an impression which is borne in on us in moral experience, the experience of ultimate moral conflict is precisely one which brings most irremovably with it the impression of objectivity: that there is nothing that one decently, honourably, adequately, *can* do in a certain situation seems a kind of truth as firmly independent of the will or inclination as any truth of morality seems.

Conflicts of obligation are peculiar in presenting a conflict between determinately specified actions; the tragic ones among them are further peculiar in lying beyond the ordinary routes of moral thought. Very many of our conflicts, however, including those which have most interested Berlin, are at a level where interpretation in action is less determinate or immediate. Values such as liberty, equality, and expressions of justice other than equality, can certainly conflict as ideals or objectives, though their connection with immediately presented courses of action may often be problematical: while, in the other direction, a choice between presented courses of action may in some cases be only indeterminately guided or shaped by appeal to these values.[4]

Still further from particular choices of action or policy are evaluations of admirable human characteristics or virtues such as courage, gentleness, honesty, independence of spirit and so forth. We know, too, that no social institution or form of society can express, embody or encourage all of them equally. One form of Utopianism – the basic form, perhaps – consists in supposing that a society could be attained in which all genuinely valuable human characteristics could be equally and harmoniously displayed. Since it is obvious that not every characteristic which has been accepted in the course of history as a virtue could be so combined, some opinions about what are virtues have to be dismissed: by the more sophisticated Utopians, dismissed as forms of false consciousness, which are revealed as false by the same reflections that yield the structure of Utopia. An easy – too easy – example is working-class deference.

That example, and others, will remind us that a critique of supposed virtues must be possible, and it should be an aim of a developed moral and social philosophy to provide one. Yet, even granted such a critique, there is little substance to the Utopian hope. Those who share Berlin's scepticism about that hope – and perhaps also some of his fears about attempts to enact it – will think that while society can move to recognise and express new virtues and ideals, perhaps even a wider range of them, nevertheless there are at the same time irrecoverable losses. As in a given choice at a given time one value has to be set against another, so also there is loss of genuine human value over time.

There is a further proposition which some of these will believe (among them, I believe, Berlin): that there is no common currency in which these gains and losses of value can be computed, that values, or at least the most basic values, are not only plural but in a real sense incommensurable. Some other people, however, sympathetic to the general drift of the argument so far, may at this point protest. To say that values necessarily conflict, and that the affirmation of some necessarily involves losses with regard to others, does not entail that they are incommensurable. The reference to *losses* does not in itself entail, on the other hand, that they are commensurable: one could register a loss in one dimension of value without comparing the amount of that loss with another dimension of value. But unless

[4] One of the several simplifying comforts offered by the purely transactional account of distributive justice which is given by Robert Nozick is that it firmly reduces this dimension of indeterminacy.

some comparison can be made, then nothing rational can be said at all about what overall outcome is to be preferred, nor about which side of a conflict is to be chosen – and that is certainly a despairing conclusion. *Some* overall comparisons can be made; and if they can, then to some degree, it will be said, these values must be commensurable.

The objection can be pressed further. When it is said that values are incommensurable, it is usually some general values such as liberty and equality which are said to be incommensurable. But this seems to imply that there is no way of comparing or rationally adjudicating the claims of these values *wherever* they conflict. But no one could believe this, since obviously there are possible changes by which (say) such a trivial gain in equality was bought by such an enormous sacrifice of liberty that no one who believed in liberty at all could rationally favour it. So either it is false that these values are, as such, incommensurable, or incommensurability is a less discouraging or, again, deep feature than had been supposed.

Against these objections, it seems that the claim that values are incommensurable – let us call it 'the claim' for short – does say something true and important; or rather, it says more than one true and important thing. There are at least four different denials which the claim might be taken to involve; they are of increasing strength, so that accepting one later in the list involves accepting those earlier:

1. There is no one currency in terms of which each conflict of values can be resolved.

2. It is not true that for each conflict of values, there is some value, independent of any of the conflicting values, which can be appealed to in order to resolve that conflict.

3. It is not true that for each conflict of values, there is some value which can be appealed to (independent or not) in order rationally to resolve that conflict.

4. No conflict of values can ever rationally be resolved.

(4) is the position which the objector elicited from the claim, and which he rightly claimed to be too despairing. But that leaves the others, and these are not trivial or shallow positions.

Among these, (1) raises an interesting question, which goes beyond that particular proposition. Obviously the claim must in some way involve (1). Yet at the same time, there is a sense in which the claim could even accept that (1) was false, and admit that a universal currency of comparison was available, without this destroying the spirit of the claim; and this shows that the relations between the claim and the issue of rational choice between values is not as straightforward as it may seem. I shall assume that the only plausible candidate for such a universal currency of comparison would be utility (in some contemporary sense of people satisfying their preferences). The most basic version of the idea that utility provides a universal currency is that all values are versions or applications in some way of utility; and in this sense the claim of course rejects the idea of a universal currency. Indeed, in this version, it is not clear that there is really more than one value at all, or, consequently, real conflicts between values. Some indirect forms of utilitarianism, on the other hand, will want it to be the case both that there is a universal currency of utility and at the same time that the various values indirectly validated by reference to utility are autonomous enough for there to be recognisable conflicts between them. It is not clear how stable or coherent views of this kind are; in any case, they are equally rejected by the claim.

Both these versions of utilitarianism have the following feature: utility is the universal currency because the appeal to it is rationally *all of a piece* with the appeal to the other values. In the strongest version, utility is, so to speak, homogeneous with the other values – they are just versions of it. In the indirect version, the appeal to it is the application to a particular case of what is their justification in general. But someone who was not a utilitarian might think that utility was indeed the only possible universal resolver of conficts, without however thinking that it was in this way homogeneous with other, conflicting, values at all. He could think that utility was another value, very different from and in certain respects perhaps even alien to other values, but that it did uniquely provide a last appeal from any conflict. I doubt that such a person could plausibly hold that utility was the only item which could ever be appealed to to resolve any conflict; he is likely to think that some other values sometimes resolve some conflicts. But he might think that utility was the only item that could always be appealed to when other appeals failed. He would have to be unduly optimistic, probably, about the sense that can be made of 'utility' itself; but – and this is the present point – he would not necessarily be going against the incommensurability claim. Although he thinks that utility can be brought in as an arbiter to situations of conflict, he sees it as too outside the other values for that fact to count as a way of measuring them. This outlook would be a wider application of one we encountered in connection with the 'tragic' conflicts of obligations, where it was suggested that there might in a particular case indeed be something which it was better, all things considered, to do, and hence there were reasons for resolving the confict in one way rather than the other, but that nevertheless that did not adequately meet the claim involved in the conflict.

(2), in so far as it is distinct from (1), seems obviously true, since unless there is a universal currency, it must surely be contingent whether there is some third value which can relevantly be brought in to decide some particular conflict. Moreover, there is a consideration similar to the one just discussed: if the deciding value were not intimately related to those involved in the conflict, we would have a decision, and a reason for it, but not one that supported any genuine commensurability of the values originally involved.

What about (3)? Here it might be wondered what processes were in question at all: how can one rationally resolve a conflict between two values by appealing to one of them? There is certainly one familiar pattern of argument which falls under this heading – that in which a conflict between values A and B is resolved, or at least alleviated, by the consideration that affirming A, though it may diminish B in some direction, will also lead to an increase of B in another. Thus proposals to increase equality, though at some cost of some people's liberty, are often defended with the consideration that they also increase some people's (not usually the same people's) liberty. Berlin himself has been very resistant to the reductionist aspects of this sort of argument, insisting that equality is one value and liberty is another. It is indeed true that they are two values, and neither can be reduced to the other; nevertheless, it is also true that increasing equality can increase liberty, and that can be one reason (besides the value of equality as a form of justice) for wanting to increase equality.

This kind of argument can, in my view, be sound; but it is not of course a type of argument which notably regards values as incommensurable: its effect is precisely to bring the values A and B *in the particular case* nearer to commensurability. The holder of the incommensurability claim, resistant as he is to reduction of one value to another, will deny that this kind of argument is necessarily or even generally available, and will thus agree with (3). However, he need not be barred, it seems to me, from coming to a sort of conclusion referred to before, to the effect that in a given conflict between A and B, the amount gained in terms of A is (say) greater than the amount lost in terms of B. This might seem like a clear admission that A and B were commensurable; but this point seems to have force, I think, only because it is assumed that if A and B have these kinds of relations to one another in a given case, this must be because there is some one thing, more of which is gained along with A, in that case, than is lost along with B. But there need be no such thing, for this kind of conclusion to be sound, and if the supporter of the incommensurability claim is right, there will not in general be any such thing.

He will support all of (1), (2) and (3), and will be impressed also by the fact that sane and honourable people can attach different importance to different values, so that they will not agree on the resolution of many difficult conflict cases. However, it is important also in describing his position to include that resistance to Utopianism which I mentioned earlier. A Utopian theorist – let us consider one who uses the notion of *ideology* – might well agree with the account *of present society* in terms of irresoluble conflict, incommensurable values and so forth; and he would be resolutely opposed to analytical philosophers and others who seek to resolve those confiicts and reduce uncertainty by systematising our morality into an ethical theory – this itself must be an ideologically polluted enterprise. However, he will think that what needs to be transcended is present society, and that in some better condition conflict will be reduced, and false values discarded. Nor does he think that this will be a purely technological achievement, as we might all agree that conflict could be reduced and less refractory values established by drugs or brain-treatments: he sees it in terms of enlightenment or insight (though grounded, no doubt, in social action). The sceptic about Utopia doubts that there is anywhere for that kind of enlightenment or insight to come from, since his understanding of values as they are gives no hope that their present incoherences could be radically transcended without loss. You might perhaps bring about a society whose values were less conflicting, more clearly articulated, more efficient; and people, once arrived in this state, might have no sense of loss. But that would not mean there was no loss. It would mean that there was another loss, the loss of the sense of loss.

A Utopian theorist of ideology, and a pluralist sceptic about Utopia, can however agree on at least one thing: that the enterprise of trying to reduce our conflicts, and to legislate to remove moral uncertainty, by constructing a philosophical *ethical theory* (in the sense of systematising moral belief) is a misguided one. The ethical theorist tends to assimilate conflicts in moral belief to theoretical contradiction, and applies a model of theoretical rationality and adequacy to moral understanding. This is wrong in more than one way. If conflict among our values is not necessarily pathological, and if even where the situation is at fault, as with some conflicts of obligation, conflict is not a logical affliction of our thought, it must be a mistake to regard a need to eliminate conflict as a purely rational demand, of the kind that applies to a theoretical system. Rather we should see such needs as there are to reduce conflict and to rationalise our moral thought as having a more social and personal basis.

In particular, in a modern complex society functions which are ethically significant are performed by public agencies and, if the society is relatively open, this requires that they be governed by an explicable order which allows those agencies to be answerable. In a public, large and impersonal forum 'intuition' will not serve, though it will serve (and nothing else could serve) in personal life and in a more closely shared existence. This is well illustrated in connection with 'imperfect rationalisation', the situation in which some difference, not further reasoned, can ground agreement in private and less impersonal connections, but may not serve, or may not continue to serve, where a public order demands a public answer. To take an example which has been recently discussed, a distinction between abortion, which is permitted, and infanticide, which is not, is one which can probably be naturally sustained in a certain context of shared moral sentiment without further reason being needed. The fact that further reason is not needed does not mean that that distinction is *irrational*. It means only that the basic distinction is more directly convincing than any reason that might be advanced for it: another way of putting it is that 'You can't kill that, it's a child' is more convincing as a reason than any reason which might be advanced for its being a reason. It may possibly be that in an open system (that is to say, in a system where explanations have to be given) where abortions are carried out by public and answerable agencies, such a context of moral sentiment can still survive, and be enough. But it may not, and a further requirement of rationalisation will be felt. If it is, then that requirement will not be a demand of pure rationality, but rather of a certain kind of public order. What this illustrates in the area of 'imperfect rationalisation' applies also to the closely analogous case of conflict.

These demands of the public order, however, have implications for private sentiment as well. There are also important needs, both of the individual and of the society, that private sentiment and the rules of the public order should not drift too far from each other. If functions which have specific moral significance (medical functions, for instance) are performed in an impersonal public sphere, and more activities which express and encourage important values are publicly conducted, some new accord must be found between private understanding, which can live with a good deal of 'intuition' and unresolved conflict, and the public order, which, unless we are to give up the ethical ambition that it be answerable, can only live with less. At the same time, the public order, if it is to carry conviction, and also not to flatten human experience, has to find ways in which it can be adequately related to private sentiment, which remains more 'intuitive' and open to conflict than public rules can be. For the intuitive condition is not only a state which private understanding *can* live with, but a state which it must have as part of its life, if that life is going to have any density or conviction and succeed in being that worthwhile kind of life which human beings lack unless they feel more than they can say, and grasp more than they can explain.

Rawls has written of a 'reflective equilibrium' between intuition (in the sense of moral conviction) and ethical theory, which it is the aim of moral philosophy to achieve. Rather, if philosophy is to understand the relations between confict and rationalisation in the modern world, it should look towards an equilibrium – one to be achieved in practice – between private and public.

ROBERT WOKLER

Rousseau's Perfectibilian Libertarianism

I

In the derelict battlefields of political theory lie the empty hulks of our discredited concepts, few of which have suffered so precipitous a fall from grace as the idea of perfectibility. At least since the time of Pelagius in the fifth century until a few generations ago our supposed capacity for self-perfection was regarded by commentators as a sign of free will or proof of mastery over our individual fates, and in the doctrines of Pico, Leibniz, Fontenelle or Wesley, whether conceived as part of a Christian rational theodicy or in a secularised form of humanist indeterminism, it has served as the shining beacon of the diverse images of our liberty envisaged by its proponents. In the eighteenth and nineteenth centuries in particular, when perfectibilian theories of human nature were most widely endorsed, the concept came to be associated with two major philosophical perspectives. The first, propounded by such figures as Condorcet, Godwin, Comte or Marx, was that of demonstrable historical progress, sometimes of the human mind, sometimes of social science, sometimes of Absolute Spirit or of our species-being, manifested in the rise of civilisations and the evolution of economic or cultural epochs. The second may be termed the doctrine of self-perfection or self-realisation, and in the almost equally diverse constructions of Kant or Hegel, Mill or Bosanquet, it has been associated with the unfolding of individual potentialities, occasionally expressed in their richest variety, more often in stricter accord with their allegedly most virtuous or rational essence. Of course to subsume the doctrines of these thinkers under such general categories – obviously neither exclusive nor exhaustive – hardly begins to explain them, and some of their features have anyway not only survived in contemporary thought but even received new impetus in the formulations of recent admirers.[1] I think it would be fair to say, nevertheless, that their perfectibilian characteristics have been largely cast aside as dead weight, and neither global nor individual perspectives of the road to perfect freedom are any longer regarded with favour by serious

[1] The best general introduction to the subject is John Passmore's *The Perfectibility of Man* (London, 1970).

political thinkers – least of all by political thinkers of a liberal frame of mind.

Since around the end of the First World War we have been taught by Hobhouse and his followers that we should be mistrustful of notions of self-perfection which ascribe true liberty only to the domination of our lower impulses by our higher faculties, and from Popper and his disciples in the period after the Second War we have learnt that the prophets of historical progress are scarcely distinguishable from the apologists of social control. Perhaps the most eloquent and incisive defence of freedom against both of those theories, however, has been set forth by Isaiah Berlin in his essays on 'Historical Inevitability' and 'Two Concepts of Liberty'. In the first of these texts Berlin argues that doctrines of mankind's ineluctable advance take account of individuals not as the agents but as the instruments of change, as minute drops in a cosmic tide of development, of which the patterns or rhythms are prescribed by laws outside human control. However much it might seem to be our destiny to undergo perfection through the operation of these laws, the course plotted by our causally determined path of development places us beyond the familiar bounds of moral responsibility and renders us no more than ephemeral embodiments of the relentless sweep of a historical 'force majeure'. In the second work Berlin has shown that doctrines of self-perfection are commonly shrouded behind a 'monstrous impersonation' of one's actual empirical self by one's real rational self. Sometimes our allegedly higher form of being or consciousness is attained by what he describes as a 'retreat to the inner citadel' where individuals so cut themselves off from their baser wants that they no longer desire anything more than to perform their duties; sometimes it is realised by a more expansive identification of one's true self with a collective entity whose very commands to its constituent parts are held to be the source of their real liberty when properly understood. Yet the perfection achieved by individuals so divided or multiplied is, according to Berlin, in conflict with any notion of the fundamental integrity of persons, denying, as it does, the inviolability of their rights and the toleration of their beliefs upon which every free society depends.

To be sure, not all liberals agree with Berlin that related issues of personal freedom are at issue in these two controversies, and some have reasserted against his views the now familiar claim that the causal determinants of actions investigated (or at any rate sought) by scientific historians are conceptually distinct from any constraints to which actions may be subjected. But it is a compelling feature of his exposition that it attempts to forge a link between the moral critique of historical inevitability, on the one hand, and the case against most versions of positive liberty, on the other, with Berlin insisting particularly upon the fact that if determinism were true then the idea of merit or desert which we attach to the optional behaviour of ordinary individuals would have no application. Positive libertarians are to a large extent prescriptive determinists, and the problems of volition, choice and responsibility that for Berlin bedevil evolutionary doctrines of human perfectibility are, on his interpretation, similarly troublesome for theories that point the way to an uplifted form of personal freedom. It is, moreover, a measure of the force of his arguments and the scope of their appeal that they have silenced the opposition at least in those quarters they attacked most directly, and such perfectibilian libertarians as have survived now lie low and still, sheltering quietly like weary soldiers bereaved of their cause.

II

In the light of the contemporary liberal challenge to the doctrine of perfectibility, then, it strikes me as odd that the author of the term – the first person, that is, who actually employed it and who indeed constructed a well known social theory in which the concept figures as a central element – should have meant by it something almost opposite to the views spurned by its critics today. When Rousseau introduced the idea in his *Discours sur l'inégalité*[2] he did not have in mind any determinist law of historical progress or any positive principle of self-realisation. On the contrary, he stressed that it was our attribute of perfectibility which had facilitated our degradation and that this trait was connected with a form of negative liberty defined as the absence of compulsion. Considered from a historical perspective, our perfectibility must have been the source not of our improvement but of our misfortunes, Rousseau argued, for it was the exercise of this distinctive human faculty which had made possible the transformation of the insignificant natural differences of our progenitors into the grave moral distinctions that

[2] It has been suggested that Turgot may have employed the term in conversation from around 1750, but apart from Grimm's reference to it (borrowed from Rousseau's manuscript) mentioned below, there is no recorded instance of its use at all, in any European language, before the publication of the *Discours sur l'inégalité* (hereafter *D.I.*) in 1755. As Jean Starobinski has noted, the word was not incorporated in the fourth (1762) edition of the *Dictionnaire de l'Académie française*, though it appears in the fifth (1798–9) edition, and he traces its first mention in a work of reference to the *Dictionnaire de Trévoux* of 1771.

form the foundation of all civilised societies. Whatever might be claimed by the philosophers of progress who employed the concept after him, Rousseau perceived a radical separation between our innate perfectibility and the putative stages of our historical advancement, for the social evolution of humanity bore witness, he wrote, to the fact that all our apparent steps towards self-perfection have in reality led to the decrepitude of the species.[3]

With regard to individual behaviour, moreover, this account of perfectibility was joined in his theory to a conception of liberty which created no formidable gulf between our higher and lower or collective and private selves but rather marked an initially very faint line between savage man and beast. According to Rousseau our species must always have had an advantage over animals only to the extent that our conduct was not naturally subject to internal mechanisms of control. Whereas all other creatures have been provided by Nature with instincts appropriate to the manner of their self-preservation, we have played an active part in the determination of how we live. We are unique in that we perform our deeds, often to our disadvantage, by exercising our liberty; animals, on the other hand, generally behave as they must in order to satisfy their impulses. It was, therefore, because our forebears would have been able to select and organise the mode of their unprogrammed response to natural drives rather than because they were endowed with any positive traits or virtues of their own that mankind alone enjoyed a prospect of development. In their original state our ancestors would have been more adroit and flexible in their way of life than other creatures, Rousseau claimed. Since the female of our species was able to move about with a child in her arms she must have found it easier to nourish her offspring than the females of most other species, and since our patterns of nutrition were not prescribed by Nature we were omnivorous and could feast on a diet of our own choice. Above all we could always decide for ourselves how best to contend with each situation – whether to confront or flee from danger, for instance – and it was, Rousseau remarked, particularly in man's consciousness of his liberty that 'the spirituality of his soul' was displayed.[4]

[3] See *D.I.*, in Rousseau's *Oeuvres complètes* (Paris, 1959–) (hereafter *O.C.*) III 142, 170–1; the *Confessions*, book 8, *O.C.* I 388; and Rousseau to Voltaire, 18 August 1756, in the *Correspondance complète de Rousseau*, ed. R. A. Leigh (Geneva and Banbury, 1965–) hereafter *C.C.*), no 424, IV 38–9.

[4] *D.I.*, *O.C.* III 142.

At least two points in this very brief sketch of Rousseau's theory may already seem problematic and require explanation before I proceed further. The first has to do with whether the idea of liberty in the *Discours sur l'inégalité* can be properly described as a negative concept, a difficulty which might appear to arise because Rousseau there identifies liberty with free will and at the same time speaks of Nature as exercising a kind of internal constraint upon behaviour[5] in a fashion some negative libertarians have regarded as either misleading or false, on the grounds that freedom applies only to bodies and constraints only to external obstacles. But leaving aside difficulties of translation, and of the dubious synonymy of 'liberty' and 'freedom' in English, I think it appropriate to speak of Rousseau's conception of liberty in this context as negative, in so far as it introduces no substantive aim or purpose to which freedom is or ought to be directed and neither entails nor implies any moral claim about the manner in which it should be exercised. His notion of perfectibility in the *Discours* lacks a positive goal largely because the account of liberty to which it is linked lacks a positive framework, and I shall try to show in a moment that Rousseau's theory is in fact rather more consistently negative in formulation than a number of libertarian doctrines to which it is often opposed. It is true that he enlarges the idea of constraint to include organic instincts together with external obstacles, but most (though not all) negative libertarians have also extended their notions of the nature of a constraint to embrace laws, contracts and compulsory enactments of various kinds, as well as physical impediments. Notwithstanding Berlin's interrelated critiques of doctrines of historical inevitability and positive liberty, the proposition that instincts are a form of constraint pertains more directly to the subject of determinism than to that of negative versus positive freedom, and no less than Berlin himself Rousseau doubted that distinctively human activities could be explained with reference to a natural cause. At any rate, suffice it to say that his conception of liberty thus far outlined amounts to little more than the claim that we are free and animals are not because we alone can choose to act as we do, a thesis unobjectionable to the great majority of thinkers usually regarded as negative libertarians, and one which many, including Tocqueville and Mill, have endorsed.

Neither should we be too much perturbed – and this is my second point – by the fact that Rousseau's concept of perfectibility is un-

[5] In the *Contrat social* (hereafter *C.S.*), book 1, chapter 8, *O.C.* III 365, Rousseau goes so far as to define the impulsions of appetite as 'slavery'.

connected with any philosophy of history that plots the advances we have made on our road to perfection. For just as we are so often reminded by Berlin and other liberals that freedom consists in the possibility of action rather than the action itself, so too perfectibility refers to a human capacity the possession of which need not ensure its fulfilment. It has long been recognised, moreover, sometimes even by those who suppose the attainment of perfection to be a finite goal within our grasp, that in becoming more perfect at what we do we may only succeed in making ourselves worse men or women, for, as both Aristotle and Aquinas, among others, have remarked, it is quite correct to speak of a perfect thief and of perfection in evil generally.[6] A somewhat different claim along these lines that focuses attention on an uplifting but again not virtuous quality can be found in one of the discussions on the *Discours sur l'inégalité*, in which the author, Mme d'Épinay, observed that, whatever the other shortcomings of male imbeciles, they might, at least in one organ, achieve what she termed 'une perfection monstrueuse'.[7] The essential point for Rousseau was that our perfectibility only made our moral advance possible, a prospect more clearly intelligible with reference to its beginning than its end and in most contexts better translated as a potential for self-improvement than as a capacity for self-perfection. Especially since it was in his view an attribute connected with our freedom its *real* development depended upon the *actual* choices individuals must have made when they adopted their various modes and patterns of life and bequeathed them to their children. Human perfectibility only ensured that there could be cumulative change in one direction or another, and it was as much compatible with the history of our degradation as it would have been compatible with the history of our progress. According to Rousseau, our forebears had indeed misapplied their freedom in the course of their evolution from their natural state in adopting social relations which debased rather than improved their habits, for just as they had grown progressively less dependent upon Nature they had equally made themselves progressively more dependent on other men. So far from having devoted our capacity for self-improvement to the task of enhancing (or even preserving) the liberty we must originally have enjoyed, we had, through our obligations undertaken in society,

[6] See Aristotle, *Metaphysica*, book 5, chapter 16, 1021b18–19, and Aquinas, *Summa Theologiae*, 1a2æ 55.3.

[7] 'Lettre de Mme d'Epinay à M. l'abbé Galiani' (1776), in the *Correspondance littéraire, philosophique et critique*, ed. Maurice Tourneux (Paris, 1877–82) (hereafter *C.L.*), XI 278.

elected to become slaves to compulsions we imposed upon ourselves.

If I find these issues less problematic than they have appeared to others, what does seem odd to me – almost as curious as the fact that Rousseau's concept should be so much at variance with the views of most theorists who later adopted the term for their own purposes – is that the connection between perfectibility and negative liberty has escaped the notice even of the great majority of his interpreters. In general, political theorists today have a fair grasp of his pessimistic evaluation of our history and recognise as the central element of his philosophy the proposition that men are naturally happy and good while the institutions fabricated by men have made them corrupt and miserable. Yet so far from joining this thesis to the doctrine of perfectibility with which it was associated in his own writings[8] most critics have come to view it as anti-perfectibilian, or 'deteriorationist' as Peacock describes it in attributing a Rousseauist philosophy to the character Mr Escot in his novel *Headlong Hall.* Together with Mr Escot, moreover, we have come, by and large, to see this bleak vision of our moral history in fatalist terms, as a 'great chain of corruption, which will soon fetter the whole human race in irreparable slavery and incurable wretchedness',[9] so that, as one of his leading nineteenth-century biographers put it, Rousseau's 'pernicious nonsense was . . . due . . . to [his] want of a conception of improvement in human affairs'.[10] The idea of perfectibility, thus divorced from his account of our decline, has been let loose to drive us on towards a more exalted goal in connection with his supposed doctrine of positive freedom, only to be thwarted and trapped by the contemporary liberal objections to this new formulation of his argument. For if self-perfection is transformed to mean the lofty pursuit of an ideal as contrasted to the mere satisfaction of desires; and if the pursuit of the ideal makes a person free just in so far as he ceases to have any desire but to attain it; then to prefer something less than this is to deprive oneself of liberty, and 'recalcitrants either conceal their preferences or end by being forced to be free in Wormwood Scrubbs or Broadmoor'.[11] With travesties such as this to feast upon it is small wonder that well trained students of political thought so frequently disgorge Rousseau's theory without having savoured a morsel.

[8] See *Rousseau juge de Jean Jaques*, Third Dialogue, *O.C.* I 934–5.

[9] Thomas Love Peacock, *Headlong Hall*, in *The Novels of Peacock* I (London, 1963) 11–12.

[10] John Morley, *Rousseau* (London, 1873) II 244.

[11] T. D. Weldon, 'Political Principles', in Peter Laslett (ed.), *Philosophy, Politics and Society*, 1st Series (Oxford, 1956), p. 32.

Eighteenth-century commentators characteristically adopted a view that is almost the reverse of this perspective of his perfectibilian doctrine. On the one hand, his contemporaries were slow to accept that a major contributor to the *Encyclopédie* – that most towering monument to progress in the period – could really suppose that our civilisations were in moral decline, and both his friends among the party of Enlightenment which he attacked, as well as his critics among the enemies of Enlightenment who might have been expected to endorse his stance, initially regarded his philosophy of history as no more than an 'ingenious paradox'[12] which did not express his authentic and sincere beliefs. At the same time these interpreters had no doubt that his concept of perfectibility was intended to draw a line between mankind and other creatures. It was so understood by Grimm, who even took advantage of the fact that he had read the *Discours sur l'inégalité* in manuscript by employing the concept himself in this sense in an issue of the *Correspondance littéraire* some months prior to the publication of Rousseau's text. It was interpreted in the same light, moreover, by Jean de Castillon in his own *Discours sur l'inégalité*, conceived as a reply to Rousseau, though in this case Castillon objected to the claim that our perfectibility had given rise to our vices and errors, adding that the trait was anyway shared by animals as well, a thesis later endorsed by Mme d'Épinay in her own commentary on the subject and by Charles-Georges Leroy in his *Lettres philosophiques sur l'intelligence et la perfectibilité des animaux*. Herder, too, read Rousseau's thesis in terms of a basic divide between our species and others, maintaining, however, in his *Abhandlung über den Ursprung der Sprache*, that the idea was superfluous to our understanding of human nature, just as the alternative concept of reason, discarded by Jean-Jacques, was indispensable.[13] Rousseau's account of perfectibility, in short, was recognised in his own day as a putative generic distinction between man and beast already evident at the root of human evolution and not as a sign of our moral pre-eminence at an advanced stage of civilisation.

12 These terms are employed by Charles Borde in his *Second Discours sur les avantages des sciences et des arts* (Avignon, 1753), p. 3.

13 See Grimm, *C.L.*, 15 February 1755, II 492; Castillon, *Discours sur l'inégalité* (Amsterdam, 1756), pp. 46, 49–50; d'Épinay, 'Lettre à Galiani', *C.L.* XI 279–80; Leroy, *Lettres philosophiques sur la perfectibilité des animaux* (Paris, 1802), pp. 59–60; and Herder, *Ursprung der Sprache* (1772), in his *Sämmtliche Werke* (Berlin, 1877–1913) V 44.

III

This idea of perfectibility in terms of an original divide between our own species and all the rest was presented by Rousseau as an alternative to natural law and social contract doctrines according to which our essential humanity was a function of other attributes – in particular, reason, language or sociability. In focusing upon these qualities as fundamental to our nature, ancient and modern thinkers had laboured under a misapprehension, on his account, for they had abstracted certain historically and socially developed characteristics of our lives and ascribed to them the status of timeless and universal principles or faculties that made the establishment and evolution of our social institutions possible. Such claims, he remarked, confused civil man for natural man,[14] incorporating in their *explicans* of human behaviour elements which could only figure in the *explicandum*. Locke, for instance, supposed that our intrinsic sociability was apparent in our natural family relationships – in the fact, that is, that the 'Conjugal Society' of 'Man and Wife' was 'more lasting, than of Male and Female amongst other Creatures' since it embraced 'the nourishment and support' of offspring dependent on their help for a specially long period.[15] Yet Rousseau replied to this contention that before domestic household units had been formed there would have been no reason for any of our male progenitors to become permanently attached to particular females after casual copulation, nor to children which they would not have recognised as belonging to them and whose birth they would neither have intended nor foreseen.[16] It was equally a mistake, he argued, to imagine that our highly complicated language systems, which were anyway almost impossible to dissociate from the social codes and principles of morality they expressed and represented, could be understood as an outward manifestation of a natural faculty. For if linguistic competence in speech was a fundamentally distinguishing mark of humanity, then we had no real grounds for regarding mutes as human and apes as not, a proposition which in the eighteenth century led Linnaeus to classify individuals abandoned in the wild as a type of being (*Homo ferus*) taxonomically different from the rest of us, and, on the other hand, prompted La Mettrie, Monboddo and Rousseau himself to wonder whether apes might not be primitive members of our species whose untrained faculty of speech had still to be perfected by ex-

[14] See *D.I.*, *O.C.* III 132 and note 12, ibid. 218.
[15] Locke, *Second Treatise*, chapter 7, sections 78–80.
[16] See *D.I.*, note 12, *O.C.* III 216–17.

perience.[17] And if it was the case that language formed no absolutely clear division between animals and men, then how could we be sure of the essential rationality of our nature, of which our use of language was generally taken to be the clearest sign? Not only were the miserably oppressive institutions we had concocted in society scant proof of any supposed rational capacity of men to select appropriate means to achieve desired ends, but it was even possible, Rousseau reflected, to view other creatures as better endowed with such a capacity than we were just *because* they showed no command of language. After all, he remarked in a letter to Hume, according to Negro observers it was a 'trick of monkeys' to pretend that they cannot speak, though they really can, 'out of fear that they might otherwise be made to work'.[18] The ascription to mankind of a positive trait or faculty was unwarranted in each of these cases, then, because it was based upon the assumption that the members of our species, and of our species alone, must always have exhibited this or that refined social quality which, in fact, only individuals in historically evolved circumstances could have come to display.

In his account of our liberty and perfectibility Rousseau opposed the natural law philosophers and social contract theorists for having gone still further in their putative definitions of our specifically human attributes. He accused Grotius, for instance, of having falsely supposed that our savage forebears must have possessed a sense of justice and injustice; he challenged Locke and Pufendorf for having wrongly claimed that we naturally recognise a right of property; and he took issue with Hobbes for assuming that we must have been able to comprehend the meaning and force of relations of authority even before we had established our first governments.[19] On his interpretation, however, the main problem with doctrines of this kind was not so much that their postulates about the nature of humanity were arbitrary when taken separately and often incompatible when taken together. It was rather that the normative political precepts framed around them were actually detrimental to the development of those attributes that truly distinguish us from animals. By positing too much in their conceptions of human nature the social philosophers

[17] See *D.I.*, *O.C.* III 146–51 and note 10, ibid. 208-14, and my 'Perfectible Apes in Decadent Cultures: Rousseau's Anthropology Revisited', *Daedalus* (Summer 1978), 107–34, from which a few adapted sentences are incorporated here.

[18] Rousseau to Hume, 29 March 1766, *C.C.* no 5129, XXIX 66. The suggestion that apes or monkeys remain silent for good reasons of their own, especially to avoid work and enslavement, appeared at least as early as 1623 in Richard Jobson's *The Golden Trade*.

[19] See *D.I.*, *O.C.* III 132, 1301.

whom Rousseau confronted in his writings had, paradoxically, perceived too little of our distinctive potentialities. They proposed justifications of authority which required that our liberty be suppressed and our perfectibility channelled along a morally decadent path, and in the course of our social and political history such justifications, he believed, had unfortunately come to serve as the legitimating principles of the dominion exercised over us by our rulers.

Despite the facts that Hobbes's political theory was focused above all on the defence of authority rather than the preservation of liberty and that Locke's doctrine sometimes described law as enlarging freedom instead of restraining it[20] – both points of view uncongenial to most negative libertarians today – there is, I think, a crucial sense, perceived by Rousseau himself, in which their political reflections are fundamentally negative in character. For the two thinkers conceived their ideas in terms of the protection rather than promotion of the interests of subjects, in a framework, that is, of the minimal conditions necessary for the maintenance of peace or the preservation of property, and in each case the essential function of government was negative in so far as it was designed to keep individuals from inflicting harm upon one another – to avoid a manifest *summum malum* rather than procure an illusory *summum bonum*, as Hobbes saw it. For Rousseau, however, the centrally negative feature of such doctrines was less their perspective of liberty than their assessments of human nature – bleak, dismal and confined by faculties more social than natural and by anxieties that could only arise in particular types of political system. Hobbes and Locke imagined that without government individuals must live in a state of perpetual conflict or inconvenience – on Hobbes's account because competition, diffidence and glory prompt them to 'endeavour to destroy or subdue one another', for Locke because each man exercises only irregular and uncertain power to punish the transgressions of others.[21] As Rousseau understood them, these conclusions, though based on different premises, were more striking for their similarities than for their differences, since both thinkers supposed that the natural condition of men – their condition of equality unfettered by a civil power – was dangerous, precarious and injurious to their interests.

20 See especially the *Second Treatise*, chapter 6, section 57.

21 See Hobbes, *De cive*, chapter 1, sections 2, 5 and 6, and *Leviathan*, chapter 13, and Locke, *Second Treatise*, chapter 9, section 127.

In his political philosophy he confronted such claims largely by contending that though they were groundless in principle they served as well-founded descriptions of how our liberty might have come to be exploited and our capacity for self-perfection turned down the moral slope of our decline. First, he maintained, on much the same grounds that he challenged all conceptions of our natural sociability, language or reason, that there was no justification for supposing that individuals in their original state must have been motivated by a sense of glory or diffidence, or a desire to secure and protect property, or indeed by any antagonistic interests of the sort described by Hobbes and Locke. Second, and on the other hand, he argued that the two theorists taken together, but only taken together and in reverse order, had provided a conceivably accurate account of the way in which our morally pernicious governments might actually have established their authority over us while making that authority appear the instrument of our common consent. For civil society, as Rousseau understood it, must at first have been a conventional artifact designed to lay the foundations of property entitlements such as Locke had supposed natural, and it must have been disputes over just those entitlements that gave rise to a state of war in the manner described by Hobbes. When the demon of private property reigns over human affairs, he remarked in the *Discours*, all men become enemies by duty and rascals by interest, finding it more lucrative to inflict harm than to extend favours.[22] He believed that agreements framed to preserve peace and protect property would in due course have been formulated, not by each of us acting rationally in a primordial state of nature, but by rich individuals in established societies seeking to safeguard their estates through a cunning hoax. The terms of those agreements might have seemed superficially plausible because they would have referred to the defence of the weak and the security of every man, but by granting to each person the legitimate possession only of what was his already their real aim was to establish order on behalf of those who owned the land at the expense of the liberty of the rest to gain the same entitlements.[23] The political authorities prescribed by Hobbes and Locke thus served the purpose of establishing a legal recognition of the differences between men in society, and so far from solving any of the problems which arose from the supposed fact that men were equal in the state of nature their true effect was to make the social distinctions between us more durable and persistent. On this reading, their doctrines were

[22] See *D.I.*, note 9, *O.C.* III 202–3.
[23] See *D.I.*, *O.C.* III 175–8.

linked to the world of politics rather in the manner that philosophical discussions at once follow and give warrant to the sexual orgies recounted in Sade's *La Nouvelle Justine*, for together with the debauched protagonists of that work the practical disciples of the political theories of Hobbes and Locke might well say of themselves, 'No sooner did we commit a horror than we sought to legitimate it.'[24] The two thinkers had inadvertently drawn an accurate portrait of the state of civil society supposing it to be a description of the state of nature, for the vices requiring remedy which they depicted were not those of our original constitution but rather those that stemmed from the very social systems they commended to us. According to Rousseau, in short, Hobbes and Locke had conceived their ideas as solutions to some problems of which those solutions were in fact the cause.[25] Even while asserting that mankind had no essence, these abstract postulators of our fundamental qualities made us appear so base and miserable that we could not but admire the peace and justice brought to us by governments which transform us from savages into citizens. And yet when we shut their splendid books and look at men outside them, what do we see?, Rousseau lamented in an unfinished composition entitled 'Que l'état de guerre naît de l'état social': 'Everyone groaning under an iron yoke, the whole of humanity crushed by a handful of oppressors; everywhere suffering and starvation, of which the rich contentedly drink the blood and tears; and throughout the world nothing but the strong holding sway over the weak, armed with the redoubtable strength of the law.'[26]

Many negative libertarians now take an equally dismal view of our political systems, even if they might be inclined to blame Rousseau rather than Hobbes and Locke for our plight. Yet if the social contract doctrines challenged by Jean-Jacques tell us more about the principles we have already come to adopt than about those that we should, our contemporary theories of historical entitlements and minimal protective associations imply a good deal more than they state about the patterns of human relations which their prescriptions are designed to maintain. Some figures commonly regarded as belonging to this tradition – Bentham and Mill, for instance – have abandoned the idea of imprescriptible natural rights; most others – including Bentham and Mill, again, as well as Constant and Nozick – have discarded Locke's conceptions of the purpose of law and the

[24] Sade, *La Nouvelle Justine, ou Les Malheurs de la vertu*, in his *Oeuvres complètes* (Paris, 1966–7) VII 37.

[25] See *D.I.*, the *Manuscrit de Genève*, book 1, chapter 2, and the 'État de guerre', *O.C.* III 184, 288 and 610, and *Émile*, book 4, *O.C.* IV 524.

[26] 'L'État de guerre', *O.C.* III 608–9.

social contract; and, not surprisingly perhaps, almost all have rid themselves of Hobbes's justification of absolute sovereignty. In so far as negative libertarians remain fundamentally concerned, however, to preserve inviolable frontiers, barriers and safeguards between persons, their philosophies continue to be imbued with many of the assumptions about our essential motives, fears and desires which Rousseau uncovered in the writings of his precursors. To that extent their views of human nature are overburdened with the weight of attributes they believe universally characteristic of our species, and, tied to these encumbrances,[27] they stand apart from Rousseau's emptier, more formal, more strictly negative conception of our distinguishing behavioural traits – unique only because, in his view, they are uncontrolled by instincts. Paradoxically, again, it is the negative libertarian doctrines so often contrasted with his allegedly positive stance which constitute the most characteristic form of the 'retreat to the inner citadel' in contemporary political thought. In the light of the argument Rousseau himself presents, we could only retreat to citadels we had already taken the trouble to construct, and we were only prompted to seek sanctuary there because we had contrived to make enemies outside.

IV

If on the one hand Rousseau opposed the social contract theorists before him for having ascribed too much to human nature, on the other hand, from a different perspective, he charged that they had actually perceived too little. For not only were they mistaken to suppose that men were universally motivated by aims both prevalent and conceivable only in civilised cultures; they were equally wrong to take no notice of the potentialities of human development. In their suppositions about the fundamental divide between man and beast they regarded our natural behaviour as in certain respects very similar to that of animals – 'nasty' and 'brutish', according to Hobbes, likely to be 'dangerous and noxious', according to Locke[28] – on grounds which did little credit to their understanding

[27] For discussions of the substantive or end-state principles implicit in the most widely discussed negative libertarian doctrine of our day – that of Nozick – see especially Thomas Scanlon, 'Nozick on Rights, Liberty, and Property', *Philosophy and Public Affairs* 6 (1976), 3–25; G. A. Cohen, 'Nozick and Wilt Chamberlain: How Patterns Preserve Liberty', *Erkenntnis* 11 (1977), 5–23; and Hillel Steiner, 'The Natural Right to the Means of Production', *Philosophical Quarterly* 27 (1977), 41–9.

[28] See Hobbes, *Leviathan*, chapter 13, and Locke, *Second Treatise*, chapter 3, section 16, and chapter 14, section 163.

of either animals or men, since creatures in the wild, Rousseau believed, were as benign and compassionate towards members of their own species as savages must initially have been towards one another. But more important in this context is his contention that animals behave in compassionate and unaggressively self-interested ways because they are bound to do so – because, that is, they lack the attributes of liberty and perfectibility which make it possible for us to become cruel and transmit the trait of cruelty to our children and their descendants. We must at first have been free not only to choose the manner of our response to the impulsions of Nature but also to develop our behaviour in a cumulative way, so that in his original condition each individual must have had the ability to improve as well as change his nature. Once he had adopted habits which no animals could share, it would have been in his power to make those habits a permanent feature of his constitution, and, in Rousseau's view, it was in fact precisely because men were able to make themselves more or less perfect rather than merely different from other creatures that they could undergo a *history* of change. After a few months every animal apart from man is already stamped with the characteristic dispositions of its maturity, he observed in the *Discours*, and after a thousand years the whole of its species is marked by the same instincts and patterns of life as the first generation. Man, however, is capable of improving his faculties, and he is also unique among animals in having what is, in effect, the same capacity to make retrograde steps and thus impair his nature.[29] By supposing that rational agents would conceive their interests in roughly the same way and pursue them in the same fashion at all times, earlier social contract theorists had wrongly supposed that men's behaviour was moulded like that of animals. They had failed to recognise the historical dimension of our nature and had overlooked the fact that we had transformed ourselves in the course of our development in ways beyond the capacity of any other known form of life. Rousseau could not accept as sufficient Hobbes's dictum that 'To make Covenants with bruit Beasts, is impossible',[30] since the divide between humanity and the rest of nature, though barely perceptible at first, was potentially much greater than that suggested by the idea of a being endowed with an ability to devise contracts. On his account we are a species apart because in the course of our evolution we have formed ourselves into the creatures we have become. Grotius, Hobbes, Pufendorf and Locke had not merely

[29] See *D.I.*, *O.C.* III 142.
[30] *Leviathan*, chapter 14.

neglected to explain how we could have attained the linguistic competence required to make and abide by compacts; they had actually omitted to notice the whole temporal scale of our moral development. For in that development, in our long process of self-domestication, as Rousseau conceived it, our collective agreements must have been accompanied by more slowly evolving forms of law – law 'inscribed not on marble . . . but in the hearts of citizens', he remarked in the *Contrat social*,[31] by custom, public opinion and all the trappings of *les moeurs* such as Montesquieu had described – which gave each State the particular kind of constitution it has. This richly textured view of how our capacity for self-perfection has been exercised, this integration of a highly optimistic idea of human potentialities with a deeply pessimistic vision of our actual accomplishments, was elaborated by Rousseau in his critique of natural law and social contract doctrines. And in the ramifications of that conception of perfectibility – borrowed as it was from an essentially theological tradition of moral philosophy and redefined in terms which anticipate the more sociological modes of argument of his successors – can be found some of his most striking contributions to eighteenth-century thought.

Of course his argument suggests that Hobbes and Locke had not entirely overlooked the perfectibility of man in their political theories, since they had unwittingly described the path our forebears might have taken when, in pursuit of their liberty, they had run headlong into their chains – when, that is, in their misguided use of their capacity for self-perfection they took the first political steps along the way of the moral decline of our species. In our subsequent history the value systems we had constructed upon the institutional base of private property had further strengthened the yoke and reinforced the bonds of our corruption, and so, too, Rousseau often reflected in his writings, had our arts, sciences and literature – those insidious forces 'weaving garlands of flowers round the chains that weigh men down'.[32] Yet while he was convinced that our natural liberty had been irretrievably lost in the course of our development he did not suppose the same to be true of our perfectibility, for if that human quality were lost as well then there would be no worldly possibility for civilised men to overcome their corruption, and the fact that persons everywhere tended to display only those vicious characteristics impressed upon them by their governments – a fact on which he so often insisted – would ensure that it was now beyond

[31] *C.S.*, book 2, chapter 12, *O.C.* III 394.
[32] *Discours sur les sciences et les arts*, *O.C.* III 7.

the power of individuals or communities to improve their condition or realise any form of virtue. In fact the whole of Rousseau's prescriptive political theory and philosophy of education depends on the assumption that however much men have been the victims of their own history they remain its authors as well, for, despite his scepticism about our civilised achievements, he believed that our perfectibility still enabled us to pursue both public and domestic modes of life that were morally superior to those of the contemporary world.

V

It is with regard to his conceptions of a better future – allegedly found in the portrait of Clarens in *La Nouvelle Héloïse*, or implicit in the schemes of the tutor in *Émile*, or expressed in the principles of political right of the *Contrat social* – that Rousseau has most often been attacked as a positive libertarian, in recent years even as a totalitarian, thinker. Almost all such charges have, in my view, been wide of the mark, not least because *La Nouvelle Héloïse* was conceived and should be interpreted as a novel with a plot and characters rather than as a moral blueprint or treatise exhorting readers to behave in one way or another, while *Émile* prescribes no active political role to the pupil and concludes with the tutor's counsel that he should perform his duties but keep aloof from urban life in particular and society in general since freedom is not to be found under any form of government. Commentators who object to the corporate essence of the civil and moral liberties contrasted to mere natural liberty in the *Contrat social*, moreover, too often neglect Rousseau's account of the fundamental rights men enjoy by virtue of their humanity alone, since he remarks both in the same work and elsewhere that any political infringement of these rights would be an act of despotism beyond the competence of the sovereign, circumscribed as it is in its authority by the laws of nature.[33] Most liberals have equally misunderstood his statement that 'Whoever refuses to obey the general will . . . shall be forced to be free.' For as is perfectly clear from their context these words were intended by Rousseau not to justify torture or violence but rather to protect in-

33 See especially *C.S.*, book 2, chapter 4, and the *Lettres de la montagne*, Sixth Letter, *O.C.* III 373, 375 and 807. In *Rousseau et la science politique de son temps* (Paris, 1950), pp. 156–61, Robert Derathé cites several more passages in a notable defence of Rousseau against some then fashionable charges of collectivism.

dividuals from such dangers, to ensure that they were in no way excluded, even by their own choice, from the deliberations of a legislative assembly whose decisions affecting them might, in their absence, he remarked, be 'absurd, tyrannical and liable to the most terrible abuse'.[34] Though there are serious obscurities and inconsistencies throughout his political theory, most of his interpreters should have fewer doubts than appear in their commentaries as to the central focus of his view of liberty in the State – which was to ensure that citizens should be autonomous agents rather than appendages of their neighbours, that they should govern themselves rather than be subject to forces beyond their control, for that was the condition of animals, enslaved, in their case, by instincts. Hobbes and Locke had supposed that the pernicious effects of our natural equality could only be overcome by the institution of a predominant power that would enforce the rules necessary for each person's security, but Rousseau's social contract was designed to provide safeguards against the exercise of just such predominant power, to protect each individual from all forms of personal dependence, as he put it several times in the text, including the passage about forcing men to be free. In this sense of a lack of dependence upon other men his conception of our political freedom is as negative as his conception of liberty in terms of our lack of dependence on Nature appears in the *Discours sur l'inégalité.* Such principles of economic equality as are introduced in the *Contrat social* do not figure there as elements of an ideal social system promoting some conception of positive liberty. On the contrary, they are justified by Rousseau only as a defence against the characteristic tendency of inegalitarian property distributions to put liberty up for auction, the poor being obliged to sell themselves to the rich and thus become subordinate and unfree.[35] So far from putting forward substantive principles at which all true republics should aim Rousseau was adamant that no specific enactments could be prescribed in advance – indeed the abstract nature of the *Contrat social* stems in part from this very impossibility of fixing beforehand the ideals citizens should pursue in the exercise of their liberty – and in that work he extended his rejection of any idea of freedom couched in terms of the pursuit of this or

[34] *C.S.*, book 1, chapter 7, *O.C.* III 364. A perceptive treatment of this subject in Rousseau's thought is provided by John Plamenatz in ' "Ce qui ne signifie pas autre chose sinon qu'on le forcera d'être libre" ', *Annales de philosophie politique* 5 (1965), 137–52.

[35] See especially *C.S.*, book 1, chapter 9, note, and book 2, chapter 11, note 1, *O.C.* III 367 and 392.

that particular end by maintaining that a truly free will could not even bind itself for the future.[36]

Neither was Rousseau especially optimistic about our prospects of achieving the forms of civil and moral liberty described in the *Contrat social*. For one thing, as he remarked in a passage that again follows Montesquieu, 'Freedom is not the fruit of all climates, nor within the reach of all peoples.'[37] For another, as he made clear in a letter commenting still further on the subject of our perfectibility, he disagreed with the Abbé de Saint-Pierre, who had claimed that human reason always tends in the direction of progress.[38] Such notions might be 'very fine for the men of Utopia', he remarked, but 'they are worthless for the children of Adam', and, quoting Ovid, he concluded, 'Video meliora proboque, Deteriora sequor.'[39] Of course, as our capacity for self-perfection remained intact, it was possible to *conceive* a better future for mankind, and even in the corrupt world we had come to inhabit, he added in a passage of *Émile*, there was no way of defining the limits of our potential development, 'no way of telling what our nature permits us to become'.[40] Yet to understand our future prospects we must begin, as Rousseau began the *Contrat social*, with the study of 'men as they are', and Jean-Jacques himself displayed little of the confidence shown, for instance, by those figures in Godwin's novel *Things as they Are* (the main title of *Caleb Williams*), whose suffering under despotic institutions was accompanied by a clear vision of 'some future period of human improvement'.

If Rousseau did not share Godwin's sanguine outlook regarding what was to come, he was at least equally sure of one thing – that it was the institutions we had created rather than the vices of our nature which were responsible for our moral decline. In his critique of doctrines of positive liberty Berlin has occasionally endorsed the claim, made by Kant in the sixth proposition of his *Idee zu einer allgemeinen Geschichte*, that 'Out of the crooked timber of humanity nothing straight can ever be made.'[41] I wonder, however, whether

36 See *C.S.*, book 2, chapter 1, *O.C.* III 368–9. Cf. the *Manuscrit de Genève*, book 1, chapter 4, *O.C.* III 296.

37 *C.S.*, book 3, chapter 8, *O.C.* III 414.

38 Rousseau had in mind here the Abbé de Saint-Pierre's *Projet pour rendre la paix perpétuelle en Europe* of 1713.

39 Rousseau to Mirabeau, 26 July 1767, *C.C.* no 5991 (and 5991bis), XXXIII (in press). The citation is from Ovid's *Metamorphoses* VII 20–1.

40 *Émile*, book 1, *O.C.* IV 281.

41 Kant, *Idee zu einer allgemeinen Geschichte*, in *Kant's gesammelte Schriften* (Berlin, 1902–) VIII 23.

this quotation may not be somewhat misplaced in Berlin's writings, partly because the *Idee* sketches a theory of progress along lines so forcefully challenged in 'Historical Inevitability', partly, too, because the sixth proposition asserts that 'man is an animal in need of a master', a claim criticised on account of its apparent illiberalism, even in Kant's day, as Berlin himself has noted elsewhere.[42] At any rate – and notwithstanding the great debt Kant owed to Rousseau's thought in so many respects – I think Jean-Jacques would have objected to this work's philosophy of history as a whole, to its proposition that men need masters in particular, and, above all, to its statement that we are naturally warped. For according to Rousseau our lives were miserable not by virtue of the crooked timbers that shaped us, but as a result of the twisted ploughs we had manufactured, the rotted citadels we had constructed, the crippling social systems we had made. He believed we were in need of liberation rather than masters, and though our rise from a morally decrepit world appeared to him uncertain, even unlikely, it was our perfectibility alone which still made liberation possible.

I am much indebted to Stefan Collini, Ralph Leigh and Hillel Steiner for their generous guidance in my preparation of this text. Its defects would at least have been less conspicuous if I had heeded their advice more closely.

[42] See Berlin, *Vico and Herder* (London, 1976), p. 199, note 1.

RICHARD WOLLHEIM

John Stuart Mill and Isaiah Berlin

The Ends of Life and the Preliminaries of Morality

I

In the introductory chapter of *On Liberty* John Stuart Mill claimed that for him utility was the ultimate appeal on all ethical questions, and that he renounced any advantage that might accrue to his argument from considerations of abstract right.[1] In 'John Stuart Mill and the Ends of Life' Isaiah Berlin challenges Mill's claim.[2] He puts it forward as his view that, though Mill avowed a commitment to utility, the commitment is not real. In support of the avowed commitment Mill was compelled to stretch the notions of happiness and pleasure to the point of vacuity. Meanwhile his real commitment was to various distinct values such as individual liberty, variety, and justice. These values may at a number of places make demands that coincide with those of utility – in so far, that is, as these themselves are coherent – but they cannot be given a consistently utilitarian interpretation.

In many writings Berlin has urged upon us a single message of great power and moment. It is that human values are necessarily many, not one, and that of the many values there is not one to which the others are properly subordinate. Values come in systems, and systems of value possess the kind of complex structure that allows the different constituent values to interact. What morality rejects is monism, and the pluralism within which it can find accommodation is a pluralism of a loose kind or pluralism without hierarchy.

It is worth pointing out that this message, which has profound and subversive implications for both practical and theoretical thinking yet to be absorbed, relates exclusively to the internal nature of an individual's morality. It says nothing about the relations between the moralities of different individuals, and specifically it does not say

[1] *Collected Works of John Stuart Mill*, ed. J.M. Robson (Toronto/London 1963–) (hereafter *J.S.M.*), vol. 18, p. 224.

[2] Isaiah Berlin, *John Stuart Mill and the Ends of Life* (London, 1959), reprinted in *F.E.L.*

that there must or even can be a multiplicity of such moralities. Berlin himself, who has always held to a version of voluntaristic meta-ethics, probably believes in this kind of pluralism too. But the pluralism here under discussion is perfectly compatible with the belief in a single system of values, to which the different systems of value held by different individuals ought to conform and upon which they may be expected to converge. The message that I have attributed to Berlin is consistent, as far as I can see, with ethical objectivism and even ethical realism.

Now, once Berlin's message is clearly before us, it is plausible to think that his reading, or re-reading, of Mill derives from it. The derivation would take roughly the following course: Berlin finds Mill a sympathetic thinker with many of whose views on moral and social topics he finds himself in deep agreement; he finds it impossible to believe that these views could be arrived at on the basis of the monistic morality that utilitarianism must insist on; therefore, whatever he may profess, Mill is not really committed to utilitarianism; rather he is committed to a pluralistic morality, moreover to a loosely pluralistic morality, and it is from this that his best thinking depends.

In this essay I want to tread a narrow path. I accept wholeheartedly Berlin's strictures upon moral monism and indeed upon anything other than a loose form of pluralism in morality. I share his high opinion of Mill, who for me also is a sympathetic thinker on moral and social topics. However, I reject Berlin's reading of Mill and I accept Mill's claim about himself. In other words, I believe that Mill did remain a utilitarian and I think that he certainly continued to think of utility as he said he did: that is, as the ultimate appeal on all ethical questions. But the crucial qualification here is, to my mind, provided by Mill himself when he goes on to say that he intends utility 'in the largest sense' or utility 'grounded in the permanent interests of man as a progressive being'.[3] For it is central to my way of thinking about Mill that this significantly extends the notion of utility, that it is vital to the understanding of Mill's revision of utilitarianism, and that it does not, as Berlin thinks, stretch the notion of utility to the point of vacuity. For me it is just this qualification, properly understood, which explains simultaneously how Mill remained a utilitarian and how he emerged as an interesting and sympathetic thinker. And, by qualifying the notion of utility as he does, Mill, to my mind, produces not only a more

[3] J.S.M., loc. cit. (note 1 above).

plausible morality, but a morality that can be more plausibly regarded as utilitarian, than that constructed upon the cruder notion or notions of utility held alike by his immediate predecessors and many of his numerous successors.

A residual question remains: Berlin insists upon the diversity of human values. Mill ascribes complexity to the single value to which he subscribes. Given that Mill in talking of complexity succeeds in doing justice to everything that Berlin has in mind by diversity, given that Mill shows that utility, properly understood, can lay claim to the appropriate complexity, is he still right to think of utility as the complex value appropriate to occupy the central place in morality? I shall not attempt an answer to this residual question.

II

In 1826 John Stuart Mill underwent a severe mental crisis, to which so much of his earlier life contributed, and from which so much of his later life was to draw benefit. Mill himself wrote of the crisis as an event in his intellectual development. It was clearly more than this, but it was also this, and it is solely as an event in his development as a moral philosopher that I wish to consider it.

One day Mill found himself putting to himself the following question:

> Suppose that all your objects in life were realised; that all the changes in institutions and opinions which you are looking forward to, could be completely effected at this very instant: would this be a great joy and happiness to you?[4]

He did not have to wait long for an answer. The question was posed, and

> an irrepressible self-consciousness directly answered 'No!' At this my heart sank within me: the whole foundation on which my life was constructed fell down. All my happiness was to have been found in the continual pursuit of this end. The end had ceased to charm, and how could there ever again be any interest in the means? I seemed to have nothing left to live for.

One striking detail about the incident, or about Mill's telling of it, is the way in which Mill frames the original question. For he does not ask, as one might expect, Do I still find the utilitarian ideal a good

[4] John Stuart Mill, *Autobiography* (London, 1873), pp. 133–4.

ideal? Am I in accord with it as a moral or political objective? Instead he asks whether the realisation of utilitarian objectives will give him pleasure, whether the satisfaction of the utilitarian ideal will in turn satisfy him, and at first this might strike the reader as a peculiarly personal or poignant touch, showing how deeply this crisis of belief affected his whole being and how it had shaken the more drily abstract way of looking at things which had been natural to him. The briefest reflection will show that this is a misinterpretation of Mill. In framing the question as he did, just what Mill shows is how firmly he still stood within the utilitarian framework. For, according to utilitarianism, it is a constraint upon morality that, for any given moral judgement, general or particular, there should be a precise match between the content of the judgement, or what it obliges an agent to do, and its motivational force, or its capacity to incite the agent – the agent, that is, who has fully understood it – to act in conformity with it. Further, utilitarianism prided itself on being a morality – indeed the only morality – which could meet this constraint. By assigning content to the moral judgement in the way in which it did – that is, as what would result in the greatest net balance of pleasure over pain for its recipients – it claimed to provide the agent with a uniquely good motive for putting it into practice – that is, the prospect of the greatest net balance of pleasure over pain for him too. Accordingly Mill was accepting one cardinal tenet of utilitarianism and using it to challenge another when he began to suspect that the fulfilment of the utilitarian ideal would not bring him happiness. As this suspicion hardened into certainty, his mental crisis peaked.

Mill's recovery from depression coincided with the attempt he made over the subsequent years to bring the content and the motivational force of utilitarianism back into line. Or – as it might more realistically be put, for Mill never really took altogether seriously the idea that there could be a morality which, once properly grasped, would prove irresistible – with the attempt he made to recapture motivational appeal for utilitarianism. Reflection must have shown that there were in principle two ways of doing this. Starting from the simple Benthamism with which he had become so thoroughly disillusioned, either he could rethink the content of utilitarian morality, so as to enhance its appeal, or he could put forward a revised account of human motivation with the aim of showing that utilitarian morality, content unchanged, had after all the capacity to move to action.

There was an evident difficulty for Mill in pursuing the second course. It would have required him to deny the most crucial experience of his life. In rewriting human motivation he would have had to rewrite his own motivation, and he would have had to say that, at the very moment when he was utterly convinced that the ideals in which he had been brought up no longer moved him, he did in fact have a motive, however best described, for acting on them, the deliverances of self-consciousness notwithstanding. In other words, Mill would have extricated himself from his mental crisis only at the expense of unlearning the lesson it seemingly had taught him, and it is no surprise that, in his attempt to recapture motivational appeal for utilitariansim, he chose the first course.

Mill's revision of the content of utilitarian morality can most conveniently be considered if it is looked upon as falling into two stages. The two stages are not chronological stages, and there are good reasons for thinking that Mill's thought is ill-suited to chronological study – which, it is no accident, his detractors greatly favour.[5] Mill was a very perceptive thinker, and he often ran ahead of himself in grasping the conclusions to which his current thinking would lead him. At the same time he was very preoccupied with the impression that his words might make on a reader, and sometimes, in order to dispel the suspicion that he had abandoned the leading ideas of his earlier years, he would use phraseology which no longer consorted well with his actual thinking. To consider then, as I propose to do, the shift that Mill effects in utilitarian morality as falling into two stages – one of which is the shift from a morality that employs a monistic conception of utility to one that employs a conception of utility that is pluralistic but with hierarchy, and the other is the shift from a morality that employs a conception of utility that is pluralistic but with hierarchy to one that employs a conception of utility that is pluralistic and without hierarchy – is not to advance a historical thesis. Evidences of the later stage are already to be found in the essay on Bentham (1838), while the earlier stage still leaves its mark on *Utilitarianism* (1861).

In explicating the revision that Mill effects upon the content of utilitarian morality, I shall do so with an eye to the two questions that may be raised about it. The first is: Does this shift in content succeed in restoring appeal to utilitarianism? The second is: Is this shift really a shift within utilitarianism, or isn't it, rather, a shift out of utilitarianism?

[5] e.g. Introduction to *Essays on Politics and Culture*, ed. G. Himmelfarb (New York, 1962); G. Himmelfarb, *On Liberty and Liberalism* (New York, 1974): cf. John Rees, 'The Thesis of the Two Mills', *Political Studies* 25 (1977), 369–82.

Finally, with Mill's revision of utilitarianism fully before us I shall draw attention to a corollary that Mill appended to utilitarianism. Its effect is to show that utilitarian morality may be set within a larger framework of ordinances. This larger framework I shall call an ethic, and that Mill proposed a three-tiered ethic is, I shall suggest, one of the most interesting, as well as one of the more neglected, aspects of his work as a moral philosopher.

III

In our consideration of Mill's revision of utilitarianism, there is one problem, which might be expected to have priority for someone out to revise utilitarianism, which we do not have to trouble ourselves with. For reasons whose adequacy need not detain us, Mill took the problem as solved. The problem is that of the transition from a purely egotistic morality, which is the form in which, according to a well established tradition, is that in which utilitarianism initially proposes itself, to a non-egotistic morality: that is, to a morality which enjoins the maximisation of pleasure but is indifferent to whom it is to whom the pleasure accrues, and, specifically, is blind to the distinction between agent's pleasure and the pleasure of others.[6] For the purposes of this essay this transition is assumed.

The first stage in the shift that Mill effects in the content of utilitarian morality consists in the move from a monistic conception of utility to a conception of utility that is pluralistic but with hierarchy. Alongside the primary principle of hedonism, or the maximisation of pleasure, secondary principles make their appearance. Examples of such secondary principles would be the education of the mind, the cultivation of sexual love and family affection, patriotism, the maintenance of personal dignity, or the attachment to beauty, and, of course, it must be appreciated that these secondary principles, like the primary principle, may be non-egotistic. Secondary principles fix the agent's ends – their ends are his ends – but there is no reason why his ends should be self-interested or exclusively for him. However, what is characteristic of this stage of Mill's thinking, and what defines it, is that secondary principles are strictly subordinate to the primary principle, and it is

[6] In two early essays – the 'Remarks on Bentham's Philosophy' (1833), which appeared anonymously, and 'Sedgwick's Discourse' (1835) – Mill sets himself against the identification of utility with selfish or self-regarding interest. In the earlier essay he uses this point as a criticism of Bentham, in the later essay he uses it in defence of Bentham against his critics. Both essays are to be found in *J.S.M.*, vol. 10.

because of this subordination that the pluralism brought about by the introduction of secondary principles is hierarchical.

In order to see how hierarchy manifests itself, let us take as the central case – for it is the clearest case – that in which a moral agent invokes utilitarian morality in order to decide how he ought to act.[7] Once we have grasped how hierarchy manifests itself here, we can use this understanding in order to grasp the effects of hierarchy in what may be regarded as derivative cases: that is, where a moral agent decides whether he has acted as he ought to have, or where a moral critic decides how others ought to act or whether they have acted as they ought to have.

Now in the central case, the moral agent in reaching a decision may consult the primary principle; alternatively he may consult one or other or more of his secondary principles. Let us suppose that he consults secondary principles. He does so, and he arrives at a decision. Then it is open to him to consult the primary principle and arrive at a decision on the basis of it. It is not required of him to do so, but, other things being equal – that is, the costs not being prohibitive – it is a rational course of action. It is so just because, should the two decisions diverge, then what he ought to do is given by the decision arrived at on the basis of the primary principle. The original decision must be abandoned. Of course, if the secondary principles have been at all carefully thought out, such divergences will be a rare thing. Nevertheless, should they occur, the primary principle operates in the agent's reasoning as though it were the only principle in the field, and this is one way in which secondary principles show themselves to be subordinate to the primary principle, or in which hierarchy manifests itself.

This way is the straightforward way, and to see the oblique way let us now suppose that the agent, in reaching a decision how he ought to act, consults the primary principle. In such a case what he will do is that he will survey the various actions that are practicable for him, he will assign to each the consequences that it is most likely to have for himself and for others, and he will calculate for each of these consequences the net balance of pleasure and pain that it is likely to produce, and then arrival at a decision will be a matter of selecting that action whose consequences maximise pleasure or produce the greatest net balance of pleasure over pain. Non-egotism is preserved

[7] For ease of exposition I write throughout as though utilitarianism were to be construed as act-utilitarianism. I tend to believe that this is correct, but all my examples can fairly readily be converted so as to concord with rule-utilitarianism.

by indifference to whom it is to whom the pleasure accrues. Now, in computing the pleasure and pain for each action, the agent will have to consider how his action interacts with the actions of others, and therefore he will need to know the courses of action on which those others who are affected by the action are embarked. However, these courses of action will themselves have been decided upon in one or other of two ways: either on the basis of the primary principle or on the basis of some one or more of the secondary principles of the person embarked on it. Let us now suppose that all the courses of action on which those others affected by the agent's action are embarked have been decided upon on the basis of secondary principles, and that this is known to the agent. All persons affected by his action are acting on secondary principles. In that case in computing the pleasure and pain that action is likely to produce the agent will surely find it natural to equate, for each person, pleasure with the achievement of the end or ends fixed by the secondary principle or principles on which that person is acting. This determines the way in which, at any rate in the first instance, the agent will consider the interaction of his action with the actions of others. But, once again, this calculation having been made, though it is not required, it is, other things being equal, rational for the agent to make a complementary calculation. This time, in computing the pleasure and pain that his action is likely to produce, the agent, one allowance apart, ignores the fact that those others whom his action affects have decided upon the courses of action on which they are embarked on the basis of secondary principles. He assumes all persons affected by his action are acting on the primary principle, and in consequence, for each person, he equates pleasure, not with the achievement of the end or ends fixed by the secondary principle or principles on which that person is in point of fact acting, but just with whatever the primary principle enjoins for him – the one allowance that the agent makes being that he still has to count as pain for each person any disappointment he might experience from frustration of the secondary principle or principles on which he is actually, if misguidedly, acting. On this new assumption the agent will arrive at a fresh decision how he ought to act, and should the two decisions diverge, it is the second decision that he should prefer. He should, in other words, act as though the primary principle operates, this time not in the agent's reasoning, but in the reasoning of others, as the only principle in the field. Here we have the other way in which secondary principles show themselves to be subordinate to the primary principle, or in which hierarchy manifests itself.

The subordination of the secondary principles to the primary principle at this stage in Mill's thinking has, as a consequence, that the ends fixed by the various secondary principles stand to the end fixed by the primary principle in a special relationship: they stand as means to end. The agent's ends are, and are to be assessed as, means to pleasure. This means–end relationship totally coheres with the motivation that prompts this first shift in the content of utilitarian morality. This motivation is essentially practical, and is best expressed by Mill when he talks of utility as 'too complex and indefinite an end'[8] for a moral agent always to have had to take stock of in calculating what he ought to do or what would be best for himself and others. Such a calculation remains a calculation about utility, but it might be more practical to arrive at an answer by working it out in terms both simpler and more definite than utility. These terms are just what secondary principles provide through fixing subsidiary aims.

If Mill's first revision of utilitarian morality makes it easier for the agent to operate, it also does more than this, and it is this additional thing it does that enhances the appeal of utilitarian morality. For the revision brings it about that an agent, in deciding what he ought to do, has no longer to regard as irrelevant a whole body of thoughts, and also the attitudes and feelings connected with these thoughts, had by him or had by others, and which must be reckoned by any sensitive person as amongst the most interesting that either he or they are likely to entertain. I refer, of course, to those thoughts which define either his ends or the ends of others, for these thoughts must now enter into his calculations in so far as he thinks of pleasure accruing to himself or to them through the satisfaction of secondary principles upon which they act. So far, but no further. This body of thoughts acquires relevance for his calculations, but the relevance is merely provisional. Once it seems to the agent that pleasure is less likely to accrue this way, once the ends of the secondary principles no longer convince him as the best means to the end of the primary principle, then these thoughts cease to have a claim upon his attention. He may, indeed he must, put them out of his mind.

The purely provisional way in which these thoughts enter into the agent's calculations, and, correspondingly, the way in which they can be appropriately displaced by the direct thought of pleasure or utility, attest, of course, to the hierarchy that at this stage constrains the new-found pluralism of utilitarian morality. But they attest to

[8] *J.S.M.*, vol. 10, p. 110.

something else as well. They attest to the degree to which the concept of pleasure, or happiness, or utility – and so far I have not found it necessary to distinguish between them – is itself found quite unproblematic. More specifically, the concept is not felt to require any of the interesting thoughts I have just referred to, or the ends fixed by secondary principles, for its elucidation. All this, however, is to change as utilitarian morality undergoes its second revision, to which we may now turn.

IV

The second stage in the shift that Mill effects in the content of utilitarian morality consists in the move from a conception of utility that is pluralistic but with hierarchy to one that is pluralistic and without hierarchy. Not merely do secondary principles appear alongside the primary principle but now they are not subordinate to it. The ends fixed by the secondary principles no longer stand to the end fixed by the primary principle in the means–end relationship. Or at least they no longer stand to it exclusively in this relationship. They also serve to elucidate it.

That the ends fixed by the secondary principle now serve to elucidate the end fixed by the primary principle has the implication that by now the latter end, or utility, has ceased to be unproblematic. And this is so. It is characteristic of utilitarianism under its second revision that utility is found problematic, but it is important to grasp how. The point is not that – or is not merely that – Mill, the moral philosopher, finds utility problematic. Rather, in his moral philosophy Mill reconstructs the fact that the moral agent finds, indeed must find, utility problematic. It then goes on to represent how the moral agent tries to resolve the problem for himself. He is represented as trying to make utility unproblematic by subscribing to secondary principles.

Why the moral agent finds utility problematic is to do with the highly abstract nature of the concept. Grasping this highly abstract concept, the agent finds that it doesn't contribute, in the way that utilitarianism leads him to believe that it should, to a decision how he ought to act. Even with all requisite information at his disposal, he will still have an inadequate grasp of what he should do to maximise utility. The abstract concept utility needs to be filled out, and this filling out can be thought of in two parts. In the first instance, the moral agent is required to have what might be thought of as a conception of his own utility. Only then can he consider how his utility is to be advanced. This conception is, however, not something that can be given to him or that he can learn. It is something that has to be formed, and it is formed through the process of trial and error. He tries out various secondary principles and finishes by subscribing to those whose ends give him or teach him what he wants. But, in the second instance, the moral agent requires that others have – that is, others form – a conception of their own utility, for only then can he consider how he is to advance their utility. And, once again, this conception is one that they have to form, they form it through trial and error, and it is codified in their secondary principles.

But it is one thing to believe that utilitarian morality cannot be successfully pursued unless each forms a conception of his own utility and that such a conception is formed through subscribing to secondary principles, and another thing, and evidently unjustified, to equate the subscription to just any set of secondary principles with the formation of a conception of one's own utility. Surely there must be some constraint upon the secondary principles subscribed to. More specifically, there must be some constraint upon the ends that these principles fix. To put the point another way: it may very well be that the pursuit of morality requires the subscription to secondary principles; but what has to be true of the secondary principles for the morality that they permit to be truly thought of as a utilitarian morality?

Actually it is an exaggeration to say, as I have said, that at this stage of Mill's revision of utilitarian morality utility is found problematic, if this is taken to mean that utility is found altogether problematic. There remains an unproblematic aspect of utility, and to mark the distinction that is at stake here it would be useful to employ the traditional distinction between pleasure and happiness. Unproblematically utility connotes pleasure, where pleasure is thought of as a kind of sensation or adjunct of sensation, and so long as utility is given this highly restricted interpretation, the moral agent may arrive at utilitarian decisions about how he ought to act without either his forming for himself or others' forming for themselves conceptions of their own utility. Such decisions are decisions about the maximisation of the privileged sensation or adjunct of sensation. It is only when the moral agent appreciates that utilitarian decisions cannot be circumscribed in this way that utility becomes problematic for him. Any issue from this problematic situation is possible only if two conditions are met. In the first place, utility must be recognised to connote more than just pleasure. It also connotes, and it must be perceived to connote, happiness. Secondly, for the concept of utility in its broader connotation to gain application, it is required that the agent and others form conceptions of their own utility. This they do, as we have seen, through subscribing to secondary principles. If, however, we now ask what these secondary principles must be like, or what is the constraint laid upon the ends fixed by secondary principles if the conception to which these principles contribute is to be regarded as a conception of the person's utility or if the morality that they help to constitute is to be regarded as a utilitarian morality, the answer is easier to find. The constraint appears to be this: the ends fixed by the various secondary principles must be systematically related to pleasure.

But to say that the ends of the secondary principles must be systematically related to pleasure if utilitarianism is to be safeguarded does not say enough. There are various ways in which the ends of secondary principles may be systematically related to pleasure. For instance, some moral philosophers would argue that the systematic relationship is to be of a conceptual kind. The ends must derive from the concept of pleasure. I wish to suggest that the systematic relationship must be of a genetic kind. And I also wish to suggest that this is how Mill thought of the matter. In other words, utilitarianism as revised by him requires that it is possible to arrange pleasure and the ends fixed by the secondary principles of a moral agent on one and the same dendrogram, where the ends lie on the branches, pleasure is at the base of the tree, and the diagram as a whole represents the emergence of the moral agent according to the best available theory of human nature.[9]

From this last point an important consequence follows. To be able to say what it is for a morality that consists in a primary principle enjoining the maximisation of utility and various secondary principles not subordinate to the primary principle to be overall a utilitarian morality presupposes that one has in one's possession a developmental psychology of a certain richness. It is only through such a psychology that one can tell whether the secondary principles appropriately relate to the primary principle. It is unnecessary to observe that Mill did not have such a psychology. He conceded the point – notably in the essay 'The Subjection of Women' – and in

[9] At two different places in his edition of his father's *magnum opus* Mill seeks to forestall those who criticise the view that evolved ends derive from the pursuit of pleasure on the grounds that the two kinds of end are unresembling, by pointing out to such critics that, when the genetic derivation is lengthy, 'the resulting feeling always seems not only very unlike any one of the elements composing it, but very unlike the sum of those elements'. James Mill, *Analysis of the Phenomena of the Human Mind*, ed. John Stuart Mill (London, 1869), vol. 2, p. 321; cf. p. 252.

at least one place he gave it as his opinion that the lack constituted the biggest single gap in contemporary knowledge.[10] However, there is a passage where he clearly recognises just what has to be the internal structure of a morality that is pluralistic and without hierarchy and also utilitarian, and how this structure presupposes a theory of human nature. I refer to the passage in *Utilitarianism*, widely ridiculed, in which Mill talks of higher and lower pleasures.[11] To see how this passage bears upon the present issue, the reader needs to orientate himself appropriately. For generally this passage is read for what Mill has to say about the difference between higher and lower pleasures, or how it is that one pleasure can vary qualitatively from another. But the passage can also read for what Mill has to say about what higher and lower pleasures have in common, or why it is that both are kinds of pleasure. Roughly, Mill's view is that higher and lower pleasures are both kinds of pleasure because they are functionally equivalent at different levels of a person's psychological development – which, of course, is also, to the same degree of roughness, just the reason why one kind of pleasure is qualitatively superior to the other. Thereby Mill throws everything on to the question of psychological development and how its levels are to be identified and what lies on each level. Given his lack of a psychological theory, Mill is naturally unable to answer these questions, but what is crucial for the proper interpretation of Mill is that he saw just what it is that was necessary if such answers were to be produced or where they were to come from.

I shall call utilitarianism under its second revision, or where its content is given by the primary principle of hedonism and various secondary principles not subordinate to but elucidatory of it, 'complex utilitariansim', and I turn to the question how, or how far, complex utilitarianism restores appeal to utilitarianism.

The crucial way in which complex utilitarianism restores appeal to utilitarianism is that it compels – it doesn't just permit, it compels – the moral agent, in deciding what he ought to do (or in coming to any related decision), to take account of what I have already called thoughts that are amongst the most interesting that human beings entertain: that is, thoughts definitive of the ends fixed

10 'Of all difficulties which impede the progress of thought, and the formation of well-grounded opinions on life and social arrangements, the greatest is now the unspeakable ignorance and inattention of mankind in respect to the influences which form human character.' John Stuart Mill, *The Subjection of Women* (London, 1869), pp. 39–40. The missing science Mill had talked about under the name 'ethology' in book 6, chapter 5 of his *System of Logic*.

11 *J.S.M.*, vol. 10, pp. 210–13.

by secondary principles, whether the agent's own or of others. And in taking account of these thoughts the agent is also required to take account of the feelings and attitudes that group themselves around those thoughts. And the account that he is required to take of these mental constellations is something that is by now ineliminable. It is not merely provisional, and it is not to be set aside in deference to some consideration which overrides secondary principles and their aims. Utilitarianism at last pays attention to man in his full complexity as a developed human being, and it would have to be a very gloomy or very dessicated self-consciousness that returned the answer 'No' to the question whether the pursuit of man's happiness, when man is thus envisaged, was an end that held the promise of satisfaction.

V

However, it might now seem that utilitarianism under its second revision, or complex utilitarianism, gains, or regains, appeal, but only at the cost of scope. Let me explain.

A moral agent, we are now told, has to take ineliminable account of both his and others' secondary principles. But this is impossible unless both he and others have secondary principles, and furthermore – for otherwise the account he takes of them would be eliminable – hold them not subordinately to the primary principle. He and they must have formed conceptions of their own happiness, and they must moreover have knowledge of each other's conceptions. But this is not a universally satisfied condition: it represents an achievement, first of all, in the life of the species, and then, secondly, in the life of the individual. Complex utilitarianism gains its appeal from the way in which it pays respect to the full faculties of man: but, by the same token, it appears to lose its hold when man has not entered into possession of his full faculties. In its attempt to do justice to the developmental nature of man, complex utilitarianism takes on or acquires a developmental nature. Or so it might seem. Is this so, and is this how Mill saw it?

Mill, we know, like his father and like Bentham, professed to think that any non-utilitarian morality was ultimately untenable. But did he think that utilitarian morality held in those circumstances – whether of general history or of personal biography – in which it did not hold appeal?

Explicitly Mill never raised the question. But implicitly – or so I believe – he must have, just because he supplied the question with an answer, and an answer which, as I have already said, constitutes one of the most interesting and also most neglected aspects of his work as a moral philosopher. For what Mill did was to set complex utilitarianism within a larger structure, appropriately thought of as a three-tiered ethic, and to each tier of which he then assigned distinct conditions under which it held or in which it obliged the agent to act in conformity with it.

On one tier of this ethic, the uppermost tier, there is utilitarianism proper, by now glossed as complex utilitarianism. Complex utilitarianism enjoins the maximisation of utility, as utility is elucidated in the moral agent's conception of happiness and in the conceptions of happiness entertained by the various recipients of his action. Complex utilitarianism holds when, or in so far as, people have indeed formed their own conceptions of happiness, know of the conceptions of others, and pursue utility accordingly. It holds just when men have entered into possession of their full faculties. On the tier below this, or the middle tier, there is simple utilitarianism, where this includes both utilitarianism employing a monistic conception of utility and utilitarianism employing a conception of utility that is pluralistic but with hierarchy. Simple utilitarianism holds when, or in so far as, men have not formed conceptions of their own happiness, and pleasure rather than happiness is what they pursue for themselves and others. It is the ethic of men whose faculties are still undeveloped. Then, on the third tier, the lowermost, there is what I shall call 'preliminary utilitarianism', and I claim that it is one of the most innovative aspects of Mill's ethical thought that he identified and found a place for preliminary utilitarianism. What preliminary utilitarianism enjoins is whatever is necessary for people either to form, or, having formed, to maintain, conceptions of their own happiness – or, for that matter (though I shall not pursue this aspect), envisagements of other people's conceptions of their own happiness. The conditions under which preliminary utilitarianism holds are disjunctive: that part which is concerned with the formation of people's conceptions of their own happiness holds when such conceptions are not fully formed, and that part which is concerned with the maintenance of such conceptions holds just when they are formed. Preliminary utilitarianism invariably holds. And, finally, when the injunctions of preliminary utilitarianism conflict with the injunctions of either simple or complex utilitarianism – whichever is relevant – then, unless the cost in utility is too severe, the injunctions of preliminary utilitarianism take priority. Education up to the point where happiness can be attained is more important than the attainment either of pleasure or of happiness.

I shall end by drawing attention to the three separate places where Mill argues for policies or practices on the basis of preliminary utilitarianism.

Two occur in the essay *On Liberty*.

The first passage is in chapter 4, where Mill, having divided the actions of the agent into the 'self-regarding' (his phrase) and the 'other-regarding' (not his phrase), exempts the former altogether from the sphere of State intervention. For this exemption might not be the verdict reached by appeal either to simple or to complex utilitarianism, and for two distinct reasons. In the first place, though it is a matter of dispute just how Mill effected the division, it seems as though self-regarding actions are not to be equated with those which in no way impinge upon others. They must be those actions which affect others, if they do, only in some discountable fashion.[12] Accordingly there is always the possibility that a self-regarding action is in its net effect more adverse than some other action practicable for the agent. Why should not such an action, on grounds of utilitarianism, either simple or complex, be the object of State intervention? Secondly, self-regarding actions, however defined, have an effect upon the agent. Why should not utilitarianism decide that those with a benign effect upon him ought to be enforced by the State and those with a malign effect upon him be prohibited? Mill's counter-argument seems to be that self-regarding actions are crucial to those 'experiments of living' without which individual conceptions of happiness would either not be formed or, having been formed, wither away.[13] Here we witness a case of preliminary utilitarianism overruling either simple or complex utilitarianism.

The second passage is to be found in chapter 2, where Mill discusses liberty of opinion, which once again is treated as total. Mill's argument in favour of total liberty of opinion appeals to two considerations: truth and rationality. In both cases the content of the appeal is subtle, but the question arises: Why should a utilitarian, even a complex utilitarian, set such supreme value on truth and rationality? These may, of course, and almost certainly will be, amongst the ends fixed by secondary principles of the various citizens. But does this fully explain the strength of Mill's commit-

[12] J. C. Rees, 'A Re-reading of Mill on Liberty', *Political Studies* 8 (1960), 113–29; Alan Ryan, 'Mr McCloskey on Mill's Liberalism', *Philosophical Quarterly* 14 (1964), 253–60; C. L. Ten, 'Mill on Self-Regarding Actions', *Philosophy* 43 (1968), 29–37; Richard Wollheim, 'John Stuart Mill and the Limits of State Action', *Social Research* 40 (1973), 1–30.

[13] *J.S.M.*, vol. 18. 261.

ment? It seems that preliminary utilitarianism must make its contribution to the argument, in that, if it does not overrule utilitarianism proper, at least it supplements it.

The third passage is in *Considerations on Representative Government.* Mill says that representative government is the ideally best form of government in that it is 'the one which in the circumstances in which it is practicable and eligible is attended with the greatest amount of beneficial consequences, immediate and prospective'. Here, it might seem, speaks utilitarianism proper. But not so. For as Mill develops the argument, he brings forward two criteria by which the merit of political institutions is to be judged. One concerns the way in which they 'organize the moral, intellectual, and active worth already existing, so as to operate with the greatest effect in public affairs'.[14] If that sounds like the voice of utilitarianism, what are we to make of the second criterion? For this concerns the way in which political institutions 'promote the general mental advancement of the community'. If this can in part be put to utilitarianism proper – and this I do not deny – in part it attests to the influence of preliminary utilitarianism.

It is not surprising that critics are to be found who will see in these passages evidence of Mill's backslidings from utilitarianism. Given their failure to perceive the complex character of Mill's commitment to utilitarianism – more complex, it now turns out, than a mere commitment to complex utilitarianism – their criticisms are altogether understandable. However, concern for the proper interpretation of Mill requires us to reject them. Properly interpreted, Mill can be shown to concur not only with Berlin's concern for a loose pluralism in morality but also with his other, no less urgent, no less generous, and certainly related, concern for the all-important value of liberty. But that is another though not all that different a story.

[14] *J.S.M.*, vol. 19, p. 392. Some interesting observations on the interlock between Mill's concern with the formation of character and his political views are to be found in R.J. Halliday, 'Some Recent Interpretations of John Stuart Mill', *Philosophy* 43 (1968), 1–17, reprinted in *Mill: A Collection of Critical Essays*, ed. J.B. Schneewind (New York, 1968).

HENRY HARDY

A Bibliography of Isaiah Berlin

Maurice Bowra once wrote of Isaiah Berlin: 'Though like Our Lord and Socrates he does not publish much, he thinks and says a great deal and has had an enormous influence on our times.'[1] Bowra's belief that Berlin rarely ventures into print has been widely held, but it does not fit the facts. He has published a great deal on a wide variety of subjects, but most of his work is of essay length, and has appeared in (sometimes obscure) periodicals and symposia, or as occasional pamphlets; much of it has been long out of print; and little[2] had been collected in book form until the publication of his four-volume *Selected Writings*. This probably explains the common underestimate of the bulk of his writings. My hope is that this bibliography, together with the four volumes of *Selected Writings*, will set the record straight.

It is likely that the list is not quite complete: though I have conducted explorations on many fronts, my searches have not been exhaustively systematic.[3] I shall be grateful for notification of errors or omissions.[4] But I do not think anything important is missing. I have excluded interviews (which do not strictly count as writings published by the interviewee), bibliographical details of translations into

[1] In a letter to Noel Annan. See Noel Annan, 'A Man I Loved', in Hugh Lloyd-Jones (ed.), *Maurice Bowra: A Celebration* (London, 1974), p. 53.

[2] Only items 112 and 148 below, apart from collectons in translation. There is a checklist of English collections at the end of this bibliography.

[3] For an informal account of how this bibliography came to be compiled, and of the genesis of the whole project of which it forms a part, see Henry Hardy, 'Editing Isaiah Berlin's Writings', *British Book News*, January 1978, pp. 3 and 5. The bibliography was first published in *Lycidas* (the magazine of Wolfson College, Oxford) No 3 (1975), 41–5, additions and corrections ibid. No 4 (1976), 42, and has been revised and updated for inclusion here and in item 165 below.

[4] I should like here to express my gratitude for help already received: Isaiah Berlin has patiently answered almost endless questions; and I have been assisted on individual points by William Beaver, Andrew Best, Michael Brock, Hugo Brunner, Kensington Davison, Victor Erlich, John Fuggles, Samuel Guttenplan, Robert Hazo, Lord Head, Arthur Lehning, Jeremy Lewis, Aileen Kelly, Anthony Kenny, Robert Kocis, Bryan Magee, Anthony Quinton, Alan Ryan (whose role in the publication of this Festschrift, despite the kind last sentence of his Preface, has of course been crucial), Hans Schenk, John Sparrow, Galen Strawson, Patricia Utechin and Nicholas Wilson.

foreign languages, and a handful of minor items, mainly non-academic letters to the Press.

It may be of some assistance to provide a rudimentary sketch-map for those who are not already familiar with Berlin's work, and wish to sample it in a non-random fashion: it is not always easy to tell from a brief bibliographical entry whether an item is substantial or not, or what its subject-matter is. It is impossible to classify definitively writings which are so remarkably free of the restrictions of conventional subject boundaries, especially since the categories that suggest themselves – in particular philosophy, political theory, history of ideas – overlap so extensively on their own account. One needs a Venn diagram. But failing that, I hope the following is a useful guide.

The contents of the four volumes of *Selected Writings*, listed separately at the end of the bibliography, provide the beginnings of a classification. But each volume lacks, for various reasons, certain items which belong in its category; and some categories are not represented as such, or at all, in the contents of any volume. So it is worth giving more complete lists here.

The major Russian essays are 30, 44, 56, 57, 63, 76, 82, 108 and 125, most of which are included in *Russian Thinkers* (157); also on Russian topics are 27, 46, 65, 67, 68 and 111.

The principal philosophical papers are 20, 25, 35, 36, 54 (with the first part of the introduction to 112), 77 and 93; 85 is a more popular article on the nature of the subject. It is somewhat arbitrary to separate these items from those which fall most naturally under political theory, namely 64, 71 (with the second part of the introduction to 112) and 81. Most of the pieces in these two groups are reprinted in *Concepts and Categories* (158).

The main essays in the history of ideas are 37, 38, the introduction to 62, 73, 74, 128, 134, 139, 143, 154, 159, 161 and the studies of individual thinkers: Marx (24 and 78), Montesquieu (58), Moses Hess (75), Vico (79, 99, 114, the bulk of 139, 152, and the more popular 115 and 130), Herder (98), Sorel (121) and Machiavelli (122); one might also include here many of the Russian essays mentioned above. Items 79 and 98 are superseded by *Vico and Herder* (148), and the majority of the remaining pieces are included in *Against the Current* (166).

There are numerous memoirs of and tributes to twentieth-century figures, mainly scholars and statesmen. All the more substantial pieces in this category are reprinted in *Personal Impressions* (167), so

I will not repeat here the list of its contents at the end of this bibliography.

The principal Jewish studies, apart from 70 and 75, already assigned to other categories, are 43, 84, 118 and 126; there are also 52, 119 and 135.

Finally, there are the musicological items 89, 110 and 124.

Much else, of course, is of interest. In particular, I have not included book reviews in this survey, some of which are essays in their own right. There is no substitute for working right through the bibliography if nothing in a particular area is to be missed. But the selection I have listed comprises the main *oeuvre* at the time of going to press.[5]

Where an item has been reprinted in *Selected Writings*, the title of the relevant volume is given in abbreviated form: *RT* for *Russian Thinkers*, *CC* for *Concepts and Categories*, *AC* for *Against the Current*, and *PI* for *Personal Impressions*.

One of the particular drawbacks of a bibliographical description is that essays or lectures which are published separately are not always readily distinguishable from full-scale books, since both have their titles printed in italics. So it may help to say that items 24, 62, 112, 148, 157, 158, 166 and 167 are books, other italicised items being lectures or essays.

Although, as I have explained, I have not included interviews, some of these are of considerable interest, and it would be unhelpful to withhold their details entirely, in deference to a bibliographical scruple. There is an interview on contemporary affairs with Henry Brandon in *Conversations with Henry Brandon* (London, 1966: Deutsch); on Malraux with Martine de Courcel in her *Malraux: Life and Work* (London, 1976: Weidenfeld and Nicolson), reprinted in the *Partisan Review* 43 (1976), 384–93; and on philosophy with Bryan Magee in *Men of Ideas* (London, 1978: B.B.C.; New York, 1979: Viking).

1929

1 'Pelican s'en va-t-en guerre: a tale of war and peace', *Pelican Record* 19 (1929), 34–6

[5] March 1979. See Addenda on p. 288 for two late items.

1930

2 'Music Chronicle', *Oxford Outlook* 10 (1930), 616–27 (under pseudonym 'Albert Alfred Apricott')
3 'Some Procrustations', *Oxford Outlook* 10 (1930), 491–502
4 Editorial, *Oxford Outlook* 10 (1930), 561–5
5 Review of Ernst Benkard, *Undying Faces*, *Oxford Outlook* 10 (1930), 628–30

1931

6 'Music Chronicle', *Oxford Outlook* 11 (1931), 49–53 (under pseudonym 'A.A.A.': cf. 2)
7 'Music Chronicle', *Oxford Outlook* 11 (1931), 131–5 (under pseudonym 'A.A.A.': cf. 2)
8 'Oglethorpe University, Ga', *Pelican Record* 20 (1931), 34–40 (unattributed)
9 Editorial, *Oxford Outlook* 11 (1931), 1–2
10 'Alexander Blok', editorial, *Oxford Outlook* 11 (1931), 73–6
11 Translation of Alexander Blok, 'The Collapse of Humanism', *Oxford Outlook* 11 (1931), 89–112

1932

12 'Music Chronicle', *Oxford Outlook* 12 (1932), 61–5
13 'Music Chronicle', *Oxford Outlook* 12 (1932), 133–8
14 Review of Leonard Woolf, *After the Deluge*, *Oxford Outlook* 12 (1932), 68–70

1933

15 Review of Havelock Ellis, *Views and Reviews: First Series*, *Criterion* 12 (1933), 295–8

1934

16 'Music in Decline', review of Constant Lambert, *Music Ho!*, *Spectator* 152 (1934), 745–6

1935

17 'Musiciens D'Autrefois', review of Bernard van Dieren, *Down Among the Dead Men*, *Spectator* 155 (1935), 732; (letter) 906

1936

18 'The Future of Music', review of Cecil Gray, *Predicaments, or Music and the Future*, *Spectator* 157 (1936), 317–18

19 'Obscurum Per Obscurius', review of T. A. Jackson, *Dialectics*, *Spectator* 156 (1936), 888

1937

20 'Induction and Hypothesis', *Proceedings of the Aristotelian Society* supplementary vol. 16 (1937), 63–102

21 'The Father of Anarchism', review of E. H. Carr, *Michael Bakunin*, *Spectator* 159 (1937), 1186

22 Review of Julius Weinberg, *An Examination of Logical Positivism*, *Criterion* 17 (1937), 174–82

1938

23 'The Development of Modern Music', review of Gerald Abraham, *A Hundred Years of Music*, *Spectator* 161 (1938), 489–90

1939

24 *Karl Marx: His Life and Environment* (London, 1939: Thornton Butterworth; Toronto, 1939: Nelson)

2nd ed. (London, 1948; Oxford University Press; New York, 1959: Oxford University Press); repr. with corrections (London and New York, 1960: Oxford University Press); trans. into French, German, Hebrew and Italian

3rd ed. (London and New York, 1963: Oxford University Press; New York, 1963: Time Inc.; [Tokyo], 1963: Maruzen); trans. into Dutch, Finnish, Hebrew, Italian, Japanese, Norwegian, Spanish and Swedish

4th ed. (Oxford and New York, 1978: Oxford University Press; London, 1978: Book Club Associates); trans. into Dutch and Japanese

25 'Verification', *Proceedings of the Aristotelian Society* 39 (1939), 225–48; repr. in G. H. R. Parkinson (ed.), *The Theory of Meaning* (London, 1968: Oxford University Press); repr. in *CC*

26 Review of Karl Britton, *Communication*, Mind 48 (1939), 518–27

1947

27 'The Man Who Became a Myth',[6] *Listener* 38 (1947), 23–5

28 Review of Bertrand Russell, *A History of Western Philosophy*, *Mind* 56 (1947), 151–66

[6] Belinsky.

1948

29 'Karajan: A Study', *Observer*, 19 September 1948, 2
30 'Russia and 1848', *Slavonic Review* 26 (1948), 341–60; repr. in *RT*

1949

31 'The Anglo-American Predicament', *Listener* 42 (1949), 518–19 and 538; (letters) 681, 813–14
32 'Mr Churchill', *Atlantic Monthly* 184 No 3 (September 1949), 35–44; as 'Mr Churchill and F.D.R.', *Cornhill Magazine* 981 (1950), 219–40; repr. as *Mr Churchill in 1940* (London, [1964]; John Murray), and in *PI*; trans. into German
33 'Three Who Made a Revolution', review of Bertram D. Wolfe, *Three Who Made a Revolution*, *American Historical Review* 55 (1949), 86–92
34 Review of G. V. Plekhanov, *In Defence of Materialism*, trans. Andrew Rothstein, *Slavonic Review* 28 (1949–50), 257–62; (letter) 607–10

1950

35 'Empirical Propositions and Hypothetical Statements', *Mind* 59 (1950), 289–312; repr. in Robert J. Swartz (ed.), *Perceiving, Sensing, and Knowing* (New York, 1965: Doubleday), and in *CC*
36 'Logical Translation', *Proceedings of the Aristotelian Society* 50 (1950), 157–88; repr. in *CC*
37 'Political Ideas in the Twentieth Century', *Foreign Affairs* 28 (1950), 351–85; repr. in *Four Essays on Liberty* (112, q.v.); trans. into Japanese
38 'Socialism and Socialist Theories', *Chambers's Encyclopaedia* (London, 1950: Newnes), vol. 12, 638–50; revised in 1966 ed. (Oxford: Pergamon), vol. 12, 640–52
39 Translation of Ivan Turgenev, *First Love* (with *Rudin*, trans. Alex Brown) (London, 1950: Hamish Hamilton); illustrated ed. (on its own) (London, 1956: Hamish Hamilton; London, 1965: Panther; Harmondsworth, 1977: Penguin); trans. into Malay
40 'Russian Literature: The Great Century', review of D. S. Mirksy, *A History of Russian Literature*, *Nation* 170 (1950), 180–3, 207–8
41 'The Energy of Pasternak', review of Boris Pasternak, *Selected Writings*, *Partisan Review* 17 (1950), 748–51
42 'A View of Russian Literature', review of Marc Slonim, *The Epic of Russian Literature*, *Partisan Review* 17 (1950), 617–23

1951

43 'Jewish Slavery and Emancipation', *Jewish Chronicle*, 21 September

1951, 17, 24; 28 September 1951, 17, 19; 5 October 1951, 13, 15; 12 October 1951, 8; repr. from Norman Bentwich (ed.), *Hebrew University Garland* (London, 1952: Constellation Books); trans. into French

44 'Lev Tolstoy's Historical Scepticism', *Oxford Slavonic Papers* 2 (1951), 17–54; repr. with additions as *The Hedgehog and the Fox* (London, 1953: Weidenfeld and Nicolson; New York, 1953; Simon and Schuster; New York, 1957: New American Library); repr. in *RT*; trans. into Italian and Japanese

45 'On Translating Turgenev', review of I. S. Turgenev, *Smoke*, *On the Eve*, *Virgin Soil*, *Fathers and Children* and *A House of Gentle Folk*, trans. Constance Garnett, *Observer*, 11 November 1951, 7

1952

46 'Generalissimo Stalin and the Art of Government', *Foreign Affairs* 30 (1952), 197–214 (under pseudonym 'O. Utis')

47 Review of Benedetto Croce, *My Philosophy*, *Mind* 61 (1952), 574–8

48 Review of Morton White, *Social Thought in America*, *Mind* 61 (1952), 405–9

49 'Dr Chaim Weizmann' (supplementary obituary), *The Times*, 17 November 1952, 8

50 'The Fate of Liberty' (letter), *The Times*, 16 December 1952, 9

1953

51 'Henderson at Oxford: 1. All Souls', in T. Wilson (ed.), 'Sir Hubert Henderson, 1890–1952', supplement to *Oxford Economic Papers* 5 (1953), 55–8; repr. as 'Hubert Henderson at All Souls' in *PI*

52 'Israel – A Survey', in *The State of Israel* (London, 1953: Anglo-Israel Association); repr. in *Israel: Some Aspects of the New State* (London, 1955: Anglo-Israel Association), and as 'The Origins of Israel' in Walter Z. Laqueur (ed.), *The Middle East in Transition* (London, 1958: Routledge and Kegan Paul)

53 'Thinkers or Philosophers?', review of N. O. Lossky, *History of Russian Philosophy*, *Times Literary Supplement*, 27 March 1953, 197–8 (unattributed)

1954

54 *Historical Inevitability*, Auguste Comte Memorial Trust Lecture No 1 (London, 1954: Oxford University Press); repr. in *Four Essays on Liberty* (112, q.v.) and in Patrick Gardiner (ed.), *The Philosophy of History* (London, 1974: Oxford University Press); trans. into Italian, Japanese, Norwegian, Spanish and Swedish

55 'Realism in Politics', *Spectator* 193 (1954), 774–6

1955

56 'Herzen and Bakunin on Individual Liberty', in Ernest J. Simmons (ed.), *Continuity and Change in Russian and Soviet Thought* (Cambridge, Massachusetts, 1955: Harvard University Press); repr. in *RT*

57 'A Marvellous Decade', Northcliffe Lectures for 1954; repr. as 'A Remarkable Decade' in *RT*; trans. into Italian

I '1838–48: The Birth of the Russian Intelligentsia', *Encounter* 4 No 6 (June 1955), 27–39

II '1838–48: German Romanticism in Petersburg and Moscow', *Encounter* 5 No 11 (November 1955), 21–9

III 'Belinsky: Moralist and Prophet', *Encounter* 5 No 12 (December 1955), 22–43

IV 'Herzen and the Grand Inquisitors', *Encounter* 6 No 5 (May 1956), 20–34; repr. as 'Alexander Herzen' in Stephen Spender, Irving Kristol and Melvin J. Lasky (eds), *Encounters: An Anthology from the First Ten Years of* Encounter *Magazine* (New York, 1965: Simon and Schuster), and as introduction to Alexander Herzen, *Childhood, Youth and Exile*, trans. J. D. Duff (Oxford, 1980: Oxford University Press); trans. into French

58 'Montesquieu', *Proceedings of the British Academy* 41 (1955), 267–96; repr. in *AC*

59 'Philosophy and Beliefs' (with Anthony Quinton, Stuart Hampshire and Iris Murdoch), *Twentieth Century* 157 (1955), 495–521

60 'Roosevelt Through European Eyes', *Atlantic Monthly* 196 No 1 (July 1955), 67–71; as 'President Franklin Delano Roosevelt', *Political Quarterly* 26 (1955), 336–44; repr. in *PI*

61 'The Furious Vissarion', review of Herbert E. Bowman, *Vissarion Belinsky*, *New Statesman and Nation* 50 (1955), 447–8

1956

62 (ed. with introduction and commentary) *The Age of Enlightenment: The Eighteenth-Century Philosophers* (Boston, 1956: Houghton Mifflin; New York, 1956: New American Library; Oxford, 1979: Oxford University Press)

63 Introduction to Alexander Herzen, *From the Other Shore* and *The Russian People and Socialism* (London, 1956: Weidenfeld and Nicolson; Oxford, 1979: Oxford University Press); trans. into Japanese

64 'Equality', *Proceedings of the Aristotelian Society* 56 (1956), 301–26; repr. in the Bobbs-Merrill Reprint Series in Political Science, No 68812, and in *CC*

65 'The Father of Russian Marxism',[7] *Listener* 56 (1956), 1063–4 and 1077; repr. as 'Father of Russian Socialism', *New Leader* (U.S.A.), 4 February 1957, 14–17

[7] Plekhanov.

1957

66 'An Episode in the Life of Ivan Turgenev', *London Magazine* 4 No 7 (July 1957), 14–24 (includes translation of Turgenev's 'A Fire at Sea')
67 'The Silence in Russian Culture', *Foreign Affairs* 36 (1957), 1–24
68 'The Soviet Intelligentsia', *Foreign Affairs* 36 (1957), 122–30 (under pseudonym 'L.')
69 (with Miriam Rothschild) 'Mr James de Rothschild: "Grand Seigneur" ' (supplementary obituary), *The Times*, 13 May 1957, 15

1958

70 *Chaim Weizmann*, 2nd Herbert Samuel Lecture (London, 1958: Weidenfeld and Nicolson); repr. in *PI*
71 *Two Concepts of Liberty*, Inaugural Lecture as Chichele Professor of Social and Political Theory (Oxford, 1958: Clarendon Press); repr. in *Four Essays on Liberty* (112, q.v.) and in part in Anthony Quinton (ed.), *Political Philosophy* (London, 1967: Oxford University Press); ed. with notes by Kimiyoshi Yura (Kyoto, 1967: Apollon-sha); trans. into Greek, Italian, Japanese, Norwegian, Spanish and Ukranian
72 'Richard Pares', *Balliol College Record* 1958, 32–4; repr. in *PI*

1959

73 *European Unity and Its Vicissitudes* (Amsterdam, 1959; Fondation Européenne de la Culture)
74 *John Stuart Mill and the Ends of Life*, Robert Waley Cohen Memorial Lecture (London, 1959: Council of Christians and Jews); repr. in *Four Essays on Liberty* (112, q.v.); trans. into Japanese
75 *The Life and Opinions of Moses Hess*, Lucien Wolf Memorial Lecture (Cambridge, 1959: Heffer); repr. in Philip Rieff (ed.), *On Intellectuals* (New York, 1969: Doubleday), and in *AC*; trans. into French

1960

76 Introduction to Franco Venturi, *Roots of Revolution* (London, 1960: Weidenfeld and Nicolson; New York, 1966: Grosset and Dunlap); repr. as 'Russian Populism' in *Encounter* 15 No 1 (July 1960), 13–28, and in *RT*
77 'History and Theory: The Concept of Scientific History', *History and Theory* 1 (1960), 1–31; repr. in Alexander V. Riasanovsky and Barnes Riznik (eds), *Generalizations in Historical Writing* (Philadelphia, 1963: University of Pennsylvania Press), and as 'The Concept of Scientific History' in William H. Dray (ed.), *Philosophical Analysis and History* (New York, 1966: Harper and Row), and in *CC*; trans. into German (in part) and Japanese

78 'Marx', in J. O. Urmson (ed.), *Concise Encyclopedia of Western Philosophy and Philosophers* (London, 1960: Hutchinson; 2nd ed. 1975)

79 'The Philosophical Ideas of Giambattista Vico', in *Art and Ideas in Eighteenth-Century Italy* (Rome, 1960: Edizioni di Storia e Letteratura); repr. in revised form in *Vico and Herder* (148, q.v.)

80 Review of Henry Vyverberg, *Historical Pessimism in the French Enlightenment*, *French Studies* 14 (1960), 167–70

1961

81 'La théorie politique existe-t-elle?', *Revue française de science politique* 11 (1961), 309–37; repr. in English as 'Does Political Theory Still Exist?' in Peter Laslett and W. G. Runçiman (eds), *Philosophy, Politics and Society*, 2nd Series (Oxford, 1962: Blackwell), and in *CC*; trans. into Japanese

82 'Tolstoy and Enlightenment', P. E. N. Hermon Ould Memorial Lecture for 1960, *Encounter* 16 No 2 (February 1961), 29–40; repr. in *Mightier Than the Sword* (London, 1964: Macmillan) and in *RT*

83 'What is History?' (letters),[8] *The Listener* 65 (1961), 877 and 1048–9

1962

84 'The Biographical Facts', in Meyer W. Weisgal and Joel Carmichael (eds), *Chaim Weizmann* (London, 1962: Weidenfeld and Nicolson; New York, 1963: Atheneum); repr. in Dan Leon and Yehuda Adin (eds), *Chaim Weizmann, Statesman of the Jewish Renaissance* (Jerusalem, 1974: The Zionist Library); trans. into French, Hebrew and Spanish

85 'The Purpose of Philosophy', *Insight* (Nigeria) 1 No 1 (July 1962), 12–15; repr. in the *Sunday Times*, 4 November 1962, 23 and 26, as 'Philosophy's Goal' in Leonard Russell (ed.), *Encore*, 2nd Year (London, 1963: Michael Joseph), and in *CC*

86 'Mr Carr's Big Battalions', review of E. H. Carr, *What is History?*, *New Statesman* 63 (1962), 15–16

87 'The Road to Catastrophe', review of Hans Kohn, *The Mind of Germany*, and G. P. Gooch, *French Profiles: Prophets and Pioneers*, *Times Literary Supplement*, 30 March 1962, 216

1963

88 Contributions to Clara Urquhart (ed.), *A Matter of Life* (London, 1963: Cape)

[8] A polemical interchange with E. H. Carr.

89 'Historical Note', in *Khovanshchina* (opera programme) ([London], 1963: Royal Opera House Covent Garden Ltd); repr. in the 1972 programme

90 'Why are these books neglected?', *Twentieth Century* 172 No 1019 (Autumn 1963), 139–47

1964

91 Contribution to *Meyer W. Weisgal* (New York, 1964); repr. as 'A Generous Imaginative Idealist' in Edward Victor (ed.), *Meyer Weisgal at Seventy* (London, 1966: Weidenfeld and Nicolson)

92 'Felix Frankfurter at Oxford', in Wallace Mendelson (ed.), *Felix Frankfurter: A Tribute* (New York, 1964: Reynal); repr. in *Quest* 1 (1965), 20–2, and in *PI*

93 ' "From Hope and Fear Set Free" ', Presidential Address, *Proceedings of the Aristotelian Society* 64 (1964), 1–30; repr. in *CC*

94 'Hobbes, Locke and Professor Macpherson', review of C. B. Macpherson, *The Political Theory of Possessive Individualism, Hobbes to Locke*, *Political Quarterly* 35 (1964), 444–68

95 'Portrait of Ben-Gurion', review of Maurice Edelman, *Ben-Gurion: A Political Biography*, *Jewish Chronicle*, 25 December 1964, 7 and 22

1965

96 Contribution to Julian Huxley (ed.), *Aldous Huxley* (London, 1965: Chatto and Windus); repr. as 'Aldous Huxley' in *PI*

97 Contribution to Ian Kemp (ed.), *Michael Tippett* (London, 1965: Faber)

98 'Herder and the Enlightenment', in Earl R. Wasserman (ed.), *Aspects of the Eighteenth Century* (Baltimore, 1965: Johns Hopkins Press); repr. as 'J. G. Herder', *Encounter* 25 No 1 (July 1965), 29–48, and No 2 (August 1965), 42–51; repr. in revised form in *Vico and Herder* (148, q.v.)

99 'Sulla teoria del Vico circa la conoscenza storica', *Lettere Italiane* 17 (1965), 420–31; repr. as 'Appendice sulla teoria del Vico circa la conoscenza storica', *Sensibilita e razionalita nel Settecento* (August 1967), 357–71

100 Review of C. P. Courtney, *Montesquieu and Burke*, *Modern Language Review* 60 (1965), 449–52

101 'A Great Russian Writer', review of Osip Mandelstam, *The Prose of Osip Mandelstam*, *New York Review of Books*, 23 December 1965, 3–4

1966

102 Introduction to Marc Raeff (ed.), *Russian Intellectual History* (New York/Chicago/Burlingame, 1966: Harcourt, Brace and World)

103 Preface to H. G. Schenk, *The Mind of the European Romantics* (London, 1966: Constable; New York, 1969: Doubleday; Oxford, 1979: Oxford University Press); trans. into Japanese

104 'L. B. Namier – A Personal Impression', *Encounter* 27 No 5 (November 1966), 32–42; repr. in Martin Gilbert (ed.), *A Century of Conflict* (London, 1966: Hamish Hamilton), and in *PI*

105 'The Great Blood Libel Case', review of Maurice Samuel, *Blood Accusation: The Strange History of the Beiliss Case*, *Jewish Chronicle Literary Supplement*, 23 December 1966, 3–4

106 'New Ways in History' (letter), *Times Literary Supplement*, 21 April 1966, 347

1967

107 Contribution to Cecil Woolf and John Bagguley (eds), *Authors Take Sides on Vietnam* (New York, 1967: Simon and Schuster)

1968

108 Introduction to Alexander Herzen, *My Past and Thoughts* (London, 1968: Chatto and Windus; New York, 1968: Knopf; ed. and abridged by Dwight Macdonald, New York, 1973: Knopf; London, 1974: Chatto and Windus); repr. as 'The Great Amateur', *New York Review of Books*, 14 March 1968, 9–18, and as 'Herzen and his Memoirs' in *AC*; trans. into Japanese

109 Comment on Richard Pipes, 'The Origins of Bolshevism: The Intellectual Evolution of Young Lenin', in Richard Pipes (ed.), *Revolutionary Russia* (Cambridge, Masssachusetts, 1968: Harvard University Press)

110 'The "*Naïveté*" of Verdi', *Hudson Review* 21 (1968), 138–47; repr. from *Atti del I Congresso internazionale di studi verdiani*, 1966 (Parma, 1969: Istituto di Studi Verdiani); repr. in *About the House* 3 No 1 (March 1969), 8–13

111 'The Role of the Intelligentsia', *Listener* 79 (1968), 563–5

1969

112 *Four Essays on Liberty* (reprints of 37, 54, 71 and 74, with a new introduction)(London and New York, 1969: Oxford University Press); trans. into Hebrew, Japanese, Portuguese and Spanish

113 Foreword to Michael Yudkin (ed.), *General Education: A Symposium on the Teaching of Non-Specialists* (Harmondsworth, 1969: Allen Lane/Penguin); repr. as 'General Education' in *Oxford Review of Education* 1 (1975), 287–92; trans. into Japanese

114 'A Note on Vico's Concept of Knowledge', in Giorgio Tagliacozzo and Hayden V. White (eds), *Giambattista Vico: An International Symposium* (Baltimore, 1969: Johns Hopkins Press); repr. in *New York Review of Books* 24 April 1969, 23–6, and in *AC*

115 'One of the Boldest Innovators in the History of Human Thought',[9] *New York Times Magazine*, 23 November 1969, 76–100

116 'Reply to Orsini', *Journal of the History of Ideas* 30 (1969), 91–5 (abstract in the *Philosopher's Index* (1969), 282)

1970

117 Foreword to R. D. Miller, *Schiller and the Ideal of Freedom: A Study of Schiller's Philosophical Works with Chapters on Kant* (Oxford, 1970: Clarendon Press)

118 'Benjamin Disraeli, Karl Marx, and the Search for Identity', in *Transactions of the Jewish Historical Society of England 22 (1968–69)* (London, 1970: Jewish Historical Society of England); repr. in *Midstream* 16 No 7 (August–September 1970), 29–49, and in *AC*; trans. into French and Spanish

119 'Weizmann as Exilarch', in *Chaim Weizmann as Leader* (Jerusalem, 1970: Hebrew University of Jerusalem); trans into Hebrew

1971

120 *Sir Maurice Bowra, 1898–1971* (Oxford, [1971]: Wadham College); repr. as 'Memorial Address in St Mary's' in Hugh Lloyd-Jones (ed.), *Maurice Bowra* (London, 1974: Duckworth), and as 'Maurice Bowra' in *PI*

121 'Georges Sorel', Creighton Lecture, *Times Literary Supplement*, 31 December 1971, 1617–22; repr. in expanded form in Chimen Abramsky (ed.), *Essays in Honour of E. H. Carr* (London, 1974: Macmillan), and in *AC*; trans. into Hebrew and Spanish; see also 132

122 'The Question of Machiavelli', *New York Review of Books*, 4 November 1971, 20–32; repr. of part of 'The Originality of Machiavelli', in Myron P. Gilmore (ed.), *Studies on Machiavelli* (Florence, 1972: Sansoni); repr. in the Bobbs-Merrill Reprint Series in Political Science, No 68813; full version repr. in *AC*

123 'Randolph', in Kay Halle (ed.), *Randolph Churchill: The Young Unpretender* (London, 1971: Heinemann)

124 'Tchaikovsky and Eugene Onegin', *Glyndebourne Festival Programme Book* 1971, 58–63

1972

125 *Fathers and Children: Turgenev and the Liberal Predicament*, Romanes

[9] Vico.

Lecture (Oxford, 1972: Clarendon Press; repr. with corrections 1973); repr. in *New York Review of Books*, 18 October 1973, 39–44, 1 November 1973, 22–9, and 15 November 1973, 9–11, as introduction to Ivan Turgenev, *Fathers and Sons*, trans. Rosemary Edmonds (Harmondsworth, 1975: Penguin), and in *RT*; excerpted as 'The Liberal Predicament' in *Dialogue* 11 No 4 (1978), 90–5; trans into Japanese; see also 138

126 *Zionist Politics in Wartime Washington: a Fragment of Personal Reminiscence*, Yaachov Herzog Memorial Lecture (Jerusalem, 1972: Hebrew University of Jerusalem); repr. in *PI*

127 Foreword to Friedrich Meinecke, *Historism: The Rise of a New Historical Outlook*, trans. J. E. Anderson (London, 1972: Routledge and Kegan Paul)

128 'The Bent Twig: A Note on Nationalism', *Foreign Affairs* 51 (1972), 11–30; trans. into Spanish

129 'Dr Jacob Herzog', *Jewish Chronicle*, 14 April 1972, 28 and 43; repr. as 'Yaachov Herzog – a Tribute' as preface to 126, and as 'Jacob Herzog' in *PI*

130 'Giambattista Vico', *Listener* 88 (1972), 391–8

131 'History as We Would Like It', *World View* 15 No 7 (July 1972), 16

132 'Sorel' (letter), *Times Literary Supplement*, 14 January 1972, 40

1973

133 'Austin and the Early Beginnings of Oxford Philosophy', in Sir Isaiah Berlin and others, *Essays on J. L. Austin* (Oxford, 1973: Clarendon Press); repr. in *PI*

134 'The Counter-Enlightenment', *Dictionary of the History of Ideas* (New York, 1968–73: Scribner's), vol 2 (1973), 110–12; repr. in *AC*

135 'A Nation Among Nations', *Jewish Chronicle*, Colour Magazine, 4 May 1973, 28–34

136 'Notes on the Foundation of Wolfson College', *Lycidas* 1 (1973), 2–4

137 'Mr Hamilton Fish Armstrong' (supplementary obituary), *The Times*, 28 April 1973, 16

138 'Fathers and Children' (letter), *Times Literary Supplement*, 12 January 1973, 40

1974

139 *The Divorce between the Sciences and the Humanities*, 2nd Tykociner Memorial Lecture (Illinois, 1974: University of Illinois); repr. in *Salmagundi* No 27 (Summer–Fall 1974), 9–39, and in *AC*; trans. into Italian

140 Contribution to *Arthur Lehning in 1974* (Leiden, 1974: Brill)

141 'Mr C. E. Bohlen: Close Study of Soviet Leaders' (supplementary obituary), *The Times*, 11 January 1974, 16

1975

142 *John Petrov Plamenatz, 1912–1975* (Oxford, [1975]: All Souls College); repr. in *PI*

143 'L'apoteosi della volontà romantica: la rivolta contro il tipo di un mondo ideale', *Lettere Italiane* 27 (1975), 44–68

144 'Performances memorable – and not so memorable', *Opera* 26 (1975), 116–20

145 Presidential Address, *Proceedings of the British Academy* 61 (1975), 71–81

146 Speech at the Official Opening of Wolfson College, Oxford, 12 November 1974, *Lycidas* 3 (1975), 3–6

147 'Sir John Wheeler-Bennett' (supplementary obituary), *The Times*, 13 December 1975, 16

1976

148 *Vico and Herder* (London, 1976: Hogarth Press; New York, 1976: Viking) (revised versions of 78 and 98, with a new introduction)

149 Contribution to John Jolliffe (ed.), *Auberon Herbert: A Composite Portrait* (Tisbury, 1976: Compton Russell); repr. as 'Auberon Herbert' in *PI*

150 'Comment on Professor Verene's Paper',[10] *Social Research* 43 (1976), 426–9

151 Presidential Address, *Proceedings of the British Academy* 62 (1976), 85–94

152 'Vico and the Ideal of the Enlightenment', *Social Research* 43 (1976), 640–53; repr. in *AC* without last section, 'The Workings of Providence'

1977

153 *Sir Harry d'Avigdor Goldsmid, 1906–1976* ([London, 1977]: privately printed)

154 'Hume and the Sources of German Anti-Rationalism', in G. P. Morice (ed.), *David Hume: Bicentennial Papers* (Edinburgh, 1977: Edinburgh University Press); repr. in *AC*

155 'Old Russia', review of Marvin Lyons, *Russia in Original Photographs 1860–1920*, ed. Andrew Wheatcroft, and Kyril Fitzlyon and Tatiana Browning, *Before the Revolution: A View of Russia under the Last Tsar*, *Guardian*, 24 November 1977, 14

156 Presidental Address, *Proceedings of the British Academy* 63 (1977), 1–11

[10] Donald Phillip Verene, 'Vico's Philosophy of Imagination', *Social Research* 43 (1976), 410–26.

1978

157 *Russian Thinkers*, ed. Henry Hardy and Aileen Kelly, with an introduction by Aileen Kelly (London, 1978: Hogarth Press; New York, 1978: Viking) (the first of four volumes of his *Selected Writings*, ed. Henry Hardy, comprising reprints of 30, 44, 56, 57, 76, 82 and 125)

158 *Concepts and Categories: Philosophical Essays*, ed. Henry Hardy, with an introduction by Bernard Williams (London, 1978: Hogarth Press; New York, 1979: Viking) (the second volume of *Selected Writings* (see 157), comprising reprints of 25, 35, 36, 64, 77, 81, 85 and 93)

159 *Decline of Utopian Ideas in the West* ([Tokyo], 1978: Japan Foundation)

160 Introduction to *Derek Hill: Portraits* (London, 1978: Marlborough Fine Art)

161 'Nationalism: Past Neglect and Present Power', *Diálogos* No 84 (November–December 1978) (in Spanish); *Partisan Review* 46 (1979) (forthcoming)

162 Presidential Address, *Proceedings of the British Academy* 64 (1978) (forthcoming)

163 'Corsi e Ricorsi', review of Giorgio Tagliacozzo and Donald Phillip Verene (eds), *Giambattista Vico's Science of Humanity*, *Journal of Modern History* 50 (1978), 480–9

164 'Tolstoy Remembered', review of Tatyana Tolstoy, *Tolstoy Remembered*, *New Review* 5 No 2 (Autumn 1978), 3–7

165 'Mr Nicholas Nabokov' (supplementary obituary), *The Times*, 15 April 1978, 16

1979

166 *Against the Current: Essays in the History of Ideas*, ed. and with a bibliography by Henry Hardy, with an introduction by Roger Hausheer (London, 1979: Hogarth Press; New York, 1980: Viking) (the third volume of *Selected Writings* (see 157), comprising reprints of 58, 75, 108, 110, 114, 118, 121, 122, 134, 139, 152, 154 and 160, and the present bibliography)

1980

167 *Personal Impressions*, ed. Henry Hardy, with an introduction by Noel Annan (London, 1980: Hogarth Press; New York, 1981: Viking) (the fourth volume of *Selected Writings* (see 157), comprising reprints of 32, 51, 60, 70, 72, 92, 96, 104, 120, 126, 129, 133, 142 and 149) (forthcoming)

Checklist of contents of collections of essays published in English

(the numbers refer to the relevant entries in the bibliography above)

112 *Four Essays on Liberty*

Introduction
37 Political Ideas in the Twentieth Century
54 Historical Inevitability
71 Two Concepts of Liberty
75 John Stuart Mill and the Ends of Life

148 *Vico and Herder*

Introduction
79 The Philosophical Ideas of Giambattista Vico
98 Herder and Enlightenment

Selected Writings

Edited by Henry Hardy in four volumes

157 *Russian Thinkers*

30 Russia and 1848
44 The Hedgehog and the Fox
56 Herzen and Bakunin on Individual Liberty
57 A Remarkable Decade
 I The Birth of the Russian Intelligentsia
 II German Romanticism in Petersburg and Moscow
 III Vissarion Belinsky
 IV Alexander Herzen
76 Russian Populism
82 Tolstoy and Enlightenment
125 Fathers and Children

158 *Concepts and Categories*

85 The Purpose of Philosophy
25 Verification
35 Empirical Propositions and Hypothetical Statements
36 Logical Translation
64 Equality
77 The Concept of Scientific History
81 Does Political Theory Still Exist?
93 'From Hope and Fear Set Free'

166 *Against the Current*

134 The Counter-Enlightenment
122 The Originality of Machiavelli
139 The Divorce between the Sciences and the Humanities
114 Vico's Concept of Knowledge
152 Vico and the Ideal of the Enlightenment
58 Montesquieu
154 Hume and the Sources of German Anti-Rationalism
108 Herzen and his Memoirs
75 The Life and Opinions of Moses Hess
118 Benjamin Disraeli, Karl Marx and the Search for Identity
110 The '*Naïveté*' of Verdi
121 Georges Sorel
161 Nationalism: Past Neglect and Present Power

167 *Personal Impressions*

32 Mr Churchill in 1940
51 Hubert Henderson at All Souls
60 President Franklin Delano Roosevelt
70 Chaim Weizmann
72 Richard Pares
92 Felix Frankfurter at Oxford
96 Aldous Huxley
104 L. B. Namier
120 Maurice Bowra
129 Jacob Herzog
126 Zionist Politics in Wartime Washington
133 J. L. Austin and the Early Beginnings of Oxford Philosophy
142 John Petrov Plamenatz
149 Auberon Herbert

Addenda

Too late for inclusion in the main list I have learnt of the following items:

160a 'Comments',[11] in Yirmiahu Yovel (ed.), *Philosophy of History and Action* (Dordrecht, 1978: Reidel), pp. 38–40
160b (with other authors) 'Is a Philosophy of History Possible?', in Yirmiahu Yovel (ed.), *Philosophy of History and Action* (Dordrecht, 1978: Reidel), pp. 219–40

[11] On Professor Kaplan's remarks.

Notes on contributors

G. A. Cohen is a Lecturer in the Department of Philosophy, University College, London.

Patrick Gardiner is Fellow and Tutor in Philosophy at Magdalen College, Oxford.

Peter Gay is Durfee Professor of History at Yale University.

Stuart Hampshire is Warden of Wadham College, Oxford.

Henry Hardy is an Editor at Oxford University Press.

H. L. A. Hart was until recently Principal of Brasenose College, Oxford.

James Joll is Stevenson Professor of International History at the London School of Economics.

Robin Milner-Gulland is Reader in the School of European Studies at the University of Sussex.

Arnaldo Momigliano was Professor of Ancient History at University College, London, until 1975. He is an Associate Member of Common Room at All Souls College, Oxford.

Alan Ryan is Fellow and Tutor in Politics at New College, Oxford.

Larry Siedentop is Fellow and Tutor in Politics at Keble College, Oxford.

Charles Taylor is Chichele Professor of Social and Political Theory and Fellow of All Souls College, Oxford.

Patricia Utechin is Isaiah Berlin's Private Secretary.

Franco Venturi is Professor of History at the University of Turin.

Morton White is Professor at the Institute for Advanced Study in Princeton, New Jersey.

Bernard Williams is Provost of King's College, Cambridge.

Robert Wokler is a Lecturer in Government at the University of Manchester, and a Visiting Fellow Commoner of Trinity College, Cambridge.

Richard Wollheim is Grote Professor of the Philosophy of Mind and Logic at University College, London.

PATRICIA UTECHIN

Index

Achaemenids, the, 140, 144, 151
Aeschylus, 145–7
aesthetics, 27, 34–9, 134
Albertini, L., 109n, 110n
Alexander the Great, 139–40, 144–5, 150–1
Alsace-Lorraine, 106, 112
Anchor, R., 38n
Annan, N., Baron, 271n
Aquinas, Thomas, St, 238
Arendt, Hannah, 111
Argives, the, 140
Aristotle, 63, 65, 122–3, 199, 238
Aron, R., 174
Aršam, 141
Artabanus, 147
Arthur, C. J., 10n, 13n
Asia Minor, 141–2, 144
Asquith, H. H., 101
Assyria, 141
Athens, Athenians, 7, 140–4, 146–9
Austria-Hungary, 103–4, 107–8, 110
Ayer, Sir Alfred J., 41
Aylen, L., 122, 131n

Baader, A., 191–2
Babylonians, 141, 143–4
Bacon, F., 201
Bakke, A., 87, 89
Balbi, N., 202, 205
Balkan Wars, the, 101
Barante, A. G. P. B., Baron de, 156, 161, 165
Bebel, A., 107
Belgium, 102–3
Belinsky, V. G., 2
Benn, M., 119, 131
Bentham, J., 78, 79n 80, 85, 87, 176–7, 179, 245, 256–7, 258n, 266
Bergamo, 209
Bergemann, F., 115n
Berlin, Isaiah: writings, 1–7, 59, 61, 221, 226, 229, 234, 237, 271–3; and philosophy, 1–2, 211–19, 221n, 272; and history of ideas, 1–2, 272; and Russian themes, 2, 272; 'A Remarkable Decade', 2; 'Two Concepts of Liberty', 2, 4, 7, 56, 57n, 175, 234; 'Does Political Theory Still Exist?', 2; *Karl Marx*, 3; *Four Essays on Liberty*, 3–8, 11n, 13n, 48n, 57n, 111n, 175, 177, 211–13, 218n; and music, 3, 273; and Jewish themes and heritage, 3, 139, 273; and freedom, 3–8, 13n, 56–9, 168, 175, 177, 211–19, 234–5, 237, 251–2; 'Historical Inevitability', 4, 48n, 55n, 211, 234, 252; and determinism, 4, 41, 44, 235; and value conflicts, 5, 7, 221–2, 225–6, 229, 253, 255; and pluralism, 5–6, 56, 221–2, 226, 253–5, 269; and free will, 41, 235, 238; quotations from, 41–2, 44, 48n, 55–8, 111, 212–14, 234; and historical method, 72; *Concepts and Categories*, 221n, 272–3; and J. S. Mill, 253–69; 'J. S. Mill and the Ends of Life', 253; *Selected Writings*, 271–3; *Russian Thinkers*, 272–3; *Against the Current*, 272–3; *Personal Impressions*, 272–3; *Vico and Herder*, 272
Berri, C. F., Duc de, 161
Berwick, Duke of, 195
Bethmann-Hollweg, T. von, 100, 104, 107–9
Bickerman, E., 145n
Bismarck, O., Prince von, 102
Bley, H., 107n
Boeotia, Boeotians, 141
Bonald, L. G. A., Vicomte de, 155, 159, 162
Bonaparte, Princess Marie, 53
Borde, C., 240n
Bosanquet, B., 233
bourgeoisie, bourgeois, 9–10, 16, 20, 21n, 25, 38, 163–4, 208
Bowlby, J., 48n
Bowra, Sir Maurice, 271
Bowring, J., 78n

Brandon, H., 273
Brecht, B., 25
Brescia, 208–9
Büchner, G., 8, 115–24, 130–3, 135–6; *Danton's Death*, 8, 115–16, 118–24, 127
Büchner, L., 118n
Burgess, A., 190n
Burke, E., 159, 204
Byron, G. G., Baron, 124, 127

Cambyses, 150
capitalism, capitalists, 9–12, 14–19, 21, 99, 104, 113, 154
Carratelli, G. P., 144n
Carthage, Carthaginians, 141
Castillon, J. de, 240
Cecil, Lady Gwendolen, 100n
Chamberlain, N., 101
Chamberlain, W., 13n, 246n
Charles X, King of France, 161
Chekhov, A. P., 116, 120
choice, 41, 44, 48, 50–2, 99–100, 111, 114, 157, 162, 170, 212–18, 226, 235
Cleomenes, King of Sparta, 148
Cobb, R., 112
Cohen, G. A., 7, 246n
communism, communists, 16–17, 175
Comte, A., 156, 233
Condillac, E. B. de M. de, 155
Condorcet, M. J. A. N. C., Marquis de, 233
conservatism, conservatives, 77, 87, 95, 109, 160, 162, 204, 206, 221
Constant de Rebecque, H.-B. (Benjamin Constant), 156, 169, 245
Contarini, G., 199, 203
contract theory, social contract, 153–4, 242, 245–6, 248, 250
Corneille, P., 30
Cowling, M., 113
Crampton, R J., 107n
Council of Ten (of Venice), 196–7, 199–203, 206
Council of Twenty-Five (of Venice), 208
Courcel, Martine de, 273
Creighton, Mrs L., 105n
Cremona, 209
Croesus, 140, 142
Crowe, Sir Eyre, 103
Ctesias, 140, 149
Cyrus, King of Persia, 139, 142–4, 147–50

Danton, G.-J., 115–24, 127, 130–3, 135–6
Darwinism, social, 104, 112
Darius, 143–4, 146–8
Debs, E., 25
Decembrists, the, 134
Declaration of Independence, American, 78
Delphi, 140
Demaratus, 140, 145
Democritus, 145
Derathé, R., 249n
Descartes, R., 73
Desmoulins, C., 123, 131–2
determinism, 4, 7, 41–4, 47, 48n, 50, 52, 53n, 74, 120, 211–13, 215–17, 219, 235, 237
Dickens, C., 135n
Diderot, D., 134
Diogenes Laertius, 142
Doctrinaires, the, 156–67
Dooley, B., 198n
Dostoevsky, F. M., 116
Driver, G. R., 141n
Dworkin, R., 86–98; *Taking Rights Seriously*, 86, 87n, 88n, 89n, 92n, 96n; 'What Rights Do We Have?', 91

Egypt, 141, 148, 150–1
Elias, J. A., 29n
Empedocles, 142
empiricism, empiricists, 66, 155–6, 168, 187
Encyclopédie, the, 240
Engels, F., 52n, 107
Engermann, S. L., 112
Enlightenment, the, 39, 53n, 159, 201, 240
Épinay, Louise-Florence, Mme d', 238, 240
equality, 7, 11, 83, 86–98, 153, 161, 163, 165–7, 195–7, 206, 208, 225, 227, 229
Erikson, E., 73
Erizzo, S., 199
ethics, 28, 34–5, 59n, 225, 230–1, 253–4, 267
Eykhenbaum, B. M., 115n, 126n, 127
existentialism, existentialists, 41, 136n

Farrar, L. L., 101n
federalism, 167
Ferguson, A., 158
Fichte, J. G., 30

First World War, the, 99–104, 106–14, 234
Florence, 202n, 203
Fogel, R. W., 112
Fontenelle, B. le B. de, 233
Foote, P., 116n
Foscarini, M., 197–8, 202–7; *Della letteratura veneziana*, 197–8
Fowkes, B., 21n
France, 103, 106, 110, 154, 156–66, 201–2
Franceschi, P., 201–2, 208
Francis Ferdinand, Archduke of Serbia, 108
Frankfurt, H. G., 41n
Freeborn, R., 115n
free enterprise, 11–12
freedom, 3–7, 12, 21–5, 52–3, 58, 61, 72, 74–5, 77, 81–2, 84–91, 98, 153, 168–71, 173, 191–2, 195, 197, 202–3, 206, 209–10, 225, 229, 233–6, 249–51, 253; Berlin's treatment of, 3–7, 13n, 56–9, 168, 175, 177, 211–19, 234–5, 237, 251–2; 'negative', 4–5, 7, 56–8, 168–9, 175–93, 237, 239, 243, 245–6; 'positive', 5, 56, 175, 177–8, 181, 193, 237, 239, 251; Kant's theory of, 8, 28–30, 34–5; Schiller's theory of, 8, 27–8, 30–9; bourgeois, 9–10, 16, 175; economic, 10–15, 87; of speech, 15, 86, 88, 96, 142; communist, 17; Freud's theory of, 41–59; denial of, 92–7; of choice, 99–104, 106–7,111–12, 114, 212–18; of action, 101–2, 104–8, 110, 114; Greek, 141–2, 145–6, 149; of the press, 161; *see also* liberalism, libertarianism
French Revolution, the, 117, 119–20, 122, 131, 159, 162
Freud, E. L., 53n
Freud, S., 8, 39, 41–50, 52–6, 58–9; *The Psychopathology of Everyday Life*, 42, 43n, 45n; *The Interpretation of Dreams*, 42; *Three Essays on Sexuality*, 46, 55n; *The Ego and the Id*, 53
Frye, R. N., 146n

Gadatas, 144
Galiani, F., 238n, 240n
Gardiner, P., 8
Gay, P., 8, 53n, 208
Geiss, I., 104n
Geneva, Genevans, 207–9
Genoa, 210
Germany, Germans, 99, 102–4, 106–13, 116
Giannotti, D., 203
Gifford, H., 135n
Gnostics, the, 55
Godwin, W., 233, 251
Goethe, J. W., 119, 121, 131n, 134
Goldman, A., 21
Goncharov, I. A., 132
Goudar, A., 205
Grabbe, C. D., 119
Great Britain, 25, 77, 94, 102–3, 105–8, 113, 155n, 183, 197, 206; political development, 157, 164, 167, 171–4
Great Council (of Venice), 200, 202–5, 207–8
Greece (classical), Greeks, 32, 122, 139–51
Grey, Sir Edward, 100–1, 105, 108–9
Grimm, F. M., Baron, 235n, 240
Grotius, H., 242, 247
Guizot, F. P. G., 156–9, 161–2, 165, 172; *Essays on the History of France*, 157–8; *History of Civilization in Europe*, 162

Halliday, R. J., 269n
Hampshire, S. N., 7, 95n, 224n
Hardy, H. R. D., 8, 271n
Hart, H. L. A., 7
Hartmann, H., 59n
Hazelhurst, C., 103n
Hebbel, F., 135
Hegel, G. W. F., 52n, 113, 134–5, 222, 233
Herder, J. G., 3, 32, 39, 240, 272
Herodotus, 140–50
Herzen, A. I., 2
Hess, M., 2–3, 272
Hinsley, F. H., 105n
Himmelfarb, G., 257n
Hippias, 142
history, historians, 2–4, 7, 61, 72–3, 112–14, 119–20, 122, 156, 164–5; of ideas, 1–2, 41; 'scientific', 2–4, 234; philosophy of, 3, 238, 240; determinist, 4; historical inevitability, 7, 99, 235, 237; Marxist, 112–13; cultural, 115–17, 134; historical materialism, 153, 210; Persian, 142–51; Greek, 142–51;

'bourgeois', 158; of Venice, 198–200, 209; historical progress, 233–4
Hobbes, T., 55, 176–7, 179, 181–3, 186, 192–3, 212, 242–8, 250
Hobhouse, L. T., 234
Hoffmann, E. T. W., 124
Holland, 210
Hugo, V.-M., 121
Hume, D., 69, 75, 155, 212, 242

Idealists, 56–8
India, 139, 151
Ionia, 142, 144, 148
Ismenias, 145

Jacobs, M., 115n, 122
Jaurès, J., 106, 109
Jefferson, T., 86
Jesus, 55
Jews, Jewishness, 3, 139, 143–4, 146, 151
Jobson, R., 242n
Joll, J., 7, 105n
Jones, E., 43n
Joseph, Sir Keith, 25
Judaea, 151

Kant, I., 8, 27–31, 34–5, 37, 39, 52n, 134, 215, 233, 251–2; *Critique of Judgement*, 34, 36
Kent, R. G., 144n
Kierkegaard, S. A., 137
Knight, A. H. J., 135
Knight, R. P., 52n, 53n

Lacroix, J. F., 131
La Mettrie, J. O. de, 241
Laslett, P., 17n, 239n
Lawrence, G., 167n
Lehmann, W., 115n
Leibniz, G. W., 55, 73, 233
Leigh, R. A., 236n, 252n
Lenin, V. I., 2, 55, 111, 112n, 114n
Lermontov, M. Yu., 8, 115–17, 124–30, 132–6; *Hero of our Time*, 8, 115–16, 124–8, 133–6
Leroy, C.-G., 240
Lessing, G. E,, 134
Lewis, D. M., 144n
liberalism, liberals, 57, 59, 77, 87–8, 90, 95, 153, 175, 179, 181, 193, 221, 235, 238; political, 8, 234; and Narveson, 10–14, 16; English, 8, 101, 109, 112, 154–6, 163, 172–4; French, 8, 154, 156–74; *see also* freedom, libertarianism
libertarianism, libertarians, 5, 10, 12n, 13, 81–2, 233–52
liberty, *see* freedom
Liebknecht, K., 107
Lind, J., 78n
Lindenberger, M., 117n, 122
Linnaeus, C., 241
Lloyd George, D., Earl, 99
Lochner, J., 87, 96n
Locke, J., 155–6, 173, 242–8, 250
Loevinsohn, E., 15n, 25n
logical positivism, 1
Lombardy, 209
Loredan, F., 206
Louis XV, King of France, 201
Louis, XVI, King of France, 201
Lukács, G., 38n, 118
Luxemburg, Rosa, 113
Lycurgus, 204
Lydia, Lydians, 140, 142–3

Macedonia, Macedonians, 150–1
Machiavelli, N., 6, 202–3, 272
MacIntyre, A., 48n
Magee, B., 135n, 271n, 273
Magnesia, 144
Maistre, J. de, 155, 159, 162
Malipiero, P. A., 202, 204
Malraux, A., 273
Manson, C., 191–2
Manuilov, V. A., 115n, 126n
Mardonius, 141
Marx, K., 18n, 19n, 21n, 24, 90, 107, 134, 158, 174, 181, 233, 272
Marxism, Marxists, 9–10, 17–19, 21, 23, 99, 104, 112–13, 158, 174, 222
Masson, A., 197n
Maxwell, J., 115n
Mayer, A. J. 104
Mayer, J. P., 167n
Medes, 148
Medici family, the, 203
Meek, R., 158n
Meiggs, R., 144n
Meredith, J. C., 34n
Mersereau, J., 115n
Mesopotamia, 141
Mignet, F. A. M., 119
Mill, J. 257n, 264n, 266
Mill, J. S., 6, 8, 75, 79n, 88, 91, 155–6, 172–4, 176, 233, 237, 245, 253–69; *Utilitarianism*, 79n, 88n, 257, 265;

On Liberty, 173, 176, 253, 268; *Considerations on Representative Government*, 173, 176, 269; *Autobiography*, 255n
Miller, R. D., 30n
Miller, S. C., 52n
Milner-Gulland, R., 8
Mirabeau, H. G. R., Comte de, 251n
Moebius, 55
Moltke, H., Count von, 110
Momigliano, A. D., 7
Monboddo, J. B., Lord, 241
Montesquieu, C. de S., Baron de, 6, 154, 166, 195, 197, 200, 203–4, 207–8, 248, 251, 272; *De l'esprit des lois*, 195n, 197, 203–4
Moore, G. E., 215
Morley, J., 239n
Morpurgo, E., 206n
Mueller, C. R., 115n, 116n
Murdoch, Iris, 135n
Murašu family, the, 141
Murray, J., 206
music, 3, 273
Musset, A. de, 127
Mycale, battle of, 146

Namier, Sir Lewis B., 2
Napoleon I (Bonaparte), 159
Narveson, J., 10n, 11–12, 14n, 16, 25n
nationalism, 3
natural sciences, scientists, 7–8, 61, 72–5, 155, 179
New Deal, the, 13n
Nicholas II, Emperor of Russia, 108, 110, 112
Nietszche, F. W., 134–5
Nisbet, R., 159, 162; *The Sociological Tradition*, 159
Nozick, R., 12n, 13, 17n, 19, 81–7, 91, 97–8, 226n, 245, 246n; *Anarchy, State and Utopia*, 12n, 81, 82n, 83n, 85n

Orchomenos, 141
Ovid, 251

Padua, 209
Pasargadae, 144
Passmore, J., 233n
Paton, H. J., 28n
Pausanias, 145
Peace, R. A., 129
Peacock, T. Love, 239
Pelagius, 233
perfectibility, 233–52
Pericles, 148–9
Perrot, J., 143n
Persepolis, 144
Persia, Persians, 7, 125, 127, 139–51
philosophy, philosophers, 10, 12n, 41–2, 45, 48, 52, 61, 72, 88, 97, 134–5, 182, 220–2, 232, 244; Berlin's writings on, 1–2, 211–19, 272; moral, 2, 34, 37, 248, 255, 258, 262, 267; of history, 3, 238, 240; of mind, 64, 155; philosophical logicians, 65; empiricist, 66, 155–6; of government, 77; social, 85, 242; 'of praxis', 113; of natural law, 242
Phocaea, 142
Phocylides, 141
Phrynichus, 142
Pico della Mirandola, G., 233
Plamenatz, J., 250n
Plataea, battle of, 140, 146
Plato, 33, 150, 204
pluralism, 2, 5–6, 56, 221, 226, 230, 253–4, 259, 261–2, 269
Plutarch, 145
Poe, E. A., 124
Poincaré, R., 106
Poland, 196
Popper, Sir Karl, 6, 234
Prelinger, E., 41n
Price, V., 115n
proletariat, the, proletarians, 18–25
property, private, 11–17, 82, 156, 158, 161, 244
psychoanalysis, 42–4, 47, 52–3, 58–9
psychology, 6, 41–3, 48, 52, 58, 74, 80, 134, 176, 264–5
Pufendorf, S., Freiherr von, 203, 242, 247
Pushkin, A. S., 119, 121, 126, 131; *Boris Godunov*, 119, 122, 131–2; *Eugene Onegin*, 125, 127
Pytharchos, 144
Pythagoras, 150
Pythius, 142

Querini, A., 201–2, 204, 206
Quine, W. V., 65

Rachels, J., 10n
Ranke, L. von, 118
rationality, 30–1, 65, 80, 173, 230, 268

Rawls, J., 10n, 78, 232; *A Theory of Justice*, 78
Rees, J. C., 257n, 268n
Renier, P., 204–5
Richards, D. G., 115n, 131
Richards, D. J., 115n
Richter, Gisela, 144
Riezler, K., 100n, 109–10
rights: natural, 7, 78, 245; basic, 77, 82, 84, 86, 91, 161, 169; Nozick's theory of, 81–5, 97; Dworkin's theory of, 86–91, 96–8; liberal theory of, 86, 96–8; political, 87, 170–1; inequality of, 161, 165; medieval, 168–9
Rilke, R. M., 128
Robbins, K. G., 105n
Robert, L., 141n
Robespierre, F.-M.-J. de, 119, 121, 123, 131
Robey, D. J. B., 195
Robson, J. M., 79n, 253n
Rodin, A., 63
Rome, 195, 197, 199, 201–2, 204, 207, 210
Roosevelt, F. D., 13n
Root, M., 145n
Rorty, A., 78n
Rosselli, J., 118
Rousseau, J.-J., 5, 7–8, 33–4, 57, 128, 134, 136, 153, 155, 169, 171–2, 175, 181, 207–9, 233–52; *Du contrat social*, 57, 169, 172, 207, 237n, 248–51; *Discours sur l'origine et les fondements de l'inégalité parmi les hommes*, 153, 235, 237–8, 240, 244, 247, 250
Royer-Collard, P. P., 156, 159, 161, 165–6
Runciman, W. G., 17n
Russia, 102–3, 105–10, 134
Ryan, A., 268n, 271n
Ryle, G., 63, 214

Sade, D. A. F., Marquis de, 245
Saint-Georges de Bouhélier, 119
Saint-Just, L.de, 123, 131, 136
Saint-Pierre, C.-I., Abbé de, 251
Saint-Simon, C.-H. de R., Comte de, 172
Salamis, battle of, 146–7
Salisbury, R. A. G.-C., Marquess of, 100
Sandi, V., 197–8, 200, 203, 206, 209; *Storia Civile*, 197–201
Sardinia, 142, 144
Sazonov, S. D., 109–10
Scanlon, T., 246n
Schafer, R., 43
Schelling, F. W. J. von, 134
Schiller, J. C. F. von, 8, 27–39; *Letters on the Aesthetic Education of Man*, 27, 30, 31n, 33, 35, 37–8
Schlieffen, A., Count von, 110
Schneewind, J. B., 269n
Schopenhauer, A., 134–5
Second International, the, 107, 109
Serbia, 102–4, 107–8
Shakespeare, W., 30, 32n, 120–2, 131
Shaw, W., 10n, 13n, 25n
Shorter, E., 112
Siedentop, L., 8
Skinner, Q. R. D., 17n, 41n
Smart, J. J. C., 78n
Smith, A., 158
Smith, J. H., 56n
socialism, socialists, 13n, 15–16, 106–7, 109, 114, 153–4, 183
sociology, 6, 8, 153, 155–60, 162, 172–4
Socrates, 271
Solon, 204
Sorel, G., 272
Sparta, Spartans, 140–3, 145, 148, 169, 197, 204
Spinoza, B. de, 55, 73
Staël, Mme de, 156, 165, 170
Stalin, I. V., 2, 131
Starobinski, J., 235n
State Inquisitors (of Venice), 196, 201–6
Steiner, H., 246n, 252n
Steiner, Zara S., 101n
Stendhal, 117n
Stern, F., 104n
Stoicism, Stoics, 5, 42
Strachey, J., 43n
Stralheim, C., 119
Suez Canal, the, 143
Susa, 143–4
Switzerland, 210

Taine, H., 135
Taylor, A. J. P., 110, 113
Taylor, C., 7
Ten, C. L., 268n
Teos, 142
Thebes, Thebans, 140–1, 145

Themistocles, 140, 143
Thersander, 141
Thiers, L. A., 119
Thucydides, 143, 145, 148
Tilly, C., 112
Tocqueville, A. de, 8, 156–8, 160, 162, 165, 167–8, 170–4, 176, 237; *Democracy in America*, 162, 165, 170, 173; *Journeys to England and Ireland*, 167n
Tolstoy, Count L. N., 2, 116
totalitarianism, 175, 178–81, 193
Tourneux, M., 238n
Trevelyan, G. M., 100n
Trilling, L., 135n
Trojan War, the, 147
Turgenev, I. S., 134
Turgot, A. R. J., 154, 235n
Turin, 198, 202
Turkey, 197

United States of America, 77, 97, 162, 167, 170, 172
utilitarianism, utilitarians, 5–7, 77–94, 96–8, 171, 173, 228, 253–69
Utopianism, 38, 226, 230

values: conflict of, 5, 7, 221–32; diversity of, 11, 58, 253–5
Vandervelde, E., 109n
Venice, Venetians, 7, 195–210
Venturi, F., 7
Verdi, G., 3
Verona, 208–9
Versailles, Treaty of, 99
Vicenza, 208–9
Vico, G., 2, 72, 75, 198n, 272
Vienna, 109, 198
Villèlle, J. B. S. J., Comte de, 161
Viviani, R., 106
Voltaire, J. F. M. A. de, 201, 208–9; *Idées républicaines*, 208–9

Waelder, R., 57n
Wagner, R., 132
Weizmann, Ch., 2
Weldon, T. D., 239n
Wesley, J., 233
White, M., 7
Wilhelm II, Emperor of Germany, 110, 112
Wilkinson, E. M., 31n
Williams, B., 7, 78
Willoughby, L. A., 31n
Wilson, Sir Harold, 114
Wilson, K. M., 103n
Wokler, R., 7
Wolff, T., 119n
Wollheim, R., 6, 25n, 268n

Xanthus, 143
Xenophon, 140, 146, 149–50
Xerxes, King of Persia, 140, 142, 144, 146–7

Zeldin, T., 112
Zen, A., 202–5
Zeno, 55
Zionism, 3
Zoroaster, 150